A Decent, Orderly Lynching

D0807413

A Decent, Orderly Lynching

The Montana Vigilantes

Frederick Allen

University of Oklahoma Press : Norman

ALSO BY FREDERICK ALLEN

Atlanta Rising: The Invention of an International City, 1946-1996 (Atlanta, 1996)
*Secret Formula: How Brilliant Marketing and Relentless Salesmanship Made Coca-Cola
    the Best-Known Product in the World* (New York, 1994)

Library of Congress Cataloging-in-Publication Data

Allen, Frederick, 1948–
    A decent, orderly lynching : the Montana vigilantes /
Frederick Allen.
        p.   cm.
    Includes bibliographical references and index.
    ISBN 978-0-8061-3637-0 (alk. paper)
    ISBN 978-0-8061-4038-4 (paper)
    1. Lynching—Montana—History—19th century.   2. Vigilantes—
Montana—History—19th century.   3. Frontier and pioneer life—
Montana—History—19th century.   4. Montana—History—19th
century.   I. Title.

HV6468.M9A55 2004
364.1'34—dc22

                                                          2004046069

The paper in this book meets the guidelines for permanence and durability of
the Committee on Production Guidelines for Book Longevity of the Council
on Library Resources. ∞

2   3   4   5   6   7   8   9   10

To the memory and the work
of
Michael P. Malone

"Justice without strength is helpless, strength without justice is tyrannical."

—Blaise Pascal

Contents

Illustrations

Maps

Author's Note

The deadliest episode of vigilante justice in American history erupted in the foothills of the Rocky Mountains during the first six weeks of 1864. While the rest of the nation was preoccupied fighting the Civil War, a small corps of armed horsemen swept through the goldmining towns of southwest Montana and hanged twenty-one troublemakers, including a rogue sheriff, creating a legend whose impact can still be felt today.[1]

Every gold discovery in the American West led to some degree of lawlessness, as stampeding prospectors rushed beyond the grasp of legal governance and had to rely on ad hoc democracies and hired-hand lawmen to keep the peace. But Montana went through a uniquely dramatic and trying experience. There, the suspected leader of the criminal element—the loose band of drifters who played havoc in the saloons and who preyed on the stagecoaches and robbed passengers of their fortunes in gold dust—turned out to be the duly elected sheriff, Henry Plummer. And what happened to him tells a good deal about human nature, or at least about the character of the men and women who inhabited the American West at the time. They would have order, with or without law. Plummer was not some woolly desperado, but a cultured, charismatic man who had enjoyed a political career in California and was newly married. He was strung up just the same.

The executions in Montana were carried out with military precision, in full public view, mostly during daylight hours, by leading citizens who did not bother to conceal their identities beneath masks or hoods. Five of the victims were tied to the crossbeam of an unfinished store at the very center of the main street of the territory's largest city, their bodies left dangling for a day like pennants of conquest. The first book published in the territory, Thomas Dimsdale's *The Vigilantes of Montana*, praised and defended the hangmen's work and heralded them as founding fathers, a portrait that endures.

To this day, the men who banded together and killed the sheriff are revered as great heroes in Montana. The shoulder patch worn by members of the Montana Highway Patrol bears the numerals 3-7-77, the mysterious warning the vigilantes posted on doors or tent flaps when they wanted to drive someone into exile.[2] A high school in Helena, the state capital, calls its football field Vigilante Stadium and its yearbook *The Vigilante*. Bozeman has a Vigilante theater company. Several of the vigilante leaders went on to successful careers as legislators, lawmen, governors, and judges. One was a founder of Creighton University, another served as U.S. senator when Montana achieved statehood. Their exploits have been written about by authors of every stripe, from hacks to Mark Twain, and even caught the attention of Charles Dickens.[3]

More than a dusty relic of the Wild West era, the events in nineteenth-century Montana resonated anew in the aftermath of the terrorist attacks on New York and Washington on September 11, 2001, as Americans found themselves in a debate about vigilante justice that would have been unimaginable the day before. Were we now at war, fighting an enemy whose soldiers we meant to kill on the field of battle? Or were we searching for criminals who should be caught and tried with the full protection of our courts of law? When President George W. Bush called for the capture of Osama bin Laden, "dead or alive," he revived a famous phrase from the Old West and imbued it with fresh relevance. The foreign policy of the United States came to include the placement of cash bounties on the heads of various wanted men, including a deposed dictator and his sons. At home, Americans seemed to agree that the need for order—for safe streets, safe travel, safe mail, and safe homes—had risen above the luxury of preserving at least some of our civil liberties. Many would have agreed with the vigilante leaders in the Rockies who chose order above the rule of law.

For all that, the vigilantes of Montana remain a matter of contention because they proved susceptible to Lord Acton's dictum. Power tended to corrupt them, and absolute power corrupted them absolutely. Contrary to popular belief, they did not disband after hanging the sheriff in the winter of 1864. They remained active for several years afterward, using the cheap, efficient tool of preemptive justice to purge the region of criminals, vagrants, and ordinary nuisances. Long after the federal government established courts and sent judges to Montana Territory, the vigilantes continued to carry out extra-legal executions, denying their targets due process and the presumption of innocence. Over a six-year period they killed a total of fifty men, many of whom were not guilty of capital crimes, some of whom were not guilty of any crimes at all.

Montana's "righteous hangmen," as one historian dubbed them, left a troublesome legacy. Later generations of Montanans, and others in the West, have occasionally invoked the romantic image of the vigilantes to justify taking the law into their own hands. As recently as 1974, the mayor of a small town in Montana resigned in terror after someone sent him a card with 3-7-77 printed on it as a political protest. In present-day rural America, various freemen, militias, survivalists, separatists, supremacists, soldiers of God, and other off-kilter types, including the most notorious mad bomber of our age, continue to define themselves in part through vigilante myth.

While unique in its deadliness, the hanging spree that began in Montana in 1864 was not some isolated phenomenon that can be neatly sequestered from the rest of the American experience. It followed on the heels of earlier vigilante outbursts in every section of the country, and led the way to later waves of violence throughout the West that pitted private armies against several categories of so-called "undesirables"—cattle rustlers, horse thieves, petty criminals, gamblers, drunks, beggars, out-of-work wood choppers and railroad hands, Chinese and other immigrants, and, later still, striking industrial miners—whose eradication was not merely condoned but applauded by a great majority of the American people. Montana's vigilantes inspired the enthusiastic support of no less a luminary than Theodore Roosevelt, who tried unsuccessfully to join them and later, as president, sang their praises, commended their courage, and used their example as his model for America's brief but potent experiment with imperialism.

For later generations of Americans, lynching has come to have an exclusive meaning: the terror that was visited on black men in the American South during the years after Reconstruction and well into the twentieth century. But in the 1800s, other forms of lynching were widely accepted and even encouraged, with insidious, lasting consequences.

To appreciate the attitude toward vigilante justice that prevailed in the American West at the time, one can read over the shoulder of Robert Fisk, the editor of the *Helena Daily Herald*, a four-page broadsheet that chronicled events in the capital city of Montana Territory. One August morning in 1883, as he sorted through the telegraph dispatches on his cluttered desktop looking for items of social and political gossip, Fisk came upon a crime story that stopped him cold.

Two days earlier, in Salt Lake City, a heavily armed black man named Harvey had run amok, killing the city marshal and wounding another man before being subdued and arrested. Hours later, a mob stormed the jail, seized Harvey, dragged him through the dusty streets, and hanged him.

Fisk was aghast. A progressive Republican, he laid out the account of Harvey's lynching in a front-page story under the stark headline "Mob Law in Utah." Afterward, he sat down and composed an editorial. "A more brutal thing we have never read," he began, "than the account of the hanging of the negro, Harvey, in [Salt Lake City] on Saturday."

Then Fisk got to the point: "We do not object so much to a decent, orderly lynching when there is particular atrocity in the crime and there can be no mistake as to the criminal. But this beating, kicking, clubbing, and dragging through the streets, both before and after death, is too brutal to allow excuse, and would better suit cannabal [*sic*] savages than men who pretend to be civilized."[4]

Reading Fisk's sermon more than a century later, one marvels at the distinction he drew between good and bad lynching. Mob violence was a terrible thing. But who could object to a *decent, orderly* lynching? Especially if the crime was atrocious and the criminal plainly guilty? What could be fairer, or easier to carry out? That he could write as he did, without the least wisp of irony or uncertainty, might have marked Fisk as a simpleton in another time and place. Yet in 1883, in Montana Territory, his thinking represented a sincere belief among respectable citizens that vigilante justice was a workable, even indispensable tool of social order. Twenty years after the establishment of a criminal justice system in Montana, Fisk kept faith in extralegal punishment. And his view was shared by vast numbers of other nineteenth-century Americans, who would not have dreamed of interfering with the constabulary and courts in their own communities, but who saw life west of the Mississippi as somehow fundamentally different.

Perhaps no other aspect of American history has been so marred by myth and cliché as the cross-continental surge that began with the discovery of

Robert Fisk, editor of the *Helena Daily Herald*. Courtesy of the Montana Historical Society.

gold at Sutter's Mill near Sacramento in 1848 and ended up giving us the staples of the dime novel and movie matinee: prospectors, claim-jumpers, dance hall girls, stagecoach robbers, sheriffs, and vigilante posses, all of them gathered in a troupe to perform in the inevitable love triangles, poker games, saloon brawls, high-noon shootouts, and rides into the sunset that form our dominant images of the Old West.

Had western expansion happened in medieval times, or in some part of the world that did not yet enjoy a written language, the caricature and distortion might make sense. For some reason—the remoteness and rugged natural beauty of the surroundings, the excitement, youth, and rootlessness of its settlers, or possibly their fondness for liquor—the American frontier has been remembered vaguely, gauzily, as fable, even while history in much of the rest of the country was being meticulously recorded. But the events that took place in Montana in the 1860s and afterward are actually well-documented (in letters, diaries, memoirs, court transcripts, mining claims, contracts, and newspaper stories, among other sources), and thus can be rescued from the accounts of nineteenth-century historians who had reason to twist the truth. As a former newspaperman, I cannot resist the impulse to trumpet the considerable amount of "news" I discovered in the course of my research: fresh information in old archives, in letters that people found in attics and shared with me, in yellowed newspaper clippings that had sat unread for decades, in oral histories gathered as a public works project during the Great Depression, in the personal papers of several prominent Montana historians, even in a forgotten section of the congressional record that revealed an act of political treachery by one of Montana's most honored pioneers.

If it is true that history is written by the victors, then Montana's early history certainly belongs to the vigilantes. They won. But it does them little justice today to confine them to folklore and leave them as thin as cardboard. They were human, as were their targets. My work aims to restore them to life and to fit them into their proper place in the mosaic of American history—including today's headlines.

This book has its origins in a trip taken by a kinsman of mine named Jirah Isham Allen. In the spring of 1862, at the age of twenty-two, Ike Allen boarded a side-wheel steamer, the *Spread Eagle*, and left St. Louis to become a fur trapper in the wilds of Montana. He traveled the length of the Missouri River to Fort Benton and spent a year out west, hunting, trading with the Crow Indians, and prospecting for gold before returning home.

Ike had good reason for making the journey. At the outbreak of the Civil War, his father enlisted in the Union Army while his older brother joined the Confederacy, splitting the family into rival camps. Rather than take sides, Ike signed up with the American Fur Company and, as the saying went, lit out for the territories.[5]

By any standard measure, Ike Allen's voyage was a failure. He found no gold and made no fortune in the fur trade. He did not seem to like the rowdy life of the saloons and dance halls. He recalled attending a Fourth of July party full of music and dancing where he was "unacquainted and felt strange [and] did nothing but look on." One of Ike's misadventures had the elements of slapstick comedy. Hearing of rich gold discoveries in the area, he and a partner bought a horse and loaded it with provisions—flour, coffee, a frying pan—for a prospecting mission on the Salmon River. As the partner swung a final piece of cargo aboard, a pair of rubber boots, the horse shied and began galloping away, spewing their goods left and right. "As far as we could see him," Ike remembered, telling the tale years later, "there was a stream of flour which resembled a white comet." Unamused, his partner threw up his hands and called off the trip. So much for undaunted courage.

Yet the West staked a claim on Ike's heart and soul. He returned to his family's farm in southern Illinois and found that he had lost patience with the seasonal rhythms of planting and harvesting. In 1870, he moved to Montana for good. He became an army scout and Indian agent, and later helped settle the Stillwater River valley. When he died in 1929, at the age of eighty-nine, he was hailed as a pioneer and buried with great pomp.

Succumbing to the lure of the frontier did not make Ike Allen very different from thousands of other men and women, of course, but he had some unusual qualities that set him apart. One was his relative lack of interest in getting rich, quickly or otherwise. While most of his fellow wanderers on the outer fringe of civilization hoped to gain their fortunes, Ike exhibited no real symptoms of gold fever. Neither was he interested in homesteading or performing physical labor or earning a wage. He never married. He seemed to enjoy life in the wilderness, even the hardship, for its own sake. The dangers of the frontier plainly excited him, yet he lacked the appetite for violence displayed by some of his contemporaries, including

The author's kinsman, Jirah Isham Allen, in 1863. Courtesy of the Montana Historical Society.

the legendary John "Liver-Eater" Johnson, whose life he once claimed to have saved. He had a respect for Indians rare for a white man of his time and place.

I began reading Ike's poems and memoirs several years ago, when my wife and I became part-time residents of Montana. I grew curious about the world he inhabited. What was it like stepping off a steamboat in Fort Benton almost a century and a half ago? What had changed since then? And what had stayed the same? As I studied the early days of white settlement in Montana, I realized that Ike had arrived, purely by coincidence, at the very moment gold was discovered. His ship, the *Spread Eagle*, had been caught and passed on the Missouri by another, faster steamer, the *Emilie*, which happened to be carrying Electa Bryan, who was about to meet and marry Henry Plummer, the villain in Montana's formative morality play.

It was Plummer's story that hooked me. What do men do, I found myself asking, when the principal bad guy in a community wears a badge? In one sense, the answer was plain. Above all else they would have order—if necessary "order without law," as one of the vigilante leaders put it. So they hanged the sheriff. Yet the more I looked into the activities of Montana's vaunted vigilantes, the more I recognized how the gold camps, seemingly such simple entities, actually contained all of the tricky cross-stitching of American society as a whole. A shootout on a dusty western street might be triggered by drunken bravado or cheating at cards, but its underlying cause could just as easily involve Civil War sympathies, or economic interests, or social class, or ethnic friction. Plummer himself was a revelation—no shallow villain, but a man torn between the good and evil sides of his character. What writer can resist that contest?

As always, I was drawn to the fundamentals of politics: Who gains power over others, and how is that power used? My research took me beyond the gold camps of Montana into many social corners of the United States in the mid-nineteenth century. I explored the thinking of the Know-Nothings, the secrets of the Freemasons, the balance of power between husband and wife in the home, the economics of small businesses from Maine to California, the mutation of Civil War passions in the West, the art of peddling influence in the hallways of Washington, D.C. And I traveled vicariously over the country's principal migratory routes of the day, by river, sea, rail, and overland trail. As I contemplated the extraordinary mobility of Americans then and now, I was struck by a note in the papers of one of my favorite characters, James Fergus, a foot-loose Scottish emigrant. His family back home remarked with astonish-ment on his constant resettlement across the North American continent—from New York to Canada to the Great Lakes to Minnesota to Colorado and finally to Montana—while they remained rooted in the same small ancestral village they had lived in for generations.[6] We Americans seem constantly to be on the move, but we insist on carrying with us certain of our values that we mean to transplant and cultivate, for better or worse, wherever we land. That was the case with James Fergus and Ike Allen, I think. And with everyone else in my story.

A Decent, Orderly Lynching

The Murdered Boy

The murdered boy's body was discovered by accident.

On a freezing December morning in 1863, a hunter named William Palmer was stalking game near the Stinking Water River in the Rocky Mountain foothills of western Montana. He climbed down from his wagon and was walking along a snow-dusted trail bordered by thick clumps of gray-green sagebrush when he flushed a grouse. As the fat little bird broke cover, beating its wings, Palmer spun quickly and took aim. Armed with a deer rifle, he had little hope of hitting the bird, but he fired anyway and was gratified when he winged his prey. The wounded grouse flew forward several yards and then tumbled to the ground.

Running toward the bird, Palmer stopped abruptly in his tracks and drew in a sharp breath. There in the brush, concealed from the trail, was a body. On inspection, Palmer could see that it was a young man, his limbs and face frozen stiff in the wintry chill. Looking closer, Palmer discovered signs of a violent death. The boy had been shot above the left eye, and his neck was mottled with rope burns, evidence that the corpse had been dragged to its hiding place. Magpies had inflicted further damage with their pecking, until the hard freeze stopped them. If not for the cold, Palmer reflected, scavenger birds and coyotes might well have torn the body to pieces.[1]

Glancing around, Palmer noticed a primitive hut about a quarter of a mile away and walked toward it, calling out a greeting. He was met by two men, a grizzled pair named George Hilderman and "Long John" Franck, who worked as herders and handymen at a nearby livestock ranch. Exclaiming over his grim discovery, Palmer asked the men to help him lift the rigid corpse into his wagon so he could carry it to the nearest town. Much to his surprise and consternation, they refused, growling that a dead body was no concern of theirs. Struggling, and a bit disquieted now about his own safety, Palmer managed to heft the body into the wagon by himself. He rode off at a brisk pace. The wheels of his wagon made an occasional high-pitched, shrieking sound as they pinched the dry, powdery snow against the hard ground, lending an eerie accompaniment to his flight.[2]

Palmer's destination was a nearby gold-rush camp called Nevada City, one of a dozen rude communes that had burst into existence during the past six months along Alder Creek, a stream on the eastern slope of the Rockies whose banks were yielding sudden, vast wealth in the form of gold dust. Arriving by wagon, cart, coach, on horseback and on foot, thousands of prospectors had swarmed to the area in a matter of days, reminding some early settlers of bees in a hive or ants in a colony. "The ground," one pioneer woman recalled, "seemed to be literally turned inside out with great deep holes and high heaps of dirt." Within weeks, tents and huts had given way to rough-hewn log cabins, and storefronts had sprouted up on the main streets of the camp. Palmer, a tall Englishman whose curtain of shoulder-length hair below a bald crown made him a distinctive sight, had opened a saloon and dance hall in Nevada City, and it was there he hastened for refuge.[3]

In spite of the dead boy's disfigurement, Palmer had a pretty good idea who he was. One of the area's leading miners, William "Old Man" Clark, a veteran of the California gold rush of 1849, had been riding back and forth through the Alder Gulch camps and nearby river valleys for the past week, searching urgently for a young man he had sent on an errand. Nicholas Tiebolt, a German emigrant, was supposed to have fetched a pair of mules for Clark from a livestock ranch. Tiebolt had been given a buckskin pouch full of gold dust to pay for the animals. But instead of returning with them, he had disappeared. Clark feared the worst.[4]

When Palmer drove his wagon with its pitiable contents into Nevada City and parked in front of his saloon, he drew an immediate crowd of curious onlookers. One of them fished through the dead boy's pockets and found a knife he had given him two years earlier, confirming his identity. Other men hastened to fetch Clark.

Some chroniclers have encouraged the belief that the frontier West in general, and Montana in particular, were so gripped by violence that the discovery of a dead body was commonplace. That was not so. On the contrary, the mining camps of the American West were largely nonviolent. The miners themselves were joined in a race to extract wealth from the ground as fast as they could. The image of the lone prospector, standing ankle-deep in a creek while fat nuggets of gold plopped into his swirling pan, was misleading. A lucky few—very few—discovered gold in the crevices of hillsides or by panning river mud. For the vast majority, mining was a collaborative effort, as men banded into teams, dug down to bedrock with picks, shoveled tons of gravel into rockers and cradles and sluices, and then funneled creek water through the mix to wash away the rocks and dirt and catch the gold dust on riffles. Many miners ended up on wages, working for those who had the best claims. The work was lucrative but also communal, which meant it was next to impossible to steal from another man without being caught.

Montana was a relative latecomer to gold fever. The great rush of 1849 had sent tens of thousands of settlers into northern California, where the hills surrendered an average of 175,000 pounds of gold every year for nearly a decade—more than half a billion dollars in all—until the yield began to play out at the end of the 1850s. San Francisco, a sleepy Mexican port with a population of eight hundred, grew quickly into an international city of 50,000. The Sierra Nevada mountain range sprouted dozens of polyglot mining settlements, which thrived for a decade and then began to shrink and empty into ghost towns as the miners fanned out across the rest of the West, hoping to strike "color," the telltale trace of ocher in the sand at the bottom of a pan that signaled the presence of gold. Leaving California, the prospectors reversed direction and headed back east toward the Rocky Mountains.[5]

Gold was struck in the present-day states of Nevada and Colorado in 1859, Idaho in 1860, and finally Montana in 1862, just as the rest of the country was convulsed by the Civil War.[6] One reason for the emergence of vigilante justice in the West was the utter confusion that surrounded the hacking out of territories and the creation of states, a clumsy process in the best of times and one that was rendered virtually incoherent as Congress and the White House grew preoccupied with war. At the time gold was first discovered in the southwest corner of Montana, the area was part of Dakota Territory, whose capital was Yankton. In 1863, it became part of

Idaho Territory, and a year after that it was split off into Montana Territory. As a result, there was no practical government—and literally no criminal code—in effect during the Montana gold rush. Towns sprang up in a matter of days, with populations swelling to ten thousand and more, void of any legal mechanism for governance. The closest thing imaginable in our own time may be Woodstock, the rock concert that spawned an instant metropolis on a mud flat in upstate New York in 1969. Had it lasted three years, rather than three days, and had the drug of choice been whiskey instead of marijuana, Woodstock might have come close to paralleling the experience of the gold-rush camps.

While some small deposits of gold were uncovered in Montana by fur trappers and prospectors in the 1850s, the first important strike occurred in the summer of 1862 on a stream in the Big Hole Basin, a valley on the eastern side of the Continental Divide, just across the Bitterroot Mountains from Idaho. The discovery is credited to John White, as is the naming of the stream. Unaware that Lewis and Clark had traversed the same ground a half-century earlier and christened the little tributary Willard's Creek after one of their party, White chose the name Grasshopper Creek because of the swarms of clacking insects that plagued him and his partners as they set up their tents and went about collecting the shallow gold, called placer deposits, that they found along the banks.[7]

The town that quickly sprouted next to the Grasshopper Creek diggings was dubbed Bannack, after the Bannock Indian tribe that frequented the area hunting buffalo. Since the Bannocks were nomadic, and did not inhabit southwest Montana on a permanent basis, the white man's arrival there did not immediately trigger the kind of clashes that were typical elsewhere in North America. One party of arriving miners gained safe passage into the area by assembling a gift package of "three oxen, some beans, flour, sugar, tobacco, pipes, etc." for the Indians they encountered on the way.[8] Many Bannock tribesmen welcomed the miners and their camp followers and established a winter lodge on the fringe of Bannack City, hoping to benefit from trading with the settlers or, in other instances, from stealing their horses.

Within a matter of weeks, miners fleeing the meager, played-out gold fields of Idaho swarmed over the Bitterroots and turned Bannack into a city of four or five hundred souls, living in tents and rudimentary huts called wickiups modeled on the familiar Indian tepee. By the autumn of 1862, Bannack's main street was lined with primitive one-story frame buildings,

Nevada City, Fourth of July, 1865, eighteen months after the discovery of Tiebolt's body. Courtesy of the Montana Historical Society.

and some settlers had built log shacks for protection against the coming winter, when snow and frigid temperatures would make mining impossible. The relative tranquility of the town surprised some of the early settlers. "There must be from twenty to thirty families here," one miner wrote his wife back in Minnesota, "and they all appear to be healthy and contented." He could see children—"little shavers"—playing hide and seek in the street in front of his cabin.[9]

What little crime took place in Bannack tended to center on the saloons, where youth, boredom, gambling, paucity of women, competing Civil War loyalties, and "forty-rod" whiskey (so named because a mere whiff of the stuff, flavored with red pepper, supposedly could stupefy a man at that distance) combined to fuel random episodes of violence.[10] Then as now, the role of alcohol in criminal mischief could hardly be overstated, with many a remorseful young man awakening in a clammy haze and swearing he would never have done it, whatever it was, had he not been drunk at the time. Even in the saloons, though, fighting was not quite as prevalent as tradition suggests, for the simple reason that most of the men were armed and thus leery of allowing angry words to escalate into a fatal encounter. A sensible man knew that even if he managed to draw his pistol and shoot first, he could still be killed, because a fatally wounded enemy might well live long enough to fire back.

Yet there was another category of crime involving the gold camps that conformed quite closely to the stereotype conveyed by popular literature and later the movies. This was the stagecoach holdup, and while these encounters were not as epidemic as we like to remember, nonetheless there were numerous bands of "road agents" who lay by the roadside in wait for passengers laden with pouches of gold dust. Typically, the robbers were most active in the autumn of a year after gold was struck, since that was when many successful miners gathered up their proceeds from several months' or a year's work and headed home for "the States" before another winter closed them in. Merchants adopted a similar schedule, carting out their profits in order to repay their creditors and bring back fresh supplies the next spring. Because gold in Montana was discovered so late in the summer of 1862, very little traffic in gold dust took place that fall. But the next year, 1863, was different.[11]

On May 26, 1863, a group of miners discovered gold seventy miles east of Bannack on Alder Creek, a small stream that ran about twelve miles from its headwaters near Old Baldy Peak to its confluence with the Stinking Water River (so named by the Indians for a sulfurous tributary, and later rechristened with the prettier but far less evocative name Ruby River), a tributary of the Jefferson that in turn joined the Madison and Gallatin rivers to create the mighty Missouri. One of the prospectors, a Scot named Henry Edgar, described in his diary how his partner, Bill Fairweather, spotted a promising sandbar in the middle of the creek and hoped aloud that it might yield enough gold "to buy some tobacco when we get to town." It proved to be one of the richest gold strikes in the West, with an annual yield of some $10 million.[12]

By the autumn of 1863, wealthy miners and merchants were traveling back and forth from Bannack to Nevada City and the other towns along Alder Gulch, and from there south to Salt Lake City or north to Fort Benton, the head of navigation on the Missouri River. These parties of rich, slow-moving travelers made an inviting target for roving bands of highwaymen, and several holdups at gunpoint were reported, creating a keen sense of alarm throughout the territory. The robbers rarely hurt or killed their victims, though, since doing so would eliminate the potential for repeating the crime. Just as many modern criminals victimize the same target over and over again, their nineteenth-century counterparts tended to spare their victims' lives, hoping that a miner or merchant would go back to work and accumulate another fortune to seize. Killing meant pursuit and possible retribution, while ordinary armed robbery usually went unpunished. Most victims accepted the harsh reality that returning to work was likely to prove more profitable in the long run than chasing an elusive adversary into the wilds of the Rocky Mountains.

Contrary to myth, life in the West was not cheap. The leading contemporary chronicler of the Montana gold rush era, an English-born professor turned newspaperman named Thomas Dimsdale, claimed that exactly one hundred and two murders were committed in Montana during the first year and half after the discovery of gold. That figure, unsupported by any documentation whatsoever, has been widely accepted ever since. But the fact is that far fewer people were murdered—only eight, by the most reliable accounting—which is why the discovery of the dead boy excited such a tremendous outcry.[13]

As Palmer was quick to relate to the crowd gathered outside his saloon, the strangest aspect of his discovery had been the refusal of Franck and Hilderman to give him a hand. They told him they did not wish to get involved, an attitude Palmer regarded not just as callous but suspicious.

Tiebolt had been on his way to the ranch where the two men worked, which suggested they had both motive and opportunity for the killing. In a matter of minutes, a large group of townsfolk in Nevada City concluded that Franck and Hilderman had committed murder. Tiebolt's body was kept on display in the wagon for the whole afternoon, allowing a procession of miners and merchants to examine the corpse's wounds. It appeared that the boy had still been alive after the shooting when he was garroted and dragged into the underbrush, meaning he must have suffered terribly.[14]

At dusk, a coffin was cobbled together, and a small group of men gathered to carry young Tiebolt to the primitive cemetery above the town.[15] In a settled community, the next step might have been an interrogation of Franck and Hilderman by the police or sheriff. But Alder Gulch was raw. The towns along the creek had been organized into districts with informally elected presidents who wielded some of the powers of local government, mostly involving public decorum. And there were miners' courts with judges who acted to resolve disputes over mining claims. But the criminal justice system, such as it was, resided in the authority of one man, Henry Plummer, the sheriff of Bannack, who lived seventy miles away. And as we shall see, the people of Alder Gulch had good reason not to want to enlist Plummer in the search for Tiebolt's killers.

As night fell, some of the men in Nevada City began agitating for direct action. Clark, who had hired Tiebolt for his fatal errand, arrived from the highest and farthest of the gold camps in the gulch, Summit, along with his partner, George Burtschy, and two other associates, Elkanah "Elk" Morse and Albert Hamilton. A tall, gray-haired, wiry man of "iron resolution," in the words of one acquaintance, Clark quickly focused the cloud of general outrage into the organization of an armed band bent on tracking down Franck and Hilderman and avenging Tiebolt's death. As Clark reminded the other men, he had been active in the quasi-military vigilante groups that operated in San Francisco in the 1850s, and he proposed adopting some of the practices and formalities used there. Accordingly, he went into the Lott brothers' general store, borrowed paper and pen, and drew up a document setting out the accusations against Franck and Hilderman.[16]

Some of the participants, describing the events years later, suggested that a virtual town meeting took place, in which an accord was reached establishing a vigilance committee. It seems more accurate, however, to say that the leaders of the town, already frightened and aroused by the spate of recent stagecoach robberies, reached a sort of critical mass and decided to form a posse bent on violence. Clark, one of them recalled later, acted like "the avenger of God."[17]

A dozen men joined the expedition. Their immediate need was fresh horses, and they turned to a rancher named James Williams for help. A stocky, laconic man with cold eyes and a tangled mane of dark hair, Williams would emerge in the coming days as the top executive officer of the Montana vigilantes. At first he merely agreed to supply horses, saddles, and bridles for the others, declining to join them. But he soon relented at their insistence. "Come on, Cap," he remembered one of them saying, calling him by his nickname, "we can't go without you." And so he went.[18]

One of the oddities of life in the gold camps was the coexistence of reputable, law-abiding citizens next door to shadowy characters with criminal records and aliases. In a pattern familiar to the point of parody, western towns typically endured sharp conflicts between the upstanding element and the saloon crowd. Alder Gulch was no exception, but there were subtleties there that elevated the situation to a level above cliché. Granted, Franck and Hilderman might have stepped directly onto the set from central casting. Franck's nickname was "Long John," a testament to his gangliness, and Hilderman was called "the great American pie-eater" because of his prodigious appetite, which he indulged by making wagers about how many pies he could eat at one sitting. On one legendary occasion, a practical joker had arranged to slip a baking tin into the stack of pies in front of Hilderman, and he rewarded the prank by biting down hard on the metal and yelping in pain and confusion.[19]

Other men, however, were harder to caricature. Franck and Hilderman worked on and off for a rancher named George Ives, who did not fit any convenient, shorthand description. Ives was born into a prominent New England family in 1834, and was reared on a farm in Wisconsin after his father picked up stakes and decided to settle on what was then the frontier. Ives's parents started an inn called Ives Grove that prospered and eventually included a tavern, post office, restaurant, and dance hall. Growing up, Ives learned how to ride and tend livestock at a nearby horse farm. Then, like so many young men of his place and time, he felt the tug of the gold rush. Defying his parents' wishes, he headed to California as soon as he turned eighteen in 1852.

Six feet tall, blond and handsome, Ives made a vivid impression. One overheated observer, encountering Ives on horseback, wrote that he sat in his saddle "like a swan on a billowy lake." For seven years, Ives toiled at various jobs in California's mining country, establishing a reputation as a skilled horseman and marksman, and as a natural leader of men. In 1859, he moved to Washington Territory and was hired by the commanding officer of an army post to prepare and supervise military packtrains. It was rumored that he appropriated some of the post's mules for himself, reporting them dead or lost and later selling them on the black market. He followed the crowd when gold was discovered in Idaho and later Montana, arriving in Bannack in February 1863.

Ives had a strong taste for whiskey, which he frequently indulged, and he developed a habit of showing off his riding skills when under the influence. He liked to back his horse into saloons and order drinks—on credit—from the saddle. He was known to pull his pistol if angered. Soon after reaching Bannack, he got into a furious row with a friend, George Carrhart, and was wounded when they exchanged pistol shots in the middle of Main Street. After recovering, Ives had a further adventure in the summer of 1863 when he joined an expedition into Yellowstone territory that ended in an ambush by Crow Indians. Once again Ives was wounded, this time in the hip. Three members of his party were killed.[20]

In the fall of 1863, Ives moved from Bannack to Alder Gulch and opened a livestock ranch that specialized in pasturing trail-weary cattle, horses, mules, and oxen. He would rehabilitate the animals for a fee or else buy them and fatten them up for resale, typically doubling the price. It was a legitimate business, but Ives's ranch, like others in the area, also fell under suspicion of harboring some of the lawless element that preyed on the stagecoaches. With their proximity to the trails that led in and out of the territory, ranches and way stations became convenient refuges for robbers. Typically, the proprietor was innocent of any direct complicity in the holdups, but Ives's violent behavior aroused a great deal of mistrust among his neighbors and made him a natural target for questioning in Tiebolt's murder. Twice during the past week, as he searched for Tiebolt, "Old Man" Clark had encountered Ives, and both times Ives had irritated him by professing ignorance of the matter while blithely asserting that the young man undoubtedly had run off with Clark's mules and money.[21]

As an indication of the spontaneous nature of the hunt for Franck and Hilderman, it is worth noting that the posse set off at ten o'clock at night in December in the foothills of the Rocky Mountains without adequate clothing or provisions. After a hard ride, they stopped around midnight to warm themselves at a ranch, then resumed their travels in the frigid darkness. Finding that Franck and Hilderman had abandoned the site where Tiebolt's body was found, they rode on toward Ives's ranch on Wisconsin Creek. In the middle of the night, they attempted to cross the frozen stream, which cracked under their weight and sent some of the men and horses plunging into the icy water. Soaked, the men's clothes promptly froze stiff. The riders kept going in this miserable condition until just before dawn, when they neared a campsite on Ives's ranch. There, palsied with cold and fatigue, they waited for first light.[22]

At dawn, as Clark, Williams, and the other riders began to approach the clearing, a dog barked, threatening to spoil the element of surprise. The men spurred their horses, rode quickly forward with their shotguns drawn, and easily captured a group of dazed men who had been sleeping on the ground in blankets and hides in front of a hut. The posse called for Franck, who emerged from the crude structure and surrendered at gunpoint. Hilderman was nowhere to be found.

The first of several decisive moments had arrived. Some of the riders, still flushed with the passion of the previous evening, and by now exhausted, cold, and hungry, wanted nothing more or less than to execute Franck on the spot. They charged him with murder, and one of them, touching his pistol, said, "Long John, you had better prepare for another world." Had they proceeded, they might fairly have been accused of a lynching.[23]

But James Williams intervened. It would not do, he warned, to act hastily or without deliberation. At first glance, he seemed an unlikely candidate to step forward as a leader. At twenty-seven, he was a good deal younger than Clark and several of the others. Born in 1834, the same year as George Ives, Williams had grown up in a farm community near Gettysburg, Pennsylvania, and left home at nineteen to join an older brother, John, in his shoemaking business. In the late 1850s, the two brothers headed west to Colorado to try their hand at mining but were unsuccessful. Another venture, farming, ended when a ruinous storm destroyed their crops.

Only in one arena did Williams stand out: his aura of command over other men. In the spring of 1863, he set out from Denver for Bannack on a wagon train. Along the way, his party joined another caravan led by Joseph A. Slade, a legendary figure of the Old West best known for overseeing a section of the Overland stage route and, as Mark Twain recounted the story in *Roughing It*, for carrying in his vest pocket the dried and cured ears of an enemy he once killed. Williams and Slade ended up competing for the captaincy of the combined wagon train, which was to be decided by vote

James Williams. Courtesy of the Montana Historical Society.

of the other travelers. When Slade protested to the members of his party that he would not be bound by the outcome, Williams took him aside and said with conviction, "I understand you say that no matter who is elected you will still be captain of this outfit. I want to say whoever is elected captain will be captain." Then he added, "Did you hear what I said?"

Williams won the trailside election and Slade accepted the outcome, even agreeing to serve as Williams's lieutenant. From then on, Williams often concluded disputes by asking others in a flat, hard voice, "Did you hear what I said?" Years later, asked about his emergence as a leader of the vigilantes, he told an inquirer simply, "I had some leather in me, I guess."[24] In the clearing outside Franck's hut, Williams took charge. He and two other riders took Franck off a short distance, sat him down, and interrogated him about Tiebolt's death. If he was not guilty, they demanded to know, why had he failed to report the awful crime? And why, they asked, did he not deserve to be hanged as an accessory?

At length, after considerable prodding and threats to proceed with his execution, Franck broke down and identified Ives as Tiebolt's killer. Ives had gotten a glimpse of Tiebolt's pouch of gold dust and shot him for it, Franck said. And, he disclosed, Ives was hiding in the nearby hut even as they spoke. With a sense of urgency, Williams went back to the clearing, entered the hut with his gun drawn, confronted Ives, and arrested him.[25]

Given the arduous trip undertaken by the posse, their sincere outrage at Tiebolt's killing, and their conviction that Franck and Ives were dangerous men, the next several hours should have been tense, with the accused culprits either summarily executed or at least securely tied up and kept under armed guard. Yet this did not happen. Ives, whether from an extraordinary ability to put up a bluff or from willful denial of his situation, treated the arrest as a genial affair and maintained a pleasant, unworried demeanor. Told he would have to return to town with the posse, he replied affably, "All right, I guess I'll have to go."[26]

The riders, evidently relieved that the arrests had been accomplished so easily, relaxed and helped themselves to coffee and warmed themselves around the campfire. Williams tried to suggest in later years that he maintained alertness. But it appears that he, too, grew lax. When the time came to leave the camp for Nevada City, Williams allowed Ives to saddle his own horse and ride without physical restraints.

For a while, Ives behaved passively. The party stopped at a ranch along the way, where they found Hilderman and captured him without incident. Afterward, on the journey home, the mood gradually became one of frolic. During the afternoon, as the men rode, they literally engaged in horseplay. They staged impromptu races, testing the speed of their horses, joshing each other and making wagers. At one point, Ives pitted his mount, a spotted Indian pony, against two of his captors' larger horses and won, outdistancing the others easily. And then he kept right on going, in a brazen bid for escape.[27]

The only way to reconcile the carelessness of the ride home with the deadly purpose of the night before may be to remember that these were mostly adventuresome men, highly spirited, and not, perhaps, the most judicious of their generation (or they likely would not have brought themselves to the gold-camp frontier in the first place). They were not trained law officers—indeed, they were not a lawfully constituted body at all. They had joined forces, to borrow a fitting cliché, on the spur of the moment. They had robust confidence in their abilities. Some were persuaded by Ives's casual behavior that he must be innocent. And Ives was not armed, the lone circumstance that would have made him seem genuinely dangerous to them. In any case, Ives's dash for freedom startled them back to their senses, and they set off in hot pursuit.

Ives gained a safe lead at first, but his pony soon tired and slowed down. Dismounting near a creek, he continued his flight on foot, running headlong down a ravine and ducking behind a stand of cedar timbers and willows in a field of boulders. More or less by luck, one of his pursuers finally spotted him crouching behind a large rock and recaptured him at gunpoint. Some of the posse renewed their bid for hanging him on the spot, but the decision held to return him to Nevada City. For the rest of the trip, Ives rode tied snugly hand and foot to his saddle in the middle of a square of guards.

Toward evening, the posse reached Nevada City, where several hundred miners and townspeople, anticipating the capture, had gathered from the other settlements along Alder Gulch. What to do with Ives and his comrades became the subject of a lively communal debate. Because of his attempted escape, many of the pursuers now believed Ives was guilty of Tiebolt's murder, and they wanted to hang him. Others argued about how to dispose of Franck and Hilderman.[28]

But on one point there was broad agreement. The prisoners would not be turned over to Henry Plummer, the sheriff. A man of considerable magnetism, admired to the point of hero worship by many in his circle of friends, handsome, well-spoken, and ambitious for high office and public respect, Plummer had won his position in an open election and served with the people's mandate. At the same time, he had managed to alienate large numbers of his fellow settlers and convince them that he was, in secret, a criminal mastermind and a direct threat to their very lives. Rarely had a politician so quickly and thoroughly polarized an American community. In coming days, its leaders meant to put him on trial along with the other suspects and try to get at the truth.

CHAPTER ONE

Maine to California

Henry Plummer was born in 1832 on the Atlantic coast of Maine, about as far from the American West as a person could get in the United States, in climate and custom as well as distance. Long before he arrived in Montana and swirled into the mists of legend, young Plummer endured a difficult childhood in "down east" Maine, on the narrow strip of land that separates the ocean from the northern pine forests. There the mists were all too real—fierce, lashing storms, driven by high winds, trailed by banks of fog that rose up a mile or more and clung to the ragged shoreline for days on end. A frail boy, Plummer suffered from chronic lung illness made worse by weather that stunted the trees and thinned the soil and made the land look like tundra. It was "no place for sissies," in the words of one local chronicler, and the simple fact that Plummer survived marked him as a young man with a streak of durability.[1]

Bone-chilling weather was not the only hardship Plummer faced. He was a member of a prominent clan, one of two dozen families that settled the Pleasant River Valley, near Maine's jagged coastline below the Canadian border, in the years just before the American Revolution. But Henry's branch of the family was poor. While other Plummers distinguished themselves as sea captains, ship-builders, and land-clearing lumbermen, Henry's father struggled to make ends meet. A lowly seaman, Moses Plummer IV bore the proud name of his father, grandfather, and great-grandfather, but he could not afford a home of his own, and his seven children, including Henry, grew up in the extended household of their grandfather, Moses Plummer III. For years, historians despaired of establishing Henry's parentage because his birth was not documented by name in the family records. Instead, it appears, he was merely listed as an unnamed son born to Moses Plummer IV and his wife sometime in the years between 1830 and 1835—an anonymous entry in the family ledger, one of a litter of whom not much was expected.[2]

The Plummers could trace their ancestry to an English linen weaver who arrived in Massachusetts in 1634, settled in Newbury, north of Boston, and built an estate valued at more than four hundred pounds by the time of his death. Four generations later, in 1768, Moses Plummer, Jr., joined a colony of pioneers, including several Quaker families from Martha's Vineyard, who settled along the Pleasant River in Maine and went to work chopping trees and diking the salt marshes to create farmland. They founded a small township, Addison, named for the English essayist and politician Joseph Addison, on the estuary that led from the ocean up to the mouth of the Pleasant River. Spreading out in the surrounding countryside, the families dug cellars, built simple but sturdy houses, grew hay, kept livestock, and battled nature. One woman, finding a black bear attacking her hog in the pen behind her house, was said to have driven the predator off by beating it with an old shovel handle. When war with the British came, in 1775, most of Addison's men joined the rebellion, and one was killed at the Battle of Bunker Hill.[3]

Despite hardship, the families of Addison proliferated. Moses Plummer, Jr., and his wife, Lucy, had nine children, and their eldest son, Moses Plummer III, fathered a dozen. The family name, originally spelled with one "m" as Plumer, gradually evolved into the more common version, Plummer, as its members spread across northeast Maine. The Plummers married into other pioneer families in the area—the Coffins, Driskos, Bucknams, Webbs, and Nashes—and formed an especially close bond with the Wass family that hailed from Martha's Vineyard and gave their name to Great Wass Island off the Maine coast. The first six children born to Moses Plummer III all married Wasses, including Moses IV, who chose Abigail "Nabby" Wass as his bride. (Today, Great Wass Island offers visitors a chance to wander through a Nature Conservancy preserve strewn with sheep laurel, Labrador tea, and jack pines, stubby trees that are "short-needled, twisted, dwarfed, and sculpted by wind and adversity into bonsai," in the words of one admirer.)[4]

By the time Maine achieved statehood, in 1820, its upper coastal region was dotted with so-called "thrifty" farms that had twenty to fifty acres in crops, plus pasturage, a yoke of oxen, a dozen cattle, and perhaps a flock of sheep. A farm family might join in the barter economy by tanning hides into leather, shaving shingles, harvesting ice, or producing boots, barrels, or ax handles. Farm wives made brooms and straw hats, or sold eggs. The principal industry was lumbering, and many farmers moonlighted as ship builders. One man built a fourteen-ton fishing boat, the *Sarah Ann*, on his farm, and then organized a "hauling bee" with thirty-eight yoke of oxen to roll it on logs several miles to the water. The sea was Maine's other great calling, and several Plummers served as sailors and ship captains, carrying lumber and forest products to the West Indies in trade for rum, molasses, sugar, and coffee.[5]

For a boy growing up on the coast of Maine, school was primitive and discipline harsh, often administered by buggy whip. But adventure abounded. Joshua Chamberlain, the great Civil War general, "considered it his duty" as a lad to climb the tallest mast of every vessel launched in the area "and hang his hat upon it," according to his biographer. Young Plummer likely did the same, clambering around on the wharves of Addison. He would have played blind man's buff, hunt the whistle, and other children's games, and watched with avid interest as the local militia drilled on the township's annual muster day. He would have picked wild blueberries in the hills above town. From his later display of skill with guns, we may assume that he learned to hunt game in the vast forests that carpeted Maine above the coast.[6]

In 1840, a federal census taker found Moses Plummer III, aged seventy-two, serving as head of a large household in Addison that included adult children and grandchildren. His son, Moses IV, was away at sea much of the time and could not afford to maintain a home of his own, so the old man provided room and board at his farm for his son's wife, Nabby, and her children, among them eight-year-old Henry. In all, there were ten mouths to feed. No written record of his childhood survives, but Henry's circumstances, living as a poor relation under his grandfather's roof, surrounded by richer and more successful Plummers and Wasses, may well have toughened him and fueled the ambition that marked his later life. In any case, his situation worsened over the decade to come. His mother died in 1844 and his grandfather in 1846, leaving him a ward of his step-grandmother.[7]

For the Plummer clan, as for so many Americans, the gold rush of 1849 proved a pivotal event. Hearing of the rich discoveries in northern California, which were certified publicly as "extraordinary" by President Polk, some of the leading men of Addison decided to form a company and make the long voyage around Cape Horn to San Francisco. They invested in a sailing ship, the *Belgrade*, that was under construction in nearby Cherryfield, and had it fitted out for the ocean trip. Along with the usual supplies, they had a small stern-wheel steamer dismantled and added to the cargo, intending to run it as a ferry up the Sacramento and American rivers to the gold fields. In all, some fifty men joined the California Mining and Navigation Company, most of them descendants of the area's pioneer families, related to each other by blood or marriage. To serve as captain, they chose Horatio Nelson Plummer, an aptly named thirty-four-year-old mariner whose branch of the family enjoyed enough means that he could afford to put up a stake and become a part-owner in the venture. In turn, Horatio Plummer hired his older first cousin, Moses Plummer IV, then fifty-six, to be the ship's steward. Nothing could have pointed up the disparity in family status more clearly: Henry's father, getting too old for such hard duty at sea, would be serving meals to his cousin and the other principals in the company, working as a crewman for wages instead of a share in the profits.[8]

On November 28, 1849, the *Belgrade* was launched and piloted down the Narraguagus River to the sea. After a brief delay to fix a leak, Captain Plummer set sail on the long voyage to the far coast of the continent. Jared Nash, a member of the company who kept a diary, recorded an auspicious beginning as good winds sped the big bark down the Atlantic coast, with the crew often "crowding on" all twenty-one sails to make fast time. The ship passed several other vessels, all pressing urgently for the Pacific and the chance to find gold. In good spirits, the men sang hymns and listened to Bible readings and sermons on Sundays, and feasted on fresh chicken and turkey on Christmas and New Year's Day. One of the men brought a fiddle to provide music.

The *Belgrade* crossed the equator on January 8, 1850, and two weeks later made port in Rio de Janeiro. There the ship's fortunes changed. According to Nash's diary, a terrible sickness laid waste to the men, giving them wracking aches followed by high fever and delirium, and in three cases death. The ship struggled for three weeks to round Cape Horn, buffeted by snow, hail, rain, and wind, pitching about in seas Nash described as "mountains high." The desperate crew reached the island of Juan Fernandez, off the coast of Chile, on March 22, and spent nearly a week there savoring fresh fruit and water and replenishing their supplies.

The winds continued against the *Belgrade*, until she finally anchored in San Francisco harbor on May 28, 1850, six full months after her launching. As the members of the company stood on deck, preparing to disembark, someone noticed that Moses Plummer was missing. A party was sent to look for him and after a brief search found him lying in his bunk, dead. The hardships of the voyage, capped by the death of the ship's steward, seemed to drain the venture of its energy. Some of the men continued on to the gold mines and prospected, but most returned home to Maine. After selling the *Belgrade* and dividing up the company's interests, Horatio Plummer made his way back to Addison, where he faced the difficult task of telling his fellow townsmen—and his kinsmen—about the tragedies that had befallen the ship.

By now, Henry Plummer's older siblings had grown up and moved away, leaving him a younger brother and sister to look after. With his father gone, he likely had to help support them and the remaining members of his grandfather's household. But it may be that Henry was too ill to work. A later examination would show that his lungs bore the telltale scars of tuberculosis, evidence of a long struggle against the punishing elements of the Maine shore. What is certain is that young Plummer eventually felt the tug of the gold fields. In 1852, when he was nineteen years old, he made his way to New York, sailed south to Panama, crossed the isthmus by mule train, and booked passage on the *Golden Gate*, a steamer bound for San Francisco. Perhaps he hoped to follow his father's footsteps and learn why they had led to death.[9]

Four years into the great rush, the trip to California was still a rough piece of business. Those who decided to cut their time at sea by crossing Panama had to stay in the squalid "hog-hole" hotels of Chagres, cover sixty-eight miles of muddy jungle by dugout canoe and mule, and hope against hope they could avoid dysentery, cholera, and other disease while waiting six weeks or more for an over-priced ticket on a fast steamer from Panama City up the Pacific coast. On the day Henry Plummer shipped out, the *Golden Gate* carried more than twice her authorized limit of passengers, with a thousand first-class travelers doubled up in cabins and half again that many jammed into steerage. The decks were teeming with humanity day and night, prompting the captain to complain of a "pandemonium of drunkenness and riot, from her departure until her arrival." The ship left Panama City on May 8, 1852, and landed at San Francisco thirteen days later. Two men died along the way.[10]

At least the place of destination had improved. The mud flats, frayed canvas tents, and wood-plank sidewalks that greeted new arrivals in San Francisco in 1849 were gone, pruned by repeated fires and replaced by brick buildings and a grid of streets. The rudiments of a zoning system were in place, nudging the gambling dens, bordellos, and saloons into separate quarters away from the residential neighborhoods and central business district. With state and municipal government in their infancy and law enforcement anemic, order of sorts was imposed in the summer of 1851 by a self-styled "Committee of Vigilance," a civilian army hundreds strong, led by the merchant elite, that lynched four suspected criminals and ran off vast numbers of scruffy young men, some of them guilty of nothing more than having a foreign accent. Still the flood of newcomers continued. Plummer was one of an estimated 65,000 passengers who landed at San Francisco in 1852, and he could count himself lucky when he found a room to rent at a boarding house on Bush Street.

Eager as he was to go northeast to the gold fields, Plummer first had to earn the money to get there. Having arrived broke, he secured a position as an accounts clerk in a business on Montgomery Street and began saving up his pay. But by now, as his new friends undoubtedly warned him, the days of striking it rich with pick and pan were gone. Gold mining had evolved quickly "from a treasure hunt to an industry," in the words of one historian, and Plummer's chances of finding a good claim and working it by himself for profit were essentially nil. By 1852, the overwhelming majority of miners were wage-earners, averaging a modest $5 a day, breaking rocks and performing hard labor more suited to felons than fortune seekers. Hefting a twenty-pound pick, swinging it overhead and driving it down into a bed of gravel, setting off sparks and stinging the hands, was muscle-breaking, agonizing work. This stark truth may explain why Plummer remained in San Francisco for several months, and why there is no record of him spending so much as a single day digging for gold during the next eight years he was to live in California. The one skill he picked up was at cards, indicating that he devoted his spare time to the faro and monte tables in San Francisco's celebrated, gilded gaming halls.[11]

In the early part of 1853, Plummer left San Francisco and made his way up the Sacramento and American rivers to the mining country on the western slope of the Sierra Nevada, the majestic mountain range that derived its name, deservedly, from the Spanish words for saw-toothed and snow-clad. The arrival of a letter addressed to Plummer care of general delivery at Nevada City (the first of several western settlements to bear the same name) was advertised in the newspaper there on July 3, 1853, suggesting that he had shared his plans and destination with friends or perhaps a member of his family back home. It was the first time his name appeared in print.

Rather than pursue a belated effort at mining, Plummer turned his hand to ranching. He and a partner named Robinson operated a small spread in the Wilson Valley north of Nevada City, raising livestock. In October 1853, they ran an ad in the newspaper saying that a large, bay-colored ox, "marked with a triangular figure on the right hip," had wandered into their corral and could be claimed by the rightful owner. Thus Plummer appeared for a second time in public print, making an honest gesture.[12]

Familiar as the tasks were from his youth, ranching did not suit Plummer, and he gave it up after less than a year. His weakened lungs made a convenient excuse for abandoning the venture, but the fact was he disliked physical labor and made a point of avoiding it whenever possible. In 1854 he moved to Nevada City and found gentler work as a salesman for a bakery. A handsome, convivial young man, now twenty-one years old and sporting a luxuriant handlebar mustache, Plummer preferred the amenities of urban life to the quiet drudgery of the countryside. Certainly his conduct in later years reflected an appetite for the buzz and bustle of saloon culture and the company of women. He liked being around other people. Standing just under five-foot-nine, he had a slight, wiry build, a fair complexion, light brown hair, and gray eyes that seemed to change color with his moods.[13]

Nevada City was by 1854 a mature town, the county seat of an area swarming with more than 20,000 settlers, the third largest population center in California. The downtown boasted twenty buildings made of brick, a Wells Fargo office, a theater, and sixty-five saloons. Construction had begun on the three-story National Hotel, today the oldest continually operating hotel west of the Mississippi River. Traveling actors and entertainers made regular visits, including the legendary Lola Montez, who performed her signature "Spider Dance" for an appreciative audience. The hilly side streets of Nevada City were lined with simple wood-frame houses, giving the impression of ordinary family life—a false impression, as it happened, since fewer than a thousand of the residents were women. Many businesses thrived by selling the individual components of domesticity to single men by hourly or daily rates: room and board, laundry, sewing, dances, and sexual companionship.[14]

The owners of the United States Bakery, Thomas Hern and Henry Heyer, hired Plummer as a salesman, and he quickly made his mark by aggressively expanding the business beyond bread and pastries into a catering service that offered, according to a newspaper ad of the time, "fresh peaches, apples, plums, figs, raisins, green peas, green corn, oysters, clams, sardines, tomatoes, and a good assortment of confectionaries, cigars, etc." Calling on new customers, notably the town's restaurants, barrooms, gambling halls, and brothels, Plummer cultivated a wide circle of friends and prospered along with the bakery. In April 1854, he bought out Hern and became Heyer's partner. Operating from their shop beneath the Dramatic Hall on Pine Street, Plummer and Heyer cooked for parties, served late dinners to the after-theater crowd, and baked the occasional wedding cake. The staff of the weekly *Journal*, pleased to have the bakery's regular advertising, tested a sample cake and pronounced it delicious.[15]

Putting down roots, Plummer bought a house, a two-room bungalow on a narrow residential street behind the business district. For the first time in his life, he owned his own home. His position in Nevada City society remains a matter of conjecture, but some historians have suggested that he began courting the daughter of a prominent merchant in this period. If so, he was treading on uncertain ground. His new wealth made him a candidate for membership in the town's mercantile class, but his close association with the owners of barrooms and bordellos put him in unsavory company. As in all towns on the mining frontier, Nevada City's saloon society competed for primacy with a fledgling middle class made up of "merchants, ministers, editors, and wives," in one scholar's phrasing, who agitated for reform and sponsored sewing bees, Sunday school classes, lectures, and a philharmonic club. California was in the midst of a recurrent temperance campaign in 1855, and the bakery's ads began carrying a motto, "Live and Let Live," that may have been meant as a plea for tolerance for its bawdier clients, or perhaps for the owners themselves.[16]

Nevada City, California, in the early 1850s. Note that almost every tree had been chopped down for lumber. Lithograph. Courtesy of the Searls Historical Library, Nevada City, California.

In the spring of 1855, fire destroyed Nevada City's other leading bakery, leaving Plummer and Heyer with a temporary monopoly and greater profits than ever. Shortly afterward, hoping to benefit from a better location, they sold their business to a man named George Lippart and used the proceeds to buy a saloon, the Polka, on Broad Street. They spent the summer refitting the new premises and opened the doors of the City Bakery on August 17, 1855, to considerable fanfare. But their good fortune did not last. A general economic downturn slowed business, most of their customers remained loyal to the bakery they had sold, and within weeks they fell into financial straits. Plummer sold his house to Heyer for $1,000 in November 1855 and apparently intended to leave Nevada City for good to return east, one more transient fleeing the boom and bust of gold country.[17]

Then an opening in law enforcement presented itself, triggering another change in career.

On November 23, 1855, Nevada City's marshal, C. B. Evans, abruptly resigned his post. One of his deputies, David Johnson, won a special election to succeed him, creating a vacancy that the city council filled by hiring Henry Plummer. How Plummer got the job is unknown, but his acquaintance with the town's demimonde probably worked to his advantage. Then as now, saloon keepers had a vested interest in maintaining friendly relations with the police, not only to soften the enforcement of various blue laws but also to encourage the patronage of lawmen as a steadying influence among a volatile clientele. Because of his work for the bakery, Plummer had become a familiar and reassuring figure in Nevada City's barrooms and bordellos. Their owners likely said a word in his behalf to the city fathers, who leavened their desire for reform with a practical recognition of the need to provide safe, discreet outlets for the appetites of a population of young, single men.[18]

Taking public office, even as a lowly constable, Plummer found himself thrust into the cauldron of California politics during an especially chaotic and ugly period. Across the nation, the rabidly nativist Know-Nothing movement was in its heyday, fueled by a surge in immigration from across the Atlantic and directed at Irish Catholics in particular. Clustering in cities by the tens of thousands, these new arrivals presented a threat to the job security and political control of native-born, working-class Americans and were greeted accordingly with hostile words and physical intimidation. In northern California, the Chinese were targeted as well. The movement's name came from an insistence on secrecy among its early adherents, who used special signs, passwords, and handshakes to protect their identities and swore to say "I know nothing" if questioned about their activities. Moving into the open in the mid-1850s, the Know-Nothings changed their name to the American Party, adopted a platform of denying the vote to immigrants, and enjoyed a brief success in legislative races in several states. In the fall of 1855, an American Party candidate, J. Neely Johnson, won California's governor's race, and though his appeal was based more on a promise of reform than on bigotry, his victory highlighted the state's division along a fault line of ethnic, religious, and class differences.[19]

As a native New Englander and erstwhile merchant, Plummer might have been expected to align himself with the Know-Nothings, but he did not. He joined the Democratic Party instead, casting his lot, broadly speaking, with the have-nots. In California as in the rest of the country, the Democratic Party of 1855 could not fairly be said to represent any unified political philosophy, nor could its constituents be strictly categorized demographically. In Plummer's region of northern California, Democrats generally tended to be wage-earners rather than business owners, miners rather than merchants, immigrants rather than natives, Catholic rather than Protestant, "wet" rather than "dry," and in a sense that conforms at least partly to today's definitions, liberal rather than conservative. Nevada City's two weekly newspapers, the *Journal* and the *Democrat*, delighted in ranting at each other in harsh partisan rhetoric that emphasized such distinctions.[20]

By embracing the Democratic Party, Plummer put himself at odds with his boss, David Johnson, and also with the top lawman in the county, Sheriff W. W. "Boss" Wright, both American Party loyalists. The Democrats, whose leadership included several of the county's lawyers, welcomed Plummer into their ranks and made him a member of the Nevada County executive committee, encouraging his political ambitions. In turn, Plummer demonstrated a talent for currying favor with older, better-established men, including Tallman Rolph, the editor of the *Democrat*, who praised him as articulate, well-mannered, earnest, and capable. In the spring of 1856, with the blessing of the party leadership, Plummer announced he would run for the marshal's position against Johnson, and the newspapers quickly took sides. Edwin Waite, editor of the *Journal* and an ardent Know-Nothing, accused Plummer of favoritism toward the saloon crowds and warned that Johnson had "arrested too many of their kind to expect any favors or votes from that quarter." The only eligible voters, Waite argued, should be residents living within the city limits, and not "swarms of outsiders" from the nearby mining camps of Alpha, Rough and Ready, Red Dog, and Rush Creek. Despite the attacks, Plummer campaigned gamely and showed a knack for bringing men to his side. On election day, May 2, 1856, he beat Johnson by a paper-thin margin, 424 to 417, and the *Journal* responded sourly that Plummer's "cursing, hiccupping and yelling" supporters, aroused by "gallons of rotgut and hard swearing," had been carted in from the camps to stack the election.[21]

Plummer now held elective office. As city marshal, he was expected "to possess a certain level of professional competence," as one authority on the era put it. In addition to such mundane duties as slowing down fast riders, keeping pigs from running loose on the streets, and reprimanding litterbugs, he bore primary responsibility for maintaining public order.[22] But he was only twenty-four years old, and his inexperience quickly showed. On the night of Friday, June 6, 1856, just a month after becoming marshal, Plummer stumbled into the sort of fracas a more seasoned lawman might have avoided. He and two companions went to a saloon, and when two of the customers there got into a drunken shoving match, rocking the bar and breaking glasses, Plummer tried to arrest them. The saloon owner, a man named Lewis, objected violently, saying he would keep the peace in his own place of business without the interference of the marshal.[23]

One of Plummer's companions, George Jordan, answered Lewis angrily on Plummer's behalf, and soon the jostling turned deadly. After an exchange of curses, the saloonkeeper pulled a pistol from under the bar, aimed it at Jordan, and fired. Jordan ducked and the bullet wounded one of the two men who had started the ruckus. Then, as Plummer watched helplessly, armed with only a nightstick, Lewis fired again, striking Jordan in the chest and killing him. In the ensuing bedlam, with the room hazy and stinking of black powder smoke, the wounded man attacked Lewis and tried to wrestle the gun away from him. Plummer flailed at both of them with his billy club and eventually managed to subdue Lewis and arrest him, while the wounded man escaped howling in pain into the night. The *Journal*, making plain its disapproval of the episode, lamented that no attempt had been made to subdue the participants "for the peace and quiet of the town."

A grand jury indicted Lewis for murder in the affair, and Plummer was absolved of any fault. Yet it was plain that Plummer had contributed to the spiral of violence that left his friend dead. One myth of the Old West was that a lawman had to be good with his gun. In truth, the great skill common to most successful sheriffs and marshals was an ability to speak soothing words to drunken men and calm them down before arguments turned violent, since the trick was not to survive a showdown but to prevent one from starting in the first place. In a word, a good lawman needed to be disarming. Plummer had failed to gain control of the situation through his bearing and tone of voice before it spun out of control. Then, in trying to make an arrest unarmed, he had invited a challenge to his authority that he could not answer. And there was the question of Plummer's choice of companion. Just hours before his death, Jordan had been arrested by a sheriff's deputy for breaking a man's jaw with a piece of lumber, and he was free on $500 bail. A marshal could not afford to surround himself with hotheaded friends who got into fights.

Further complicating matters, Plummer's rude apprenticeship took place at the very moment San Francisco was seized by political crisis, as another vigilance committee, again led by prominent businessmen, began cracking down on a city government run by Irish Catholic, working-class Democrats. Depending on the sympathies of the historian, San Francisco's political machine was either famously corrupt, modeled by its leader, David Broderick, on New York's Tammany Hall, or the victim of the same irrational fears that incited the Know-Nothings elsewhere in the country. (Actually, it was both. William Tecumseh Sherman, who was running a bank in San Francisco at the time, during a break in his army career, believed the city's culture of greed afflicted men on every rung of the social ladder. "It seems that nobody is proof against this country," he wrote in a gloomy letter to a business partner. "The temptation of large profits is the soul of gambling and business here has partaken of that character. My opinion is the very nature of the country begets speculation, extravagance, failures, and rascality. Everything is chance, everything is gambling.")[24]

California had been admitted to the Union as a free state as part of the Compromise of 1850, and while its politicians were drawn inexorably into the bitter debate over slavery that ensued in the rest of the country, they had narrower concerns as well. Politics in northern California tended toward the parochial, centered more on patronage, spoils, and personal advancement than principle. As in some modern American cities, the business community in San Francisco believed its City Hall was riddled with waste and graft, and complained bitterly of padded payrolls and excessive taxes. Ethnic and class distrust added to the friction. The trouble in San Francisco began when a professional gambler named Charles Cora took his mistress, a beautiful prostitute named Arabella Ryan, to the theater. Her presence offended the sensibilities of the federal marshal for northern California, William Richardson, a hero of the Mexican War, who was sitting nearby with his wife and daughter. Richardson asked the theater manager to expel Cora's companion and complained loudly when the man refused. A few days later, Cora and Richardson encountered each other and traded insults, culminating in a sidewalk duel in which Cora shot and killed the marshal with a derringer.

As Cora sat in jail awaiting trial, one of San Francisco's firebrand newspaper editors took up the cause of the fallen lawman and began agitating for a lynching. James King was no ordinary journalist, but a fiery polemicist whose flamboyance extended to his own name. Not content with a common surname, he fashioned an aristocratic title of sorts and began calling himself James King of William, adding his father's name to his own. His paper, the *Bulletin*, railed against corruption in general and Broderick's political machine in particular. When Cora's trial ended in a hung jury, King of William accused the city's officials of bribing the jurors to protect Cora and went so far as to encourage the lynching of the sheriff.

King of William also directed his invective at a Democratic politician and rival newspaper editor named James Casey, creating another feud that ended badly. Casey had served a term in New York's famous Sing Sing prison after selling furniture that belonged to his mistress, and he was understandably sensitive about references to his record. When King of William published a detailed account of the matter, an enraged Casey confronted him on the sidewalk and shot him, inflicting a fatal wound.

Within days, the Committee of Vigilance was revived, led by an imposing businessman named William Tell Coleman, a millionaire contractor and veteran of the 1851 movement known for his sober, deliberate approach to the inherently incendiary question of imposing extralegal justice. Operating from a sturdy building guarded by hundreds of sandbags and four cannon on the roof, the committee quickly organized a private army of some six thousand men. On May 22, 1856, its members seized Cora and Casey from the jail and hanged them in full public view from a crossbeam on the second story of their headquarters. In coming days, they hanged two other men, drove dozens of others into exile, including Broderick, and took charge of City Hall.

In their time, the San Francisco vigilantes were widely applauded for their actions in imposing reform. Governor Johnson found himself power-less to intervene and saw his political career collapse overnight, since it was mostly his own American Party supporters who swelled the ranks of the insurgents and ignored his authority. A few voices were raised in protest, Sherman's among them, complaining that San Francisco was now gov-erned "by an irresponsible organization claiming to be armed with absolute power by the people." Sherman, who served as head of the state militia, resigned in frustration when he discovered that the vast majority of men under his command supported the vigilantes and would not take up arms against them. Certainly the vigilantes enjoyed a broad popular mandate, as even their critics conceded that their actions cleansed City Hall of "a bevy of political bullies," the phrase one historian used to label the ward-heelers and ballot-stuffers of the Democratic machine. In effect, the vig-ilantes staged a coup on behalf of honest elections and civil service, and then retired from the field of battle with political control safely in their hands for a decade to come.[25]

Watching the events from a distance, Plummer was profoundly affected. Closely aligned with the Democrats, and still smarting from the Ameri-can Party's attacks on him during his campaign for marshal, Plummer formed a deep distrust of vigilante justice, seeing its contempt for the rule of law as a direct threat to his friends, his new profession, and even his personal safety. In a sense, he saw the vigilantes as a posse of his political enemies, bent on overriding his authority. The Know-Nothings were to prove a short-lived phenomenon, their nativist passions quelled by a decline in immigration, and many in their ranks were drawn off into the newly formed Republican Party. But for Plummer, the clash between Democrats and Know-Nothings was the baptism of his political career.

Plummer recovered his bearings after the saloon shooting and went about his business as a lawman, keeping order, tracking fugitives, collect-ing fines and property taxes, issuing licenses, and trying to prevent fires. He suffered a dramatic embarrassment in this last duty on July 19, 1856, when a blaze that started in a blacksmith shop swept uphill from lower Main Street and destroyed half of Nevada City in a matter of hours. Fanned by a strong breeze, the flames consumed scores of wooden buildings, gutted many of the brick and stone structures, including the new courthouse and its "escape-proof" granite jail, and claimed ten lives. Afterward the city council adopted an ordinance, to be enforced by Plummer, requiring all public buildings to be equipped with a full barrel of water and two buckets.[26]

The saloon fight and the fire had the effect of widening the rift that already existed between Marshal Plummer and Sheriff Wright. Immediately after the election, Wright had hired Plummer's defeated opponent, David Johnson, as his deputy, and many in Nevada County regarded the sheriff and his men as having greater authority than Plummer. Fairly or not, the Know-Nothings enjoyed a better reputation than the Democrats for supporting and enforcing law and order. Following the violent partisan clash in San Francisco, the mood of political distrust in northern California reached a fevered pitch, with adherents of the Democratic and American parties viewing each other as little better than criminal classes. It was a situation made for misadventure.

Because of the damage it suffered in the fire, Nevada City's jail was no longer escape-proof. Until it could be rebuilt, security would have to reside in a padlocked wooden door and a lone guard, both easily defeated. In October 1856, Plummer arrested an accused armed robber named Jim Webster, who promptly escaped into the cool autumn darkness by digging a hole under the brick wall of his cell and smashing the padlock on the outer door while the guard was off having dinner. Plummer tracked him down and returned him to jail, only to have him escape a second time in the company of two brothers named Farnsworth, also charged with robbery. Plummer meant to bring in all three, but first he approached Sheriff Wright and insisted that the county pay his expenses, since the escapees were county prisoners. Wright agreed, then demanded in turn that he be part of the posse.[27]

Plummer had an idea that the prisoners might be hiding at a cabin in nearby Gold Flat, where Webster had asked to stop and speak to a friend after his first capture. Despite the urgency of the situation, however, the marshal seemed in no hurry to begin the manhunt. He told Wright he had chores that would tie him up until late in the day, and Wright agreed to join him at five o'clock at the quartz mill near the stable. As the hours passed, several men rode into Nevada City to warn that they had seen horses tied up in a forested ravine near the cabin, and at least two of them spoke directly to Plummer. The wanted men, it appeared, were right where the marshal expected them to be. Still he delayed. It was the afternoon of Monday, November 3, 1856, the day before the national election, and

Plummer watched with interest as his fellow Democrats busied themselves preparing for a torchlight rally in support of their presidential candidate, James Buchanan. On the morrow, Buchanan would win a lone,
hapless term in the White House, a last stop on the nation's long, dismal
march to civil war.

At five o'clock, Plummer sent word to Sheriff Wright that he was still
busy, asking for a delay of another half-hour. Plummer made no secret
that he would have preferred leading a small, stealthy party, perhaps just
himself and his top deputy, Bruce Garvey, to pursue the fugitives. He may
have hoped the sheriff would grow tired of waiting or be called away to
some other duty. But at five-thirty, when Plummer and Garvey mounted
their horses and crossed the bridge leading out of town, Sheriff Wright
came hastening after them. The three men rode together for about an
hour until they neared the cabin in Gold Flat, where Plummer motioned
for the others to halt.[28]

In the quiet of the woods, Plummer suddenly heard the sound of other
horsemen behind him. He spun around, saw riders approaching, and was
furious when Wright admitted that he had arranged for three friends to
follow him. One of them was David Johnson, Plummer's defeated rival for
marshal. The sheriff plainly had not trusted Plummer enough to ride alone
with him and had organized a small posse of his own. Given little other
choice, the wary group of six joined forces and pressed ahead with their
business, Plummer taking the lead and stalking quietly into the ravine until
he spotted the getaway horses staked to trees in the twilight. He gave a low
whistle to call the others forward.

In that same instant, Plummer sensed another group of men nearby, perhaps only fifteen or twenty feet away, and stiffened as one of them shouted,
"Don't come any closer!" Behind Plummer, David Johnson yelled back,
"What are you doing here?" An anxious voice answered with the same
question, and a second later both sides opened fire in a quick, lethal fusillade of fifty or more shots—a deafening explosion punctuated by the
sounds of bullets and buckshot slapping through pine boughs and thudding
into tree trunks and banks of earth.

It was Plummer, by all accounts, who first realized the awful truth, that
the enemy fire was not coming from the fugitives but from a group of
interloping innocents—a vigilante group that had despaired of the lawmen
ever arriving and taken matters into their own hands. In a flash of muz-
zle fire, Plummer recognized one of their number as a prominent young

lawyer named Wallace Williams, the scion of one of Nevada City's leading families. "Stop firing!" Plummer shouted. "You're killing your friends!" Afterward, horrified men from both parties came forward, combed the ground in the dark, and found the body of Sheriff Wright, dead of gunshots to the chin, neck, and chest. David Johnson, they learned later, had managed to make his way on foot to the home of one of the vigilantes, where he lay mortally wounded.

The next day, a coroner's jury convened to try to sort out the fatal confusion of the previous evening. For the first time, Henry Plummer's words were recorded, giving posterity a chance to hear him speak and to judge his answers. He said he and Sheriff Wright had been standing side by side when they first heard shouting in the ravine and assumed it was Webster, the escaped prisoner. When the first shots rang out, Plummer added, "Wright and I stepped back a few feet toward the horses. The shots started coming fast and thick now, and I saw a man jump behind a big stump in the center of the ravine. Wright ran for him. This man put his pistol out and fired and Wright fell." Plummer said he did not know the man by name, but recognized his face and knew he was not one of the fugitives. "Almost immediately," the marshal continued, "I recognized Wallace Williams by the flash of Garvey's gun. I called him by name, and told him to stop, that he was shooting his friends. There were a few shots after this, near where Johnson was attempting to come down. They stopped and we all came together. Someone brought a candle. Then we knew it was a mistake."

Other witnesses supported Plummer's account. The only important conflicting testimony came from Hamilton McCormack, one of the men who had spoken to Plummer in town, who said he had warned Plummer about the group of men keeping watch over the horses in the ravine. The damaging implication was that Plummer had taken advantage of the situation to lead his rival, Wright, into harm's way. But this made little sense. Plummer had done his best to discourage the sheriff from joining him in the first place, and then had stood by his side in deadly jeopardy when the shooting started. McCormack was a good friend of the sheriff's and might well have wanted to plant a seed of doubt about Plummer's motives, given the antagonisms of the time and place. Certainly that would account for McCormack's response when one of the lawyers at the inquest asked if Plummer had been drunk on the afternoon in question. "I cannot tell," McCormack replied with casual spite, "when Henry Plummer is drunk or not."

The coroner's jury wasted little time in returning a verdict of accidental death. And there the matter might have rested, with Plummer vindicated, except that Wallace Williams had a bone to pick with him. In his testimony, reported prominently in the partisan *Journal*, Williams suggested that Plummer had run like a coward at the sound of the first shot. His exact words were, "I suppose Plummer took to his heels and ran after he fired." Understandably, Plummer was outraged at the accusation. By every account, including Williams's, it was Plummer who had recognized the other party and called a halt to the shooting, something he could not very well have done if he had been running away. And one of Williams's party testified that Plummer was standing beside the sheriff when the firing stopped.

Plummer insisted on writing a letter responding to Williams, which ran in the *Nevada Democrat* on November 19, 1856, two weeks after the incident. "I would gladly forget all the deplorable events of that tragedy," he wrote, "but I cannot permit the sneering insinuations to go unnoticed." Williams, he said, had invented a "gratuitous insult" purely and simply "to inflict on me an injury." In the stuffy language of the era used by men who considered themselves gentlemen and observed the code of the duel, Plummer concluded that "unlike Mr. Williams, my own courage is dependent on my own testimony under oath, not on the trumpeting of the press. I will leave this subject with the hope that he may enjoy the reputation for which he longs and I such as I deserve."

Williams answered with a letter of his own in the *Journal* six days later, accusing Plummer of acting like a "spoiled child" in disputing him. But Williams made it plain that he did not wish to pursue the feud. He suggested coyly that it was "self-preservation" and not cowardice that impelled Plummer to run away, adding, "There are times when it is valiant to retreat, for instance when a man is so situated as to be a target for others to shoot at with no chance to act defensively, [and] then it is fool-hardy to stand." With this exchange of public letters the matter ended.[29]

Once again, Plummer stood exonerated by a coroner's jury and, for the most part, by the court of public opinion. But once again, he also stood center stage in an incident that had claimed innocent lives. Wright and Johnson, albeit fierce partisans, were widely respected as lawmen, their funerals attended by hundreds of mourners. At a minimum, Plummer's distrust of Sheriff Wright, rooted in the politics of the time and place, had created delay and sowed deadly confusion for which Plummer had to share some of the blame. And, of course, Webster and the Farnsworths, the three fugitives, had gotten clean away during the mishap, with consequences that would be felt in the future. Still, Plummer clearly did not intend to sulk or slink away. Within the stiff prose of his letter lay a hot defense of his reputation and a cry for recognition of his bravery. It does not seem too much to say, in the language of our own time, that Henry Plummer was displaying an ego.

In the months ahead, Plummer redoubled his efforts to do his job well. He demonstrated a knack for tracking down wanted men, bringing in so many fugitives that the *Journal*, the opposition newspaper that delighted in flaying him, grudgingly applauded his "considerable ingenuity" in making the arrests, typically without resistance. The compliment was especially generous because Plummer had just cited and fined Edwin Waite, the editor, for not having the requisite barrel of water and buckets in his office for firefighting. In May 1857 Plummer was reelected marshal by a comfortable margin, 417 to 305.[30]

Plummer's political career appeared to be back on the upswing. At the Nevada County Democratic convention in August 1857, he was one of five men nominated as candidates for the state assembly, the lower house of the California legislature. If successful, he would go to Sacramento with a chance to trade his marshal's badge for higher office. But there were disquieting signs as well. During his race for reelection, Plummer's enemies openly accused him of taking money—and orders—from the proprietor of one of Nevada City's leading brothels. In the fall campaign, the *Sacramento Union* ran an article, attributed to a fellow Democrat, saying Plummer had split the party by aligning himself with the saloon crowd and becoming "the leader of the reckless, rowdy gang of gamblers and loafers" while ignoring the "quiet and respectable" wing of the party.[31]

More damaging still, anonymous handbills were distributed in Nevada County accusing Plummer of planning to vote against the interests of the miners by supporting wage cuts and foreign ownership of mines and mills. Plummer was also "in favor of early spring rains," the handbill said, because he wanted to discourage creek and river prospectors. Tallman Rolph, the editor of the *Democrat*, the local party organ, responded to this last attack with sarcasm, assuring miners that Plummer had never taken a position on rain, early or otherwise, "and further, that he has not been in the last dog fight, and has had no hand in the next war; that he is in favor of good diggings, with the bed rock of a proper pitch, water the year round, an equitable temperature, an addition to our moonlight nights, and an immediate reform and general improvement in everything."[32]

Rolph's light touch notwithstanding, Plummer discovered he was indeed the subject of a hostile faction in the party. The miners, his natural constituency in previous elections, believed the accusations and lost faith in him. On Election Day, September 9, 1857, while his four fellow Democratic nominees won seats in the assembly, Plummer went crashing to defeat, the victim of dissident Democrats who cast their votes for a Know-Nothing. His career, so recently promising, lay in tatters.[33]

There was worse to come.

CHAPTER TWO

"A Seducer" on Trial

In the spring of 1857, a young couple, Lucinda and John Vedder, moved to Nevada City from an outlying farm and rented a small house Henry Plummer owned on Spring Street. They quickly gained a reputation for violent arguments and physical abuse. John Vedder, who worked nights as a card dealer in a gambling house, suspected his young, pretty wife of seeing other men and occasionally had her followed. Both had quick tempers. Once, when he forgot to bring home some coal, she gave him a dark look and he cursed her in front of a friend. Another time he struck her and pinched her nose. They stayed together mostly because they had a year-old daughter.[1]

Aside from a few brief meetings when he stopped by to pick up his personal effects, including a fishing line, Plummer had little contact with his tenants. During celebrations on the Fourth of July, 1857, John Vedder was injured in the forehead by a bottle rocket, nearly losing an eye. He called on David Belden, a local lawyer, to file a civil suit on his behalf, and Belden, a prominent Democrat and a friend of Plummer's, soon found himself playing the reluctant role of referee in the Vedders' stormy marriage. In August 1857, Vedder told Belden that his wife seemed intent on divorcing him and expressed worry about losing custody of their little daughter. The couple reconciled a few days later.[2]

Around the middle part of September, a week after Plummer's defeat at the polls, Lucy spotted a man tailing her as she walked down the street.

That night, she confronted John and accused him of spying on her. Furious, he pulled his Bowie knife, held it to her throat, and told her he had a good notion to kill her. The next day, a terrified Lucy sent for Plummer, who still held his post as city marshal, and asked him for protection and advice about a divorce. Plummer fetched Belden and brought him to talk to her about the legalities of separation. Lucy told Belden that John had abused her, but she also cried and said they loved each other, and Belden urged her to try to work things out.[3]

That night, Lucy told her husband about Belden's visit. John was furious and went to see Belden in the morning, demanding to know who had intervened and invited the lawyer to his house. Alarmed at Vedder's anger, Belden refused to answer. Vedder suspected the truth anyway, and from that point on he treated Plummer with wary hostility. A few days afterward, Lucy packed up some clothes and took a room at the Hotel de Paris, a modest, one-story frame lodging a block from her house. She went back home each day to fix John his meals, but spent her nights at the hotel with their daughter.

The dissolution of the Vedders' marriage, a sad, combustible, but entirely commonplace affair, took an unusual and fateful turn when Plummer, concerned about Lucy's safety, rented the room across the hall from hers at the Hotel de Paris and began spending nights there. By today's standards, perhaps, Plummer's action might be seen in a benign, protective light. But in the mid-nineteenth century, when a husband was widely presumed to hold dominion over his wife, Plummer's move aroused suspicion all over town. There is no evidence that any liaison occurred between Plummer and Lucy Vedder. Indeed, one of Plummer's former deputies, Pat Corbett, stayed in the room with him, acting as a sort of chaperone. Still, people gossiped, and John Vedder fumed.[4]

One morning a few days later, Vedder went to his wife's room at the hotel, collected their small daughter, and took her with him back to the house. Later that day, he ran into a couple of friends and told them he meant to kill Plummer for having an affair with Lucy. He showed one of them his knife and said he preferred using it to a pistol. Alarmed, another friend wrote a letter to Vedder's father in Sacramento, warning that his son was on the verge of serious trouble. For his part, Plummer also spoke to several people, telling them he knew John Vedder had suffered a "hard lot" but warning that he could face prison for kidnapping his child. And in a very different tone, chilly with menace, Plummer said he was keeping a

The Hotel de Paris in Nevada City, California, where Lucy Vedder moved and Henry Plummer followed. Courtesy of the Searls Historical Library, Nevada City, California.

close eye on Vedder and did not intend to let him draw first blood. "He told me," one of Plummer's friends said later, "that he knew everything Vedder had said or done and had no intention of letting Vedder shoot him down, that Vedder might be lucky and get one shot, but that would be all." Plummer's ability to sound reasonable in one breath and ominous in the next, a trait that would manifest itself time and again in coming years, had taken root.[5]

Vedder began making preparations to leave Nevada City and return to his father's home in Sacramento. He told the milkman to stop deliveries. He offered some of his furniture, including a rocking chair, for sale to friends. On the afternoon of Thursday, September 24, 1857, he took his daughter back to the ranch where he and Lucy had lived before moving to town and asked the owner, Van Young, to guard her in case Lucy and Plummer tried to take her.[6]

The next morning, Vedder went to Belden's office and told him he wanted divorce papers drawn up, served, and processed that very day. To Belden's eye, he seemed agitated and preoccupied. Belden agreed to prepare the paperwork. A couple of hours later, Vedder returned to Belden's office, and together they went to the house on Spring Street to have Lucy sign the documents. As they left, Belden warned John not to try to see her again, and he answered hotly, "Do you think I'm a damn fool? She can go to hell her own way." They went to the courthouse and by three o'clock in the afternoon the papers had been recorded.[7]

In the late afternoon, Vedder went to the Hotel de Paris and took a seat in the small dining room there. The owner, noticing that he seemed pale and had no appetite, asked Vedder if he was sick. Vedder answered that he was fine but left without touching his food. He next went to the Empire Stable and arranged to rent a horse. Around dusk, he was walking along Broad Street when he spotted a friend, George McFadden, on the steps of a rooming house, and asked if he could borrow a pistol. Volunteering to get him one, McFadden excused himself, walked to a nearby store, went to the owner's bedroom in the back, and appropriated a revolver he knew to be kept under the pillow. Moments later, he rejoined Vedder and handed him the gun. Vedder, who had no holster or gunbelt, tucked the weapon in the outside pocket of his jacket.[8]

Vedder rode out to Young's ranch to check on his daughter. He had agreed to surrender custody to Lucy as a condition of the divorce, but now he apparently changed his mind. He asked the rancher to keep her, then rode back to town and returned his horse to the stable. Around midnight, he went to his home on Spring Street. The house was a tiny wood-frame structure, painted white, with a sitting room in front and a kitchen in back, each about twelve feet square. A long, narrow stairwell led from the back of the kitchen down to an alley behind the house, where there was a privy and a high wooden fence. Instead of going to the front door, Vedder began climbing the back steps in the darkness.

Lucy Vedder also had dinner at the Hotel de Paris that evening, about an hour after her husband. Plummer's associate Pat Corbett dined with her and then accompanied her back to the house, where she finished packing her belongings. Corbett made a fire for her in the kitchen stove, and stayed with her as she waited for John to return with their daughter. She meant to take the child with her on the 2 A.M. stage to Sacramento, if he got back in time. Several hours passed, and shortly before midnight Plummer showed up to spell Corbett. He and Lucy sat in chairs on either side of the stove, talking quietly.[9]

Moments later, neighbors heard four rapid gunshots splitting the stillness of the night. In the next minute, Plummer ran from the kitchen through the front room of the house and into Spring Street, blowing his police whistle. Lucy followed an instant later, crying out that her husband had been shot. The first man to arrive on the scene, a neighbor named Thomas Couts, found Vedder lying on his back at the bottom of the backstairs, barely alive, with a small, fresh bloodstain on the left side of his white shirt. By his side, just visible in the candlelight, was a Colt revolver. Couts picked the gun up and was about to examine it when Pat Corbett rushed in and declared, "I'll take that pistol." He stuck it in his belt.[10]

Soon the area at the foot of the back steps was crowded with neighbors and onlookers. Lucy returned and tried to comfort Vedder. But he was already dead. A constable, J. C. Mallory, arrived a few minutes later and found Lucy in tears, saying Plummer had shot her husband. Mallory put a pillow under Vedder's head and closed his eyes. Several men then carried Vedder's body up the back stairway and placed him on a straw mattress in the front room. Around the same time, adding a sort of exclamation point to the night's rush of events, the sharp crack of a lone, mysterious gunshot could be heard echoing several blocks away in the direction of the Methodist Church.[11]

After leaving the house on Spring Street, Plummer made his way up the hill to the courthouse and knocked on the door of the jail. His deputy,

Bruce Garvey, was with him. A jailer, Charles Van Hagan, answered the door and asked Plummer what he wanted. Plummer said he wanted to give himself up. Van Hagan asked what had happened. After refusing at first to explain, Plummer told Van Hagan and another jailer that he had been "in a fuss." John Vedder, he said, had climbed up the backstairs, stepped into the kitchen, pointed a pistol at him, and shouted, "Your time has come!" Plummer was not sure who fired first, only that he had fired several times and believed he hit Vedder. A few minutes later, someone called through the jail window that Vedder was dead. Oddly, Plummer then announced defiantly to the jailers that no man could scare him. He held out his hand and demanded to know if they could see it tremble. They could not. They took him into custody.[12]

In the hours before dawn, the house on Spring Street was finally secured, the doors nailed shut by order of the coroner in preparation for an inquest in the morning. Lucy Vedder was taken to a neighbor's house, then back to the Hotel de Paris to rest and gather herself. In the morning, before the hearing, several members of the coroner's jury went to the house to look for evidence, and they were struck by the absence of any indication that Vedder had fired his gun at Plummer. There were no bullet holes in the walls of the kitchen or front room of the house. A puncture mark was found in a gate in front of the house, but it was an old one, covered with a coat of paint. Meanwhile, an autopsy showed Vedder had been shot twice, once fatally in the chest and a second time in the arm, and two other balls were found lodged in the privy and the wooden wall at the bottom of the steps—accounting for all four shots. Doctors examining Vedder's body concluded that his wounds appeared to have been inflicted from above.

At the inquest, Lucy Vedder tried to corroborate Plummer's story. Her husband had stepped into the kitchen with his pistol drawn, she swore, and shot at Plummer. Pat Corbett turned in the gun he had confiscated from Vedder's side and demonstrated that it had been fired. But their accounts were not very convincing. If Vedder had shot in Plummer's direction, where was the bullet? It seemed to many observers that Corbett must have fired the gun himself to bolster his friend's case for self-defense, accounting for the final gunshot of the night before. Later during the hearing, a neighbor, James Ballard, testified that he had seen the four shots as they were fired while he lay in bed in a nearby, unfinished house that had no blinds. The trajectory of all the shots, he said, was downward.

It was difficult not to conclude that Plummer had heard Vedder coming up the backstairs of the house, assumed his intent was sinister, and fired first, down the darkened stairwell, killing him before he had a chance to act. As a matter of criminal law today, a prosecutor might very well decline to bring charges against a police officer in Plummer's position. But in Nevada City, California, a century and a half ago, the judge bound Plummer over to the grand jury and set his bail at $8,000. According to the *Journal,* long his adversary, "Plummer's course and conduct [have] been generally condemned," an assessment that seems to have been accurate. The *Sacramento Union,* also hostile to Plummer, reported matter-of-factly that "an intimacy" had existed between Plummer and Lucy Vedder, giving that rumor the gloss of established truth. In the mining camps around Nevada City, men who might have scorned Vedder as a lowly wife-beater under other circumstances took his side and voiced sympathy for him, calling Plummer a "seducer." A miner at the San Juan settlement expressed the prevailing view when he told friends, "A man who would take another's wife away and then shoot him down like a dog, ought to be hung."[13]

In the days after the inquest, a shaken Lucy Vedder gave up custody of her daughter to her husband's father, Vulcan Vedder, in Sacramento. She left Nevada City and moved down the valley several miles to the town of Auburn. Then, on the night of Sunday, October 11, 1857, she turned up at Vulcan Vedder's house, asked to visit the child, and moments later spirited her away to a nearby friend's house. Within the hour, a crowd assembled outside the house and threatened to seize the little girl by force. Lucy and her daughter wound up in police custody overnight. In the morning, a judge ordered her to return the child to Vulcan Vedder pending a formal hearing, an indication that the court doubted her fitness as a parent.[14]

On October 15, 1857, the Nevada County grand jury indicted Plummer for murder. He pleaded not guilty, and David Belden, who agreed to act as defense counsel, asked for a change of venue because of the widespread feeling against his client. Judge Miles Searls denied the motion for the time being, but acknowledged that it might have merit and agreed to revisit the issue at trial, which he set to begin on Monday, December 21, 1857.[15]

As Belden feared, seating an impartial jury proved difficult. On the first day of jury selection, a pool of one hundred potential jurors yielded only seven qualified panelists, as scores of others admitted or revealed bias. Judge Searls invited Plummer's lawyer to renew his call for a change of venue, but much to the court's surprise, Belden declined. One of the seven jurors selected was a man named George Getchell, who hailed from the same part of Maine as Plummer, and Belden apparently believed he represented a promising vote for acquittal. Five more jurors were picked over the next two days, and the first witness was called on Wednesday afternoon, two days before Christmas.[16]

The trial largely paralleled the coroner's inquest. The prosecution focused on evidence that Vedder had not fired his gun, a point Belden was hard-pressed to refute. Pat Corbett gave a confusing account of his custody of Vedder's pistol, saying he first examined it under a street lamp a few minutes after the shooting and saw a broken cap in the cylinder, indicating it had been fired. But before turning the gun over to the coroner's jury the next morning, he added, he had taken it to a gunsmith named Davis who examined it and in the process dropped the pieces of the cap out of the cylinder, accidentally destroying the evidence. Asked about the single, final gunshot late on the night of the killing, Corbett insisted he had not heard it and knew nothing about it.

By far the most dramatic moment came on the second day of the trial, after the state rested, when the defense called Lucy Vedder to the stand. As before, she said she and Plummer had been sitting on either side of the stove in her kitchen on the night of the incident, Plummer with his head tilted back and his hands over his eyes. "I heard someone coming up the stairs very fast," she testified. "I thought it was Mr. Vedder by his step. He opened the door and stepped in, and saying to Mr. Plummer, 'Your time has come,' fired a pistol. As he fired his pistol, Mr. Plummer raised out of his chair and fired at him as he was in the act of stepping out of the door." She offered no ready explanation for the discrepancy between her version of events and the physical evidence and testimony that contradicted her.

The ensuing cross-examination created quite a stir. Prosecutor Henry Meredith approached the witness with an accusatory air. Had she not told her father-in-law that she was happy with Vedder? That her husband provided well for her? Had she not admitted that Plummer promised to pay for a divorce so he could marry her himself? That Plummer wanted to set her up in a bordello so he could live off her? Lucy vigorously denied all of these allegations, but it was plain from the prosecutor's questions that she had talked with the elder Vedder several times after the shooting and that he meant to turn those conversations against her and Plummer. "He said he would spend his last dollar or last drop of blood to have Plummer convicted," she explained, trying to stop the onslaught.[17]

But the state had the last word. The prosecutor rose, holding a document in his hand, and asked Lucy if she recognized it. "Yes, I know it," she replied wearily. "Yes, I signed it." The document, admitted as Exhibit A over the strenuous objections of Plummer's lawyer, was an affidavit, signed by Lucy Vedder in Sacramento on December 4, three weeks earlier, stating that Vulcan Vedder had asked her only to "tell him the truth relative to the murder of his unfortunate boy," and that he had made no threats or inducements against her to do otherwise. "I have told him nothing but truth," it concluded. Moments later, the state put Vulcan Vedder on the stand, and he testified that Lucy had told him "the object of Plummer killing [John] was to get her to a bad house. . . ." The reason Plummer was at the house on Spring Street that night, Vedder added, was to sleep with Lucy. And his son, he said, was shot dead at the foot of the back steps before he ever started to climb them. He glared at Plummer, sitting nearby at the defense table, as he spoke.[18]

On cross-examination, Belden tried to show that Lucy had talked to Vedder's father and signed his paper because she was desperate to placate him and regain custody of her daughter. But the damage was done. The affidavit she signed sounded almost like a confession. Belden did not call Plummer to the stand, possibly because he feared even greater harm from questioning by the prosecutors. Testimony was concluded late on the afternoon of Christmas Eve, and Judge Searls ordered a recess the next day so that all of the parties could observe the holiday. Court reconvened on Saturday, December 26, 1857, for closing arguments and the judge's instructions to the jury. Deliberations began about 9:30 that night and continued the next morning. In the early afternoon, the jury returned and pronounced Henry Plummer guilty of murder in the second degree.[19]

The shortcomings of Plummer's defense strategy were fairly obvious during the trial, but the worst miscalculation came to light only after the jury returned its verdict. Getchell, the juror from Maine, had not been a good bet for a vote for acquittal. On the contrary, according to several acquaintances who now came forward, he had been severely prejudiced against Plummer from the beginning. On Wednesday, December 30, the day the judge set for sentencing, Belden came into court and charged Getchell and two other jurors, Gideon Denny and Green Jamieson, with expressing bias against Plummer before the trial began. The state asked for time to review the accusations, and Judge Searls deferred sentencing.

During the first week of 1858, Plummer's lawyers filed affidavits from several friends and acquaintances of the three jurors asserting that they had prejudged his guilt. "The people ought to take Henry Plummer out of jail and hang him," one man quoted Getchell as saying a day after Vedder's death. Judge Searls pondered the matter for two weeks before rejecting Belden's plea for a new trial. On January 18, 1858, he sentenced Plummer to twelve years at hard labor at San Quentin. But signaling his doubts about the sturdiness of the verdict, he freed Plummer on a $10,000 bond while Belden prepared an appeal to the California Supreme Court. On the same day, Plummer resigned as marshal.[20]

Fair-minded observers, especially those with a perch in modern times, may wonder how Plummer lost a case that seemed to embody the heart and soul of reasonable doubt. The defense put on an abundance of witnesses who testified about Vedder's animus toward Plummer, and about his threats and menace of arms. Plummer's version of events did not ring entirely true, granted, but even if he had ambushed Vedder at the alley wall it was still a matter of killing an armed intruder. Why were the jury—and the public at large—ready to believe the worst of Plummer? To a large extent, the answer seems to have been his reputation. By the time of the Vedder incident, Plummer had been closely linked with Nevada City's saloon and brothel crowd for more than three years. His friends and political supporters came from the netherworld, and it was easy enough to believe that he had beguiled Lucy Vedder and meant to set her on a life of prostitution because so many of the people in his circle were doing exactly that as their way of making a living. It was guilt by association.

Once the transcript was completed, the California Supreme Court wasted little time in reversing the verdict and ordering a new trial in a new venue. Perhaps Plummer was due a political break, for he certainly got one. The court's unanimous opinion was written by Justice David Terry, a legendary figure of early statehood in California, an ex-Texas Ranger turned Know-Nothing who made his reputation by standing up to the vigilantes of San Francisco during the events of 1856. On one memorable occasion in Governor Johnson's office, Terry had confronted William T. Sherman and demanded that he take up arms against the businessmen of the Vigilance Committee. When Sherman demurred, Terry sat glowering at him in disgust, a scene Sherman recalled vividly in his memoirs. If anyone was primed to detest mob psychology and to take the side of a victim of vigilantism, it was Terry. The prejudiced jurors who convicted Plummer, he wrote heatedly, were guilty of "an offense little short of murder itself."[21]

On September 16, 1858, almost a full year after Vedder's death, Plummer stood trial again, this time in Marysville, a mining town in Yuba County about thirty miles west of Nevada City. The testimony was virtually the same as before, and so, surprisingly, was the verdict. A fresh jury found Plummer guilty of murder in the second degree. It may be that Marysville was close enough to the original venue that the taint of Plummer's reputation remained a factor. And the state introduced a new witness, a friend of Lucy Vedder's who claimed the widow kept a photograph of Plummer, possible evidence of a romance. The era's presumption in favor of a husband, even an abusive one, remained pervasive. The legal standard of self-defense was not as liberal as today. Still, the conviction came as a shock. The judge sentenced Plummer to ten years at hard labor, and this time the prospects of an appeal looked dim.[22]

Plummer's health, robust since his recovery from childhood lung problems, took a turn for the worse under the strain. His appeal failed, and on February 22, 1859, he reported to San Quentin to begin serving his time.[23]

San Quentin, 1859. Like most things in California at the time, the prison on the bay north of San Francisco was caught in the struggle between the state's political factions. Not that the gaunt pile of stones looked like much of a prize. Built in 1854 to replace a floating jail, the two-story stockade might have come straight from the pages of Charles Dickens. Its dank, gray walls held nearly six hundred prisoners, jammed four to a cell, sleeping on filthy straw and wearing rags instead of uniforms. The kitchen stank of stale codfish, "putty" bread, and green meat. Discipline was enforced by leg-iron and whipping post, and disease and food poisoning ran rampant. Signs warned that prisoners caught trying to escape would have their sentences doubled. Many tried anyway.

The prison was run by a private contractor, who profited from hiring out the convicts and, according to periodic scandal, from selling pardons. The state intervened from time to time, but the legislature found little public support for spending the money needed for reform. In 1858,

Democrat John Weller succeeded the hapless Neely Johnson as governor and sent a commission to investigate conditions. Finding "brutality, vice, corruption, filth, and mismanagement . . . enough to make the heart sick," the commission's report prompted Weller to seize control of the prison by force and compel improvements. The ousted administrator sued, and the matter was still ricochetting through the courts a year later when Henry Plummer arrived for processing.[24]

Like all new inmates, Plummer was stripped naked and searched intimately. Convict Number 1573 stood five-foot-eight-and-a-half, weighed one hundred and fifty pounds, had two moles on the back of his neck, another under his left shoulder blade, and bore an ugly scar on his left forefinger. Three other fingers on his left hand were permanently crippled, curled inward by scar tissue from a deep cut. The purpose of the examination, beyond teaching a lesson of deliberate indignity, was to compile an inventory of identifying characteristics in the event of escape. In Plummer's case, it gave evidence of a severe injury inflicted in some episode missed by the Nevada City newspapers, a further indication of the volatility of his brief career as a lawman.[25]

The medical examination also disclosed Plummer's chronic lung illness, and in this he was lucky. The prison doctor, Alfred Taliaferro, insisted that Plummer sleep in the sick bay on the ground floor instead of a cell, and he made Plummer his assistant, sparing him from the chain gang and the quarry. Granted the status of a trusty, Plummer was given the run of the infirmary and allowed to perform errands for Dr. Taliaferro outside the prison.[26]

A few days after Plummer entered San Quentin, the state Supreme Court ordered the old prison administration restored to power. The private contractor returned and resumed the practices of hard labor and strict discipline. He fired Dr. Taliaferro and other officials aligned with Governor Weller. A small prison break ensued in May 1859, followed by a major insurrection on June 26, 1859, in which fifty inmates captured two guards and scattered through a gate into the hills above Point San Quentin. They were recaptured in a bloody manhunt that left several convicts dead. After order was restored, the prison remained in a lockdown, with inmates confined to their cells.

On July 1, with several inmates injured and in need of medical attention in the infirmary, Dr. Taliaferro was recalled to service, giving Plummer back his patron. A few days later, the doctor sent Plummer to fetch some medical supplies from his home in nearby San Rafael, and Plummer was caught in a fierce squall on the way back to the prison. Soaked to the skin, he caught a chill and fell sick. He awoke the next morning with a high fever, a wracking cough, and a pillowcase spattered ominously with blood. Dr. Taliaferro diagnosed consumption—tuberculosis—the dreaded infectious disease that could run through a confined population like wildfire if unchecked. Plummer was placed in quarantine in the infirmary, and Dr. Taliaferro monitored him closely. On July 14, 1859, Taliaferro and the prison's other physician, T. B. Heiry, sent a petition to Governor Weller stating that Plummer was fatally ill and had only five or six weeks left to live. They urged his release from confinement.

Plummer's friends joined the campaign for clemency. One of his lawyers wrote the governor asking for a pardon, as did a prison guard who saw Plummer on a daily basis and attested to the severity of his condition. In Nevada City, Plummer's old deputy, Pat Corbett, secured more than a hundred signatures on a petition that cited Plummer's ill health and also expressed doubt about his guilt. "The fatal occurrence," it said, "took place without entraps other than the female, the cause of the tragedy." A number of lawyers and law officers signed, including the marshal of Marysville, the site of Plummer's second trial. Corbett made an appointment to see the governor in Sacramento and presented the document to him in person. Dr. Taliaferro wrote another note to the governor, in a highly personal vein, saying he sympathized "very deeply" with Plummer and asking the pardon "in order that he may die among his friends."[27]

On August 15, 1859, Governor Weller issued the pardon, citing Plummer's "imminent danger of death" while pointedly ignoring any comment on his guilt or innocence. The next day, Plummer walked out of San Quentin a free man, having served slightly less than six months. He returned to Nevada City within the week, and the remarkable thing was that he did not die. Indeed, he did not appear very sick at all. He was up and about in days, showing no trace of consumptive disease. A fair guess is that Plummer had faked the extent of his illness, parlaying a severe head cold and the genuine evidence of lung damage from his youth into a ticket out of prison, perhaps cinching his case by exploiting a cut or some other source of blood in the infirmary to supply the stains on his bedclothes. Fully recovered, he was hired by his friend and successor, Marshal E. O. Tompkins, to be a constable on Nevada City's police force. A month later, in a nice irony, Plummer arrested one "Ten Year" Smith, an escapee from San Quentin, after recognizing him at a restaurant.[28]

Plummer's return to law enforcement did not excite comment one way or the other from Nevada City's newspapers, but it soon became clear that a majority of his fellow citizens strongly disapproved. In May 1860, Marshal Tompkins ran for reelection and was soundly trounced amid rumors that he planned to resign in Plummer's favor if he won. Plummer abruptly found himself out of work. One can only wonder at his reasons for thinking he could go home and resume his career as if his conviction for murder had never happened. Perhaps he was deceived by the sincerity of those who supported him and considered him innocent. The prison guard he befriended, for instance, wrote the governor that Plummer was "a gentleman worthy of sympathy." Or he may have persuaded himself that his pardon was warranted by merit as well as mercy. His ability to charm men of influence like Dr. Taliaferro may have emboldened him to hope he could alter public opinion and repair his reputation. Plainly a measure of arrogance was at work. Other men might have seized on the West's boundless opportunity for reinvention by adopting a new identity and moving to a new town. Or they might have gone back home, leaving their legal travails a continent behind. Plummer thought he could get back what he had lost.[29]

At his trial, Lucy Vedder had described an incident that gave a glimpse into Plummer's personality. One morning after she moved into the Hotel de Paris, she said, her husband came barging into the room, angry and abusive, threatening to hit her. The commotion drew Plummer from his room across the hall and he intervened, asking Vedder if he would not be ashamed to strike a woman. Vedder answered hotly that he would strike his own mother if she treated him as badly as his wife did. Plummer somehow managed to pacify Vedder on that occasion, speaking quietly and forcefully to him, until at last they left the room together, "laughing, apparently good friends," in Lucy's words. Plummer had developed the lawman's necessary ability to soothe an adversary, and he placed too much faith in it. He seemed to think he could handle Vedder, when the truth was he had only calmed Vedder's rage for the moment.

However much he wished it, Plummer did not have the ability to sway the people of Nevada City. Jobless, chastened, he joined the rush eastward over the mountains to the Comstock Lode, near present-day Carson City, Nevada, in the late spring of 1860, and took up prospecting. He spent the summer there, digging for gold and silver, filing several claims. In the fall, he returned to Nevada City and resumed mining in the northern

California foothills. He showed off a chunk of gold-laden quartz to a reporter from the *Democrat,* prompting a story that he had struck it rich. Still active politically, he joined a Democratic club that supported Stephen Douglas for president.[30]

These grasps at respectability did nothing to rehabilitate Plummer in the eyes of his fellow townsfolk. As if to fulfill the worst opinions of his detractors, Plummer slipped deeper into the saloon world where he had always felt welcome. He began drinking heavily, gambling, and spending nights in a bordello, keeping company with a prostitute. The *Journal,* casting a disapproving eye on Plummer and his companions, warned of the "increasing immorality of the people of our good city," who were gambling and drinking "from daylight to dark and even till the small hours of the morning." Plummer's lapse into utter disgrace started on the evening of February 13, 1861, at a whorehouse called Irish Maggie's on Pine Street, not far from his old bakery. Plummer was upstairs in a bedroom with a woman when another customer, W. J. Muldoon, banged on the door demanding to be let in. According to newspaper accounts, Plummer opened the door, exchanged curses with Muldoon, and then struck him heavily on the head with the butt of his pistol. Dazed and bleeding profusely, Muldoon ran from the scene, nearly lost consciousness on the street, and was taken into a bookstore where a doctor was summoned to stitch a gash in his scalp. For a time it was feared he might die. No arrest was made, but Plummer feared the consequences of the encounter and slipped out of town to return to his silver claims at the Comstock Lode. He kept in touch from afar for the remainder of the winter, and when it seemed Muldoon had recovered Plummer returned. He made a conspicuous show of befriending Muldoon and spending time in his company—a prudent tactic, as it happened, because Muldoon took an unexpected turn for the worse and died several weeks later. Plummer was not charged.[31]

The outbreak of the Civil War in the spring of 1861 added one more ingredient to the combustible stew of life on the mining frontier. Along with gambling disputes, romantic jealousies, and ordinary male bravado, sectional prejudices now helped fuel the inevitable fights that broke out wherever men gathered and drank too much. Though many of his fellow Democrats supported the Confederacy, Plummer's loyalties lay with the North. At about two o'clock in the morning of the last Sunday in October 1861, Plummer was drawn into a savage altercation in the foyer of Ashmore's brothel in Nevada City. A Southern sympathizer named William

Riley slashed him with a knife, cutting through his hat and laying open his scalp. Plummer responded by drawing his pistol and killing the man.

Once again, Plummer was jailed, this time in jeopardy of a lengthy prison sentence he might have to serve to completion. He was also gravely wounded, with a deep laceration running three inches along his hairline. A surgeon was summoned to dress the cut, and for the next two days Plummer remained in bed in his cell, too weak to stand for more than a moment at a time. The jailers understandably relaxed their watchfulness and allowed him visitors. On the third evening after the incident, Plummer's lover presented herself claiming to be his wife, and the jailers showed her into his cell. Moments later he dashed into the street and disappeared. A brief, unsuccessful manhunt was called off around midnight.

Despite the evident daring of Plummer's escape, it appears to have taken place with the tacit blessing of the authorities, who did not wish to bear the expense of trying him again on criminal charges. Writing in the *Democrat,* editor Tallman Rolph, Plummer's onetime advocate and political ally, called his disappearance "prudent," given the widespread antagonism toward him. Bidding him adieu with a cruel but candid assessment, Rolph added, "If Plummer shows as much tact in staying away from the county as he did in leaving the jail, the community should have no particular reason to deplore his departure as the cost of an expensive trial would probably result in leaving him here, a most useless if not dangerous man."[32]

In other words, his old friend was saying, good riddance.

Still in critical condition, Plummer somehow made his way across the Sierra Nevada to Carson City, capital of the newly created Nevada Territory, where the Comstock discovery had generated a sudden influx of some ten thousand fortune-seekers, replicating the early days of the gold rush of 1849. On arrival, Plummer called on a friend from his earlier visits named Billy Mayfield, a professional gambler and petty criminal who agreed to hide him while he recovered from his wound. That Mayfield was a thunderous, passionate supporter of the Confederacy did not deter Plummer in the least. He was desperate.

For a day or two, Plummer stayed in Mayfield's cabin, confined to bed as he waited for his cut to close. His escape, while quietly applauded by many in Nevada City, nonetheless resulted in a warrant for his arrest, and the California prison authorities launched an inquiry into rescinding his pardon. Carson City's sheriff, John Blackburn, got word that Plummer might be in his jurisdiction and began looking around and asking questions. His suspicions settled on Mayfield, who denied knowing Plummer's whereabouts. Fearing discovery, Mayfield moved Plummer to another friend's cabin, placed a mattress atop the rafters, and sealed him above a false ceiling with enough food and water to last several days.[33]

Over the next two weeks, Blackburn and Mayfield encountered each other several times, the sheriff's suspicions growing steadily as Mayfield repeatedly professed ignorance. At last, on the night of November 18, 1861, the two met in a saloon, where the fuel of whiskey accelerated their game of cat and mouse into a furious exchange. Blackburn threatened to arrest Mayfield for harboring a fugitive and then attempted to do so, grabbing the smaller man in an arm-lock and tugging him toward the door. Resisting, Mayfield pulled a knife and stabbed the sheriff several times in the chest, mortally wounding him.[34]

Understandably, Plummer's next moves are not well documented. With his protector, Mayfield, awaiting trial for murder, Plummer disappeared from Carson City. Rumor had him in Salt Lake City, San Francisco, then Walla Walla, Washington, and one newspaper account even said he had been captured and hanged. In all likelihood, he found a hiding place and stayed put, since the winter of 1862 was one of the coldest in memory and made travel nearly impossible. What is certain is that eight months later, on July 24, 1862, Plummer signed the guest book at the Luna House hotel in Lewiston, on the western border of today's state of Idaho. There, dozens of gold camps were sprouting to life as the discovery of "color" across the Rocky Mountains continued to feed a prospecting frenzy after the spring thaw.[35]

Why Plummer used his real name when he surfaced, and accurately listed Nevada City, California, as his last place of residence, is difficult to fathom. Granted, he was in a remote place, a corner of Washington Territory nearly four hundred miles by road and river from the capital at Olympia. But he was still a fugitive from justice, vulnerable to arrest. The West was full of men using aliases, whether fleeing the law or Civil War conscription or an abandoned family, and Plummer could easily have slipped into their ranks. It may be that he was so familiar by now to so many other men on the mining frontier that trying to hide his name was useless. He was traveling in the company of two men, William Ridgley and Charles Reeves, who had escaped from San Quentin, and they may have decided that the best way to avoid capture was by force of arms and fearsome reputation. Or perhaps, despite all that had happened, Plummer still clung to a willful hope of establishing himself anew on a fresh stage, away from the social and political complications that undid his career in northern California. In short, he may have thought he had done nothing wrong. According to one vague account, Plummer took a public stand against lynching a murder suspect in Lewiston during the summer of 1862 and succeeded in standing off a mob, an action, if true, that would have fulfilled the role he once saw for himself as a man of command and of law and order.[36]

In any case, Plummer traveled in the Idaho "diggings" for a month under his own name before checking back into the Luna House on August 23, 1862. One of his fellow guests was an itinerant dance hall proprietor named Pat Ford, who followed the migrant miners with a tent supplying a band, liquor, and a few girls who would dance for a fee. One night in early September, Ford staged a party at Oro Fino, one of the nearby gold camps, and Plummer attended along with Ridgley and Reeves. Whatever new start he might have been contemplating, old devils still toiled within Plummer. He and his friends got drunk and began roughhousing, until Ford ordered them to leave. They responded defiantly by throwing glasses and upending tables before heading off to a corral where they had left their horses. Ford followed, according to several accounts, and opened fire on the departing men, wounding Ridgley in the legs and killing Plummer's horse. Plummer and the others returned fire, killing Ford.[37]

The number of deaths in Plummer's wake now stood at four—twice that number if one counted the accidental victims of his various misadventures—and his place in western history was secured. Up to now, he had always spelled his name with one "m" as Plumer, in the family tradition. As if to mark his passage into folklore, his name now was typically misspelled with an extra "m" in the newspapers, and he made his way into legend as Henry Plummer. In serious jeopardy of lynching at the hands of Ford's friends and customers, the very saloon crowd he once had counted as his electorate, Plummer fled the area. At the same time, Billy Mayfield resurfaced in Idaho, having escaped from prison after standing trial and being convicted for the murder of Sheriff Blackburn. On October 6, 1862, Mayfield led a notorious raid in nearby Florence, Idaho, riding at the head of a mob that shot up the mining town, plundered its hotels, bars, and stores, and filled the night air with rebel yells and hurrahs for Jeff

Davis and the Confederacy. Because of his earlier association with Mayfield, Plummer was widely reported to have participated in the raid, and
the false assumption was born among some chroniclers that he favored the
Southern cause in the Civil War.[38]

Fallen into bad company and bad habits, Plummer might easily have
drifted off at this point into a criminal life, camping in the wild, riding
with a gang and robbing stagecoaches, taking his place alongside Jesse
James and other desperadoes who clothed their venal purposes in a veneer
of Civil War loyalties. Indeed, some of the men who wrote western history in the nineteenth century believed so and said so, appropriating
Plummer's story and turning it into fable. The wonder, then, is that he
was about to emerge on the other side of the Rocky Mountains, a very
real figure, and a man transformed.

CHAPTER THREE

Wooing Electa Bryan

At the outbreak of the Civil War, the sum total of white men living in the present state of Montana probably numbered fewer than one hundred. Aside from fur trading and the work of missionaries, nothing had attracted settlement since the Lewis and Clark expedition a half-century earlier. The name "Montana" did not yet exist. The western end of the area rose up and undulated along various ranges of the Rocky Mountains, while the eastern half lay flat, a vast shelf of the Great Plains, hot in summer, frigid in winter, gummy from snowmelt in the spring, pleasant for a few days each autumn. The gold-mining diaspora finally reached western Montana in the summer of 1862, sending its fractious infantry of prospectors swarming into the foothills all the way from the Canadian border down to the pothole geysers of Yellowstone country.[1]

Among the resident population at the time were the Stuart brothers, Granville and James, who were born in Virginia, grew up in Illinois and Iowa, ventured to California in 1852, and had been headed back east when the Mormon conflict of 1857 drove them north over the Continental Divide into the southwest corner of present-day Montana. "As soon as we had crossed the divide," Granville Stuart wrote, "a wonderful change appeared in the country. Instead of the gray, sagebrush-covered plains of the Snake River, we saw smooth, rounded hills and sloping bench land covered with yellow bunch grass that waved in the wind like a field of grain." In search of gold, the Stuarts spent the next two years exploring the streams of the Rocky Mountain foothills, eventually making a permanent camp in the Deer Lodge Valley at a spot on the Clark Fork River they called Gold Creek. Prolific diarists, they chronicled the coming of civilization, such as it was, to an unspoiled land.[2]

The path from the gold mines of Idaho led east across the steep, forested terrain of the Clearwater and Bitterroot mountains, over mile-high Lolo Pass on the present border of Idaho and Montana, into a modest settlement called Hell Gate on the Clark Fork River about three miles south of modern-day Missoula. The western portion of Montana was then part of Washington Territory, and as fresh settlement began to quicken, the legislature in Olympia created a huge jurisdiction, Missoula County, to bring the rudiments of local government to a sixty-mile stretch along the Clark Fork River from Hell Gate to Gold Creek. An election was held on July 14, 1862, and the thirty voters who cast ballots chose James Stuart as sheriff and his brother, Granville, as a county commissioner. It was on a trip to Hell Gate two months later to set up the county's administrative offices that Granville Stuart encountered Henry Plummer.[3]

Far from seeming a desperado, Plummer gave Granville Stuart the impression of a gentleman. At Beaver Dam Hill, Stuart wrote, he and his companion, Frank Woody, "met two fine-looking young men. One of them said his name was Henry Plummer, the other was Charles Reeves." They said they had come from the Idaho diggings and asked about the new gold discoveries east of the Continental Divide. "They rode two good horses and had another packed with their blankets and provisions," Stuart recorded. "We liked their looks and told them that we were only going down to Hell Gate and would return to Gold Creek in a few days." Stuart invited them to ride along, and they accepted.[4]

The Stuart brothers were nobody's fools. In August, they had participated in the first execution in Montana, hanging a man they suspected of arriving on a stolen horse. In his diary, James Stuart confided that he could recognize a "bad man" when he saw one—not a widely accepted forensic skill in our own day and time, obviously, but an indication that the Stuarts tried to be observant and keep up their guard against trouble. Plummer and Reeves rode home with Granville Stuart and stayed with the Stuarts in Gold Creek for nearly a week without arousing their suspicions. Granville Stuart even mended Plummer's shotgun, which was snapped at the grip, accepting his explanation that he had cracked it on a tree coming through the mountain forests. Frank Woody noted that

Granville Stuart, pioneer and chronicler. Courtesy of the Montana Historical Society.

Plummer and Reeves both liked whiskey, but that did not make them very different from most other men, and they drank in moderation during their stay. In sum, Plummer displayed social skills that deflected any hint of his past activities, and he showed he could still ingratiate himself with men of authority and discernment.[5]

As their visit with the Stuarts drew to a close, Plummer and Reeves made plans to head south to the newest gold fields in the Beaverhead Valley in the southwest corner of Montana.[6] In the summer of 1862, as war gripped the East, Montana resembled a kind of switching station, with newcomers arriving from all directions and scurrying back and forth across the Rockies, searching every creekside for gold, one hot rumor of discovery tumbling on the heels of another. Generally speaking, parties arrived by one of four main paths. Western miners, bypassing the meager diggings in Idaho, came east over the Rockies into western Montana, many of them using a rudimentary wagon trail cut by Lieutenant John Mullan for the army and named after him. From the south, where the "Pikes Peak or Bust" legions had exhausted Colorado's deposits, men took shortcuts through Indian territory along the Yellowstone River or came up through Utah and gathered their wagons in the bottlenecks of the mountain passes of southwest Montana. With the blessing of Congress and the army, Captain James Liberty Fisk led a wagon party of 117 men and 13 women from Minnesota west across the Great Plains, completing the first successful overland journey through eastern Montana. And steamboats sailed from St. Louis up the Missouri River to the head of navigation at Fort Benton, a crude little port in north-central Montana above the Great Falls portaged by Lewis and Clark.

It was not possible at the time (nor is it necessary now) to keep precise track of these various pilgrimages. On arrival, most of the parties dispersed, their members hastening off in smaller groups to whatever discovery sounded most promising at the moment. The point is that large numbers of people of highly varied background began converging on Montana as the next mining Mecca, making it a dangerous place for Plummer. He and Reeves left Gold Creek on September 21, 1862, headed south for Bannack, the boomtown in Beaverhead Valley, but there is no record that Plummer ever arrived there. Instead, he parted company with Reeves, switched directions entirely, and headed north to Fort Benton. His intention can only be inferred, but Fort Benton was a gateway out of the region, the start of the water route taking steamboats or smaller mackinaws

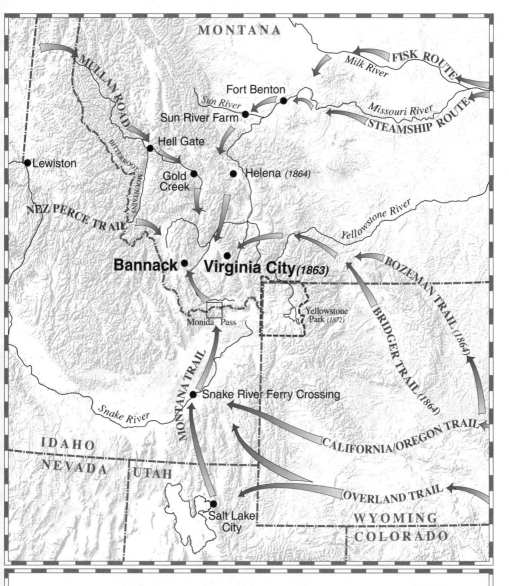

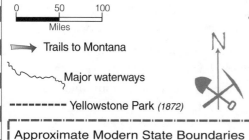

Early Routes to the Montana Gold Fields

0   50   100
Miles

→ Trails to Montana

〜 Major waterways

--------- Yellowstone Park *(1872)*

Approximate Modern State Boundaries

N

• Western miners came east along the Mullan Road or along Indian trails.

• Gold seekers came from the south through Utah and Idaho or shortcuts to the Yellowstone River.

• The Fisk wagon train came west from Minnesota.

• Steamboats sailed from St. Louis up the Missouri River to Fort Benton.

downstream to St. Louis. Fearful of being recognized, no doubt, and feeling lucky to have survived a week undetected under the gaze of a sheriff, Plummer evidently meant to leave the West for good.

In early October 1862, Plummer arrived at Fort Benton with a new companion, a burly, hard-edged man who called himself Jack Cleveland. How and where Plummer encountered Cleveland remains a mystery, as does the exact nature of their relationship. But the man's real name was John Farnsworth, and he turned out to be one of the accused robbers who had broken out of jail when Plummer was marshal of Nevada City, California, in 1856, during the fateful episode that left Sheriff Wright dead. Plummer can hardly have been pleased to see this reminder of his past life, and the wonder is that he agreed to travel with Cleveland. He may have had no choice. A fair guess is that after chancing on Plummer along the road from the gold camps to Fort Benton, Cleveland saw an opportunity and decided to stick close to his old adversary. Plummer was rumored to have a cache of gold dust hidden somewhere after his decade of off-and-on gambling and prospecting, and Cleveland might have meant to find it by dogging Plummer on his way out of the West. Plummer may well have wished to shed his unwanted company, but short of killing him in cold blood there appears to have been little he could do about it.[7]

Fort Benton was not much of an oasis. Operated as a trading post by the American Fur Company, it more closely resembled an Indian camp than a military base. The fort itself, built of adobe and named for Senator Thomas Hart Benton, the champion of western expansion, enclosed about an acre and a half and contained a few modest wooden buildings. One visitor, surveying the scene in 1862, wrote sarcastically that it was little better than a livery stable, occupied by "Indians, half breeds, horses and wolf dogs, living together in the same high inclosure in *fragrant* and harmonious fellowship." In early October, when Plummer and Cleveland got there, the steamers had long since departed for the return trip to St. Louis, leaving before falling river levels trapped them over the winter. Mackinaw boats, with their shallower drafts, could still make the trip, but their captains had heard reports of violent encounters with Indians along the riverbanks downstream and refused to embark. The passengers who had arrived in summer were gone, headed off to the diggings. What Plummer and Cleveland found was a thinly populated outpost, closing down for winter, affording them no way out.[8]

Sketch of Fort Benton, with river traffic. Courtesy of the Montana Historical Society.

Faced with the prospect of confinement at Fort Benton until the spring thaw, Plummer was open to almost any alternative, and he took a keen interest when a man named James Vail, the manager of the U.S. government's Indian farm on the Sun River, some sixty miles to the west, arrived a few days later looking for help.

Vail's attempts to "civilize" the Blackfeet—to teach them farming, commerce, Christianity, and a written language—had not gone well. From the point of view of the Blackfeet, his mission seemed to be to subdue and conquer them, or at least to reduce them to domesticity and women's work. They were restive, as were most Plains Indians. A row of dominoes had fallen earlier in the year when a large band of eastern Sioux were pushed out of Minnesota by army troops and retreated west into Dakota Territory, causing agitation among the various tribes in their path all the way into Montana.

Vail feared for his family's safety in the coming winter months. He rode to Fort Benton looking for men to join him and live at the farm, guarding against raids by the Blackfeet. He found two ready recruits in Plummer and Cleveland.[9]

In the spring of 1862, five months before Vail's encounter with Plummer and Cleveland, the docks of St. Louis were teeming with voyagers bound for the new Eldorados of the West. The grandest of the steamships, the *Emilie*, a four hundred-ton side-wheeler, had cabin space for eighty-five first-class travelers, who paid $100 each for a ticket through to Fort Benton, three thousand meandering miles upstream. Unlike some of the scruffy western prospectors who rode mules or walked to Montana, the passengers on the steamers tended to be men of substance. Many had banded together and formed mining companies, bringing along equipment and horses. Samuel T. Hauser, who would become one of Montana's pioneer capitalists and a territorial governor, recorded with satisfaction in his diary that he had been introduced to three doctors, two engineers, two ministers, and a professor. "A large proportion of the balance," he added, "are Gentlemen." Glancing around the ship's salon one evening, he counted ten men reading, seven playing cards, checkers, and dominoes, and four writing at a table.[10]

The chancellor of Washington University also made the trip on the *Emilie*, along with his wife, on his doctor's advice to seek a change of pace and climate. Chancellor Joseph G. Hoyt had a high opinion of his shipmates: "as fine a set of men, with a few whiskey-loving exceptions, as were ever seen together on a steamboat." But he could not help noticing one party that seemed out of place. James Vail, a twenty-four-year-old schoolteacher from Ohio, was on his way to the Indian farm at Sun River, along with his wife, Martha Jane, their two children, Mary and Harvey, and Martha Jane's younger sister, Electa Bryan. Writing an account of the trip for the *St. Louis Democrat*, Hoyt explained that Vail was expected to oversee the government's attempts to civilize the Blackfeet, Piegan, and Blood Indians. "We have little faith in the success of the enterprise," he concluded bleakly.[11]

A family with two small children was unusual enough on the Missouri, but the real oddity in the Vail party was the presence of Electa Bryan. Freshly uprooted from life on a farm in Hancock County, Ohio, she was a demure, unsophisticated young woman, just turned twenty, and unmarried. She was attractive, by most accounts, described by Francis Thompson, a fellow passenger who befriended her, as "pure" and "pretty." Her sedate existence in Ohio had been disrupted by the death of her father and a subsequent clash with her common-law stepmother, persuading her to join her sister's family on their trek west. She planned to help with the children and the farm work and perhaps eventually teach school. Thompson, whose path was to cross hers at several crucial moments in the coming months, found her spirited and determined.[12]

The *Emilie* sailed from St. Louis on May 14, 1862, under the command of the legendary Joseph La Barge, a longtime captain with the American Fur Company who had formed a new partnership and was now competing with his old employer. Indeed, all of the steamers on the Missouri that spring were in hot competition, since their passengers urgently insisted on being the first to reach the new diggings and stake their claims. Thompson, a well-born young banker, kept a diary of the trip, recording the curiosities and excitements of the race up the river. Passing through Missouri, he noted the "burned and ruined buildings" along the riverbanks that marked skirmishing in the state in the early weeks of the Civil War. At various stops, the roustabouts in their striped shirts would rush ashore to collect wood, hoping to scamper back aboard before encountering troops from either side.

For many of the passengers, it was the first time they had seen Indians. At Fort Randall, in the southeastern part of today's South Dakota, Thompson met a large contingent of Sioux. "The men were finely formed," he wrote, "strong and lusty, and were clothed with breech-cloth and a robe thrown over their shoulders, so arranged as to show any scars they had received in battle." Large groups of agency Indians swarmed the ship at forts along the way, hoping for commerce or handouts, often alarming the passengers. Hauser, taking a jaded view of the white man's purposes, believed the trading posts had been established "to swindle the Indian out of the fruits of his labors or hunts." Others, looking through the cruel lens of their era, merely saw savages—"gross in all their appetites," as Chancellor Hoyt unsparingly put it, "revengeful, treacherous, and bloody." The clash of cultures was overwhelming at times. Thompson, watching a group of hungry Indians on his boat disembowel an elk and eat its liver and unborn fawn raw, could not help expressing revulsion at conduct so foreign to his sensibilities.

Perhaps the Sioux were equally appalled at the behavior of the whites. When they saw their first buffalo, a large bull swimming in the river, most of the *Emilie's* passengers ran to their cabins to get their rifles and began shooting from the main deck in a frenzy. When the beast was finally hauled on board, examination revealed it had been struck only seven times out of several hundred shots fired. The fusillade was so undisciplined and reckless that Captain La Barge had to post strict orders limiting future shooting. In Dakota Territory, the passengers marveled at the huge herds of buffalo filling the river. "The water seemed alive with them," Thompson observed, "old bulls, cows, and calves swimming in the eddy formed by the body of their mother, and the wheels of the steamer had to be stopped, lest the paddles be broken on the horns of the animals."[13]

All of these wonderments, the jewels of the greatest voyage America had to offer in the nineteenth century, were subordinate to the goal of speed. Several ships had embarked ahead of the *Emilie*, and Captain La Barge intended to catch them. Travel was impossible at night, because of the river's shallow channels and floating tangles of fallen trees, but at first light each day the *Emilie's* boilers were stoked red hot, her tall funnels belched dark smoke, and her paddles churned the water. On June 4, 1862, near Fort Berthold, in the western part of present-day North Dakota, she overtook a smaller, slower rival, the stern-wheeler *Spread Eagle*, amid loud cheers and catcalls from both decks. Responding, the *Spread Eagle's* captain got up a fresh head of steam, reclaimed the lead, and then took direct aim at the side of the *Emilie*, meaning to ram and disable the paddle wheel. As his passengers looked on in alarm, La Barge let out a mighty oath in French, reached for his rifle, pointed it straight at the other captain, and might well have shot him had his son not grabbed his arm and restrained him. The *Spread Eagle* hove lightly into the *Emilie's* side, breaking three timbers but leaving the wheel intact, and La Barge soon passed again for good. A passenger on the *Spread Eagle*, Jirah Isham Allen, innocently recalled those on the deck of the faster ship "waving us a fond good-bye as they passed."[14]

Completing her journey, the *Emilie* passed beneath the white cliffs of the Missouri, the towering walls of sandstone that had captivated Lewis and Clark, rising above both banks, as solid as marble monuments to the eye and as delicate as sand castles to the touch. On June 17, 1862, Captain La Barge steered the *Emilie's* bow onto the riverbank and made landfall at Fort Benton. The cargo was off within a day, and the passengers organized themselves into parties headed for the diggings. The Vails joined the members of Thompson's mining company and another party for the sixty-mile trip west to the government farm on the Sun River. Vail hired one of the ship's crew, nineteen-year-old Joseph Swift, Jr., of Philadelphia, to come along and work for him at the farm.

Making fast time, the group reached its destination in two days, only to discover that the rope-tow ferryboat had sunk, making it impossible to cross the river. Thompson could see the farm buildings inside their cottonwood palisade across the stream and observed drily that while the station had many cattle and a few horses, "no Indians were taking lessons in agriculture." The next day, after refloating and repairing the ferry, the group hauled their wagons to the other side. The mining parties continued on their way west, and by nightfall the Vails were alone in their new home.[15]

Assessing his situation, Vail could not have felt much encouragement. The lone employee he found at the farm was an Indian named Iron who acted as a hunter and general handyman. The Vails' residence, a meager log cabin, was "not fit to live in," according to one visitor, and there was "no crop of much consequence." The weather already had turned hot and there were mosquitoes and rattlesnakes to contend with.

In late summer, around the time Henry Plummer was making his way from Idaho into Montana, sudden rains broke the drought and the Sun River flooded, badly damaging the farm's crops. Worst of all, the Blackfeet showed no intention of cooperating. Among the most implacable of the Plains Indians in their hostility to white encroachment, and coming from a nomadic, warrior tradition that relegated all domestic work to women, the Blackfeet viewed the government farm with scorn and trepidation. Behind its ill-repaired walls, the Vails kept a few rifles and a lone, tiny cannon, timid defenses should the Blackfeet decide to rid themselves of a threat to their way of life.[16]

Having succeeded in his recruiting trip to Fort Benton, Vail hastened back to the farm with Plummer and Cleveland in tow, hoping no mischief had taken place while he was gone. He found the place intact and showed his two new helpers the small cabin they would occupy during the winter. He put them to work fixing fences, chopping wood, and doing other chores around the farm. And, of course, he introduced them to his family.[17]

As it happened, the Vails' outpost did not come under attack from the Blackfeet. Instead, the weather changed and the soft warmth of a western autumn soothed away the many tribulations of summer. The Vails and their new companions settled into a peaceful rhythm of quiet days and nights along the Sun River, watching the cottonwoods turn yellow and high snows coat the tops of the Rocky Mountain Front off to the west. Plummer began courting Electa Bryan, and she returned his affections. Francis Thompson, reflecting later on their improbable romance, speculated that Electa, "isolated in a palisaded log house with no companion of her own sex, excepting her married sister," welcomed Plummer's attentions because of loneliness. That he was a dashing figure with a proven aura of magnetism may be closer to the mark, especially since her interest in him remained ardent even after he confided his troubled past to her.[18]

Explaining Plummer's reciprocal affection is more difficult. Given his previous experience with dance-hall women and prostitutes, a simple farm girl in a brown calico dress might not have been much of an attraction. Had he merely seduced her, their entanglement could be dismissed as a matter of sport on Plummer's part. But his intentions proved honorable. He proposed to her, and she accepted. Perhaps he meant to protect her from the clumsy advances of Jack Cleveland. Or he may have thought marriage would provide some form of refuge while he remained in the

West. Tempting as it is to search for an ulterior motive, it appears Plummer simply fell in love.

What did they have in common? Very little, at first glance, except that one must not ignore the bond of two people who shared the experience of having picked up stakes to go west. Plummer's appetite for risk was amply evident, but in her own quiet way Electa had demonstrated equal pluck by boarding the *Emilie*, rejecting the safe if dull prospects of spinsterhood in Ohio for the complete unknown of an outpost on the border of the Blackfeet nation. The Vails were a devout Methodist family, and it may be that Electa felt the tug of the Redeemer as she contemplated a future with Plummer, mending his life. Whatever the reason, in the days ahead Plummer came to have a change of heart about his plans. Now, instead of waiting for the spring thaw and fleeing back east, he meant to stay in Montana and take up the challenge of regaining his respectability. He had never entirely given up his ambition for a proper career and a decent life, and Electa rekindled his hope of settling down.

The Vails were not so easily convinced. Plummer told them he thought it would be best for him to leave the farm for the winter, taking Cleveland with him. Supplies were thin, and the Vails would have a better chance of surviving without two extra mouths to feed. The Blackfeet had withdrawn, eliminating the need for protection. Plummer planned to head south to Bannack, the mining camp in the Beaverhead Valley, where he and Cleveland could expect to find provisions if the passes were open and supply trains got through from Salt Lake City. Then in spring, he said, he would come back to claim his bride. If Martha Jane and James Vail did not believe him, they had only to wait and see if he kept his word.[19]

In November 1862, Plummer and Cleveland set off for Bannack, nearly two hundred miles to the south. Their path took them past Beaverhead Rock, the landmark famously recognized by Sacagawea during the Lewis and Clark expedition as a signpost of her native Shoshone people, who befriended the Corps of Discovery and helped its members cross the Rocky Mountains.

Riding through arid foothills covered with dun-colored grass and faded green sagebrush, Plummer and Cleveland followed the Beaverhead River until they reached its tiny tributary, Grasshopper Creek, and turned up to the diggings. There they found a muddy main street fronted with a few rough-hewn log storefronts and cabins so small they more closely resembled sheds, their doors so low a man had to duck his head to enter. The creek, not quite narrow enough to jump across, had a footbridge leading to a meadow called Yankee Flats, where Minnesotans from the Fisk party and other northerners had pitched their tents and built cabins. The Civil War sympathies of the several hundred settlers were much in evidence, with Union loyalists complaining about the unruly "secesh whiskey rowdies" living on the other side of the creek. "I verily believe that two-thirds of the people here are infidel and 'secesh,'" one woman wrote home to her father, equating what she considered twin evils.[20]

In addition to the sharp gulf of war passions, the camp was divided more subtly by social distinctions. The settlers from the Fisk expedition and those who arrived by steamboat via Fort Benton, having brought goods, equipment, and money, tended to look down a bit on the men who came from California and Pikes Peak without much to their names. As in all camps, the merchants bore greater responsibilities than the miners, since they had creditors to satisfy in order to buy fresh supplies. The miners could afford the risk of looking for gold, gambling it away, and then looking for more.

In their memoirs, many of the settlers who spent the winter of 1862–63 in Bannack remembered a lawless, violent place, but their contemporaneous letters and diary entries reflect a more sedate existence. Granville Stuart moved to Bannack from Gold Creek with his brother to open a butcher shop, and he recorded his satisfaction with the cabin they bought, calling it "quite cozy and home-like." A fireplace occupied one corner, with two bunk beds along the other wall. A pair of shelves with a calico curtain served as a cupboard, he wrote, and "another shelf holds our five books and James's tobacco pipe and pouch. The table and some stools complete the outfit." After an early cold snap, the winter grew mild, and food and supplies arrived from Utah. With two fiddlers in town, there were regular dances. The men put on their best flannel shirts, soft collars, and neckties, and paid $5 apiece in gold dust to take turns dancing with the thirty women in camp. Still, Stuart noted, drinking and gambling were the leading leisure pursuits, and there were enough rough types in town to make others nervous. "It became the custom," he wrote, "to go armed all the time."[21]

Arriving in Bannack on November 22, 1862, the Stuarts found Henry Plummer already there, settled in a cabin. He and Cleveland had split, and

Bannack in the 1860s. Courtesy of the Montana Historical Society.

their relationship had turned openly antagonistic. According to several observers, Cleveland now spoke rudely to Plummer when they encountered each other and often offered—only partly in jest, it seemed—to whip him in a fight, shoot him, or otherwise best him in man-to-man skirmish. One night at a saloon, drunk, Cleveland boasted, "Plummer is my meat," meaning he thought he could take his adversary at will. For his part, Plummer responded soothingly, like an exasperated parent, as if Cleveland's bluster were just that, and he was able to keep the heckling from escalating into physical violence.[22]

As the winter months passed, Plummer bent to his goal of making a respectable place for himself in the gold camp's hierarchy. "He speedily became a general favorite," according to one account, admired for his purported expertise as a miner and often approached for counsel about the quality of various claims. Because of the mild weather, prospecting continued off and on through Christmas of 1862, with each new discovery triggering a small stampede. "Men might be seen running," pioneer settler Edwin Purple recalled, "as if their lives depended upon reaching the point, across the creek, up the steep hills, panting for breath, never stopping an instant . . . with two wooden stakes ready to stick in the ground to mark the bounds" of a claim. By common assent, enforced by written contracts and by an informal miners' court with an elected judge, claims were one hundred feet along the creekside and had to be worked regularly, except in winter, to be maintained. Most of the gold lay close to the surface, in shallow stripes along the banks, ten to twelve feet above the water line. According to Granville Stuart, the deposits were fairly easy to dig out. Several times, he said, he saw miners pull up sagebrush plants by their roots, shake off the attached sand and fine gravel into a pan, and sift out the gold dust in the water of the creek. "This caused the saying at Bannack," he explained, "that 'we could pan gold out of the sagebrush.'"[23]

These placer deposits—pronounced "plasser," from the Spanish word for shoal—yielded modest wealth with a modicum of effort for quite a few individual prospectors, but the hillsides around Bannack turned out not to contain many of the deeper quartz veins that constituted a genuine lode. There was little large-scale, cooperative mining, with elaborate sluices and rockers, of the sort that typified northern California, where many miners worked regular hours for wages.

In Bannack that winter, the men had a good deal of free time on their hands between spurts of discovery, and as a result the poker and faro tables stayed crowded and busy in the camp's saloons. Plummer proved adept at gambling, displaying a stony demeanor that earned admiration, not resentment, from other players. James Fergus, a Scot who arrived with the Fisk expedition from Minnesota, called Plummer "an inoffensive, gentlemanly man," which squares with other descriptions.[24]

An unresolved question is just how much the other men knew about Plummer's past. Cleveland, for all his bravado, fell quiet if anyone asked about the source of their trouble. The Stuarts remained unaware of Plummer's record, or at least failed to mention it in their diary, and other contemporary sources are silent on the subject as well. Yet it seems highly unlikely that Plummer was considered a completely upright citizen, innocent of any wrongdoing. Scores of California miners were among the settlers in Bannack that first winter, and few could have failed to recognize Plummer and recall at least some of his difficulties. A tattooed ex-convict named Cyrus Skinner ran one of the most popular saloons in Bannack, the Elkhorn, named for the adornment over its door, and he had been in San Quentin at the same time Plummer was there as a trusty with the run of the prison infirmary.[25]

The best guess is that Plummer was known as a man with a checkered past, but deserving of another chance. As Nathaniel Langford, third-in-command of the Fisk expedition, explained in his memoirs, "It is charitable to believe that Henry Plummer came to Bannack intending to reform, and live an honest and useful life." Cleveland, on the other hand, alienated most of the men he met. By Langford's account, he was regarded around Bannack as "a desperado of the vilest character," a bully who drank too much, started arguments, and tried to intimidate others with his size and readiness to fight. Edwin Purple called him "perhaps the worst" of the rough crowd. He liked to make other men call him "chief" and humiliate them if they refused. When a man from his hometown of Galena, Illinois, recognized him as John Farnsworth, Cleveland admitted his true identity and then convincingly threatened to kill the man if he told anyone.[26]

Around the first of January 1863, in the midst of a fierce snowstorm, a man named George Edwards left Bannack to check on his livestock in the nearby countryside. When he failed to return after two days, friends went looking for him and found his clothes stuffed in a bloody bundle in a badger hole upstream on Grasshopper Creek. This was Bannack's first killing, and suspicion fell on Cleveland, who suddenly seemed to have extra gold dust to spend. As we have seen, barroom thuggery was fairly commonplace in the frontier West, but premeditated murder was not, and feeling against Cleveland ran high. Had Bannack been organized at the time as a county, as Missoula was to the north, a duly elected sheriff might have arrested Cleveland. But Bannack lay just east of the Continental Divide in a remote corner of Dakota Territory, hundreds of miles from the capital at Yankton, and it lacked any law enforcement apparatus whatsoever. A butcher named Hank Crawford, who "caroused around a good deal" himself, as one associate put it, was entrusted to clean up the occasional brawl, but he had no arrest powers and took no steps to deal with Cleveland.[27]

Late on the morning of January 14, 1863, Plummer joined a small group of other men around the wood stove in the saloon at Goodrich's Hotel, taking refuge from an icy snap of weather. Cleveland came in, already drunk, and began bellowing about the scoundrels he knew from "the other side," meaning California and Idaho, and how he meant to get even with some of them. This was dangerous talk, and Plummer eyed him coldly. Cleveland fixed his attention on a man named Jeff Perkins and started berating him about a debt, claiming Perkins owed him money from some previous association in California. Perkins objected that he had repaid the obligation, and Cleveland seemed momentarily assuaged. But soon he was cursing again and touching his pistol, renewing the accusations and threats. Plummer now spoke firmly, telling Cleveland to sit down, be quiet, and behave himself. The debt had been repaid, Plummer said, and the matter was closed. Perkins, thoroughly frightened, took advantage of Plummer's intervention to leave in search of a sidearm.

The lull held for a few more minutes, until Cleveland grew red-faced once more and spat out a new stream of oaths and threats. With this last provocation, according to witnesses, something in Plummer snapped. "You son of a bitch," he said, standing abruptly and facing Cleveland, "I'm tired of this." He drew his pistol, fired one shot into the ceiling, then a second into Cleveland's abdomen.[28]

Cleveland fell to the floor and looked up at Plummer, astonished. "You won't shoot me when I'm down?" he begged.

"No," Plummer answered. "Get up."

As Cleveland struggled to get to his feet, Plummer shot him twice more, in the chest and head. Cleveland fell again, bleeding heavily, and lay still on the floor. Two bystanders took Plummer by the arm and led him away, warning him urgently that he had made serious trouble for himself

Goodrich Hotel, where Plummer shot Cleveland. Courtesy of the Montana Historical Society.

and ought to flee Bannack. Plummer left the bar and wandered back to his cabin, seeming dazed.

Someone fetched Hank Crawford from his butcher shop, and he arrived at the Goodrich Hotel bar to find Cleveland slumped on the floor, conscious but near death. Crawford asked why no one had volunteered a bed for the wounded man, and when he got no answer he offered his shop and helped carry Cleveland there. After getting Cleveland onto a table, Crawford went to Plummer's cabin to borrow a pair of blankets, not wanting to soak his own in Cleveland's blood. What happened next has become a matter of dispute. By Crawford's account, he found Plummer in a highly agitated state, demanding to know whether Cleveland had said anything about him on his deathbed and threatening to go and finish the job of killing him if he had. Presumably, Plummer feared that Cleveland meant to expose some aspect of his past that might undo his plans for marriage and a new life in Bannack.

Yet it is hard to imagine what that revelation could have been, given the broad general awareness of Plummer's reputation. As it happened, Cleveland suffered for about three hours and expired without uttering a word about Plummer. His dying words were about himself. "Poor Jack has got no friends," he said. "He has got it [death] and I guess he can stand it."

Plummer remained sequestered in his cabin during the next several days, waiting to see how the town would respond. James Fergus, who helped make Cleveland's coffin, wrote in his diary of his surprise that the victim "was shot in cold blood in mid-day, and the murderer is still at large, untried, unpunished, and no one molests him." Others may have shared Fergus's unease, but many in Bannack believed Plummer had acted in self-defense, or at least had performed a hard piece of business that benefited the camp by eliminating its most notorious bully, a suspected killer. "It was thought by many," Langford reported, "that Plummer merely anticipated Cleveland's intention by firing first." The better acquainted the settlers were with Cleveland, it seemed, the more sympathy they felt for Plummer. In any case, no move was made to arrest or discipline Plummer, and he remained free to come and go as he pleased. Those who remembered his days as a politician could shake their heads and remark how far he had strayed from his early ideals, when he stood out as an adamant opponent of vigilante justice.[29]

CHAPTER FOUR

The New Sheriff

Around the time of Henry Plummer's fatal confrontation with Jack Cleveland, a small group of Bannock Indians appeared near the gold camp and set up tepees on a hillside beyond Yankee Flats. A branch of the Shoshone tribe, they were considered "friendly," in the parlance of the day, though that word hardly does justice to the intricate and unequal relationship that existed between two very different peoples—as Plummer was about to witness.[1]

In the heyday of the fur trade, white men who hoped to thrive in the West learned to accommodate themselves to the Indians whose lands provided their livelihoods. As in any form of commerce, a smart businessman dealt fairly, kept his word, and cultivated good relations with his customers. In many instances, this extended to marriage, as the most ambitious white settlers forged family alliances with the dominant tribes. Granville Stuart married a Shoshone Indian woman named Aubony who bore him eleven children and, according to his brother, was "a fairly good cook, of an amiable disposition." But when the gold rush erupted, the need to do business with the Indians faded and these "squaw men," as they were known, began to lose their prestige and positions of influence. The arrival of white women in the West triggered a fundamental change of attitude that branded intermarriage with a social stigma.[2]

This abrupt switch of status was unknown to the Indians, of course, and many tribes remained perfectly willing to pair off their daughters with white men. Plummer's companion from Idaho, Charles Reeves, settled in Bannack that first winter and arranged to "marry" one of the young women from the small tribe of Bannocks after they arrived in mid-January. But Reeves considered the union little more than the acquisition of a seasonal sex partner and treated the woman accordingly. Like Plummer, Reeves was well-spoken, capable of charm, and prone to violence. He grew up in western Pennsylvania, ran away from home, lived for several years in Texas, and arrived in California in time to become an early inmate at San Quentin. Serving five years for theft, he escaped, was recaptured, then escaped again for good in December 1854. He remained at large for the next eight years and eventually wound up prospecting with Plummer and joining him in the gunfight that killed Pat Ford. Plummer apparently steered clear of Reeves after arriving in Bannack, hoping to avoid old associations.[3]

One night about a week after Reeves claimed his Indian bride, she fled his cabin in tears and ran back to her lodge, claiming he had abused her. Reeves followed, demanding her return, and was rebuffed by one of the Bannock elders. The next evening, angry and drunk, Reeves and an accomplice, Charley Moore, went back to the Indian encampment and emptied their revolvers into the tents, wounding one of the tribesmen. Not satisfied, they circled back to town, drank a few more rounds, collected another ally, William Mitchell, and returned to the Indian lodge. Again they fired indiscriminately into the tents, and this time their volleys proved lethal, killing three Bannocks and a white bystander, a French fur trader drawn by curiosity after hearing the initial gunfire. "The squaws and children set up the most dredful [sic] howling I ever heard," miner James Fergus wrote his family back home, describing the aftermath. Not surprisingly, the terrified Bannocks folded their tents that very night and were gone by morning, carrying their dead with them.

Hearing the gunfire and learning of the carnage, Bannack's white settlers were deeply upset, though not for reasons that would fit today's sensibilities. The loss of Indian life meant little to them. While dismayed by the senseless assault, their real concern was that Reeves's attack might provoke some kind of retaliation and place white lives in jeopardy. Many pioneers, inflamed by tales of Indian torture in the popular literature of the day, had a fear of Indians that bordered on psychotic dread. Fergus, condemning the work of the "drunken rowdies," fretted that "hundreds of naked mounted savages are ready to revenge the murder of their kindred, and pick off every straggler that comes in their way." A devoted husband

and father, Fergus yearned to have his family join him and recoiled at any act of stupidity or violence that might discourage them.[4]

As it happened, this particular Bannock tribe lacked the numbers and the will to respond in kind. (Other Shoshones, provoked by white intrusion on their lands, did carry out raids on white settlers, and were targeted in turn for retribution by the U.S. military. A week after the incident in Bannack, on January 29, 1863, two hundred miles to the south, a band of Shoshones became the victims of one of the deadliest massacres in American Indian history, as Colonel Patrick E. Connor and his California Volunteers stormed a winter camp and killed some two hundred and fifty men, women, and children at Bear Creek, in the southeast corner of present-day Idaho. The slaughter was widely commended at the time for promoting white settlement.)[5]

Reeves and his two companions, fearing the wrath of their fellow townsmen, beat a quick retreat into the foothills above town late on the night of the shooting. On their way, they picked up Plummer, who was frightened of reprisals for his own act of killing several days earlier, now that the settlers' anger had been stirred. The four men rode sixteen miles north to Rattlesnake Creek, where they stopped around dawn and made a rude bivouac in a thicket of willows.

In Bannack, first light found dozens of men milling in the main street, vowing to conduct a search for the killers. When it became evident that their quarry had escaped, a small posse of four men, including O. J. Rockwell, a friend and partner of Fergus's, set off in pursuit. Tracking fresh hoof marks through the snow, they made swift progress and approached the encampment about midday, demanding surrender. Reeves shouted back his refusal. Evenly matched and heavily armed, the two sides found themselves in a stalemate, neither able to advance on the other without drawing fire. As the afternoon lengthened, Plummer assumed the role of negotiator. He and his party had no wish to continue their flight into the winter vastness of the Rockies with a posse in pursuit, he said. They would give up their guns and return to Bannack, but only with a guarantee that they would receive a trial by jury. Their pursuers, faced with the prospect of going home empty-handed to gather reinforcements and resume the hunt from scratch, agreed to the concession.[6]

Arriving back in Bannack, the captors kept their word. No new ill feeling had been ignited toward Plummer, and he was tried and exonerated within hours by an informal tribunal. He spoke in his own behalf and swore that Cleveland carried a grudge from their days in California and meant to kill him, an account that satisfied most of his fellow townsmen.[7]

The case against Reeves, Moore, and Mitchell was taken far more seriously. They would have to stand trial for murder, the first proceeding of its sort ever held in southwest Montana. A messenger was sent to Godfrey's Canyon, ten miles away, where some of the leaders of the Fisk expedition were building a sawmill, summoning them to take a hand in conducting the affair. One of those who answered the call was Nathaniel Langford, an ambitious young banker who had served as third officer of the overland party. Virtually all of Bannack's five hundred residents were gathered in Main Street when he arrived that evening, Langford recalled, making it "apparent from the first that the current of popular opinion [was] set strongly against the prisoners." The crowd wanted to act as a mass jury, as had been the practice in other western gold camps when miners convened to settle a pressing civil or criminal matter. Typically they would elect a judge, hear testimony, shout down any long-winded arguments from counsel, and reach a swift verdict so they could return to their claims and keep digging. As vehicles of crowd psychology, voting by simple majority and unencumbered by the niceties of reasonable doubt, these juries of the whole tended to be far more likely than a regular jury of twelve to convict.

But a standard jury trial had been promised to Reeves and the others, and Langford argued in favor of proceeding with it. In his memoirs, published in 1890 and steeped in a fair bit of melodrama over the years, Langford described a frantic scene, with desperado friends of the defendants openly vowing to kill jurors and waving their guns around, firing rounds in the air, threatening serious mayhem and resembling, in his words, "some of the riotous gatherings in Paris in the days of the first revolution." In truth, while the crowd in Bannack was rowdy, Reeves, Moore, and Mitchell did not have many friends agitating in their behalf, and certainly no organized faction of gunmen.

After a good deal of shouting back and forth, the crowd grudgingly agreed to hold a jury trial the next morning in an unfinished log building on Main Street. By acclaim, J. F. Hoyt of Minnesota was elected judge, and Hank Crawford, the butcher, was chosen sheriff, giving him a sturdier position as the town's lawman. A jury of twelve, including Langford, was picked, and two of the town's handful of lawyers agreed to act as prosecution and defense. With tables and chairs arranged in the traditional pattern, the scene resembled an orthodox courtroom and the participants acted accordingly, even though they enjoyed no formal legal standing whatsoever.[8]

William Mitchell was tried first and acquitted when he was able to show that he had not fired his gun during the attack on the Indians. The jury nevertheless voted to banish him from town as a nuisance. Reeves and Moore were then put in the makeshift dock. By seven o'clock in the evening, the two sides had argued their cases, and the jury began its deliberations with Langford as foreman. By Langford's account, the culpability of the two defendants was never in doubt. But a lengthy argument ensued over the verdict, he said, because his eleven fellow jurors were scared of retaliation at the hands of the defendants' supporters. In the end, Langford said, his was the only vote for guilt, as the others refused to risk doing their duty.[9]

Actually, given the prevailing attitudes toward the victims of the killing spree, a likelier explanation is that few of the jurors believed Reeves and Moore deserved hanging. Their attorney argued—feebly—that their actions were justified because Indians had killed some of their friends who were headed west to California in 1852, a decade earlier. This "meager" excuse, as shopkeeper Edwin Purple termed it, "induced the jury to look with some leniency upon the act." Shortly after midnight, concluding five hours of argument, Langford relented and agreed to a compromise verdict. The lives of Reeves and Moore would be spared, but they would be banished from the area and their property would be seized to compensate the court. As in all gold-rush camps, the most appropriate and convenient tool for punishment—a penitentiary cell—did not yet exist.[10]

The defects of the verdict became immediately evident. In the middle of winter, banishment was impractical for the simple reason that the men had nowhere to go. Mitchell wandered the hills outside Bannack for a few days and then, cold and hungry, simply returned to town, where no one had the heart to force him back into the wild. Reeves and Moore were packed off to Deer Lodge, a hundred miles to the north, and told to stay there until the Rockies became passable in spring. After seeing Mitchell on the streets of Bannack, however, a group of townsmen met and agreed to rescind the banishment of Reeves and Moore, believing it unfair to punish them and not Mitchell. Exhausted, filthy, and ill from living in a crude hut and subsisting on coffee and dried meat, the two crept back to Bannack, embittered by their experience.[11]

The unraveling of the case led to serious trouble by clouding the duties of Crawford, the newly chosen sheriff. The initial verdict called for the defendants' property to be confiscated and sold. Accordingly, Crawford gathered up all of the guns belonging to Reeves, Moore, Mitchell, and also Plummer, and sold them at public auction. Plummer, having been acquitted, was furious and protested the sale. When the banishment of the others was revoked, the miners' court ordered Crawford to retrieve the guns of all four men and return them. Crawford did so, which stripped him of compensation for his duties during the trial. To cover his expenses, he then tried to sell a horse that had belonged to Jack Cleveland, but this created another ruckus when a half-owner of the horse came forward and challenged the sale.[12]

Adding to the tension, Crawford began telling friends he feared Plummer meant to kill him to prevent the disclosure of any confidences Cleveland might have uttered on his deathbed. Crawford said he was worried that Plummer, a quick draw, would contrive some confrontation as an excuse to pull his pistol and shoot him. A poor hand with a gun, Crawford stood little chance of surviving such an encounter, and he surrounded himself with two or three heavily armed friends whenever he went out on the streets of Bannack. Plummer sent word protesting that he intended Crawford no harm, but that did little to allay Crawford's anxiety.[13]

For a time, the two men maintained an uneasy truce. Having served as a marshal himself, making the inevitable enemies by collecting fines, Plummer may have felt some empathy for Crawford's situation. There is no evidence that he had any actual designs on Crawford's life, and it is difficult to fathom what he could have hoped to gain by gunning down the town's ad hoc lawman. Still, Plummer was by now a man with a formidable reputation for violence, and Crawford's fear could hardly be dismissed as irrational. Walter B. Dance, a prominent merchant in Bannack, told a story of encountering Plummer on Main Street one day that winter and immediately pulling out his big Bowie knife and beginning to whittle. Plummer affected a hurt expression and asked, "Why do you always begin to whittle when you meet me?" And Dance responded evenly, "Because I never intend that you shall get the advantage of me."

As the weeks passed, the feeling between Plummer and Crawford evolved into a feud. Their friends exchanged ugly words in the saloons on a pair of occasions, and rumors flew back and forth that one side or the other was planning an ambush. According to Edwin Purple, who operated a dry goods store on Main Street, Plummer kept a cool demeanor and displayed "little of the bragadocio [sic] or slashing style of manner that characterized the behavior of his comrades." Wearing a well-fitted coat made of black broadcloth, Plummer cut an elegant figure and spoke "in a low, quiet tone of voice, a habit which never deserted him." But when Plummer got angry, Purple added ominously, his gray eyes "grew black and glistened like a rattlesnake's."[14]

As ever, winter was a long season in Montana, its icy tedium to be endured with strong drink and strong talk. At one point, Plummer complained that Crawford was spreading gossip about him keeping company with an Indian woman, a story he thought was designed to injure his engagement to Electa Bryan. For his part, Crawford came to believe that he had to kill Plummer or be killed, and by early March of 1863 the two men had begun, in effect, to stalk each other.[15]

One morning in broad daylight, in the middle of Main Street, Plummer stood resting with one foot perched on a wagon wheel, cradling a rifle in his arm, looking out for his adversary. Crawford stepped from the door of a restaurant behind Plummer, balanced his rifle on a log projecting from the corner of the building, and fired. The ball struck Plummer in the right elbow, traveled along his forearm shattering the bones, and lodged in his wrist. Spinning around, Plummer cursed Crawford and shouted defiantly, "Fire away!" Crawford fired the second barrel and missed, and Plummer was helped to his cabin.

Then as now, shooting a man in the back was considered a cowardly act, and Crawford found himself swiftly ostracized. In the moments after the shooting, he rushed into Edwin Purple's store through the back door, so overwrought he was visibly shaking. He went from there to a friend's cabin where he hid behind several sacks of flour until dark, fearing reprisal from Plummer's allies. Within days, seeing that the town had turned against him, Crawford fled to Fort Benton for protection and later slipped aboard a mackinaw that took him back east.[16]

Plummer's show of nerve in standing his ground and inviting Crawford to shoot a second time became the stuff of legend and cemented his reputation for physical courage. But he barely survived the encounter. His arm, full of bone shards, quickly swelled to three times its normal size and he developed a severe fever. He was given into the care of Dr. Jerome Glick, a well-trained surgeon who urged amputation. Plummer refused, saying he would just as soon die as live with only one arm. According to

Dr. Glick, Plummer's friends threatened to kill him unless he saved Plummer's arm *and* his life. Thus inspired, the doctor operated, digging out countless bone fragments but failing to remove the ball, which was caught in Plummer's wrist. For several days, Plummer lingered near death, until finally his fever broke and he began a slow, painful recovery.[17]

On March 3, 1863, just before the shooting in Bannack, Congress created Idaho Territory, gathering together most of the modern states of Idaho, Wyoming, and Montana and forming them into a single, massive entity that covered 325,000 square miles, an area bigger than Texas. As a nice irony, Congress then adjourned without appropriating any money for the new government, without providing it any civil or criminal codes, and without designating a capital.[18]

This mischief was the work of a lobbying battle between James Ashley, a congressman from Ohio who chaired the powerful House committee on territories, and William H. Wallace, a delegate from Washington Territory with political ambitions in the gold rush West. One of the strangest aspects of western politics in the nineteenth century was the ardent desire of established cities to rid themselves of jurisdiction over lands inundated with new settlers during gold rushes. The reason was the threat that large clusters of new voters would dominate territorial elections and gain enough clout to move the capital and seize the trappings of power. The city fathers of Olympia, the capital of Washington Territory, wished to lop off the gold areas to their east, ridding themselves of new, competing populations in the Boise Basin and along the Salmon River. For their own part, the men in the new settlements eagerly embraced the idea of becoming a separate territory because they had a legitimate need for access to governance that went beyond mere politics. The Idaho camps were three hundred miles from Olympia, while Bannack's territorial capital, Yankton, was even farther away to the east and unreachable in winter.[19]

Ashley wanted to craft a territory with smaller boundaries that would suit the political ambitions of his protégé, Lieutenant John Mullan, the army surveyor who in 1853 had cut the Mullan Road, a wagon trail, through six hundred miles of wild country from Walla Walla, Washington, to Fort Benton. But Wallace hoped to be appointed governor of the new

James M. Ashley, chairman of the U.S. House committee on territories. Courtesy of the Montana Historical Society.

territory himself, and as a close friend of President Lincoln's he persuaded the Senate to adopt his larger version of the map. With all parties preoccupied by war, the House and Senate remained deadlocked until the last night of the session, when the upper chamber sent Wallace's plan to the House with no time for debate, compromise, or refinement. The House reluctantly assented, and President Lincoln signed the badly flawed act into law the next day. A week later, on March 10, 1863, he appointed Wallace governor of the newly formed Idaho Territory.[20]

Bannack was now part of Idaho, and Plummer would recuperate in a new jurisdiction. But as a practical matter, the gold camp remained every bit as remote from governance and the rule of law as before. Wallace chose to travel to his new posting via the sea route from the East Coast to Panama, across the isthmus, up to San Francisco, from there to Portland, Oregon, and then east through Washington Territory by coach. It was not until July 10, 1863, four months later, that he got to Lewiston, on the border of Washington and Idaho, and proclaimed it the territorial capital. Only then did he take up his duties.[21]

Around the first of April, meanwhile, the weather in Montana broke enough to allow travel and the resumption of prospecting. James Stuart led a party into Yellowstone country while his brother, Granville, traveled to Gold Creek for fresh supplies to sell, including chewing tobacco he peddled for $15 a pound. James Fergus shook off the torpor of winter and began mining again and sending letters to his wife in Minnesota, urging her to pick up stakes and bring the family west to join him. He worked from dawn to dusk six days a week, he wrote her, and on Sundays he took his picks and shovels to the blacksmith for repair, washed his laundry, bathed, wrote letters, and bought supplies. Flour was a fairly expensive $8 per hundredweight, butter $1.25 a pound, and eggs $1.50 per dozen. Fergus lived on bread, beef, beans, rice, dried apples, and a little pork when he could afford it.[22]

Like the Stuarts, Fergus was a temperance man who avoided the saloons and gave his spare time to writing, creating a vivid portrait of life in the West. At the age of forty-eight, nearly three decades after leaving his native Lanarkshire, Scotland, Fergus sent his father and brothers a photograph showing his white beard and bald pate and described himself with candid good cheer as: "Americanized, tinged with the cares of business and the frosts of 27 years [abroad]—somewhat eccentric to be sure, and wearing more hair on [my] face than Americans generally, and following the dictates of no man, or set of men." For those who might wonder what drove a man from his homeland to America, and then from east to west across the continent, Fergus had a compelling explanation. "I like the prairies and the western country and people," he wrote, "for I am tired of seeing . . . land covered with stumps and stones. I want more elbow room . . . more freedom, more generosity, more wages for work, bigger souls and fewer cults. . . . " Having abandoned the Presbyterian Church of his youth, Fergus delighted in calling himself "an infidel," but in truth he was a very thoughtful man with a strict code of personal morality. All he required to make life complete was the company of his beloved wife, Pamelia, and their children, Mary Agnes, Frances Luella, and Andrew. He was saving his gold dust to pay for their trip to join him.[23]

By the middle of spring, traffic in Montana had resumed the pace of the previous fall, with parties arriving daily from almost every direction. The Missouri River remained too low to allow passage by steamboat, but all other routes were open and Bannack gained hundreds of new settlers, more than doubling in population. Surviving contracts show a lively trade in claims along Grasshopper Creek. The first itinerant preacher, said to be a black man, arrived, as did sacks of long-delayed mail and bundles of newspapers with accounts of the ebb and flow of the Civil War. A prevalent rumor, that the Confederates had stormed Washington, D.C., and captured President Lincoln as a prisoner of war, was finally dispelled. A group of Masons met and applied for a charter to form a lodge.[24]

This freshening of activity brought with it a renewed fear of crime, especially the threat of highway robbery. Parties traveling on the trails between the settlements or out of the region faced the specter of masked men popping out from behind a rock, getting "the drop" on them, and stealing their pouches full of gold dust or U.S. Treasury notes at gunpoint. A couple named Davenport were surprised during a picnic just outside Bannack on their way to Fort Benton and relieved of some $300 in gold dust by a bandit who introduced himself politely as "the robber of the glen." The actual number of such encounters was impossible to tally, given the remote locations and confused accounts of the victims, and it may be that the perception of danger was greater than the reality. Fergus wrote home that the road from Bannack to Fort Benton was "infested by robbers" but cited only two specific incidents. Similarly, Langford talked breathlessly of "wholesale plunder" while giving few details.[25]

Yet the fear was real enough. Settlers did not know each other very well and often believed they were in jeopardy whether they were or not. A traveler risked losing his entire stake, a year's worth of grueling work, in the flash of an eye, without recourse of any kind. In their journals, Granville Stuart and Edwin Purple describe a trip they took together for protection from Bannack to Deer Lodge in April 1863; Purple states that his companion had less than $20 with him, while Stuart confides that the actual amount was closer to $3,000. A smart man did not advertise his bankroll, even to a friend.[26]

In Bannack, the period of calm that followed Plummer's shooting ended in dramatic fashion on the afternoon of May 17, 1863, when two gamblers at the Elkhorn got into a scrape and emptied their pistols at each other, creating a melee that left two men dead and several others injured. The particulars of the fight were predictably muddled by a haze of alcohol, but the key point was that an innocent bystander, George Carrhart, died in the crossfire. In the same week, an unarmed Indian was shot and killed for no apparent reason by one of the town's rough characters. As before, the absence of any machinery for trying and punishing those responsible frustrated and infuriated the town's leaders. Langford complained that it was "dangerous to pass along the streets, where stray bullets were not an exception," a worry shared by many citizens who felt threatened by the lack of a policing authority to control the saloon crowd.[27]

With no sign of activity on the part of the new territorial government, Bannack's elders decided to take matters into their own hands and hold an election to fill several vital positions. Walter Dance was serving as president of the mining district at the time, a job he held by general acclaim with duties that loosely resembled those of a small-town mayor. At a meeting of about a hundred and fifty townsmen on May 21, 1863, Dance gained agreement that a vote would be held in three days to choose a judge, sheriff, and coroner. Investing the election with as much formality as he could, Dance assigned polling monitors and official counters to tally the paper ballots.

Largely healed by now, though his right arm remained stiff and immobile, Plummer announced his candidacy for the job of sheriff. He campaigned energetically over the next seventy-two hours, asking for votes, and proved to be a very sympathetic figure. He had conducted himself, in Purple's phrase, "with the utmost propriety" after being shot, and his reputation for past violence seemed to work in his favor, since his fellow townsmen could appreciate the need for a man who commanded fear and respect to serve in the post. On Election Day, May 24, 1863, Plummer defeated his opponent, Jefferson Durley, with a handy majority of the 554 votes cast, completing a most improbable return to public office.

In his only known comment on this reversal of fortune, Plummer approached Langford, who doubted his fitness, and asked for a fair chance to do the job, telling him, "I will show you that I can be a good man among good men. This is a new life before me." Langford wrote later that he was swayed by Plummer's evident sincerity, though not, he added, ultimately convinced.[28]

CHAPTER FIVE

The Dillingham Killing

Two days after his election as sheriff, Henry Plummer loaded a small buckboard with provisions and set off alone for the two-hundred-mile trip north to Sun River. He meant to fulfill his promise to marry Electa Bryan, a decision that came from his heart and not his head.[1]

Under the best of circumstances, Plummer would have had his work cut out establishing his position as Bannack's new lawman. His reputation did not set well with some of the town's leaders, and his intention to turn a new leaf would have to be proven. A few weeks working with the other newly elected officeholders—judge B. B. Burchette and coroner J. M. Castner, two well-respected men—might have gone a long way toward reassuring the town that he planned to enforce and uphold the law. As it was, Plummer barely stayed long enough to pin on a badge. Setting the stage for trouble, he named a chief deputy, D. H. Dillingham, who was utterly untested, to be in charge while he was gone. Then he appointed several deputies who did not know each other well or entirely trust each other, including three men generally reputed to be "toughs"—Ned Ray, Buck Stinson, and Jack Gallagher. And he left before they could sort out a pecking order.[2]

Various theories have been put forth over the years about Plummer's motive in giving badges to men known for their fierce dispositions and handiness with fists and pistols, but the obvious answer seems to be that he was now physically unable to defend himself. With both of his hands damaged, he could not easily draw or fire a gun, and he needed surrogates to enforce his authority. Indeed, before the sheriff's job came along, it was far from clear how Plummer would be able to support himself at all, since his injuries prevented him from mining, dealing cards, or other manual pursuits. During his period of recuperation, facing the prospect of permanent disability and desperate to secure a livelihood, Plummer formed a partnership with two of Bannack's least savory characters, Cyrus Skinner, the proprietor of the Elkhorn saloon, and Charles Ridgley, his former companion in Idaho, in the ownership of several mining claims. The fact that the two men were escapees from San Quentin did not bother him. He needed them to make a living.

Until the unexpected chance to serve as sheriff arrived, Plummer apparently hoped to make his way as a mine owner. To that end, he gave a remarkable interview to an itinerant newspaperman in the days just before the election. Having no idea that he was about to return to public office, Plummer spoke with surprising candor to a reporter from the *Sacramento Union,* the journal that had been a thorn in his side during his time as a politician in northern California. Making no effort to conceal his identity, he freely discussed his earlier life and described his dealings with Skinner and Ridgley. He argued, persuasively, that he and Ridgley had fired their guns in self-defense during the shootout in Idaho that left Pat Ford dead. Plummer took the traveling correspondent around to see his claims and bragged about their yield. From a single day's work, the journalist wrote later, "I saw $3,800 in neat amalgam in the retort."[3]

It was not at all unusual for miners to boast about the quality of their holdings, of course, either to attract a labor force to help them dig or to exaggerate the value of a claim for the benefit of a gullible investor (or both). But Plummer went far beyond the boosterism of the typical gold-camp settler. He escorted the reporter all around town, making introductions, glad-handing, and generally playing the role of leading citizen. "No man stands higher in the estimation of the community than Henry Plumer," the *Union* dutifully reported, using a spelling of his surname familiar to readers in northern California. It seemed Plummer's hunger for acclaim outweighed his need for prudence. He talked openly about his third mining partner, a young man from California named Edward Richardson, saying they had struck the "richest claim" in all of Idaho Territory on a fifty-foot stretch of Grasshopper Creek and had turned down an offer of $25,000 for half of it. It sounded very much like a sales pitch.

Whatever his intent, Plummer's bluster had the effect of advertising his association with bad company. Not only were Skinner and Ridgley fugitives from justice, it turned out that Richardson was a wanted man too, on suspicion of murder. Handsome and well-spoken, the son of a judge in northern California, Richardson had served a term in San Quentin as a teenager for receiving stolen property and later was arrested in Nevada for questioning about a fatal shooting. He escaped jail in Carson City with a $750 bounty on his head and fled to Bannack, arriving sometime in the early spring. There he shot and killed a man in a bar fight, recording the town's fifth homicide.[4]

Why would Plummer affiliate himself with a criminal element if he hoped to regain his respectability? The answer appears to be a matter of timing. Had he known he stood to be elected sheriff, he might well have behaved more discreetly. He would not have entangled himself with the likes of Skinner, or at least he would not have broadcast that entanglement to the world. Absent a crystal ball, though, and facing an uncertain future with little hope of pursuing a career, Plummer evidently figured he could join forces with Skinner and the others, make enough money to survive, and perhaps eventually sell off their claims for a profit. The one constant was Electa Bryan. He seemed determined to get back to her, one way or the other, and marry her. But he now found himself hastening to her side as a lawman who was in partnership with criminals, and who had just spilled his secrets to a newspaper.

Adding another tick of bad luck to his timing, Plummer began his journey to rejoin Electa on the eve of one of the greatest gold discoveries ever made in the Rocky Mountains. From the moment of the first thaw in the spring of 1863, teams of prospectors had been crisscrossing the territory looking for "color." The most celebrated group, led by James Stuart, ventured into the area along the Yellowstone River and found hostile Crow Indians instead of gold. After missing a planned rendezvous with Stuart, another, smaller team of six miners struck out on their own and also encountered the Crows, who captured them along the Yellowstone just north of the present park boundary. According to legend, their lives were spared by the theatrics of one of their number, William Fairweather, a wild-haired, wild-eyed man who professed the ability to handle poisonous snakes with impunity. As he delighted in recounting the story afterward, Fairweather spotted a rattlesnake during their ride to captivity, grabbed it off the ground, shoved it inside his shirt, and then pulled it out and waved it at the Crow leaders with great dramatic effect just as the Indians were deciding his fate. As a result, the Crows allowed Fairweather and his companions to depart in peace.

Relieved of most of their food supply, but still armed and on horseback, the members of the Fairweather party abandoned their quest along the Yellowstone and headed back west toward Bannack, away from the Crows. Crossing the Gallatin River and then the Madison, the men examined the banks of the various tributary creeks they encountered, alert for traces of gold dust. As they passed between the Tobacco Root and Gravelly mountains, west of today's town of Ennis, they found encouraging signs. "We are in gold country," Henry Edgar recorded in his diary, "and we want to find where it comes from." They climbed to the highest nearby point, a rounded peak they called Mount Baldy, and began prospecting downstream, hunting for the source of the traces of dust. On the evening of May 26, 1863, two days after the election in Bannack, the six prospectors made camp along an unnamed creek. After dinner Fairweather stuck his shovel in gravel near a promising piece of rimrock and famously wondered aloud if he would find enough gold to afford a plug of tobacco.

After panning two or three shovels of loose rock, the prospectors realized they had discovered a major deposit. "We talked over the find and roasted venison till late . . ." Edgar wrote, "and a more joyous lot of men never went more contentedly to bed than we!" His companion Harry Rodgers, a man of fewer words, allowed simply, "God is good." As Plummer was beginning his nuptial journey to Electa Bryan's side, six men went to sleep about seventy miles away knowing they were rich.[5]

To plumb their wealth, Fairweather and the others would have to return to Bannack for supplies, and they would face the tricky challenge of recruiting enough men for the hard work ahead of them without triggering a free-for-all dash that would swamp their findings and force them to share their discovery with hundreds or thousands of others. For two days, the party remained at the diggings, panning gold and marking hundred-foot claims along the creekside. To record their claims in writing, they had to give the place a name, and Edgar chose Alder Gulch because of the bushes that lined the banks of the brook. They broke camp on May 28, 1863, and arrived in Bannack two days later, "the raggedest lot that was ever seen," according to Edgar. Making a poor job of guarding their secret, they feasted that evening on ham, potatoes, and fresh eggs from Salt Lake City, bought new clothes, paid for everything in gold dust, and then expressed surprise when word flashed through town that they had hit a big strike. "Such excitement!" Edgar wrote in his diary, amazed that strangers had surrounded him in a saloon demanding to know about his "horse load of gold."

On June 2, 1863, as they prepared to leave Bannack and return to their discovery, the six miners found themselves in the vanguard of a crowd of more than a hundred vagabonds insistent on following them and sharing their good fortune. Granville Stuart arrived in Bannack that day from Gold Creek and recorded his amusement at the sight of the "big stampede" rushing along in Fairweather's wake. "They were strung out for a quarter of a mile," he wrote, some on horseback and some on foot, tottering under the weight of heavy packs. "The packs had been hurriedly placed," he added, "and some had come loose, and the frightened animals [were] running about with blankets flying and pots and pans rattling . . . and the hillside was strewn with camp outfits and grub."[6]

By the time this disheveled corps reached Beaverhead Rock, about halfway to the diggings, Fairweather and Edgar and the other discoverers realized that they would have to reach some accommodation with their pursuers or face chaos upon arrival. They called a mass meeting and agreed to lead the way. But unless their claims were honored, Edgar warned ominously, "our horses will die at the end of the picket ropes before we stir a foot toward the place." The settlers nominated a portly lawyer named Samuel McLean to represent their interests, and he negotiated an agreement that the six discoverers would be allowed to keep two claims apiece, while the others would enjoy the customary right of making a single claim each. The deal might not have sounded very generous to the discoverers, except that it secured them a combined twelve hundred feet of proven claims on the richest stretch of the biggest gold strike in the mountain West.[7]

Even with a written agreement in place, the rush to Alder Gulch remained an unruly affair, with men on horseback riding ahead of those on foot to get the best claims. Various groups allied themselves by ethnicity or old friendships from earlier mining ventures. One of the discoverers, Barney Hughes, was an Irishman, and he gathered together a band of his countrymen to safeguard his claims. Another discoverer, Tom Cover, had been at Pikes Peak, and he surrounded himself with familiar faces from Colorado. "There was such a stampede as I never saw before or since," Edgar observed. "The men on horseback left their pack horses, and men on foot threw down their blankets and grub and flew." Happily for the gold-crazed horde, Alder Gulch proved richly blessed with deposits. Good claims were abundant up and down the fourteen-mile course of Alder Creek from its confluence with the Stinking Water River nearly to the top of Mount Baldy. Tents were thrown up, wagons pried apart for cabin walls, and by sundown on Saturday, June 6, 1863, a half-dozen pockets of rude settlement were in place.

The next day, a Sunday, miners gathered and held informal elections to pick a president, judge, and recorder of claims in each of these districts, and to begin the work of writing up rudimentary laws and laying out boundaries. The task of creating an ad hoc government did not always go smoothly. One group was assigned to draw up plans for a 320-acre town site, and because many of the men hailed from the South they decided to give it the name Varina City in honor of Varina Davis, the wife of Jefferson Davis, president of the Confederacy. When the paperwork reached the pen of the district judge, Dr. Giles Gaylord Bissell, a Connecticut-born, Yale-educated physician and ardent supporter of the Union, he furiously scratched out the name and vowed that "no such blot" would stain the new settlement. Instead, he christened the town Virginia City, thereby ensuring endless confusion with its namesake in Nevada Territory. Another district was called Nevada City, sowing further mix-ups with the town in northern California.[8]

The first days of white habitation in Alder Gulch were a furious race to find and record claims, and then to begin the hard labor of shoveling gravel into sluice boxes, washing away the dirt, twigs, and lighter ore, and capturing gold dust on the brushy riffles at the bottom. Molly Sheehan, who went to Alder Gulch with her father around the time of her eleventh birthday, recalled making the trip from Bannack by a wagon "creaking in the warm sunshine amid a hovering cloud of alkali dust over ground [that was] tobacco brown, through endless stretches of parched, gray-green sagebrush." On arriving, she saw swarms of rough-clad men with long hair and flowing beards and listened as "the sound of brawling, insults, oaths echoed through the gulch." Hour after hour, men chewed into the earth with their picks and shovels, hefting ton after ton of rock into the sluices, taking as much as a thousand dollars a day from some claims. Two weeks after the first wave of miners arrived, fire swept the length of Alder Gulch, wiping out the pretty alder bushes and coating the area with embers and soot, darkening the riverbed rocks of red jasper, mica, and rose quartz. Many of the miners were perfectly content with the devastation, since the denuded creek banks would now be easier to reach and explore.[9]

The riches of Alder Gulch almost emptied Bannack. The gold camp on Grasshopper Creek had housed some four or five hundred souls over the winter and then burgeoned to more than a thousand in early spring. Now Bannack found itself collapsing. Not only was the strike at Alder Gulch vastly bigger, but the quality of the gold dust was better, valued at $18.50 per ounce, half again as much as Bannack's. The *Sacramento Union* published its story about Bannack on June 17, 1863, quoting Plummer and predicting that the town would rival Salt Lake City in size before the year was out. Instead, in the words of Edwin Purple, Bannack was "as quiet as a graveyard," in danger of becoming a ghost town.[10]

And Henry Plummer was still absent.

In the last part of May 1863, after spending the winter in San Francisco, Francis Thompson returned to the Vail family's compound on the Sun River. He was headed east to Fort Benton to meet a shipment of supplies from St. Louis that he hoped to sell in Bannack, and he looked forward to spending a few days visiting with the friends he had made during his journey up the Missouri the summer before on the *Emilie*. The river's current was too strong to permit crossing when Thompson first arrived, but he hailed James Vail in a loud voice and the two men shouted greetings over the roar of the water. Even at a distance, Thompson could tell that Vail was upset.[11]

Accomplishing his crossing the next day, Thompson found a family riven by discord over Electa Bryan's plans to marry Plummer. Martha Jane Vail took Thompson aside just moments after greeting him and begged him to intercede. Plummer was due to arrive any day, and the Vails feared Electa meant to fulfill her engagement in spite of Plummer's violent past. At age twenty-nine, Thompson had enjoyed a fair amount of seasoning before coming west, and the Vails hoped he might be able to influence Electa when they could not. A native of Massachusetts with an impressive lineage—his mother was an Adams—Thompson had worked for several years in the 1850s as a bank collector in the Midwest, trading paper notes at a discount for gold coins and transporting thousands of dollars from city to city. He was accustomed to carrying a large revolver for protection,

Francis Thompson. Courtesy of the Montana Historical Society.

though he had never been called on to use it. Thompson's wanderlust was born in his distaste for formal education, first as a student—he paid for his tuition by tending fires at the public schoolhouse, and was compensated in "diluted form," as he put it, by receiving the ashes for use as fertilizer at his father's farm—and later as a teacher who found only tedium in the classroom. He worked for a time in his family's foundry and then accepted an invitation to work for a bank in Cincinnati.

Thompson's job, in brief, was to persuade clerks at state banks to redeem paper notes in gold, a transaction many resisted. "At one of the northern towns of Ohio," Thompson recounted in his memoirs, "was a belligerent cashier who sent word down to Cincinnati that he would pound the life out of the next 'land shark' who presented any of his notes for redemption." Assigned by his boss to confront the cashier, Thompson had the inspiration of asking a female acquaintance to accompany him when he called at the bank and was gratified to find that the man dared not make a scene in front of a lady. Without having to resort to fisticuffs or worse, Thompson left with $10,000 in gold coins and the satisfaction of knowing he had outwitted a potential adversary. With his sharp eyebrows and strong, aquiline nose, Thompson presented a formidable appearance, but he relied more on diplomacy than bluster in his business dealings. Like so many other men who survived the inevitable testy encounters of western travel and commerce, he was a teetotaler.

During his travels, Thompson demonstrated a knack for meeting and befriending influential men, including Abraham Lincoln, a lawyer in private practice at the time, who interviewed Thompson as a potential witness in a civil suit. Thompson attended the Republican convention in Chicago that nominated Lincoln for president and visited him later at his office in Springfield, Illinois. He found the candidate musing over a basketful of editorial cartoons, including one that showed him pounding the body of Stephen Douglas into rails, "which seemed to tickle his fancy." Thompson went to the inaugural in 1861, but he spurned service in Lincoln's army, dismissing the commanding officers as "little youngsters," and instead joined the exodus up the Missouri to the gold camps of the West. He prospected for several weeks in the fall of 1862 without success before deciding to spend the winter in the relative comfort of San Francisco.[12]

Having heard about Plummer's fatal confrontation with Jack Cleveland during his return from the West Coast, Thompson agreed to speak to Electa to try to persuade her to call off the wedding. But she stood by Plummer. "To her unsophisticated soul," Thompson wrote later

> he was a pure, good man, persecuted beyond all endurance, and the fatalities which had surrounded him were such that in no instance was he to be blamed. The little blind god had taken complete possession of her soul. She said that she loved Mr. Plummer, that she knew he loved her, that she had the utmost faith in him, that the terrible stories of him were told by men not worthy of belief.

She fervently believed, Thompson concluded, "that she could never be happy unless she married him."[13]

Complicating Thompson's task, Joseph Swift, the young passenger from the *Emilie* who had stayed to work for the Vails, volunteered his own expressions of admiration and affection for Plummer, reinforcing Electa's resolve. But Thompson talked to her about Cleveland's death and argued that even if the shooting had been justified, it was further evidence of Plummer's violent nature. Why rush into marriage, Thompson asked, with a man who seemed so determined to die young? "I counseled her not to rashly make a change which was of so much importance in her life," Thompson recalled, especially when doing so would bring distress to her family and friends. Thompson urged Electa to go back east for the season, "and in the fall if she and Mr. Plummer remained of the same mind, he could then go and meet her."[14]

After resisting for a day or two, Electa finally broke down and accepted Thompson's advice. She began packing her clothes for the trip home, much to her sister's relief. But the Missouri River remained too shallow for steamships to reach Fort Benton, and for the time being Electa was forced to remain at the farm. Thompson settled in, too, awaiting the arrival of his supplies. Some eight or nine steamships were reported bunched at anchor below the Milk River, two hundred miles east of Fort Benton, stymied by the Missouri's low water level. Major Henry W. Reed, the Indian agent who had recruited the Vails, and who was also their minister back home in Ohio, was among those expected to arrive, bringing supplies and money for the farm. Electa had hoped he might perform her wedding ceremony.

Waiting at the farm, Thompson occupied himself observing the sundries of daily life on the invisible border that marked the line between white and Indian domains. He and the Vails mourned the death of Iron, the farm's handyman, who was killed by Bannocks on a hunting trip. "He was the best Indian I ever knew," Thompson wrote in simple tribute. On another day, Thompson and Mrs. Vail were confronted by a Blackfeet tribesman searching for his runaway wife. He vowed that if he found her he intended to kill her or cut off her nose and ears—a punishment, Thompson recorded, "which Indian law permitted." He and Mrs. Vail answered that they had not seen the woman. An hour later, when she arrived at the farm, they gave her a blanket and some provisions and urged her to keep going into the mountains to the west. "We had determined that no murder or maiming should be done in our midst," Thompson wrote, "and hoped that she would reach some Flathead camp."[15]

On June 2, 1863, the same day the six discoverers of Alder Gulch were leaving Bannack with a small army at their heels, Plummer arrived at the Sun River farm. Thompson, who had never met him, marveled at the favorable first impression Plummer made, writing that "when I saw him I could but wonder if this could be the young desperado whom people so much feared." Plummer was modest, dignified, and devoid of swagger, Thompson wrote, and above all "seemed devoted to Miss Bryan." In no time, Electa reversed herself and announced that she intended to proceed with the marriage after all, a decision Thompson benignly accepted because of the obvious joy it brought her. Plummer, it seemed, could infatuate almost anyone.[16]

The Vails, overwhelmed by the couple's determination to marry, abandoned their objection to the union but asked that Plummer and Electa agree to wait until Major Reed, as the family minister, could arrive and perform a proper Methodist ceremony. Plummer had little choice but to go along. Unaware of the gold discovery at Alder Gulch and diffident about the need to return to his post as sheriff, Plummer settled into the routine of the Vail household and seemed content to let the days drain away. He joined the family in a trip to the Great Falls of the Missouri, thirty miles to the southwest, where they saw an eagle's nest that Thompson thought might have been the same one observed by Lewis and Clark. After camping overnight, the party visited all of the falls, then returned to the farm in time to chase off a party of ten Flathead Indians they found helping themselves to the larder.[17]

A few days later, Plummer and Swift rode to Fort Benton to make inquiries about the steamships stuck downstream. They learned that wagon trains had been dispatched to retrieve the cargoes, since no one could predict when the Missouri's current would swell enough to allow navigation above the Milk River. The news meant it might be many more days, perhaps weeks, until the passengers arrived overland at Fort Benton. Displaying a level of patience absent in so many of his life's earlier turns, Plummer returned to the farm and continued to bide his time. Finally, more than two weeks after his arrival, he grew restive and demanded that the wedding proceed. The Vails relented and sent word to St. Peter's mission, a nearby Jesuit outpost, that they required the services of a cleric.[18]

On June 20, 1863, with Father Minatre presiding, Electa Bryan and Henry Plummer were married at the Sun River Indian farm, with young Swift as best man and a good-natured Thompson standing in as bridesmaid in place of Martha Jane Vail, who could not bring herself to participate. "The pretty bride was neatly gowned in a brown calico dress," Thompson wrote, sounding a bit like a society-page columnist, "and was modest and unassuming in appearance." Plummer was "dapper," Thompson added, wearing a blue suit mended here and there with buckskin, a checked cotton shirt, and a blue necktie. Swift wore sheep's gray pants, a red and white sash with a gray flannel shirt, "and was under the necessity of wearing moccasins both of which were made for one foot." Completing the bridal party, Thompson sported moleskin trousers, a black cloth coat and vest, and buffalo-skin shoes.

The ceremony, Thompson recorded, was lengthy and formal. Afterward, the family tucked into a wedding breakfast of buffalo hump and cornmeal bread, and then Plummer and his bride climbed into the farm's "ambulance," a four-wheel wagon pulled by four Indian ponies, and set off to begin married life in Bannack.[19]

Alder Gulch continued to fill. James Fergus, the faithful Scot who missed his wife, estimated that by mid-June 1863, some 1,800 settlers were in residence, making good use of the twenty dry goods stores and "grog shops" he counted along the main street of Virginia City. Fergus had abandoned Bannack and staked a claim that was panning out well, as the saying went, yielding $25 to $50 a day in gold dust. He had two men working for him for wages and guessed that he would clear $2,000 by the end of the summer.[20]

Along with prospectors, provisioners were flocking to the gulch as well, hauling boots, tents, tools, whiskey, beef, flour, cloth, coffee, tobacco, and other notions and sundries, all priced as high as the market would bear. The economy was fairly simple. Miners created wealth by digging it out of the ground and spending it freely on their needs and wants. "Gold dust was the sole medium of exchange," Granville Stuart recalled, valued at $18.50 an ounce. Merchants of all stripes, from butchers to bartenders, kept small, finely calibrated scales on hand to measure out the currency of the realm, which the miners dipped out of tightly sewn buckskin pouches.

A shot of whiskey cost twenty-five cents, as did a pound of the best beef. A typical grocery list included eggs at $1.50 a dozen, coffee at ninety cents a pound, along with flour, bacon, sugar, butter, salt, potatoes, and dried fruit and vegetables, all at comparably hefty prices. Lumber went for fifty cents to $1 a foot, picks and shovels cost $8 to $10 apiece, dried apples were 50 to 75 cents a pound, and one enterprising fellow sold boots at a price that escalated by an ounce of gold dust per shoe size. A stove that might have fetched five or six dollars back east went for $250. At one point during the summer of 1863, an observer counted 150 wagons massed in a bottleneck at the Snake River in eastern Idaho, waiting for the ferry on their way from Denver and Salt Lake City to Montana.[21]

The riches of Alder Gulch lifted it above the Bannack and Idaho diggings to a level closer to California's gold rush, with a populace swelling daily; yet the place remained entirely beyond the reach of legitimate government. The main thoroughfare of Virginia City was named Wallace Street in honor of the newly appointed territorial governor, William Wallace, but that worthy had not taken office or even reached the farthest border of his new jurisdiction. The districts in the gulch—Summit, Highland, Junction, Adobetown, Nevada City, Virginia City, and a few smaller settlements—chose presidents, judges, and claims recorders, but no formal system of law enforcement was in place. Plummer's chief deputy, D. H. Dillingham, held a tenuous claim on the position of acting sheriff, but his authority did not seem to extend beyond the rapidly emptying confines of Bannack. The miners in Alder Gulch gave the job of sheriff to a man named Dick Todd, whose lack of standing may be reflected in a description of him written by one of the district presidents: "He was a stupid, ignorant fellow."[22]

The Alder Gulch strike introduced a greatly heightened fear of trailside robbery into daily life in Montana, because many more travelers were now venturing back and forth between stops in the area, because they were making the trips more often than before, and mostly because they had vastly more gold dust to be robbed. The seventy-mile trip from Bannack to Alder Gulch gained a particular reputation for danger because the isolated trail offered so many opportunities for ambush. In the latter part of June 1863, Dillingham came to believe that some of his fellow deputies were involved in planning robberies, and he warned several parties of travelers to beware of them. Edwin Purple talked to him and quoted him as saying, "There is [sic] a lot of robbers about this town, and I intend to nip some of them one of these days. I have overheard them, talking over their plans, and am going after them."[23]

Dillingham's harshest suspicions fell on Buck Stinson, a barber by trade who worked a chair in the front corner of the Elkhorn, Cy Skinner's saloon. Unlike his patron, Stinson had no criminal record. But he was known to be handy with a gun, and he had begun keeping company with a rough-edged, hard-drinking gambler named Hayes Lyons. The two spent a lot of time on the trail traveling back and forth between Bannack and Alder Gulch, and Dillingham thought he knew why.

One of Bannack's richest and most respected settlers, a lawyer named George Washington Stapleton, was planning a trip to Alder Gulch with two other men when Dillingham took him aside and shared his sense of uneasiness about Stinson and Lyons. "Wash" Stapleton mentioned the warning to his companions, and one of them rashly repeated it back to Stinson, triggering a blood feud between the two deputies. Stinson loudly denied any criminal involvement or intent, and vowed to get even with Dillingham for slander. Stapleton, a veteran of the Pikes Peak rush and later a prominent figure in Montana's territorial legislature, decided to make the trip despite the possible danger. He encountered Lyons at Rattlesnake Creek and, as he told the story afterward, felt as uncomfortable in his presence as a man caught napping in church during the sermon. Lyons demanded to know if Stapleton had heard that he and Stinson intended to rob him. Stapleton swore ignorance. He had only $100 in greenbacks on his person in any case, he added, and Lyons was free to take it if he wished. Lyons gruffly told Stapleton to keep his money and be on his way.[24]

This encounter might well have been forgotten, one of countless nervous exchanges between parties of jittery armed men meeting on western trails, except for what happened next. On the morning of Monday, June 29, 1863, a hearing was underway in a makeshift courtroom in Virginia City. The venue, a conical tent made of tree branches to provide shade from a hot sun, sat next to the rushing current of Alder Creek. Inside, Dr. William L. Steele, a physician and the president of the mining district, was trying to sort out a disputed claim. Crouched by his side, a young man called Charley Forbes acted as court reporter, making notes on the testimony. The session was a more or less jovial affair, as Steele later recalled it, with each side attempting to curry his favor with promises of cigars and "valley tan," a potent kind of whiskey. Steele, who had no formal training in the law, struggled with some of the terminology and betrayed bewilderment at one point over the word "nonsuit," much to the amusement of the lawyers. Lending a further touch of informality, Steele was wearing a borrowed hat

Dr. William L. Steele, judge of the miner's court. Courtesy of the Montana Historical Society.

a size too small whose band he had enlarged by slitting it in several places, allowing random cowlicks of his hair to sprout out like a porcupine's quills.[25]

The court's genial mood was interrupted when Stinson and Lyons burst in rudely and announced that Dillingham had just arrived in town. They directed the news to Forbes, who jumped up and hurried out of the tent with them. Moments later the three men rushed up to Dillingham on Wallace Street with their pistols drawn, cursed him as a liar, and opened fire, hitting him in the thigh and chest. Dillingham fell "like an empty sack," by one account, and bled to death within minutes.[26]

Even by the archest notions of Wild West anarchy, this was a flagrant act: the cold-blooded murder of a lawman in broad daylight on the main street of town, with dozens of witnesses looking on. Up to now, all of Montana's fatal episodes had contained at least some grain of the familiar, with blood spilled through drunken rage, greed, stupidity, or in the case of the Indians, racial antipathy. But the assassination of Dillingham was different—a sober, calculated act, bereft of any evident human sentiment save sheer meanness.

Rushing from his tent, Steele ordered the three gunmen arrested. They were taken into custody by Jack Gallagher, another of Plummer's deputies, and trussed up in logging chains in a nearby building. Their guns were confiscated. Drawn by the sound of gunfire, scores of miners poured into the streets, buzzing with horrified excitement and demanding a swift, severe response. As in the case of Reeves and Moore when they shot up the Indian lodge, a sharp debate broke out over the best way of conducting a trial. A large majority of onlookers argued in favor of forming themselves into a jury of the whole rather than trying to pick an ordinary jury of twelve. Ignoring the delays and safeguards of standard practice, the crowd also insisted on beginning the proceedings immediately. Dr. Steele agreed to serve as judge along with two fellow physicians, Drs. Bissell and Rutar.

A large wagon was pulled to the foot of Wallace Street to serve as an open-air tribunal, with the three judges presiding from the front seat. Jurors crowded around, lining the street, including the spot where Dillingham had fallen, and strained to hear the arguments and testimony. What seemed an open-and-shut case quickly turned complicated, as a mystery arose over the identity and actions of the third gunman, Charley Forbes. Several witnesses had heard Forbes shout, "Don't shoot! Don't shoot!" at the very moment Dillingham was struck. Some thought he had yelled these words even as he fired the fatal shot into Dillingham's chest, but others were just as certain that he had withheld fire. Adding to the confusion, Gallagher, the deputy sheriff, reported that he had examined Forbes's pistol and found that it was not fired.[27]

Confronted with these doubts about Forbes's guilt, the judges agreed to try him separately, after Stinson and Lyons. Their decision appears to have been motivated in part by a sense that Forbes, though a newcomer to the area and not known to many of the other settlers, had the looks and demeanor of a gentleman. In the mid-nineteenth century, many people believed they could discern a man's character by his appearance. Phrenology—the study of the shape of the skull as a determinant of personality traits, including criminal tendencies—remained a popular pseudo-science, and newspapers of the era often described accused criminals as looking like brutes or having an evil eye. With their rough manners and scruffy faces, Stinson and Lyons fit the prevailing image of killers and were treated accordingly.

Forbes, on the other hand, was "a splendid looking fellow" who stood "straight as a ramrod," in one observer's words, and he spoke like a well-educated man. For that reason, and perhaps because Dr. Steele had liked him and given him a position of trust as a recorder in his court, Forbes's case was set aside. The trial of Stinson and Lyons proceeded, and by noon the next day the two stood convicted of murder by assent of the public jury. When Dr. Steele called for the crowd's will on sentencing, a loud cry went up, "Hang 'em!" Accordingly, the three judges solemnly condemned Stinson and Lyons to death by hanging and ordered the immediate erection of a scaffold on the edge of town. Men were sent to dig their graves.[28]

Taking his turn in the dock soon afterward, Forbes spoke convincingly in his own behalf and protested his innocence of any involvement in Dillingham's death. He explained that he had rushed off with Stinson and Lyons not to participate in the murder but to try to prevent it. He had called out for the others not to shoot. He emphasized the point that his gun had not been fired. No transcript was made of his testimony, but a breathless chronicler called it "one of the finest efforts of eloquence ever made in the mountains." And surely it must have been, because the crowd ignored all evidence of his complicity and voted to acquit him. A group of friends and supporters surged forward to shake Forbes's hand and congratulate him on the verdict.[29]

The public defender during these proceedings was a legendary character named H. P. A. (for Harry Percival Adams) Smith, a well-known frontier lawyer whose tremendous oratorical gifts were often overwhelmed by his chronic drunkenness. Smith had abandoned his family and his legal practice in Maine to join the rush to Pikes Peak, where he served as a probate judge and had the honor of naming the city of Denver after a friend, James W. Denver, the governor of Kansas. After a famous incident when he lost thirty town lots in the space of ten minutes while playing poker under the influence, Smith left Colorado and made his way to Montana hoping for a fresh start. Volunteering his services in the Dillingham case, he argued effectively on Forbes's behalf and rejoiced at his acquittal, weeping openly and crying, "My boy! My boy!" while hugging Forbes around the neck.[30]

The dramatic outcome of Forbes's trial gave Smith an unexpected opening to revisit the verdicts against Stinson and Lyons from the day before. Even as Forbes and his supporters celebrated, guards led the two condemned men from the unfinished log building where they were being held, placed them in shackles on the bench of a wagon, and began pulling them slowly through town toward the newly raised gallows. Stinson kept a stony demeanor, but Lyons broke into tears and cried aloud for mercy, and one of his friends began reading a letter he had written to his mother begging forgiveness for his errant ways and promising reform if he were given another chance. Responding with tears of their own, several women in the crowd called out for the men's lives to be spared. Smith chimed in, arguing that it would be unfair to hang the two men after their alleged accomplice had been exonerated.[31]

Some in the crowd now demanded another vote on the death sentences of Stinson and Lyons. Dick Todd, the nominal sheriff of Alder Gulch, who had custody of the condemned men, abruptly stopped the wagon in the middle of Wallace Street and called for a voice vote of ayes and nays on the question of hanging them. The crowd, thinner now but still about a hundred strong, shouted at full volume on both sides of the issue. Unsure of the outcome, Todd next asked those who favored execution to file one way up the street while those opposed marched the other way. When this exercise also failed to establish a clear resolution, Todd tried to get the crowd to form two lines and pass by a pair of monitors to be counted, a procedure that broke down as unruly participants on both sides maneuvered to be counted two or three times or more. The situation teetered on the verge of mayhem when Gallagher, the deputy sheriff, rode his horse into the middle of the crowd and called out in a commanding voice, "Let them go! They're cleared!" an order he punctuated by waving his gun. Todd gave up, ceding authority.[32]

As the crowd backed off, Stinson and Lyons were freed of their chains, set in tandem atop an Indian pony, and warned to ride away quickly. Someone spurred them into a gallop. By now Dr. Steele had started for his cabin a couple of miles down the gulch. It bothered him a great deal, he admitted afterward, to have sentenced the two defendants to death, knowing their hanging would dismay and disgrace their families. They were young men, he reflected, capable of reform and decent lives. Walking home in a "melancholy reverie," as he later described his mood, he was startled to look up and see the two ride by him in a blur, Lyons waving and calling out, "Bye, Doc!"

As he reflected on Dillingham's murder in later years, Steele came to believe that it was Forbes who had fired the fatal shot, and that he did so with cold calculation, yelling "Don't shoot!" as a deliberate means of creating confusion and getting off the hook. Forbes slipped away from Alder Gulch in the hours after his acquittal, never to be heard from again. But some in the gold camp believed they recognized him as Edward Richardson, the fugitive and mining partner of Henry Plummer. Reconstructing the crime, Steele concluded that Richardson had conspired with the other two assailants to silence Dillingham, and then had conspired *against* Stinson and Lyons by having Gallagher, the deputy sheriff, reload his confiscated pistol so it appeared not to have been fired. In Steele's theory, Stinson and Lyons were low-ranking members of a criminal band, dispensable after killing Dillingham, while Gallagher and Richardson enjoyed superior status and looked out for each other. Only after Forbes was acquitted did Gallagher seize on the crowd's confusion and agitation to help free Stinson and Lyons.[33]

There was no way of proving this theory, of course, and many in Alder Gulch ignored the finer points and simply believed that three desperadoes had gotten away with murder. Fergus wrote his wife in disgust, saying the defendants "belonged to a group of highwaymen and it was a crime to let them go." Giving explicit expression to the sense that justice had been mocked, someone hand-painted a sign that said "Graves to Let" and placed it beside the two freshly dug holes in the ground. A story made the rounds that Stinson and Lyons had stopped there as they left town, pausing to relieve themselves as a parting gesture.[34]

The Fourth of July, 1863, fell on a Saturday five days after Dillingham's death. Fergus recorded it as a somber occasion in Virginia City, with sympathizers on both sides of the Civil War holding their tongues, afraid of setting loose passions in a place raw with emotion. No one yet had the news of the Union victories at Vicksburg and Gettysburg that would turn the tide against the Confederacy.[35]

Many settlers now believed that organized criminal activity had gained a hold in Bannack and Alder Gulch, with more incidents likely to come.

The capricious outcome of the Dillingham affair shook their faith in the capacity of their infant criminal justice system—and the informal democracy behind it—to act effectively in curbing or punishing crime. They wondered about their absent sheriff, Henry Plummer. And a few began to think about taking the law into their own hands.

CHAPTER SIX

"Cut-Throats and Robbers"

Sometime in the first week of July 1863, Henry Plummer returned to Bannack with his new wife and set up housekeeping in a tiny log cabin. The majority of townspeople welcomed him home with enthusiasm, eager to have him take up his duties and enforce the law. In time, some of them would come to believe that he had been involved in D. H. Dillingham's death, and even that he might have ordered it, but for now he enjoyed the same broad support that had earned him election as sheriff six weeks earlier.

George Chrisman, a well-respected shopkeeper, gave Plummer a corner of his store on Main Street to use as an office, a gesture of obvious trust. Chrisman's store was "the news bureau, the university, the social settlement of the hamlet," one settler remarked, "to which intelligent, genial companionship and a wide fireplace gave cheerful welcome." Nathaniel Langford, who kept his misgivings about Plummer to himself, acknowledged a "marked change" in the sheriff's behavior as he worked to reassure his constituents and regain their confidence. "There was much apparent sincerity in his conduct and professions," Langford recalled. "He forsook the saloons, and was seldom seen in the society of his old associates. His duties were promptly attended to." Acting to extend his authority to Alder Gulch, Plummer made the two-day ride back and forth from Bannack to Virginia City several times during the summer and fall, making a good impression on the settlers at the new diggings. One man who lost his bedroll and coat on the trail recorded in his diary that Plummer volunteered to help him search for the items, adding, "He appears to be a very nice man. I like him very much."[1]

Plummer was now thirty-one years old, a fully mature man with scars to show for a hard life on the fringes of frontier society. The fingers of his left hand were permanently crippled and his right wrist ached with recurrent pain from the bullet lodged there. He dressed well, though somberly, typically in black, and some people remarked that he rarely removed his hat, even indoors. Not many knew that he meant to hide the deep knife scar along his hairline.[2]

There is no record of his trip home with Electa, but then as now, summers in western Montana could be utterly glorious, with the heat of day melting away rapidly as soon as the sun went down and with nights spent by campfire under a blanket or two. Reading the diaries and memoirs of the many pioneers who traversed the American West in the nineteenth century, one is struck by the pivotal role played by chance. An unexpected calamity could always plunge a traveler into terrible crisis—an Indian attack, a child bouncing out of a wagon and under a wheel, a husband taking sick and dying, leaving a wife to fend for herself, or a mother dying and leaving an infant to be suckled by other women. In the absence of mishap, though, western travel then could be as pleasant as a camping trip is today. Young Molly Sheehan remembered riding north from Denver to Montana in the summer of 1863 lying contentedly in the back of her father's wagon atop a mattress covered with blankets and a comforter, like a princess on a divan, with a view most evenings of "gorgeous sunsets gilding distant mountain peaks." Knowing that they arrived safely, we may assume that Electa and Henry Plummer rode home slowly in their wagon past rushing rivers and mountain majesties in the daylight hours, and spent their nights beneath the stars, enjoying an enviable honeymoon.[3]

Once settled into their cabin in Bannack, the Plummers' routine became a good deal more prosaic. With their dirt floors and sod-covered roofs, early log cabins were hard to keep clean, and their interiors could be gloomy. Installing even a single window, the pane no larger than a sheet of stationery, was considered a luxury. Water had to be hauled by tin bucket from Grasshopper Creek, and ordinary chores—cooking, cleaning, mending clothes—could take all day. Given her strict religious upbringing, Electa apparently preferred not to break the tedium by attending the weekly dances held in Bannack, where one of her husband's deputies, J. B.

"Buzz" Caven, liked to play his fiddle. She was rarely seen about town. Still, life in Bannack offered pleasanter circumstances than the isolation and rigors of the Indian farm at Sun River.[4]

Plummer attended closely to his job. With more than half its populace gone to Alder Gulch, Bannack was unusually calm, and the sheriff's duties turned out to be mostly administrative. He started a subscription for the construction of a jail, asking residents to contribute $2.50 each. A surviving document with Plummer's signature shows that he carried out a sale of property on August 10, 1863, at the direction of a miners' court. He helped settle the estate of George Carrhart, one of the victims of the double slaying in the Elkhorn saloon the previous May, and learned that he himself was one of the beneficiaries, inheriting a share of a claim on the Dakota Lode, the richest bar in the area.[5]

And Plummer showed he had learned some lessons about handling people. William Pemberton, an early settler in Virginia City and later the chief justice of the Montana Supreme Court, recalled acting as defense attorney for an accused thief Plummer had arrested. Pemberton won the case, and as payment for his services he expected to be given the man's horse. But Plummer insisted that the lawyer first pay a stable fee. When Pemberton hotly refused and threatened to make trouble, Plummer calmed him down and got him to agree to put the horse up for auction, which fetched enough money to pay the stable fee and also put a nice profit in the lawyer's pocket.[6]

Throughout the summer of 1863, settlers continued to pour into southwest Montana. Typically, they came first to Bannack, drawn by accounts of the mining discoveries of the year before, and then promptly decamped for Alder Gulch after hearing of the larger gold deposits there. With the Missouri too shallow for navigation until late in the summer, overland parties made their way by various routes from all points, with the heaviest traffic coming west on the Oregon Trail to Salt Lake City and then taking a sharp turn to the right, due north. Mormon freighters sent hundreds of wagons rolling up through Idaho, over the Continental Divide at 6,832-foot-high Monida Pass, and into the Beaverhead River valley, carrying all manner of human and commercial cargo.

Close behind the provisioners came providers of services: tree cutters, cabin builders, blacksmiths, brick-makers, cooks, teamsters, herders, the occasional lawyer, doctor, preacher, and teacher, and of course women of all callings. Molly Sheehan, the precocious eleven-year-old, remembered seeing "fancy ladies," as she called them, walking along the sidewalks in

Virginia City or sitting by their doors in dressing gowns, smoking cigarettes and signaling their availability. In the hurdy-gurdy houses, a miner could dance with a woman for a dollar and buy her a drink after finishing their waltz or schottische or quadrille. Miners who failed to exhaust their earnings on whiskey and women could always lose money later at night playing poker, faro, monte, euchre, old sledge, cribbage, and other card games.[7]

Families made money taking in boarders for $16 or $18 a week. Molly Sheehan's father bought a small house on Wallace Street and lodged two of the original "discovery men," William Fairweather and Henry Edgar. As James Fergus regularly reminded his wife, she and their daughters could make a decent living, around $1,000 a year, providing domestic services such as sewing, cooking, and laundry. In Virginia City, which survives today as a living museum and tourist attraction, the window of an old dentist's office still displays the tools of the profession as they were used in the mid-nineteenth century: an array of pliers.[8]

The surge of settlers also promoted a lively industry in the countryside around the gold camps, as ranchers operated stations that provided food and lodging to travelers of the two-legged and four-legged variety alike. By the late summer of 1863, two stagecoach lines, A. J. Oliver's and Peabody & Caldwell's, were running between Alder Gulch and Bannack, stopping at Pete Daly's place or Robert Dempsey's on the Stinking Water River, or at Rattlesnake Ranch near Bannack. The stagecoach drivers typically switched horses at the ranches so fresh teams could keep a fast pace.[9]

Generally speaking, prices were high, a matter of supply and demand inflated by the value of the gold dust. The first Catholic Mass in Virginia City was conducted by Father Joseph Giorda, an itinerant Jesuit priest who learned an important lesson about gold-camp economics during the offertory. He accepted a thin trickle of dust from each of his congregants and did not think much of the size of the collection until the next day, when he was shocked to receive a bill for $40 for stabling his horse. When he protested that he could not afford to pay, the dust in his purse was weighed and turned out to be worth several hundred dollars.[10]

Perhaps the most precious thing the settlers craved was news—letters from family and friends, above all, and word about the war. Telegraph wires connected the east and west coasts and cities in between, but they did not yet extend to the mining camps of Montana, and the sense of remoteness gnawed at everyone. "Napoleon was not more of an exile on

St. Helena," Langford wrote with his customary flourish, "than the newly arrived immigrant from the States, in this recess of rocks and mountains." Newspapers from California took three or four weeks to arrive, eastern papers even longer. Granville Stuart did not learn of the Confederate surrender at Vicksburg until July 30, 1863, twenty-seven days after it took place. The *Sacramento Union's* incriminating story about Plummer had yet to surface in Montana by late July. And nothing was known of the new territorial government.[11]

On July 10, 1863, Governor William H. Wallace finally arrived at Lewiston, the small city on the border of Washington and Idaho, and proclaimed it the provisional capital of Idaho Territory. He had little interest in serving as governor, perhaps because the salary of $2,500 was so meager, and immediately began making plans for a territorial election in which he intended to run for the post of delegate to Congress. In addition to better pay—$6,000 a year—the job would enable him to return to Washington, D.C., where he could lobby on behalf of his new constituents for federal funds, services, patronage, and other niceties that had been ignored in the rush of creation.[12]

One of Wallace's first acts was to send the territory's federal marshal, Dolphus S. Payne, to conduct a survey of the huge new jurisdiction. Among other things, Payne was asked to carry out a census and organize the various mining clusters into counties. Staunch Republicans both, Wallace and Payne set out to recruit party loyalists as candidates for the territorial legislature and for county and federal offices.

Payne made his way east across the panhandle of northern Idaho and crossed the present western border of Montana, the crest of the Bitterroot Mountains, around the first of August 1863. He arrived at Gold Creek, Granville Stuart's settlement on the Clark Fork River, on August 7, and introduced himself as the new marshal. "His business," Stuart recorded, "is to estimate population, resources, etc., and to establish election precincts through this part of the country, which is now Idaho Territory."[13]

Payne's next call was at Bannack, where he looked up Nathaniel Langford. Operating a sawmill, Langford had prospered by ferrying lumber to the burgeoning camps at Alder Gulch, where hewn logs for cabins and shops brought a premium price. Langford was president of Bannack's chapter of the Union League, a Republican organization fiercely dedicated to the Union cause in the Civil War, and Payne wanted him to run for the territorial legislature. By now, though, many in Bannack and Alder Gulch had come to doubt the benefit of belonging to a territory so vast, and Payne's report that the capital would be Lewiston confirmed their fear of isolation from the seat of government. Already, Langford told Payne, there was talk of sending a delegation to Washington to ask Congress to sever the area east of the Bitterroots from Idaho and make Bannack and Alder Gulch the nucleus of a new territory. In fact, Langford confided, he had been asked to head the delegation.[14]

Prevailing on him to hold off, Payne urged Langford to stand for election to the territorial legislature and promised to give him a say in matters of patronage in the "eastern district," the portion of the territory east of the Bitterroots. Specifically, Payne told Langford he could nominate a deputy federal marshal for the area, and Governor Wallace would forward the name to Washington, D.C., for approval.

In his memoirs, Langford insisted that by now he held deep suspicions of Plummer, believing him to be involved in some form of criminal enterprise. On several occasions, Langford wrote later, Plummer's face betrayed a "weatherbeaten appearance" first thing in the morning, evidence that the sheriff had been out and about overnight instead of home in his cabin. "Where had he been?" Langford wondered. "What was the character of that business which could woo him from his home, to face the angry elements, and require his return and appearance on the streets by daylight?" Another time, Langford wrote, he was visiting a livestock ranch in the area and saw a fine saddle horse that was strange to him. Making inquiries, he was told it belonged to Plummer, who often exercised it but never rode it to town. "Why was he keeping this horse, unused, and away from public view," Langford asked, "if not for the purpose of escaping from the country in case of failure of his criminal enterprise?"[15]

Good questions, perhaps, but the fact is Langford did not give any indication whatsoever of harboring such qualms at the time of Payne's visit. No discernible, organized criminal activity was taking place during the summer months of 1863, and Plummer's reputation had not suffered any evident public erosion. If Langford knew something incriminating about Plummer, he did not disclose it to Payne. Indeed, Langford and the vice president of the Union League, William Rheem, suggested Plummer's name to their thirty-odd members for the post of deputy marshal and

Samuel T. Hauser, who warned against making Plummer a deputy federal marshal. Courtesy of the Montana Historical Society.

gained a unanimous vote in his favor. Payne agreed to recommend Plummer for the job.[16]

The first sign of trouble came a few days afterward, when Langford mentioned the League's endorsement to a friend, Samuel T. Hauser, one of the area's leading miners. Hauser was aghast and reacted fiercely. It would not do, he warned, to promote Plummer to federal office. The sheriff was a dangerous man, Hauser argued, too cozy by far with the saloon crowd, and complicit, it appeared, with the men who had murdered Dillingham. If the criminal class in the gold camps had a champion, Hauser added, it was probably Plummer.

Hauser's broadside against Plummer took Langford aback, not least because it came from a man of such imposing stature. Hauser had come west on the *Emilie* to escape the Civil War passions of his native Kentucky. He joined James Stuart's prospecting trip to Yellowstone County and was one of the men injured in the attack by Crow Indians. In later years, he started a bank, amassed a fortune in mining, real estate, and ranching, and became one of Montana's richest and most powerful capitalists. In 1885, he was appointed territorial governor by President Grover Cleveland. Of particular significance, he was a Democrat.

Some historians have assumed that Plummer fell victim to partisan politics. As a Democrat, they reasoned, he could not be trusted by the Republicans who held territorial office, and thus was spurned for federal office. But the truth is that Plummer's support of the Union cause was widely known in Bannack and Alder Gulch and made him more than acceptable to Langford, Rheem, and other Republican leaders, as reflected by their endorsement of him. His undoing actually came at the hands of a fellow Democrat, Hauser, which made it all the more stinging.[17]

For the first time, a prominent citizen had given voice to serious apprehensions about Plummer and argued against advancing his career as a lawman. Langford took Hauser's words to heart and spoke to the sheriff soon afterward, telling him the Union League planned to withdraw its support of his appointment as deputy marshal. "We sat down upon an ox-shoeing frame," Langford recalled, "and talked over the whole matter." Plummer was furious, according to Langford, believing he had been betrayed. And so it must have seemed, since Plummer saw his hope for higher office thwarted by nebulous accusations he had no chance to confront or rebut. "He said many provoking things," Langford recalled, "and used many oaths and epithets."

When Langford refused to reconsider, Plummer stood up and said to him coldly, "Langford, you'll be sorry for this before the matter ends. I've always been your friend, but from this time on I'm your enemy. And when I say this, I mean it in more ways than one." Then he turned to go.

According to Langford's memoirs, the two encountered each other a few more times but never again spoke.[18]

Plummer retained his job as sheriff. His repudiation by Hauser and the ensuing angry exchange with Langford did not become a matter of wide public knowledge, at least not right away, and no formal charges were leveled against him. No attempt was made to remove him from office. He continued to carry out his duties, much as he had before. If anything, Plummer seemed more determined than ever to cling to his position of authority, a point he made with dramatic emphasis by carrying out a public execution. Two mining partners named Peter Horen and Lawrence Keeley fell into a bitter dispute about the division of proceeds from the sale of their claim on Grasshopper Creek, and on the morning of August 19, 1863, Horen shot and killed Keeley at their cabin. Plummer arrested Horen and brought him before a miners' court, which convicted him and sentenced him to death. Judge B. B. Burchette ordered the sheriff to build a gallows and hang Horen, and Plummer did so on August 25, 1863.[19]

The scaffold, two tall timbers with a crossbeam supporting a noose, stood on a spare, windswept hillside about two hundred yards from Bannack's main street, plainly visible from town. Given his own close calls in the past and his distaste for summary justice, Plummer's willingness to carry out the sentence seems out of character, but apparently he had little choice in the matter. Horen became the second man executed in Montana, after the accused horse thief hanged by the Stuart brothers a year earlier at Gold Creek. Among white settlers, Keeley's was the eighth homicide in a year— a rate that fell far short of the numbers of men reported killed in Montana by contemporary chroniclers, even though it would have qualified as a murder spree in a sedate city back east.

The execution demonstrated that Plummer was still acting as the town's de facto lawman. His deputies were considered a decent lot for the most part, now that Buck Stinson and Jack Gallagher had become inactive. Edward Richardson had disappeared and Cyrus Skinner, the ex-convict who ran the Elkhorn saloon, had moved to Alder Gulch, ridding Plummer of his two most disreputable associates. He continued his mining operations, forming a new partnership with judge Burchette and four other respected men. He often rode out of Bannack to give advice to other miners and help assess their findings.[20]

Still, Hauser's censure had a corrosive effect on Plummer's reputation, as did the belated arrival and circulation of the *Sacramento Union* article.

As summer deepened, miners and merchants alike were beginning to make plans to travel home to "the States" with a season's accumulation of gold dust. Some had families to support, others had debts to satisfy, and quite a few had both. Fergus, hoping to arrange for his family to join him, sent his wife $1,000 and warned her to keep the money a secret from his creditors back in Minnesota.[21] Fear of trailside holdups, always keen, reached new levels that bordered on paranoia. As the settlers talked among themselves, trying to determine safe ways out of the territory, word of Hauser's suspicions and Langford's confrontation began to ripple in wider and wider circles. Langford considered Plummer's angry words to him a threat of physical violence and kept up his guard accordingly. The murky past that had made Plummer seem a good candidate for sheriff three months earlier took on a darker hue.

Even his close friends came to have doubts.

After serving cheerfully in Plummer's bridal party, Francis Thompson returned to the serious business of trying to track down and retrieve the supplies he had arranged for his brother to ship up the Missouri River from St. Louis. Through the summer, steamboat traffic remained stuck below the Milk River, two hundred miles east of Fort Benton, and several captains elected to unload their cargoes on the riverbank and go home rather that wait for rains to swell the current.[22]

By the middle of July 1863, it was plain to James Vail that the money he so desperately needed to keep running the Indian farm at Sun River would not be arriving. He concluded that he could not pay young Joseph Swift for his year's labors and offered instead to give him some of the farm's livestock to sell. On July 17, Thompson and Swift bade farewell to the Vails and set off together to pursue their fortunes. They spent their first night camped on the Dearborn River, each man propped against a tree after supper to write in his diary, and it struck Thompson that a passing Indian might think he had stumbled upon a literary salon. At Deer Lodge, Swift sold the six oxen Vail had given him, while Thompson found letters from his brother indicating that six tons of goods had been shipped up the river on the steamer *Shreveport* and now presumably sat abandoned beside the Milk River.[23]

With a renewed sense of urgency, Thompson and Swift continued their travels south to the mining camps, where Thompson decided that Bannack, not Alder Gulch, would provide the best market for selling his merchandise. He did not explain in his memoirs why he chose a dwindling town of three hundred over a thriving area of several thousand to open a business, but it seems likely that he was influenced by Plummer, who continued to extol the mining potential of Grasshopper Creek. In any event, Thompson and Swift traded their belongings for a wagon team and circled back north, returning to the Indian farm on the Sun River on their way to search for the missing supplies. With the drought continuing, they found near-famine conditions. Thompson reported seeing "not a spear of grass within miles of the camp, the country being so dry." Settlers around Fort Benton, according to Granville Stuart in his diary, had been reduced to "a semi-starving condition."[24]

At Sun River, the Vails were on the verge of giving up their mission. Their cows had gone dry, and they had no flour or sugar in their larder. The idea of following Thompson and Swift to Bannack and reuniting with Electa and Henry Plummer appealed strongly to them, and they began making preparations for the move. Meanwhile, Thompson went on to Fort Benton, where he paid $8 a bushel for corn for his pony, "and the poor suffering beast did not know enough to eat it." Thompson himself felt "completely used up," he confessed, exhausted by more than a month of hard travel with very little to show for the effort. After sending Swift to the Milk River to reclaim the supplies, Thompson packed his two-wheel "go-devil" cart to return to Bannack and establish his dry goods store there.[25]

On August 26, 1863, the day after Plummer carried out the execution of Peter Horen, Thompson was at Deer Lodge buying food and supplies for the last leg of his trip to Bannack. A storekeeper asked where he was headed, and when Thompson answered, the man grew alarmed. Hostile Indians had been spotted along the seventy-mile trail to the south in recent days, he explained, and it was not safe to travel alone. A party of a dozen white men were camped about a mile from town looking for someone to guide them to Bannack, the shopkeeper added, and he suggested that Thompson might be wise to join them.

"I drove down to their camp," Thompson recalled, "and told them I was going to Bannack and would like company, as the Indians were very ugly on the route." The leader of the group was a well-spoken man named "Doc" Howard who claimed to have been trained as a physician at Yale. He and another member of the party, James Romaine, struck

Thompson as "educated men of agreeable manners," and he gratefully assented to ride with them. One of their number was suffering from a bad back and Thompson let him ride in his cart. In return, Thompson recounted, "I was not permitted to even take care of my horse, but was their guest." He was impressed by the group's cook, a fellow named Red who prepared first-rate meals. The men had come east over the Bitterroots from poor diggings around Lewiston and were headed for the promising discoveries of the Beaverhead valley.

Thompson spent four pleasant days traveling south with his new companions, bedding down on the last night in a haystack at a farm just north of Bannack. The next morning, he walked into town and chanced upon Henry Plummer on Main Street. Thompson described his trip and volunteered that some of his party said they knew Plummer and "were old friends of his and spoke very highly of him." Plummer asked their names and appeared upset and agitated when Thompson told him. "Thompson," the sheriff replied sharply after a moment of silence, "those men are cut-throats and robbers! There will be hell to pay now!" He warned Thompson not to associate with them any further.

Plummer's outburst left Thompson "thunder-struck," in his words, because it was so vehement and unexpected, and because it triggered a disturbing question. Thompson could not help wondering how Plummer "knew so much about these people." If they were such bad characters, what was Plummer's connection with them? And why had they spoken so highly of him? "They speak well of me," Plummer explained, "for they don't dare do otherwise." Thompson dropped the matter, assuming Plummer meant the men respected his position as sheriff. But the episode continued to trouble him. Thinking back, he realized that "Doc" Howard had elicited quite a bit of information from him—that his supplies had been dumped at Milk River, "and that I did not have any money to pay the freight bills, and would not be in funds until I [sold] the goods." Had he not sounded convincingly destitute, Thompson reflected, he might well have been robbed on the trail by men who claimed to be on intimate terms with his friend Plummer.

Thompson was still puzzling over the exchange two days later when an even bigger surprise greeted him. Plummer's wife, Electa, announced abruptly that she was moving back east. She emerged from her cabin on the morning of September 2, 1863, with a small valise holding her clothes, and boarded the stagecoach bound for Salt Lake City. She told Thompson that she was lonely, with Plummer away so often on business, and she planned to go home and wait for him to join her in the autumn.[26]

Thompson did not know what to believe.

CHAPTER SEVEN

The Reluctant Chief Justice

As she climbed aboard the stagecoach for Salt Lake City, Electa Plummer left behind a town buzzing with questions. Just two months after marrying, this shy, demure young woman was abandoning a husband who had utterly captivated her and swept her off her feet. Why? Her stated reason for leaving, loneliness, made no sense. Often as he might be away, Henry Plummer still regularly returned to her and lived with her in their cabin. She would surely feel more alone if she went back east by herself. And why would she leave just as her sister and brother-in-law, Martha Jane and James Vail, were making their way from the Indian farm with their children to take up residence in Bannack? Her friend, Francis Thompson, planned to make his home nearby and open his new business in Bannack, and Joseph Swift was expected to arrive shortly as well with the long-lost cargo of goods. Why quit family and friends for the unknown?

Rumors began swirling immediately. Was she pregnant? There is no evidence that she was. She never had a child by Plummer, and if she miscarried in the coming weeks she kept it a secret. Was she carrying home a cache of gold dust? Some contemporaries wanted to think so, just as Jack Cleveland once had dogged Plummer hoping to find his hidden treasure. But there is nothing to suggest that Plummer had any fortune at all. As we have seen, he had a hard time making a living after his hands and arm were injured, and his circumstances in Bannack after returning with Electa were modest at best. If he did have a hoard, the fruits of the sort of criminal enterprise that Sam Hauser, Nathaniel Langford, and others were beginning to suspect, would he ship it back east in the care of a young woman traveling alone through hostile territory?

More curious still, what of Electa's statement to Thompson that her husband planned to join her in the fall? The first day of autumn was just around the corner. If Plummer planned to quit as sheriff and return east, why not do so right away and accompany Electa on her journey? If he had loose ends to tie up before leaving, why would she not have waited for him? Tempting as other conjectures might be, the most plausible conclusion about Electa Plummer's departure has to be that she learned something about her husband's affairs, and that the knowledge upset her and drove her away. Perhaps she hoped to lure him into joining her and abandoning his activities.[1]

When her stagecoach left, Plummer rode alongside on horseback, apparently hoping Electa might change her mind and return with him to Bannack. They traveled together this way for several days, south through Beaverhead Valley and over the high plateau of Monida Pass into Idaho, past the spectral vision of the Grand Tetons in the distance to the east, eventually arriving at the ferry across the Snake River near the present-day city of Idaho Falls. There, in an encounter laden with symbolism, the Plummers met a party coming the other way.[2]

To serve as chief justice of the Supreme Court of Idaho Territory, President Lincoln had chosen a former congressman from Ohio named Sidney Edgerton, a radical Republican whose gaunt cheeks, fierce glance, and graying beard gave him the appearance of an Old Testament prophet. Edgerton had been forced to wait months to begin his journey west, not knowing which city Governor William Wallace would choose as the territorial capital. Finally, on the morning of June 1, 1863, Edgerton gathered his wife, children, and several other members of his extended household, and set off from Tallmadge, Ohio, for his new posting. He still had no idea of his ultimate destination, but time was growing short and he felt pressed to get started. He hoped to receive a telegram somewhere along the way telling him where to find the governor and establish his court.

Edgerton's wife, Mary, did not relish the thought of leaving home. She would have to say farewell to her mother, a twin sister, ten other siblings, and scores of friends, trading the settled existence of small-town life for the hazards and privations of the gold-rush frontier. But as her daughter, Martha, explained, she was a woman "whose own wishes were always subordinate to those of her family," and she gamely agreed to pull up stakes and support her husband's new career. Her one insistence was that the party take the overland route, because the prospect of sea travel frightened her and made her physically ill.[3]

For Edgerton, at age forty-five, change and challenge were a way of life. Born in Cazenovia, New York, in 1818, he was a sickly child who came so close to dying his mother sewed a set of clothes for his coffin. His father, a schoolteacher, went blind and then died when Sidney was only six. Finding she could not make ends meet as a seamstress, his mother sent Sidney and his five older brothers and sisters to live with various relatives. By age eight, Sidney was boarding with an aunt, relieving his loneliness by immersing himself in the books in her library. Eventually he found work as a teacher. Though his parents were unable to leave him anything of material value, they did pass along an ardent commitment to the abolition of slavery, a cause young Edgerton embraced completely.

In 1844, with all of three dollars in his pocket, Edgerton moved to Akron, Ohio, and began reading the law under the supervision of a prominent attorney, Rufus Spalding. After earning a degree from the Cincinnati Law School, Edgerton opened his own law practice in Akron and soon took an active interest in politics. Not surprisingly, perhaps, given the grim nature of his childhood, he could not accept the solaces of the church. He declared himself an agnostic, a stance that very nearly undid his courtship of Mary Wright, the daughter of a prosperous and devoutly Congregationalist family in Tallmadge, Ohio, five miles from Akron. But the two were eventually married, and Edgerton became active in the movement that took the place of religion in his life, the crusade to end slavery. He served as a delegate to the Free-Soil Convention of 1848, when fifteen thousand fellow believers gathered in Buffalo, New York, and created a political party that nominated the first abolitionist candidate for president.

Moving to Akron, Edgerton built his law practice into a success, and he and Mary started a family. In 1852, Edgerton was elected prosecuting attorney of Summit County on the Free-Soil ticket, and four years later he was chosen as a delegate to the first convention of the new Republican Party. He was elected to Congress on an abolition platform in 1858 and reelected in 1860, serving in the House of Representatives during the four

Sidney Edgerton, chief justice of Idaho Territory. Courtesy of the Montana Historical Society.

years that saw the United States slip from intractable political disagreement into civil war.

Edgerton's opposition to slavery, the South's "peculiar institution," was no faint, philosophical preference, but a fierce belief that qualified as a moral commitment and bordered on mania. In 1859, after John Brown led his famous, failed raid on the federal arsenal at Harper's Ferry, Virginia, hoping to incite and arm a slave rebellion, Edgerton traveled at his own expense to try to see Brown in captivity and help arrange his affairs before his execution. The commanding general refused to let Edgerton see Brown and sent him packing back to the railroad station. A cordon of Virginia militiamen lined the route, shouting angry threats to kill him. From that moment on, Edgerton viewed southerners in general, and Confederate soldiers and sympathizers in particular, with an attitude of open contempt and hostility that belied the gentler side known to his family. His daughter, Martha, remarked many years later on her surprise at seeing her father arm himself with a cane that hid a slender sword when he went out in public. He carried it onto the floor of Congress as well.

In 1862, Edgerton's political career was undone by the cruelties of gerrymandering. Ohio lost two seats in Congress after the 1860 census, and Edgerton was thrown into a new district dominated by his mentor, Rufus Spalding. After failing to gain renomination, Edgerton retired, and President Lincoln rewarded his service to the Republican Party by naming him chief justice of the new Idaho Territory. During the spring of 1863, Edgerton assembled a group to accompany him on his mission, which he hoped would include mining and business opportunities to supplement his modest salary as a judge. Along with his wife and four children, the small colony also included Edgerton's twenty-nine-year-old nephew, Wilbur Fisk Sanders, his wife, Harriett, their two sons, and Edgerton's niece, Lucia Darling. Henry Tilden, the teenage son of a family friend, and a young woman named Almarette Geer, who helped care for the Sanders children, completed the company.[4]

Edgerton's group ventured to Cleveland by train, and from there took a boat across Lake Erie to Detroit. Mary Edgerton's severe seasickness during the crossing confirmed the wisdom of her insistence on making most of the trip by land. They continued by train through Chicago to the western rail terminus at St. Joseph, Missouri, where they boarded a steamboat and sailed upriver to Omaha. There the members of the party bought provisions for the passage west in ox-drawn wagons. The women outfitted themselves in the latest frontier fashion: oilskin masks and goggles with colored glass and wire screens designed to protect their faces from the sun and the harsh alkaline dust of the trail. Demonstrating high spirits, Mary Edgerton wrote her sister that the trip had been surprisingly pleasant so far, at least the rail portion, as they crossed rolling prairies matted with carpets of wildflowers.[5]

Aside from the occasional river crossing or rumor of Indian activity, the Edgerton party enjoyed an uneventful passage west, making leisurely time as the men walked alongside the oxen. Like modern tourists, several of the group's members marched off to see Chimney Rock, the landmark spire along the Platte River in western Nebraska, and broke off a small piece for a souvenir. In sharp contrast to the harrowing experiences of so many pioneers, the company benefited from unusually good weather—and from the good luck of avoiding accidents and illness. One morning,

Edgerton slipped and fell while jumping down from the front seat of his wagon as it rolled along, but he was able to dive between the wheels and escape being crushed. Mary Edgerton had little more to worry about than her husband's decision to shave off his thick, tangled eyebrows to keep them from collecting trail dust. "I wish you could see Sidney," she wrote home. "He took my shears, and cut off his eyebrows a few weeks ago, and it does make him look funny enough. They are beginning to grow out again now."[6]

When the group crossed into the central part of modern Wyoming, its pace grew more difficult, as the men and oxen strained to climb the long, sloping shelf of the Continental Divide. Edgerton's daughter, Martha, would recall hearing the animals moaning from thirst in the night. In the second week of August 1863, roughly the time Henry Plummer thought he was about to become a deputy federal marshal, the Edgerton party reached South Pass, a small settlement at the foot of the Wind River Mountains where the trail crossed the Continental Divide at 7,550 feet. A telegraph operator there told Edgerton no word had arrived yet about the capital of Idaho Territory.[7]

Edgerton pressed on, leading his party west. A day or two later, on August 15, 1863, the telegraph man from South Pass came riding up at a gallop to announce that notice had been received at last. The capital would be at Lewiston. This was welcome news, Harriett Sanders recorded in her diary, because "it will be far pleasanter and the provisions much cheaper than at Bannack," the other likely choice. While others in the party rejoiced, however, Edgerton recognized that getting to Lewiston before the snows began would be a very dicey proposition. Their destination was more than four hundred miles distant, with the towering Sawtooth and Salmon River mountains blocking the way, and already the weather was turning cool at night.[8]

For the next two weeks, the company made slow work descending the western slope of the Rockies, crossing the southwest part of present-day Wyoming into Idaho. We may presume that Mary and Sidney Edgerton kept each other warm at night, for she became pregnant with their fifth child during this part of the trip, at the age of thirty-six. On September 2, 1863, Edgerton's party reached the trail at Blackfoot Creek that led north toward Bannack. At first, Edgerton meant to continue west and complete the journey to Lewiston. But the realities of place and season discouraged him, and he decided to go to Bannack instead. Weather permitting, he could continue from there to Lewiston, but if the snows came early his family would spend the winter in one of Idaho Territory's populated enclaves.[9]

So it was that on Sunday, September 6, 1863, the Edgerton party arrived on the eastern bank of the swift, dark Snake River, a few miles north of Idaho Falls, and waited to cross over on the ferry and follow the trail to Bannack. They met Plummer and his wife, Electa, coming from the other direction and exchanged pleasantries. One of the stagecoach drivers took the Edgertons aside and told them the sheriff was a man with a violent past. The Edgertons' eldest daughter, Martha, then thirteen, confided later that she was thrilled at this first encounter with a desperado—"a bad man," as she put it, "one who was quick on the draw." But if the other members in her party shared her sense of excitement, they failed to make note of it. Mary Edgerton did not mention the Plummers in her next letter home, and neither of the diarists in the group, Julia Darling or Hattie Sanders, put down a word about them. The portent of the encounter seems to have been lost on both sides: the sheriff with the criminal record going one way, the former congressman with the highly developed moral code and the authority of the federal government coming the other.[10]

Like other pioneers, the Edgertons were concerned about Indians, illness, and accidents, and not very much about the threat of robbery. It was only parties *leaving* the gold camps who faced the menace of armed highwaymen, since those just arriving carried nothing of immediate value to a criminal. The Edgertons had no particular reason to be careful in sizing up the parties they met on the trail west, and they treated their encounter with the Plummers accordingly. A few days afterward, on their way north from the Snake River to Monida Pass, the Edgerton party met another famous figure from the gold camps, George Ives, and found him utterly charming. Ives visited with the Edgertons at their camp near Market Lake and dazzled them by showing off a sack full of gold dust and nuggets, giving them a glimpse of the wealth of the new Xanadu they were about to enter. It did not occur to them that Ives might be dangerous.[11]

After crossing Monida Pass, the Edgerton party pressed on to Bannack, arriving on the afternoon of Friday, September 18, 1863. As they gazed down on the town from the top of a hill, they were less than impressed. "'Bangup' is a humbug," announced little Jimmy Sanders, aged five, and no one argued. As Lucia Darling recorded in her diary, "the view was not an inspiring one," consisting of scattered log cabins and stores and the gallows on the facing hillside. "I think there was not one of us," Martha Edgerton wrote later, "who did not feel a keen sense of disappointment at the prospect. Not a ray of sunlight enlivened the scene. The grey clouds above and around us made the bare mountains and the log cabins between them look extremely forbidding."[12]

Nevertheless, it would be their home for the coming months. Talking with townsmen he met over the weekend, Edgerton concluded that it was too late to start out for Lewiston. On September 22, four days after reaching Bannack, he bought an abandoned log building for $400 at a sheriff's auction and began fixing it up as a home for his family. Hattie and Wilbur Sanders bought a smaller cabin nearby.[13]

Looking back on his early days in Bannack, the striking thing about Edgerton's conduct is that he made no attempt whatsoever to establish his authority as a federal official. Plummer had returned, without Electa, and resumed his duties as sheriff with Edgerton's evident blessing. It was Plummer who signed the bill of sale when Edgerton bought his house. On his first weekend in town, Edgerton happened on a miner's court in progress and watched the proceedings with avid interest, investing the tribunal with his tacit approval.

In later years, Edgerton asserted that he could not take up his position as chief justice because there was no one in Bannack to administer the oath of office to him. This finicky insistence on form strikes a modern observer as pretty thin gruel, more of an excuse than an actual impediment to action. Most likely, Edgerton took the view that the mining camp's informally elected officials—president, judge, coroner, and sheriff—were performing satisfactorily without his interference. He would have seen the gallows and heard of the recent execution of Peter Horen, and he probably concluded that adequate instruments of law and order were in place. According to his wife's first letter home from Bannack, written on October 4, 1863, Edgerton had been busying himself with carpentry, adding partitions as bedroom walls in his new house and crafting furniture. Perhaps he placed a higher premium on securing a safe, comfortable home for his family for the coming winter than on trying to hold court without the benefit of law books and bailiffs. Until a territorial legislature was elected and convened to adopt a code of laws and organize a court system, Edgerton would be on his own.[14]

It also seems that Edgerton caught a dose of gold fever. Writing to her mother, Mary Edgerton described how a pair of miners invited her husband to visit their claims and "shake a pan of dirt" to harvest an ounce or two of the glittering dust. Edgerton got about $40 worth of dust on his first try and $30 on his second, and soon he was investing in claims up and down Grasshopper Creek. The Edgerton women fixed up their houses and tended to their cooking and cleaning, resolutely determined to keep up their spirits. Mary Edgerton wrote home pining for the taste of fresh fruit and butter, then added bravely, "Now don't think that I am finding fault because I can't have such things as I have spoken of. We don't think of them very often, only when we are talking about the folks at home. We are perfectly contented without them." At night, the family slept by the whooshing sound of Grasshopper Creek's waters running through the miners' wooden sluice boxes.[15]

Not long after the Edgertons settled into their new home, Captain James Liberty Fisk arrived in the area with his second large company of settlers from Minnesota. He stopped first at Fort Benton, then led a large contingent to the diggings at Alder Gulch and Bannack. Finding Edgerton in residence, Fisk presented him with the expedition's small howitzer, which he no longer needed after passing safely through Indian country. Fisk left immediately to return home by the stage route through Salt Lake City, and Edgerton stored the cannon under his bed. He had no evident need for the weapon, but his acceptance of it suggests that in at least one respect he accepted and acknowledged his role as the lone representative of the federal government in the region, even while declining to hold court as a judge.[16]

For a time, it appeared that Plummer meant to bow to his wife's wishes and join her back east. She had chosen a farming community near Cedar Rapids, Iowa, as her destination, because she had distant relatives living there. Just after she left, Plummer sold a part interest in his most profitable mining claim for $1,500, to be collected in his absence by his patron,

Mary Edgerton, wife of the chief justice. Courtesy of the Montana Historical Society.

storekeeper George Chrisman. In mid-September, Plummer sold his cabin to his brother-in-law, James Vail, who had packed up his family and vacated the Indian farm at Sun River. For some reason, though, Plummer did not leave. He continued to board with the Vails in his old cabin and take his meals there, and he kept up his duties as sheriff. Francis Thompson, the family friend, boarded there as well, keeping whatever misgivings he felt about Plummer to himself.[17]

The most vexing question about these early days of autumn in Bannack is what to make of the town's attitude toward Plummer. By now Nathaniel

Langford had broken with Plummer, sharing his friend Samuel Hauser's suspicion that the sheriff was too cozy with the rough faction in town, and perhaps a criminal himself. Did Langford share these beliefs with Edgerton? The record is silent. As president of the Union League, Langford was the leading Republican figure in Bannack, and he undoubtedly would have welcomed Edgerton and wanted to talk politics with him. Plainly the two men found common ground in the Civil War, both of them fervently dedicated to the Union cause and appalled at the number of Southern sympathizers in the area. But another topic may well have claimed their closer attention. Langford believed that the most pressing issue in the gold camps east of the Bitterroot Mountains was the need to break away from Idaho Territory and escape reliance on a government headquartered at Lewiston, hundreds of miles away. One reason Edgerton refused to hold court may have been an agreement with Langford that the cause of creating a new territory would be boosted by the absence of a legally constituted and fully operational court system. Leaving law enforcement in the hands of a man like Plummer might well have served their purposes by advertising the need for a new, separate territory.

Before one accuses Edgerton of tolerating or encouraging criminal activity for political gain, however, it is vital to note that not much actual crime was taking place in and around Bannack during the period while he settled in. Writing home on Sunday, October 18, 1863, a month after arriving, Mary Edgerton told her sister that Bannack was "very quiet and orderly for such a mining town—much more so than I expected to find it." Other contemporary accounts convey the same sense of calm. Fear of travel between Bannack and Alder Gulch remained high, as always, and rumors flew in the saloons about one party or another having narrowly escaped mischief on the trail. One settler complained in his diary that he had encountered "a hard looking set of men" near Robert Dempsey's ranch on the Stinking Water River. Yet he was not robbed. Indeed, not one armed robbery was reported anywhere in the present-day state of Montana at any time during the four weeks immediately after Edgerton's arrival. Suspicion of Plummer remained pretty much just that—suspicion—with no hard evidence that he was engaged in criminal enterprise.[18]

Perhaps no one had a harder time coming to grips with the issue of Plummer's real character than Francis Thompson, who lived under the same roof with the sheriff, broke bread with him on a daily basis, and continued to find him warm and compelling, "a loveable man," in Thompson's candid phrase. Plummer had warned him to steer clear of "Doc" Howard and his crowd, an admonition Thompson appreciated and at the same time found suspicious. As he reflected on Plummer's advice, Thompson was nagged by the thought that the sheriff had been talking not merely about Howard's past reputation but also about his future intentions. "I became certain," Thompson wrote later, "that [Plummer] knew of the plans of the road agents before they were carried into execution." If so, this was a harsh indictment indeed from a close friend.[19]

For Thompson, and for many other settlers who knew and liked Plummer, dealing with the sheriff took on the nuances of living inside a crime novel as they tried to balance their growing distrust of him against the lack of solid proof that he had done anything wrong. Inevitably, they began acting like detectives, looking for clues. Thompson kept an especially close watch on Howard and his men, anxious to see if they were the villains Plummer made them out to be and what trouble they might be planning to make.

In mid-September, Howard and three other members of his party, James Romaine, Chris Lower, and Billy Page, signed on as hired hands with a trader named Lloyd Magruder, who came east over the Bitterroot Mountains from Elk City, Idaho, with a large pack train of dry goods. A handsome, dark-haired man with blue eyes and an affable manner, Magruder set up shop in Virginia City and with Howard's help sold out his entire inventory in three weeks, clearing some $12,000 in gold dust. On October 5, 1863, Magruder left Bannack in company with Howard and the others for the return trip to Idaho, and Thompson was left to wonder about his safety. If Howard and his men were indeed "cut-throats and robbers," as Plummer had said, why did the sheriff let Magruder set off with them?[20]

Or maybe it was not that simple. It seemed that Plummer and Magruder had been acquainted years earlier in California and did not entirely trust one another. A veteran of the 1849 gold rush, Magruder was an off-and-on merchant whose ventures in various towns in the Sierra Nevada ultimately left him in debt. He was living in Marysville in 1858 during Plummer's retrial for murder, working as a lawyer and part-owner of the weekly newspaper there, trying to rebuild his fortunes, and he would have been familiar with the case against Plummer and its outcome. If Plummer warned him against traveling with Howard and company, the words might have fallen on deaf ears.[21]

Adding political spice to the stew, Magruder had presented himself in Bannack and Alder Gulch as a candidate for territorial delegate to Congress, the job that Governor William Wallace coveted for himself. A native of Maryland and the son of a plantation owner, Magruder was running as a Copperhead, a Democrat in strong sympathy with the South, eager to see the Union make peace even if it meant the continuation of slavery. A reluctant Congress had instituted federal military conscription (on March 3, 1863, the same night Idaho Territory was created) in an effort to replenish the ranks of the Union armies, and by summer antidraft riots had resulted in New York and other northern cities, giving the Copperheads a powerful issue. In Lewiston, the pro-Republican newspaper, the *Golden Age,* denounced Magruder for belonging to the "filthy den" of secessionists and urged his defeat. No newspaper was yet in operation east of the Bitterroots, and there is no record of the reaction that Republican leaders like Edgerton and Langford had toward Magruder. But it seems fair to say they would have been glad to see him leave. Did they, too, bear some responsibility for failing to warn him about his companions?[22]

Mining camps in general, and Bannack in particular, were places where contradiction took easy root in the arid soil. Men were judged by appearance, yet they were also allowed the freedom of alias and endless reinvention. A caste system separated miner and merchant, yet many men practiced both professions, and class boundaries were porous. Immigrants were the targets of prejudice, yet typically were allowed to vote on thirty days' residency. Men worked to create the comforts and succor of domesticity, then picked up and left town for good on a moment's whim. Rumor sent men scrambling on fool's errands, stampeding to empty claims, and those same men returned and lusted for more rumor. It was possible to like a man while holding a dark thought in the back of your mind that he might be capable of killing you. Settled society offered a hundred small tests that allowed one man to take another's measure and deal with him accordingly. The frontier West did not. Still, the fact remained that a man of consequence—a candidate for Congress, carrying a small fortune—was heading off into the forested wilderness with a pack of very dangerous men.

Perhaps Plummer tried to give Magruder some kind of warning about the company he was keeping. Perhaps Langford, Edgerton, and other Republican leaders sent a signal to Magruder that he ignored, advising him not to set off across the Bitterroot Mountains with men of bad reputation. Or perhaps not.

CHAPTER EIGHT

A *Rashomon* Night

Dolphus Payne, the federal marshal, completed his travels around Idaho Territory in September 1863 and reported back to Governor William Wallace in Lewiston. The population of the gold camps seemed weighted in favor of the Democrats, Payne warned, and might well doom Wallace, a Republican, to defeat in his bid to become the territorial delegate to Congress.[1]

Fortunately for Wallace, Congress had limited the vote to men in residence before March 4, 1863, the day the territory was created. The narrow franchise had the effect of denying the vote to thousands of men, a majority of them Democrats. The election was called for October 31, 1863, and Wallace won handily. A later investigation would show that Payne had acted to guarantee the outcome by padding the vote totals from Fort Laramie, the military post near the eastern border of present-day Wyoming. Wallace apparently was unaware of this helpful fraud, which Payne undertook in hopes of becoming governor himself once Wallace vacated the post to return to Washington, D.C. Thanks to the stacked deck, Republicans also won narrow majorities in both houses of the territorial legislature.[2]

As it happened, the political maneuvering proved to be unnecessary, at least in the case of Lloyd Magruder, the Copperhead candidate for territorial delegate, because he had disappeared. After departing from Bannack on October 5, 1863, Magruder was expected back in Lewiston by midmonth. When he failed to return on time, his family, friends, and supporters began to fret, and the Democrats chose another nominee in his place. His wife, Caroline, who had married him at sixteen and joined him in the gold rush to California, feared she might now be a widow, facing the prospect of raising their four young children alone.[3]

Late on the night of October 18, 1863, a man walked up to the desk in the lobby of the Luna House hotel in Lewiston and asked to buy four tickets on the morning stagecoach bound for Walla Walla, Washington. The clerk explained that the stage line did not issue tickets, but simply took money and made reservations in the names of those traveling. He asked the man to print the names in his ledger. Looking a bit rattled, the man did as he was told and quickly left, saying his party was staying at the Hotel de France a few blocks away and could be picked up there. From his office just off the lobby, the proprietor of Luna House, Hill Beachy, watched the exchange with interest. The man buying the tickets seemed to be shielding his face with his collar, a gesture Beachy found suspicious. He checked the ledger and found unfamiliar names with the ring of aliases.[4]

In the early hours of the next morning, Beachy and his clerk saddled their horses, rode by the Hotel de France, and watched from the shadows as the four men loaded their things onto the stage. The men had covered their faces with scarves, making it difficult to recognize them. Beachy's first thought, he said later, was that they might be planning to rob the stage. But that concern was assuaged by the evident weight of their luggage. It seemed they had valuables of their own to protect. Having no grounds or authority to stop them, he allowed the coach to leave.

Still, Beachy remained troubled. As one of Magruder's closest friends, he entertained a nagging worry. Could the four men have some knowledge of Magruder's whereabouts? Were they possibly involved in his disappearance? The men had arrived on horseback, and Beachy began searching for their stock and gear at Lewiston's various stables. Several hours later, at a remote pasturage called Tammany Flat, he discovered a horse and saddle he recognized as belonging to Magruder. Rushing back to town with this highly incriminating evidence, Beachy arranged for a formal complaint to be drawn up and got the territorial secretary, William B. Daniels, who was acting as governor while Wallace campaigned, to sign letters to the governors of California and British Columbia seeking extradition. On October 23, 1863, Beachy was sworn in as a deputy sheriff and took off in pursuit of the four suspects.[5]

Just how quickly word of the evident foul play involving Magruder got back to Bannack and Alder Gulch is hard to say. Unlike Lewiston, the gold camps east of the Bitterroots still had no telegraph service. The difficulty of travel between Lewiston and Bannack was a matter of record, but the fact is that small parties did make the trip on a regular basis, at the rate of roughly one per day, either by the direct route over the rugged Nez Perce Pass or by the longer trail north on the Mullan Road and down through Deer Lodge. It seems safe to assume that by the latter part of October 1863 settlers in Bannack and Alder Gulch would have heard that Magruder was missing and presumed dead.

Closer to home, meanwhile, on October 26, 1863, two hooded men armed with shotguns held up Peabody & Caldwell's stagecoach on its trip from Virginia City to Bannack. The target of the robbery was a character named "Bummer Dan" McFadden, an Irish miner who had struck it rich, and the odd way in which the crime unfolded became the talk of the town. As his nickname suggested, McFadden had gained a reputation as a lazybones who "bummed" food and drink from other miners in the early days of settlement at Bannack. But McFadden demonstrated an unexpected burst of initiative during the winter of 1863 and got hold of a lucrative claim on the area's richest lode, the Dakota. Later he joined the rush to Alder Gulch and had good luck there as well, staking a high-yielding claim on Bummer Dan's Bar. After a season of hard work, McFadden was ready to head back to "the States" with a cache of gold dust rumored to be worth thousands of dollars. Fearing mischief if his plans were too widely known, McFadden decided to leave town at night on foot and catch the stagecoach along its route.[6]

On October 25, 1863, Peabody & Caldwell's stagecoach departed from Virginia City for the daylong trip to Bannack. The regular driver had reported in sick and was replaced by a substitute named Billy Rumsey. The morning dawned dark and foreboding, and soon a snow squall enveloped the coach and its passengers. Because of the storm, the stage made slow progress to its first stop, a way station on the Stinking Water River. The travelers found the corral empty, the stock scattered by the driving snow, and had to spend two hours searching before they could round up fresh horses. Hastening to the next stop, Robert Dempsey's ranch, they found McFadden waiting to join their party and welcomed him into the coach.

Because of the storm and the delay in finding stock, the stage did not arrive at Rattlesnake Ranch, the last stop before Bannack, until sunset. The corral had been emptied for the night, and the passengers were forced to wait until morning to continue their journey. The proprietor of Rattlesnake Ranch was a man named Bill Bunton, a native of Missouri whose father had been ruined in the Panic of 1837 and moved the family to Oregon to try to rebuild his fortunes. Young Bunton came of age working on a farm in northeastern Oregon with his parents and siblings, and briefly owned a spread of his own before opening a saloon in Lewiston in 1862 to service the flood of prospectors there. A drinker and gambler with a quarrelsome reputation, Bunton killed a man during a fight over a bet on a horse race, and while he was found to have acted in self-defense—the familiar verdict in drunken clashes—he fell into a legal feud with his victim's friends and family and decided to relocate east of the Bitterroots.[7]

Bunton opened the Rattlesnake Ranch as a livestock operation in partnership with Frank Parish, a Tennessean who was perhaps best known for having taken a Bannock Indian wife who weighed more than two hundred pounds. Parish furnished a legendary anecdote one day while dealing with a group of prospectors who suspected he had found a rich discovery and demanded that he share his good fortune. "I've got a big thing," he admitted with a deadpan expression, and then led his inquisitors to his ranch and pointed out his wife. Parish suffered frostbite during the winter of 1863 and was in such poor physical condition afterward that his friends did not expect him to live out the year.[8]

The two partners were judged to be decent hosts, and one visitor described Bunton as "the soul of hospitality," generous in pouring whiskey. Accommodations at the ranch were far from luxurious—guests provided their own bedding and slept on a hard-packed dirt floor in front of a large fireplace—but the kitchen turned out hot meals and the place served the rudimentary purpose of offering travelers protection from the elements. In the autumn of 1863, the two partners hired Erastus "Red" Yeager to work as cook and barkeeper—the same man who had accompanied Francis Thompson into Bannack with "Doc" Howard in September, provoking the warning from Henry Plummer that he was in bad company.[9]

The travelers who arrived at the Rattlesnake Ranch on the night of October 25, 1863, spent the evening drinking whiskey and gambling and did not get much sleep before first light. Rumsey, the driver, abstained and was up early to search for fresh horses. Oddly, the ranch's wranglers were unable to locate the herd, and Rumsey eventually had to rehitch the tired team that had brought the stage to the ranch the night before. Setting off for Bannack at mid-morning, the passengers enjoyed a final round of whiskey offered up by Bunton and were surprised when he decided at the last minute that he would join them, riding up top on "the box" with Rumsey in the cold, blustery weather.

The stage made slow progress because of the harsh conditions and depleted horses, and after an hour Bunton climbed down to ride inside the coach with McFadden and the other passengers. Rumsey was alone on the bench moments later when two hooded men on horseback rode swiftly out of the gloom, aimed shotguns at him, and ordered him to halt. He obeyed, and the passengers were told to step out of the carriage and line up on the ground with their hands in the air. The gunmen recognized McFadden and directed their attention to him, ordering Rumsey to disarm him and collect his gold dust. After giving up a pair of navy revolvers, McFadden reached into his coat pockets, pulled out two pouches, and handed them over. One of the gunmen then cursed McFadden, accused him of concealing his main cache, and threatened to shoot him unless he surrendered his gold. A sullen McFadden took off his coat, unfastened a shoulder strap, and pulled a large buckskin purse full of gold dust up from its hiding place in his pants. He handed it to the driver, who turned it over to the robbers.

With a stern warning not to tell anyone what had just happened, the gunmen rode off, leaving the stage to resume its trip to Bannack. Arriving in the afternoon, McFadden and the other passengers ignored instructions and reported the incident to anyone who would listen. "Unusual excitement in town today," Granville Stuart recorded in his diary on October 27, 1863. "News has just arrived that the coach that left here [Virginia City] for Bannack on the twenty-fifth was held up by highwaymen and the passengers robbed." He reported that McFadden had lost $2,500.[10]

As they recounted the incident, McFadden and the other victims made a point of describing what they considered curious behavior on Bunton's part. Ordinarily a fairly composed man, he had appeared on the verge of panic during the robbery and had begged the two gunmen not to kill him, saying several times, "For God's sake, don't shoot! Take what I have, but don't kill me!" This pleading struck the other passengers as theatrical, intended for their benefit to make certain that Bunton was considered an innocent victim, when perhaps he was not.

The holdup of the Peabody & Caldwell stage marked a new era in the gold camps. Up to now, trailside robberies had been largely a matter of rumor. The handful of documented cases had occurred outside the corridor between Alder Gulch and Bannack, and they had seemed entirely random. This latest crime had been very carefully planned. It took place within ten miles of Bannack, targeted a specific individual who was known to be carrying a large hoard of gold dust, and appeared to involve one or more principals of a way station, the refuge all travelers had to be able to trust if they hoped to carry their fortunes back home to family and creditors.

And there was one other oddity about the robbery. As Stuart put it in his diary, "So far as I can learn no steps have been taken to discover who the robbers are or to punish them." For some reason, Sheriff Plummer did not seem eager to catch the bad guys.[11]

Suspicion of Plummer was accelerating, fueled by a peculiar pattern his critics thought they detected. Miners and merchants were leaving for "the States" in large numbers, laden with gold dust they had amassed during the spring and summer. In Bannack, a traveler would come into George Chrisman's general store or some other business and discuss his departure plans within earshot of Plummer or one of his deputies. Often, it seemed, Plummer would then find himself called away on sheriff's business, or to inspect a new mining claim, just as the party was leaving by stagecoach. Was it simple happenstance if the stage was later held up? Or was Plummer out there somewhere directing a criminal operation? Neil Howie, a miner who later served as the sheriff of Helena, claimed that Plummer approached him one day, commiserated over the rigors of mining for a living, and then added cryptically, "I can tell you an easier way." Howie refused to listen.[12]

One episode in particular helps explain the confused but increasingly wary attitude toward Plummer in the gold camps. Sam Hauser, the widely respected settler whose distrust of Plummer helped undo his chances of becoming a deputy federal marshal, was making plans in early November 1863 to return east to St. Louis. After recovering from the injuries he suffered at the hands of Crow Indians during his venture into Yellowstone territory, Hauser had spent the summer working a profitable claim on

Alder Creek, accumulating a substantial amount of gold dust. He meant to take the money home, and he also agreed to take along a cache of dust valued at $14,000 belonging to his friends Granville Stuart and Walter B. Dance, the store owners, to repay their creditors. On the morning of Friday, November 13, 1863, Hauser stepped onto the stagecoach bound from Virginia City to Bannack and was surprised to find Plummer sitting across from him.

Concealing his discomfort, Hauser chatted with Plummer as if nothing were amiss. As the coach passed through some of the tight spots on the trail, Hauser said later, he imagined that Plummer's confederates might be lurking there, bent on robbery, though his stronger suspicion was that Plummer intended to wait and carry out the crime on the road from Bannack to Salt Lake City. When the coach arrived in Bannack without incident, Hauser breathed a sigh of relief.[13]

The passengers, including Plummer, alighted and went into Goodrich's Hotel to have a drink and visit with their friends. Hauser was planning to make the trip east with Nathaniel Langford, the successful lumberman and Republican politician, who greeted him with evident concern and asked about Plummer's presence on the stage. Nothing had happened, Hauser reported, but they would have to be on their guard constantly in the coming days. Langford agreed. In recent days he had encountered two of Plummer's deputies, Ned Ray and Buck Stinson, and he believed they were shadowing him, trying to learn the details of his departure.

Hauser's immediate concern, he confided in Langford, was the safe-keeping of the gold dust in his possession. He and Langford intended to spend the night in Bannack and travel the next day with a group of Mormon freighters to Salt Lake City. Their money, a tempting target, would have to be guarded overnight. Much to Langford's surprise, Hauser abruptly interrupted the buzz of conversation at Goodrich's bar and announced in a loud voice that he was carrying a large supply of gold dust. Then he turned to Plummer and asked him to take custody of the buckskin sack full of money. "I've got fourteen thousand dollars in this bag, which I'm going to take to the States with me," he told Plummer, "and I want you, as sheriff, to keep it for me till I start."

Langford pulled Hauser aside and demanded in a sharp whisper if he had lost his mind. This was akin to asking the fox to guard the henhouse, Langford pointed out, entrusting "so large an amount to a man of such doubtful reputation." In Langford's telling, Hauser answered him with breezy reassurance, pointing out that Plummer could not very easily keep the money, since it had been given to him in front of several witnesses, many of them Bannack's most prominent citizens. If he failed to return it, his complicity would be obvious and the debate about his honesty would be answered once and for all in the negative. Faced with this "bold strategy," as Langford called it, Plummer accepted the money and placed it in the safe at Chrisman's store until morning.

The next day, Plummer returned Hauser's buckskin sack and also made a point of offering him a bright red scarf to keep him warm on the trip, a gesture Hauser interpreted as an attempt to mark him as the target for Plummer's band of highwaymen. "It was the common custom of Mormon freighters to extend their day's journeying far into the evening," Langford explained later. "Plummer was cognizant of this fact, and there can be no doubt that his purpose in presenting Hauser with the scarf was that he might single him out from the rest of the party after nightfall."

As Hauser and Langford prepared to leave Bannack on the afternoon of November 14, 1863, a miner arrived in town with news of a possible silver discovery and called Plummer away to examine it. Believing that the sheriff had invented an excuse to track them, and that he meant to way-lay them along the trail, Hauser and Langford briefly considered abandoning their journey. But they concluded that they would face the same risk whenever they set off, and decided to proceed. "As a precautionary measure," Langford wrote, "I carefully cleaned my gun, and loaded each barrel with twelve revolver balls."

Departing late from Bannack, after nightfall, Hauser and Langford kept their guns cocked in their laps while they rode. They caught up with the Mormon freighters, who had left in the afternoon, at a place called Horse Prairie about twelve miles south of Bannack. A fierce snow squall and plummeting temperatures had halted the freighters' progress and forced them to make camp. After yielding his blankets and sleeping spot in one of the wagons to another traveler who was ill, Langford tried to make himself comfortable on the ground in a buffalo robe. Too cold to sleep, he arose in the middle of the night and wandered the perimeter of the camp acting as a sentry. In his memoirs, he claimed to have seen four spectral figures in masks, lurking near the camp in a stand of willows, who rode off after he spotted them. One of them, he said, was Plummer.[14]

The problem with this tale is that it competes with another version in Langford's very own book. As in *Rashomon,* the classic Japanese film that

Nathaniel Langford, author of *Vigilante Days and Ways*. Courtesy of the Montana Historical Society.

has become a synonym for the subjective nature of memory, Plummer's actions invited differing interpretations. On the afternoon he and Hauser were preparing to leave Bannack, Langford recounts elsewhere, Plummer made an excuse to leave town—not to investigate a silver discovery, but to check on the health of Frank Parish, the rough sort who ran Rattlesnake Ranch, the livestock operation and way station on Rattlesnake Creek. According to Langford's rival account, Parish had fallen seriously ill and Plummer was worried that, if he died, his famously hefty Bannock Indian wife might round up his horses and take them off to her tribe.[15]

This alternate explanation for Plummer's departure aroused an entirely separate set of suspicions, because some of the men in Bannack believed that he was indeed going off in search of rich new silver deposits, and they feared he meant to cut them out of the action. To them, the story about Frank Parish's ranch was just an alibi intended to cover a lucrative prospecting venture. Among this latter group of skeptics was Sidney Edgerton. In addition to his appointment as the territory's chief justice, Edgerton had come to Montana hoping to make money in mining, not as an active prospector but as an investor in well-paying claims. He desperately wanted a piece of Plummer's find.

Edgerton's nephew, Wilbur Sanders, the young lawyer, had been a passenger on the same stagecoach that brought Hauser and Plummer from Virginia City to Bannack. Unlike Hauser, who said he felt uncomfortable riding with the sheriff, Sanders described the journey as entirely commonplace. Writing about the trip years afterward, Sanders insisted that he felt no uneasiness at all. To him, Plummer was simply the well-established sheriff, "in many respects the most conspicuous citizen of eastern Idaho." Sanders had been visiting Virginia City as part of a three-member delegation hoping to buoy support for the move to ask Congress to slice off the gold camps east of the Bitterroots into a new territory, and he was pleased at the positive response.[16]

Upon arriving in Bannack, Sanders declined to join the others who went into Goodrich's Hotel for a drink. Instead, he was intercepted by an acquaintance, Samuel McLean, a fellow lawyer who had come to the gold camps from Pikes Peak. It was an "open secret," McLean reported to Sanders, that silver deposits had been found, and a race was on to find and stake claims before all of the good discoveries were taken. Some of the area's best-known miners were in Bannack that Saturday afternoon with their horses saddled, frequenting the various saloons, and McLean believed they must be celebrating and planning to return to their discoveries. After leaving Goodrich's Hotel and depositing Hauser's buckskin sack into safekeeping, Plummer had joined the other riders, and McLean urged Sanders to speak to him and find out what was happening.[17]

"I went to [Plummer] and asked him where he was going," Sanders recounted. "He told me that he and his party were going that evening to the ranch of Parish, Bunton and Company on Rattlesnake Creek . . . where they would remain all night." The next day Plummer and his associates planned to ride farther east toward Blacktail Deer Creek in search of the herd of horses that required protection from theft by the Indians. "The story was a plausible one," Sanders concluded, and he said as much to McLean. Sanders had been at the ranch that morning and could see with his own eyes that Parish's condition was grave.

Though disposed to trust Plummer, Sanders pressed him with further questions, repeating McLean's assertion that a treasure hunt was afoot and asking to join it. "All right," the sheriff replied, "get your horse and come along." But Plummer continued to insist that silver mining was the last thing on his mind. If it would make Sanders feel any better, Plummer added, he would promise to reserve a claim in his name if one were found, "as certainly as if [you] were there." Satisfied at last, Sanders told Plummer he believed him and said good-bye.

Sanders retired to his office and was still there about an hour later, in midafternoon, when his uncle came to the door accompanied by McLean, Francis Thompson, and a man named Leonard Gridley, who had joined the Edgerton party as it came west. The group spoke sharply to Sanders, warning him that he had been duped by Plummer and insisting that he follow the sheriff to make certain they were not cut out of the silver claims. The composition of this group was odd, to say the least. McLean had surfaced before, as the lawyer who stepped forward to negotiate an agreement over claims between the Alder Gulch discoverers and their army of pursuers the previous summer. His experience then had been successful, and it was hardly surprising that he wanted to play a similar role again, assuming a new wave of discoveries was about to unfold. But McLean was also a prominent Democrat, a friend of the notorious lawyer H. P. A. Smith and of miner "Wash" Stapleton, other veterans of Pikes Peak who had little use for Republicans and the Union cause. How a pair of abolitionists as fierce as Edgerton and Sanders could have linked interests with McLean and his friends remains a mystery. It is worth noting that a year later, after the tumultuous events that led to the creation of Montana Territory, Sanders and McLean faced off in vigorous battle as their parties' rival nominees in the first election for territorial delegate to Congress. Perhaps it suffices to say that gold and silver fever could be intense enough to numb even the most ardent partisanship.

Thompson, whose ambivalence about Plummer continued to deepen, had at last received his missing cargo of dry goods and opened his store in Bannack. His young partner, Joseph Swift, finally returned on November 9, 1863, completing an arduous trip from Milk River, where he rescued the shipment that had been abandoned in late spring. Thompson recorded in his memoirs that it ended up costing him more to transport the goods, $4,762, than it had to buy them in the first place. As he went about setting up shop, Thompson got a helping hand from Plummer, who advised him to stack his bulkiest packages along the front wall for protection in the event of an attack. There were "likely to be rough times ahead," Plummer warned him, once again leaving Thompson to wonder if the sheriff knew more than he was saying about criminal activity in the area.[18]

Though he still boarded with Plummer at the Vails' cabin and remained fond of him, Thompson found himself drawn closer into Edgerton's circle. He considered the chief justice and his nephew to be "intimate friends," and he took their side in the unfolding atmosphere of suspicion on the afternoon of November 14, agreeing that Sanders ought to follow the sheriff and stick close to his side. Browbeaten by his uncle and friends, Sanders assented to shadow Plummer and left his office to collect his blankets and a revolver while the others went in search of a horse for him to ride.[19]

Unhappily for Sanders, the stables of Bannack were all but empty that afternoon, their stock having been exhausted by townsmen who witnessed the freshening of activity and hoped to get in on the action. The only mount available for rent was a diminutive, balky mule, barely tall enough to keep a rider's feet from dragging in the dirt. Plummer left Bannack in the late afternoon riding a fine horse, and Sanders, a well-dressed and dignified young man, set off in pursuit atop an animal not much bigger than a large dog. Many years later, a rueful Sanders vividly recalled the laughter and mockery that accompanied his slow departure from Bannack. Before he managed to reach the end of Main Street, his progress ground to a complete stop for nearly half an hour as the mule went rigid and refused to take another step. By the time Sanders finally whipped the animal to the crest of the hills outside town, dusk was falling. Eventually he gave up, dismounted, and tugged the mule along with a rope, making his trek by foot.

Sanders' destination was the Rattlesnake Ranch, where he expected to find Plummer, and the antic comedy of his journey ended abruptly when he arrived there to find no trace of the sheriff. The same cold snap and sudden snow squall that had stopped the Mormon freighters at Horse Prairie, south of Bannack, also swept down with a vengeance on the hills north of town, making Sanders' eight-mile hike from the crest of the hill to Rattlesnake Creek a tortuous passage that left him sodden, foot-weary,

Wilbur Sanders, reluctant prospector and prosecutor. Courtesy of the Montana Historical Society.

and badly chilled by the time he finally found the way station. Banging on the door, he was admitted by Erastus "Red" Yeager, the cook and one-time companion of "Doc" Howard and his gang. Sanders, unaware of Yeager's association with men now suspected of murder in Idaho, accepted the hospitality of the Rattlesnake Ranch with gratitude. Yeager put his mule into the stable for the night and led Sanders to the blazing fire in the way station's main room. A doctor, who had been fetched to attend the ailing Parish, was asleep—passed out, in Sanders' judgment—on a straw mattress in front of the fire, as was the ranch's other part-owner, Bill Bunton. Parish was sleeping fitfully in a room in the back, in poor condition but still alive. Yeager invited Sanders to share his straw pallet by the fire, and Sanders gratefully assented. He asked Yeager where Plummer was, and Yeager answered that he had no idea. The sheriff had not come to Rattlesnake Ranch that night. Unsettled by the news, but too tired to pursue the matter, Sanders fell asleep.

Adding further confusion to the jumble of events, another person was out after dark that night, and he too had quite a story to tell. Henry Tilden, the young family friend who had accompanied the Edgertons from Ohio to the gold camps, was sent to fetch a missing cow thought to be at a pasturage south of town. Unable to find the animal, Tilden was riding his horse back toward Bannack around dusk when he encountered three mounted men wearing masks who stopped him, held him at gunpoint, frisked him, and then let him go with a curse after discovering that he had no money. Frightened out of his wits, Tilden spurred his horse into a full gallop and began racing toward town, only to crash blindly into a mining ditch, where he fell from his saddle and was knocked unconscious. Regaining his faculties a moment later, Tilden resumed his ride, dazed and bruised, calling for help at the top of his lungs. He went directly to Sanders' cabin, where Hattie Sanders listened to his breathless story and then took him to see Edgerton. Much to their surprise, he said he had recognized one of the men who accosted him as Henry Plummer.

Tilden's guardians did not believe him, at least not at first. He was only fifteen or sixteen years old, new to the West, and perhaps susceptible to an overactive imagination. How could he possibly have identified the sheriff, wearing a mask in the dark in the midst of a violent snowstorm? Tilden's answer, that he recognized Plummer's revolver, was unconvincing. Hundreds of men wore revolvers, and the weapons were so similar as to be indistinguishable under such conditions. Tilden added that he had seen the flash of a red lining inside Plummer's overcoat, a detail that seemed a bit more convincing. Still, Edgerton had strong doubts about his young charge's version of things and told him to keep the matter to himself for the time being.[20]

The events of the night were not quite finished. At Rattlesnake Ranch, around midnight, Sanders was awakened by the sound of a man shouting to be heard over the wind and pounding on the door. Yeager arose from the mattress they were sharing and admitted Jack Gallagher into the room.

Since serving as one of Plummer's original deputies and involving himself in the trial of the men who gunned down D. H. Dillingham, Gallagher had kept a low profile. He no longer served as a deputy but remained close to Plummer and was part of his circle of friends. Gallagher was described by those who knew him—when he was sober—as a handsome, well-spoken man. "He was tall and striking looking," according to Molly Sheehan, the bright eleven-year-old who rode in the same wagon train with him from Denver to Bannack. "He spoke in a pleasant, quiet voice, and praised me for reading so well." The young girl liked to recite passages from the Bible and *Uncle Tom's Cabin,* and Gallagher enjoyed listening. When he drank, on the other hand, Gallagher could be a holy terror, and his role in guiding the crowd to acquit Dillingham's killers had left him with a bad reputation among many of the settlers. As he entered the Rattlesnake Ranch on the night in question, he was loud and unhappy, complaining that he had been riding for hours looking for Plummer without success, exhausting himself and his horse.[21]

Yeager showed Gallagher into the ranch's main room, dark now except for the glow of the fire, and invited him to put down his blankets and sleep. But Gallagher began agitating for food and drink and refused to take no for an answer. It was late, Yeager answered, and the household was in some disarray because of Parish's illness. No meal had been prepared. Gallagher replied that he was famished and would have to eat something, even if it were just some bread. And he wanted whiskey. Afraid to argue further, Yeager went to fetch a bottle of whiskey and a pan of cold boiled beef, which Gallagher wolfed down. He told Yeager he had worn out his horse and wanted to trade for a fresh mount from the ranch's stable.

The commotion aroused the other sleepers, including Bunton. Taking an interest in the talk of a horse trade, Bunton suggested that Gallagher might want to buy one of the fresh horses in the stable that belonged to A. J. Oliver's stagecoach company. In exchange for his old horse and $60 in cash, Bunton said, he would be willing to make the trade. That he would be dealing away a horse that did not belong to him apparently did not upset Bunton's scruples, and he and Gallagher closed the bargain. It was at this point that Sanders piped up from the mattress on the floor, asking Gallagher if knew where Plummer was.

According to Sanders, his question triggered a violent response. Gallagher pulled his pistol, aimed it at Sanders' head, cursed him, and threatened to shoot him. Giving his account of the exchange many years after the fact,

Sanders offered no ready explanation for the fury he unleashed by asking a man he barely knew about the sheriff's whereabouts. The implication was that Gallagher had some guilty knowledge of Plummer's activities and meant to silence anyone who expressed curiosity. In his version of the encounter, Sanders said he leapt to his feet, dashed to the nearby bar, and seized the shotgun he had seen Yeager place underneath the counter. He pointed the gun at Gallagher, who dropped his pistol, tore open the buttons of his overcoat, and dramatically invited Sanders to shoot. Yeager and Bunton quickly intervened, according to Sanders, and the men calmed down. Bunton told Gallagher he was out of line, and eventually a chastened Gallagher apologized to Sanders and insisted on buying him a drink. Ordinarily a teetotaler, Sanders said he thought it prudent to accept the offer. "Gallagher was profuse in apologies," Sanders wrote, "and as soon as I could withdraw from the conversation, I returned to the fireplace."

Gallagher rode off into the night on his newly acquired horse, but returned after a couple of hours complaining that the snow squall was blinding and travel impossible. He fell asleep by the fire and the household finally enjoyed a few hours of calm until daylight. At that point two of Sanders' friends came looking for him, concerned about his safety after hearing of young Tilden's experience the previous evening. Sanders left Rattlesnake Ranch and returned to Bannack without incident, bringing a quiet end to a chaotic night.

Reconciling these various accounts is no easy matter. Certainly there was no reason for Plummer to have held up a lone rider just outside Bannack if his real target was the rich purse being carried by Hauser and Langford on the trail to Salt Lake City a good deal farther south. Why risk being seen on the wrong side of town? Why jeopardize a lucrative hold-up with a clumsy dress rehearsal? One may speculate that some group of armed men encountered Tilden on the trail in the midst of the squall and decided to stop and frisk him, an action that may or may not have been intended as a robbery. Since they took nothing from him, Tilden might have been subjected to what amounted to an identity check at a roadblock, and he might have overreacted. His recognition of Plummer was vague at best, as reflected by the fact that his family thought at first that he must be confused and mistaken.

Similarly, Langford's account of seeing Plummer at Horse Prairie must be met with skepticism. He made no report of the incident at the time, and no one in Bannack knew of it until he returned the following spring.

In his own detailed version of the encounter, published many years later in his memoirs, *Vigilante Days and Ways,* Langford wrote in strangely guarded language that he and Hauser "afterwards ascertained" that the four men in the willows were Plummer, Buck Stinson, Ned Ray, and George Ives. Langford carefully avoided any claim to have made an eyewitness identification, and one wonders how he could have recognized any masked men, given the storm, the darkness, the distances involved, and the various visual obstructions.[22]

Sanders' confrontation with Gallagher, meanwhile, raises some very puzzling questions. While Sanders would prove himself to be a man of considerable gumption in the coming weeks, one nevertheless must ask if he really dashed across a room to grab a shotgun while Gallagher held him at the point of a pistol. It seems more likely that Gallagher, a bully, spoke rudely to him and perhaps cursed and threatened him upon being asked about Plummer. And it may be that Gallagher touched his sidearm or even took it out and waved it about, but he does not seem to have been aiming it directly at Sanders with lethal intent, or else the story might well have ended abruptly with Sanders' death. The degree of actual menace posed by Gallagher, that is, remains debatable. More important, Gallagher's presence at Rattlesnake Ranch undermines the notion that Plummer was riding at the head of some posse of armed robbers tracking Hauser and Langford on the road to Salt Lake City south of town. Gallagher was looking for Plummer—and making quite a dramatic show of his search—to the *north* of Bannack, in the vicinity of the ranch where Plummer had said he was going. Granted, Gallagher might not have known what Plummer was doing that night, but then why would he have reacted so violently to Sander's question? And if he was meant to be a decoy, why did he act so abusively toward the subject of the deception?

Whatever the case, Plummer returned to Bannack the next day, acting perfectly normal. He had ridden beyond Rattlesnake Ranch in the storm, he said, and stayed out in the wild all night. His goal of finding and protecting the ranch's herd had been relieved when Parish survived the night and seemed to be recovering slightly. No new silver claims were filed by Plummer, or anyone else, in the aftermath of their supposed discovery. Hearing of Tilden's misadventure, meanwhile, Plummer went to the express office where the young man worked and asked with evident concern about the incident. Could Tilden identify his assailants? No, Tilden replied guardedly, he could not. The sheriff went about his business.

Still, when all was said and done, the events of the night of November 14, 1863, raised suspicion of Plummer to fresh heights. He had not been where he said he would be when Sanders came looking for him. In private, Tilden continued to insist that he had recognized the sheriff, and his family could not shake his certainty. The reason he told the sheriff he could not identify his assailants was because he feared the consequences of accusing Plummer to his face, not because he had any doubts. After their conversation, according to Edgerton's daughter, Mattie, young Tilden was more frightened of Plummer than ever, and "every night after closing hours he ran the whole distance to his boarding house."[23]

On a Sunday afternoon shortly after the eventful night, Edgerton paid a call on Francis Thompson at his store. As the two men talked of recent events, Thompson went to the front door and carefully locked it. "Judge," he asked, "who is doing all this business?"

Edgerton paused for a moment, looked around the room, and said, "I think I know . . ."

Before he could say anything further, Thompson blurted out, "*Henry Plummer!*" One of the sheriff's closest friends now believed him to be guilty.[24]

CHAPTER NINE

The Southmayd Robbery

If Henry Plummer realized that he was now regarded with alarm and suspicion by many of the leading men of Bannack and Alder Gulch, he gave no sign of it. About a week after the strange events of November 14, 1863, the sheriff and his sister-in-law, Martha Jane Vail, called on the Edgertons and invited the chief justice and his family to come to their cabin for Thanksgiving dinner. Edgerton's teenage daughter, Mattie, recalled staring at Plummer with rapt fascination as he came into her house, sat down, took off his hat, and laid it on his knee. "It was unusual at that time for the average miner to take off his hat as a concession to good manners when entering a house," she wrote later. Plummer seemed a bit ill at ease, she added, possibly because of her open scrutiny of him. He tilted his chair back against the wall and let Mrs. Vail do most of the talking.[1]

The Edgertons accepted the invitation, according to Mattie's recollection, because they had a high opinion of Mrs. Vail and did not wish to offend her by refusing. It may be, too, that their distrust of Plummer had not yet matured into a firm belief that he was involved in criminal activities. In any case, Mary and Sidney Edgerton donned their best clothes for the affair—the judge wore a white shirt for the first time since coming west—and went to the Vails' home determined to enjoy themselves. Their niece, Lucia Darling, accompanied them, along with Hattie and Wilbur Sanders. Writing to her sister a few days later, Mary Edgerton marveled at the meal. "We had an excellent supper," she reported, "equal to any that we ever had in Ohio. I tasted butter for the first time since we came here and it was a treat I can tell you," a luxury the Edgertons themselves could not afford. Hattie Sanders remembered dinner as "delicately cooked and with all the style that would characterize a banquet at 'Sherry's.'" Plummer had arranged to ship the turkey all the way from Salt Lake City, she said, at a cost of $40.[2]

To the Edgerton women, at least, Plummer did not appear to present much of a menace. Hattie Sanders described him lyrically in her memoirs as "slender, graceful, and mild of speech. He had pleasing manners and fine address, a fair complexion, sandy hair, and blue eyes—the last person one would select as a daring highwayman and murderer." In a letter home shortly after the dinner, Mary Edgerton called him "a very feminine-looking man." Wilbur Sanders was effusive in his praise of Plummer's conduct, remarking that the sheriff had been "the soul of hospitality" at the dinner, full of good conversation and easy humor. If any of them feared Plummer, or wondered how he could afford to pay for such a sumptuous meal, they did not mention it at the time.[3]

Nor was there any ready explanation for the obvious thaw in relations between Plummer and his sister-in-law. The previous spring, Martha Jane Vail had been adamant in opposing her sister Electa's marriage to Plummer, to the point of boycotting the small ceremony and leaving Francis Thompson to serve as bridesmaid. Now, it appeared, the two were warm friends, with Plummer living under the Vails' roof as a welcome member of the family. Whatever his wife's reason for leaving, it apparently had not infected Plummer's standing with the Vail family. Some historians have gone so far as to speculate that Plummer and his sister-in-law had a budding romance of some sort going on, an idea that seems far-fetched given her sharp devotion to the code of morality taught by the church. More likely, Plummer's proven ability to charm and beguile people had worked on her as it did on so many others who came within his reach.[4]

In some quarters of the community, Plummer's reputation seemed not to have been damaged at all. He continued to exercise his authority as sheriff from a desk in the front corner of George Chrisman's store on Main Street, and by all accounts he enjoyed Chrisman's complete trust. Chrisman, in turn, was one of Bannack's most respected men, chosen as a county commissioner in the territorial elections at the end of October 1863.

How far Plummer's jurisdiction extended beyond Bannack is difficult to gauge. Several of the mining districts in Alder Gulch had chosen sheriffs of their own, but their degree of independence and influence was an open question, and only a few had won election as Plummer did. After the gold camps east of the Bitterroots were organized into a single county as part of Idaho Territory, Plummer may have considered himself sheriff of the whole region, and his travels from Bannack to Alder Gulch appear to have been meant to establish his position there. His deputies continued to roam throughout the gold camps, their actions "acquiesced in rather than approved," in Francis Thompson's phrase.[5]

Around the time of Plummer's Thanksgiving party, a miner named Leroy Southmayd arranged passage from Virginia City through Bannack to Salt Lake City. As he and two other passengers stood in the street beside the A. J. Oliver & Company stagecoach, preparing to board, they drew the interest of a weathered old prospector named "Tex" Crowell, who seemed to be sizing them up. As always, a traveler carrying gold dust had to be cautious, and Southmayd and his companions remarked to each other on their discomfort at being observed so closely. At their first stop, Laurin's ranch, on the Stinking Water River, the passengers were further disquieted to encounter George Ives, the handsome rancher with the reputation for drunken bullying.[6]

As Wilbur Sanders noted in his memoirs, Ives could be utterly charming. His encounter with the Edgerton party near Monida Pass two months earlier had been perfectly pleasant, and they took him to be a gentleman. It was Sanders, an otherwise level-headed lawyer, who described Ives as sitting astride his horse "like a swan on a billowy lake." But other Montana pioneers told convincing stories of brushes with Ives that left them badly frightened. Colonel C. A. Broadwater, a wealthy cattleman and later a territorial governor, swore that he once escaped robbery at Ives's hands by outriding him on a fast horse. Bill Sweeney, one of the original discoverers of Alder Gulch, claimed that Ives bragged to him about taking $500 in gold dust from a traveler at gunpoint. No fewer than six memoirs written or dictated by early Montanans describe violent exchanges with Ives. At the time of Southmayd's journey, many settlers believed that Ives was cruising the trails between Bannack and Alder Gulch, staking out the way stations and measuring up the parties he encountered with robbery in mind.[7]

Southmayd and the other passengers left Laurin's without engaging in much conversation with Ives, but they did hear him say that he was riding ahead to Cold Spring ranch, another stop on the trail to Bannack, because

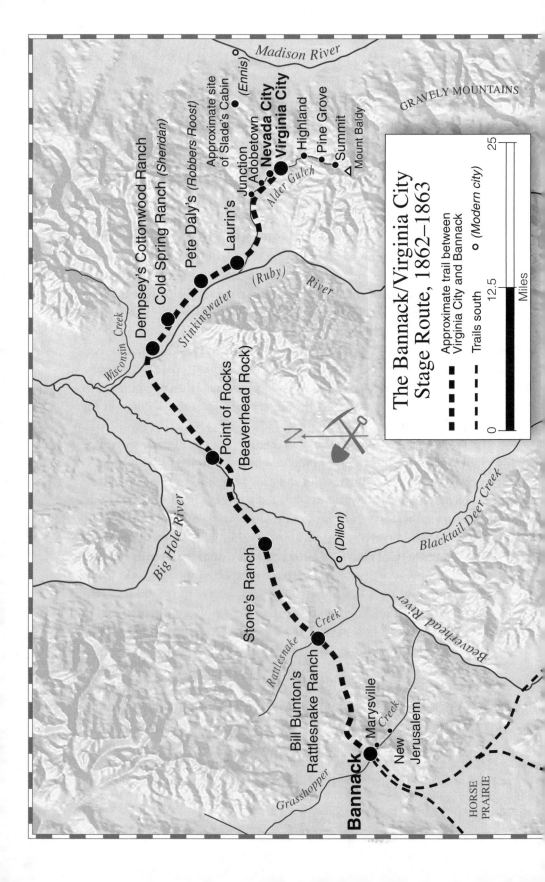

The Bannack/Virginia City Stage Route, 1862–1863

he expected to meet Tex Crowell there. The notion that Crowell, the man who had checked them out in Virginia City, was on the trail and in contact with Ives left them very uneasy. They made it safely to Beaverhead Rock, the landmark associated with Sacagawea, and spent a nervous night at a way station there.

Around eleven o'clock the next morning, Southmayd's party was on the road to Bannack when three masked men burst from concealment and halted the stage at gunpoint. Recounting the episode later, Southmayd described the three assailants as dressed identically in blue-green blankets that covered them from head to toe, and wearing masks of various fabrics with slits cut for their eyes and mouths. Their horses were draped in blankets as well. Despite the disguises, Southmayd said, he recognized all three of the gunmen: Ives, "Whiskey Bill" Graves, and Bob Zachary.

Unlike so many other reports of highway robbery that were clouded by vague details or second-hand telling or the passage of time, Southmayd's was given immediately and with vivid particulars. Ives had aimed a shotgun directly at him, he said, and he could look straight down the barrel and imagine the hot buckshot erupting and tearing into his flesh. As the man in charge, Ives had directed Zachary to dismount and disarm the passengers, and Southmayd said he could feel Zachary trembling with anxiety as he took his pistol. Moving from one passenger to the next, Zachary took $400 in gold dust from Southmayd, smaller amounts from the other two passengers, and several small pouches that the driver, Tom Caldwell, was carrying for friends and customers of the stage company. Next, the robbers rifled through the mail, looking for letters and packages containing gold dust. At length, Ives dismissed the victims, telling them curtly, "Get up and skedaddle."

According to Southmayd, he took a risk and looked directly at the three gunmen as he and the others climbed back on the stage. Ives noticed him and warned, "Drive on. If you don't turn around, and mind your own business, I'll shoot the top of your head off." With those words hanging in the air, the driver set the stage moving and the victims rode on to Bannack.

At the express office on Main Street, the passengers were greeted by Plummer, who noticed their obvious distress and asked if the stage had been robbed. Recognizing the sheriff, Southmayd jumped down from the coach and began to describe the details of the crime. Before he could say very much, he was interrupted by Gaylord Bissell, the Yale-educated doctor who presided over the miners' court in Virginia City. Bissell, who

Gaylord G. Bissell, who warned against trusting Plummer. Courtesy of the Montana Historical Society.

was visiting in Bannack, belonged to the ranks of those who distrusted Plummer. He took Southmayd by the arm and pulled him a short distance away. You must be very careful what you tell the sheriff, Bissell warned, since he might well be in league with the assailants. The safest course, he added, would be to profess ignorance of the men's identities.

Declining to heed the judge's counsel, Southmayd returned to Plummer's side and resumed his narrative.

"I think I can tell you who it was that robbed you," Plummer volunteered.

"Who?" Southmayd responded, intrigued that the sheriff seemed so knowledgeable about the affair.

"George Ives was one of them," Plummer said.

"I know," Southmayd said. "And the others were Whiskey Bill and Bob Zachary, and I'll live to see them hanged . . ."

Plummer soon excused himself, and Judge Bissell admonished Southmayd for revealing too much. The sheriff had been testing him, Bissell said, and his willingness to accuse Ives and the others by name had placed him in jeopardy. "Leroy," Bissell added ominously, "your life is not worth a cent."

As it happened, Southmayd spent the next three days in Bannack unharmed in any way. He did not see Plummer again. What the sheriff did in response to his accusations, if anything, is not recorded in any account of the period. But when Southmayd made preparations to go back to Virginia City, he was alarmed to find that two of Plummer's deputies, Buck Stinson and Ned Ray, intended to make the trip on the stagecoach with him. He did not trust either man, and especially not Stinson, who had escaped justice in the killing of D. H. Dillingham. Determined to travel in spite of the evident risk, Southmayd borrowed a double-barrel shotgun from the express agent and arranged for Tom Caldwell, his fellow victim on the trip to Bannack, to serve as driver on the return leg as well. Caldwell also borrowed a shotgun, and he and Southmayd agreed to defend themselves aggressively if the deputies made any provocative moves. A final passenger, a teenage boy, completed the uneasy party that departed from Bannack.

The stage passed without incident over most of the trail back to Alder Gulch, until it arrived at Cold Spring ranch on the Stinking Water River. There, on the patch of packed dirt in front of the way station, stood two of the suspected robbers, Graves and Zachary, along with a third man,

Aleck Carter. As Southmayd and Caldwell tensed, they were surprised to hear Stinson call out rudely to the men on the ground, saying, "Ho! You damned road agents!" Southmayd had no idea if the deputy was taunting the men, accusing them, or warning them. When the deputies made no move to arrest the men, he grew deeply frightened. "Tom," he whispered to Caldwell, "we're done for." The driver sighed in assent.

To Southmayd's surprise and relief, the three armed men did not attempt to confront them. Two of them, Graves and Zachary, put down their guns and went inside the ranch house. Carter, an occasional associate of Ives's, slung his shotgun around on his back and entered the frame building as well. Joining them inside for the evening meal, the passengers from the stage observed that Zachary was either drunk or doing a good job of pretending to be. He had a bottle of whiskey and insisted that the others drink with him. As soon as fresh horses were rounded up, the passengers hastened back to the stage and Caldwell drove them away. But before they were out of sight of the way station, Graves, Zachary, and Carter rode up alongside and one of them yelled, "Halt!" Believing that robbery or perhaps even murder was at hand, Southmayd brought his shotgun up from his lap and took direct aim at Carter. Caldwell had his gun cocked and ready as well, and leveled it at Graves. For one long moment, it seemed a shootout would ensue.

Then Carter threw up his hands. "We only want you to take a drink," he protested. "But you can shoot and be damned if you want to." As Southmayd and Caldwell held the men at gunpoint, Carter offered them a bottle of whiskey. They merely touched it to their lips, thinking it might be poisoned. An instant later, the three suspected highwaymen spurred their horses into a gallop and sped away on the trail, shouting farewell.

Unnerved by these events, and uncertain what role Stinson and Ray might be playing in them, Southmayd and Caldwell gave serious thought to abandoning the stage and making their way forward on foot through the brush, away from the trail to Alder Gulch that seemed to hold such menace. Eventually, Caldwell convinced Southmayd that they could hold their own against Stinson and Ray if the necessity arose. Caldwell asked Stinson to ride with him up on the "box," and Stinson reluctantly agreed. Southmayd rode in the carriage, keeping an eye on Ray. Seeing that they were being treated as suspects, Stinson and Ray objected and swore that they had no evil intent. "Gentlemen," Stinson said with formality, "I pledge you my word, my honor, my life, that you will not be attacked between this [place] and Virginia City."

With that, Southmayd related, Stinson began singing at the top of his lungs and continued to do so until Ray relieved him, and the two kept up their chorus all the way to Virginia City. It was their signal to the robbers, Southmayd was convinced, to stay away from the stage.[8]

With the arrival of Leroy Southmayd and his party back in Virginia City, word of the odd behavior of Sheriff Plummer's deputies soon circulated. It seemed plain that Stinson and Ray were in league with a pack of highway robbers, quite possibly with Plummer's consent and connivance. And even if Plummer was innocent of direct involvement in the robbery of the stagecoach, why had he failed to pursue the accused? Why was no one arrested? Why was Plummer not enforcing the law? A further layer of trust was stripped away.

In the first week of December 1863, another stagecoach robbery took place and another piece of incriminating evidence fell into place. A freighter named Milton S. Moody loaded three wagons for the trip south to Salt Lake City and signed on seven passengers, among them John Bozeman, the famous trailblazer, and a wealthy miner named Melanchthon "Lank" Forbes. The party represented the richest prize yet, having some $80,000 in gold dust hidden in canteens tucked away amid their luggage and other freight. One morning on the trail to Red Rock, the passengers were finishing breakfast beside a bend in the road when they overheard men's voices. Alerted to nearby company, the members of the party drew and cocked their guns and had the advantage when two riders came forward and proffered greetings, introducing themselves as Steve Marshland and "Dutch John" Wagner. (A native of Germany, Wagner drew his nickname from his word for home, *Deutschland,* and not from any connection with the Netherlands.) The two explained that they were in search of missing horses, an account some in the Moody party doubted, believing the pair had been planning to ambush them. In any case, Marshland and Wagner were permitted to ride away after the brief exchange.

Two days later, in Red Rock Canyon, two masked gunmen swept down on the wagon train and forced it to halt. One of the riders held a shotgun on the driver of the lead wagon while the second began a search of the passengers and their belongings. The second man started slitting open the luggage with a knife and soon found $1,500 in Treasury notes bundled in a carpetbag. But he did not think to examine the contents of the canteens and missed the greater treasure in gold dust. When he came to the last wagon, he stepped up on its bench and pulled open its curtain. Lank Forbes was hiding inside and fired his pistol into the robber's side, severely wounding him. Cursing in pain, the startled robber fell to the ground, struggled to get up, and stumbled into the woods. The noise of the gunshot made the first robber's horse rear, causing him to miss as he fired both barrels of his shotgun in the direction of the wagon drivers. In the confusion, Moody reached down into his boot, grabbed a pistol he had concealed there, and shot at the first robber, hitting him in the shoulder and sending him racing away at a gallop.

The two robbers managed to keep their masks on during the melee and escaped without anyone making an eyewitness identification. But the members of the Moody party were pretty sure their assailants were Marshland and Wagner, and they would know for certain if they ever crossed paths again, because both men were now marked by their wounds. Gaining his composure afterward, Moody reflected that he and the other passengers might have had a chance to capture the robber who ran away on foot if any one of them had jumped on his abandoned horse and chased him down. In the frenzy of the moment, no one had thought to do so. But it would be hard for a man with a chest wound to get away on foot in the winter, and Moody believed they would meet again.[9]

The accelerating pace and violence of these robberies provoked an understandable surge of fear among the settlers in the gold camps. Jittery about travel in the best of times, the miners and merchants now had to contend with gangs who seemed all too willing to kill their victims. If there once had been a sort of tacit understanding that highwaymen would spare lives in exchange for the swift surrender of gold dust, that day was now gone.

As if to punctuate the point, a newcomer to the gold camps named Anton Holter survived a harrowing encounter on December 8, 1863, on the outskirts of Alder Gulch. Holter was a cigar-smoking Norwegian of imposing aspect—he later became a leading businessman and bank director in Helena—who spoke English with an accent that bordered on parody. Whenever he saw a good business opportunity, a friend once said, Holter could be trusted to "yump" on it in a hurry. But as he approached the gold camps for the first time, he had yet to make his success, and the two men who accosted him at gunpoint near the Stinking Water River were unhappy when he produced only $10 in greenbacks. They cursed him and warned him not to travel again with such a puny purse. They motioned angrily for Holter to ride away, and as he started to remount his horse he happened to glance up. He saw one of the men leveling a pistol at his head. Holter ducked instinctively and flinched as a bullet tore through his hat and creased his scalp. The man took closer aim and pulled the trigger again. This time the gun misfired, and Holter managed to escape by running away on foot. He later identified the man who tried to kill him as George Ives.[10]

The terror aroused by this spiraling criminal activity was accompanied by another strong emotion—anger. In their diaries and letters home, it was rare for the men who settled the gold camps to disclose much about their emotional states. In modern parlance, they did not tend to share their feelings. Granville Stuart, the pioneer miner turned shopkeeper, made a terse entry in his diary on November 30, 1863: "There is certainly an organized band of highwaymen around here and something will have to be done soon to protect life and property." James Fergus, the Scot who wanted his wife to join him, tried to send her treasury notes and gold dust on at least two occasions, only to have his envelopes arrive empty. He wrote his former congressman in Minnesota urging the federal government to "ferret out the mail robbers" on the route to Salt Lake City.[11]

What these expressions and others failed to convey was the utter fury that so many men felt toward the robbers. Beyond the obvious frustration of losing a season's hard-earned fortune at gunpoint, the men hated the very idea of being intimidated and physically threatened. Not just in robberies, but in violent encounters with rough sorts in saloons and way stations and elsewhere, men often found themselves embroiled in ugly clashes that involved menace by firearms or fists or plain bullying. Conrad Kohrs, who went on to become Montana's leading cattle baron, described an incident that exemplified the problem. A sturdy young man who had left his native Holstein, Germany, at fifteen to go to sea, Kohrs became a butcher's apprentice and arrived at Bannack in 1862. He was one of the settlers who advocated the capture and punishment of Charley Reeves and Charley Moore for the drunken spree in which they shot up the Bannock Indian village and killed four people. After returning from their banishment and recovering their health, Kohrs discovered, the two men carried a grudge against him.

As Kohrs related the story in his memoirs, he stopped in a saloon in the Deer Lodge valley during a cattle-buying trip in the spring of 1863, where he chanced to run into Charley Moore and some of his friends. "Moore . . . stepped up to me, called me all the vile names he could think of, spit in my face, and half a dozen of the highwaymen stood around pointing their pistols at me," Kohrs recounted matter-of-factly. "I was obliged to stand all this abuse for at the first sign of resistance I would have been shot."[12]

Kohrs revealed nothing more of his response, but it is easy enough to imagine the impotent rage that anyone, especially a strapping, headstrong young man, would feel at such provocation. Thomas Dimsdale, the English schoolteacher turned newspaperman, wrote that Plummer once challenged a man to step outside a saloon and fight, and the man responded, "I'm a coward and no fighting man, and I will not go out of doors with anybody." The depths of these mortifications are perhaps best left to novelists and filmmakers to explore—one thinks of *Straw Dogs,* as well as countless Westerns—but are no less real for lack of discussion and self-examination by the victims. The miners' courts of Bannack and Alder Gulch served fairly effectively in mediating disputes involving claims and contracts, but were ill equipped to deal with crime, civic order, and public safety in general. The idea of law enforcement awaited the arrival of legally constituted government (and adequate taxation to support a police force, court system, and prisons). In the meantime, many decent men concluded that they would have to take direct responsibility for defending themselves.[13]

In the last weeks of autumn, 1863, settlers in Bannack and Alder Gulch began talking guardedly among friends they believed they could trust about forming a vigilante force. The specifics of these conversations were not recorded, for obvious reasons, but it is certain they took place. Quite a few of the settlers had been in California during the previous decade and had witnessed or participated in the vigilance movements of 1851 and 1856. The swift, sweeping success of those private armies in imposing public order made them a very appealing model and tended to overwhelm any qualms the men might have felt about operating extralegally and violently.

Wilbur Sanders, acting as a representative of his uncle, the territory's unsworn and oddly passive chief justice, made several trips from Bannack to Alder Gulch in the final weeks of 1863, rallying support for the pend-

Conrad Kohrs. Courtesy of the Montana Historical Society.

ing effort to create a new territory east of the Bitterroots. As he consulted with the leading men of the gold camps, Sanders disclosed later, several of them broached the subject of the escalating wave of stagecoach robberies and the dangerous question of organizing some form of resistance. "With increasing certainty," Sanders wrote, these leaders confided in him their suspicions about the names of the guilty parties, "and strangers in the country who had gained each other's confidence began to consult as to the protection of their enterprises and themselves." The first stirrings of a vigilance movement had begun, with Sanders as a party to the discussions.[14]

Justice Edgerton, meanwhile, was making plans to go to Washington to press Congress and President Lincoln in person for the creation of the new territory. It is difficult to assess Edgerton's motives across the divide of a century and a half, but he seems to have had his own interests in mind as well as the public's. He hoped to be appointed governor of the new territory, an outcome he could best pursue face to face with the president. Perhaps, had he asserted his authority as judge at once upon arriving in Bannack, Edgerton might have built up enough of a court system to cope with the crime wave that gripped the gold camps as the onset of winter approached. Another pointed question is whether Edgerton could have, or should have, taken steps to discourage the sort of talk his nephew was hearing about vigilantism. Because he meant to get to Washington, Edgerton may have found himself drawn to the idea of an extralegal presence that would protect the trails and help smooth his passage. In any case, it was plain enough by mid-December 1863 that no one felt safe in the countryside, and Edgerton was forced to postpone his travels.

In this climate of fear and mistrust, the mutilated body of young Nicholas Tiebolt was discovered. The posse led by "Old Man" Clark and James Williams arrested George Ives for the crime and brought him into Nevada City, bound snugly hand and foot to his saddle after his attempt at escape, shortly after dark on the night of Friday, December 18, 1863. As word spread of his capture, several dozen men gathered in the mining camp's main street, talking excitedly about what to do next. The arresting officers favored conducting a trial and gained a consensus in their favor, even though some voices warned of the flawed outcome of previous people's courts and urged immediate hanging. A spirited debate ensued over the trial's venue. Remarkably, Ives was allowed to speak in his own behalf and asked to be tried in Virginia City, the next mining camp up the gulch, where he kept an office and had friends. In wary resistance to his wishes, the members of the posse voted to hold the trial in Nevada City, where they felt more secure. Unable to reach quick agreement on the form of the tribunal, the exhausted riders appointed guards to keep watch over Ives and the two material witnesses, "Long John" Franck and George

Hilderman, and retired for the night. They would figure out the details in the morning.

During the night, a lone rider set out from Nevada City on a fast horse, bound for Bannack. George Lane, known by the cruel nickname "Clubfoot George" for a deformity of his right foot, worked as a cobbler at the store in Virginia City operated by Walter B. Dance and the Stuart brothers. A friend of Plummer's, he was hurrying to tell the sheriff of Ives's arrest and warn him of the coming swirl of events that threatened to pull everyone into its undertow.[15]

CHAPTER TEN

The Ives Trial

On the morning of Saturday, December 19, 1863, a pale sun worked to thaw the last of a thin snow cover on the main street of Nevada City, the gold camp on Alder Creek. By noon, the frozen crust atop the primitive thoroughfare had melted into "gumbo," the leaden, sticky mix of mud and clay that placed the soil of southwest Montana in a class of its own, nearer concrete than ordinary dirt. During a winter warm spell, the streets of Alder Gulch turned into pools of glue, caking the boots of men and the hooves of beasts and slowing traffic to a crawl. Drawn by the news that George Ives was to be put on trial, hundreds of men gathered in Nevada City that morning, not so much milling around as stepping carefully and trying to find a dry place to stand.[1]

The night before, Wilbur Sanders had watched with interest as the posse brought Ives into town. After completing the latest in his round of meetings meant to build support for the creation of a new territory, Sanders planned to return to his home in Bannack, where he looked forward to spending his first Christmas in the Rocky Mountains with his wife, Hattie, and their two young sons. As he listened to the debate about what to do with Ives, Sanders was struck by the posse's instinct to act on a democratic basis, with a vote to be taken on when, where, and how to conduct the trial. Letting the accused killers have a say in the matter seemed dangerously open-minded to Sanders, and in fact the idea was soon abandoned. John and Mortimer Lott, the brothers whose store served as headquarters when the posse was organized, argued successfully that the trial should be held in Nevada City, the venue nearest the spot where young Tiebolt's body was discovered.[2]

After Ives and the two other prisoners were shackled and placed under guard for the night, Sanders began to walk the short distance up the road to Virginia City, the largest of the Alder Gulch gold camps, where he would spend the night with a friend before catching the stagecoach in the morning. As he neared his destination, Sanders encountered a succession of lawyers hurrying to Nevada City to represent the accused men. One of them, James M. Thurmond, invited Sanders to come along, telling him "there was an opportunity for me to make a good fee, as [the defendants] had plenty of money." It seemed the pending trial would be a bonanza for Alder Gulch's small coterie of lawyers, and Sanders was disturbed to see that Ives appeared to have the market cornered. John D. Ritchie, a tenacious advocate in spite of his long battle with tuberculosis, was on his way to Nevada City, along with H. P. A. Smith, the flamboyant litigator whose oratory had helped acquit one of D. H. Dillingham's killers.[3]

As he went to buy his ticket for the stage the next morning, Sanders was intercepted by a friend who told him the Lott brothers urgently wanted to see him in Nevada City. Sanders replied that he would be passing through Nevada City in just a few hours, since it lay along the stage's route to Bannack. That would be too late, his friend said. Sanders was needed in Nevada City immediately. Agreeing to leave at once, Sanders borrowed a horse and covered the two miles to the nearby settlement in a matter of minutes. He went into the Lott brothers' store and found them in an agitated state. Ives was hiring all the lawyers in Alder Gulch, they said, and there was no one left to act as prosecutor. They implored Sanders to take the job.[4]

Acting as the people's attorney in a murder trial was not a role that appealed very much to Sanders. His uncle, Sidney Edgerton, had declined to take up his duties as Idaho Territory's chief justice, excusing himself on the ground that he had not been administered the oath of office. It would have been easy for Sanders to follow suit and avoid the pitfalls of attempting to administer justice in a place that had no formal criminal code, no legally constituted system of law enforcement, no bailiffs or other courtroom personnel, nor any of the other rudiments of the judicial system in place back home in "the States." The lone aspect of the coming tribunal that would seem familiar was the prospect of matching wits with opposing

Mortimer Lott in 1862. Courtesy of the Montana Historical Society.

counsel, a bank of clever and determined lawyers. And the stakes could hardly be higher. One misstep and Ives might well be acquitted, free to get even with Sanders in ways the imagination hesitated to explore.

At age twenty-nine, Sanders had practiced law for several years, but almost exclusively in civil matters. Born in New York state, he was the son of Sidney Edgerton's older sister, Freedom, whose name suggested the extent of the family's commitment to the American Revolution. Sanders attended public schools in New York and then moved to Akron, Ohio, to live with his uncle and study law. He was admitted to the bar in 1856. Two years later, he married Harriett Peck Fenn, known as "Hattie," and they had two sons, James and Willie. With the outbreak of the Civil War, Sanders enlisted in the Union Army and served under James A. Garfield, the future president, a fellow Free-Soil Republican who organized the

Forty-second Ohio Volunteer Infantry. There are conflicting accounts of the reason Sanders withdrew from military service in 1863—his family claimed that his health was failing, while a friend said he quit in protest of enforcing the Fugitive Slave Act—but it seems most likely that his uncle simply recruited him to join the family on its journey west.[5]

Years later, Sanders could recall the songs he sang with his cousin, Mattie Edgerton, along the trail to Montana: "There's a Light in the Window for Thee, Brother," and "The Soldiers Are Gathering from Near and from Far." He had a booming voice, one that occasionally embarrassed his family in church and apparently was better suited to the open prairie. At the Snake River ferry, Sanders had been outraged at the exorbitant charge for crossing and was nearly swept away trying to ford the river before he changed his mind and agreed to pay. He had a strong jaw line that seemed to emphasize his stubborn streak.[6]

On arrival in Bannack, Sanders settled his family into a small cabin, and Hattie made a few dollars cutting up a prize Belgian rug she had brought from Ohio and selling the strips to various saloons in town. Sanders operated as a secretary and factotum for his uncle, helping accumulate mining claims and organizing the movement to split the Montana mining camps away from Idaho Territory. It is far from clear that Sanders had anything to gain by agreeing to act as prosecutor in the Ives affair. Yet he took the job. He told the Lotts he would serve, and he made it clear that he intended to act forcefully. He had heard about the unraveling of the earlier people's courts and vowed to avoid a similar outcome. "I had made up my mind," he wrote in his memoirs, "in light of all this history and from my knowledge of human nature . . . that if I should prosecute any case, I would push it with the utmost vigor, and if the guilt of the accused was certain, that the retribution should be swift, and absolutely remorseless." He had given the matter a good deal of thought, it seemed, and believed that a timid approach would invite disaster.[7]

It was late morning by the time Sanders emerged from the Lott brothers' store, and he found a raucous public meeting underway on a patch of open ground between Main Street and Alder Creek. Don Byam, a doctor who served as judge of the miners' court in Nevada City, stood atop a freight wagon, presiding over a session meant to establish the rules for the trial. Ives's lawyers shouted to be heard, as did several self-appointed advocates, and hundreds of settlers crowded around to listen, shout responses, and vote on how best to proceed.

Dr. Don L. Byam, judge of the people's court that tried George Ives. Courtesy of the Montana Historical Society.

As in previous attempts at conducting trials, the first issue was whether to try Ives before an ordinary jury of twelve or to allow the whole crowd to render a verdict by common assent. Ives's lawyers argued vigorously in favor of a regular jury with six or twelve members, whose verdict would have to be reached unanimously and beyond a reasonable doubt. A majority of the crowd disagreed, and eventually a compromise was reached. The full assembly of settlers would have the final say in the matter, but a pair of twelve-member juries, one chosen from Nevada City and the other from Junction, a nearby gold camp, would serve in an advisory role.

As these matters were debated, Sanders excused himself and went to interview his prime witnesses. William Palmer, the English saloon owner who had discovered Tiebolt's body, agreed to testify despite his fear of reprisals at the hands of Ives and his friends. "Long John" Franck, the gangly herder whose refusal to help Palmer fueled suspicion that he was an accomplice in the killing, had become Ives's principal accuser and would be the main witness for the prosecution. Sanders worried about Franck's credibility and how he would fare during cross-examination. George Hilderman, the other defendant, struck Sanders as a feeble-minded old man, not likely to have taken a significant hand in any of the events surrounding Tiebolt's death. Sanders decided to postpone Hilderman's trial until later and deal first with Ives.

Returning to the public arena, Sanders discovered a fresh argument raging over a motion that lawyers be excluded from any participation in the trial. Ives's defense team had grown to four, with the addition of Alexander Davis, a well-respected attorney, and it seemed to many in the crowd that a conviction would be very hard to obtain in the face of their collective legal wiles. Sanders chose this moment to climb up on the wagon and introduce himself as counsel for the prosecution. "The crowd looked at me curiously," he wrote later, with due modesty, "as if taking the measure of my ability to cope with the great lawyers of established reputation who were on the other side, and they did not give any sign of satisfaction . . ." Actually, as recognition spread that Sanders was the nephew of the territorial chief justice, his role in the proceedings created quite a stir, investing the prosecution with a sense of legitimacy. After he had spoken, the crowd voted in favor of allowing counsel on both sides.[8]

Thus far, the name of Henry Plummer had not been uttered. Nevada City had its own sheriff, Robert Hereford, who took charge of guarding the prisoners and maintaining general order as the miners discussed and debated the matters of procedure. He was assisted by the sheriff of Junction, Adriel Davis. Suddenly the sheriff of Virginia City, J. B. "Buzz" Caven, mounted the wagon and asserted that an advisory jury of twelve men should be named from his town as well, since it was a main population center of Alder Gulch. Caven was a familiar figure, a fiddler and family man who settled in Bannack in the early days, and he was widely presumed to be a friend and ally of Henry Plummer's. After serving as one of Plummer's deputy sheriffs during the summer of 1863, Caven moved to Virginia City and was chosen sheriff of the mining district there in early September.

The sight of Caven atop the wagon, advocating a role in the trial for men from Virginia City—men who were Ives's friends and neighbors—aroused Sanders to speak in fierce opposition. Enlarging the advisory jury to a cumbersome thirty-six members was a poor idea, Sanders argued. What was to prevent the addition of juries from all the other mining camps in the gulch, all the way up to the top of Mount Baldy? As the camps closest to the crime scene, Nevada City and Junction deserved representation on the juries, Sanders said, but there was no such justification for including Virginia City.

Caven responded by reading aloud a list of twelve men he proposed to serve as jurors. He waved the paper at Sanders and demanded to know if he had anything to say against the character or quality of the men. Taking the bait, Sanders replied that he did not know any of the men personally but was aware of their reputations and therefore did not wish to know them. With that cavalier insult, an arcane dispute about advisory juries turned ugly. Caven stepped directly to Sanders' side and said ominously, "I will hold you personally responsible for that remark"—a thinly coded invitation to a duel. Recognizing the significance of this sudden escalation, Sanders wrote later that "the whole tumult of the Ives trial arose in that moment." Had he backed down, Sanders believed, all of the miners who knew and liked Ives and thought him no worse than a bully when drunk would have been emboldened to take his side in the trial. Listening to the shouts and catcalls of Ives's sympathizers—a group he described as "the good fellows" and "the boys"—Sanders decided he must answer in kind. He told Caven he accepted the challenge and would be happy to meet him in mortal conflict as soon as the trial was over.[9]

Impressed by Sanders' show of gumption, the crowd voted down the idea of a third advisory jury and cleared the way for the trial to begin. The

J. B. "Buzz" Caven, deputy sheriff who challenged Wilbur Sanders. Courtesy of the Montana Historical Society.

point had not been the number of men who would serve on a jury panel, of course, but a test of Sanders' resolve. In the mining camps of Alder Gulch, the sheriffs tended to be men of limited authority, their duties consisting largely of handling deeds and other paperwork for the miners' courts. They were not law enforcement officials in the modern sense, with responsibility for patrolling the streets, investigating crimes, or making arrests. Plummer was the exception. With his background as a city marshal, his aptitude for tracking fugitives, and his force of personality as a leader, he had appointed deputies and asserted a degree of authority in Bannack that was highly unusual. If he could somehow extend his reach into Alder Gulch, there was no telling how the Ives affair might turn out. Hereford and Davis, the sheriffs of Nevada City and Junction, could not maintain order in coming days unless the hundreds of men arrayed in front of them voluntarily obeyed them. The same was true of Sanders.

With the preliminaries concluded, Judge Byam called a brief recess for lunch. While he and the other principals went off in search of a midday meal, a group of miners began assembling the components of an outdoor courtroom. Moving to a more convenient site, they chose a spot on the east side of Main Street in front of a two-story wood-frame building. The audience, which numbered more than a thousand by most estimates, would be able to observe from surrounding rooftops as well as from the street. A large Schuttler wagon was pulled up and parked to provide seating for Judge Byam and his counterpart from the Junction mining district, Judge Wilson. A second wagon was placed beside it to serve as a witness stand. Benches from a hurdy-gurdy house were arranged in a semicircle for the advisory jurors. William Pemberton, a young lawyer from Virginia City, was named court reporter and given a table and chair beside the wagons. While the sun melted the rutted slush in the street, Pemberton recalled later, the air remained cold enough that he had to take notes wearing his gloves. A large bonfire was built with wood appropriated from a nearby store.[10]

Sanders was still reeling from his exchange with Caven. He had stood off the threat of physical confrontation for the time being, but it seemed the trial would be filled with such clashes, which might easily trigger a fight with fists or even guns. Some men had a knack for soothing their adversaries and sidestepping encounters before they got out of hand. Not Sanders. He took offense easily, replied in kind, and lacked the guile to think quickly and cunningly on his feet. There was no disputing his courage, just his judgment. It was easy to get his goat. As he prepared for opening arguments, Sanders took steps to protect himself. He borrowed a pair of Colt police revolvers and slipped them into the deep side pockets of his overcoat. And he sent a note to a friend in Virginia City, the freighter and merchant John Creighton, asking him to come with all of the men he could round up.

Sensing that Sanders needed help, Judge Wilson took him aside during the lunch break and gently suggested the wisdom of obtaining co-counsel. There was a miner in Junction, Wilson said, who might be able to help. Sanders agreed to be introduced and never forgot his vivid first impression of Charles S. Bagg: "a short, stubby, hairy, fatherly-looking man, somewhat rude, of dilapidated garb, whose bootlegs did not have sufficient fiber to stand up, and into one of which he had vainly essayed to tuck one of the legs of his pantaloons." This apparition, Sanders added, spoke intelligently and expressed an ardent desire to bring Ives to justice. In his memoirs, Sanders insisted that he was entirely satisfied to have Bagg's assistance, but it seems more probable that Sanders took on a partner because he had little choice. As a miner, Sanders conceded, Bagg would be able to reach the crowd and speak to them on their level, using a common touch Sanders himself plainly lacked. That Bagg was a Democrat and Southern sympathizer gave him another point of reference with many of the settlers.[11]

Arriving at the makeshift courtroom around midafternoon, Sanders was struck by the size of the audience. He measured the crowd at more than a thousand, perhaps as many as fifteen hundred, mostly miners but also freighters, merchants, butchers, tree-cutters, mechanics, and gamblers, sitting on the dirt roofs of adjacent cabins or standing in the muck in the street. They were well behaved for the most part, craning their necks for a good view and shushing any random comments from their neighbors so they could hear the words of the participants. Ives was to be tried first, by himself, and was brought from confinement in a nearby store with a logging chain held tightly around his legs by a padlock. His demeanor remained as seemingly unperturbed as it had during his arrest, and several observers remarked on his evident confidence. Some of his friends were in the crowd, among them "Tex" Crowell and Aleck Carter, shouting occasional words of encouragement.

Sad to say, the notes made by Pemberton and his assistant recorder, W. H. Patten, have not survived. But in his memoirs, Pemberton, who went on to serve as chief justice of Montana's territorial Supreme Court, gave a useful insight into the empathy that a surprising number of observers felt toward Ives. As a neighbor in Virginia City, Pemberton kept an office in the same building as Ives and occasionally visited with him. He liked Ives and could not believe him guilty of the crime of murder. In obvious error, Pemberton wrote that Ives did not drink, and it may be that the young lawyer's favorable impression was colored by ignorance of Ives's violent behavior when under the influence. Molly Sheehan, the observant young woman, recalled having Ives as a boarder in her family's cabin and admiring the way he looked in his long blue soldier's greatcoat. "I went on to notice," she added, "that he stood head and shoulders above most of the men who gathered around our table, that unlike the others he was smooth-shaven, and that he was blond and handsome." As we have seen, a man who comported himself as a gentleman was granted a good deal of leeway in the nineteenth century, not least if he happened to be handsome and charming.[12]

While most of the actors in the trial filled conventional roles, the same could not be said for the fifty or so armed men who ringed the periphery of the open-air courtroom and kept a close watch on the crowd, cradling rifles and shotguns. The two sheriffs, Hereford and Davis, were so manifestly outnumbered by spectators that they required assistance from a security force closer in size to a platoon than a team of bailiffs. The head of this small army was James Williams, the leathery rancher who had led the posse that captured Ives and returned him to Nevada City. By what authority he now served was an important question. The spectators were free to vote for procedures and the participants were free to follow them as they wished, but no legal machinery existed to *enforce* any of it, including a verdict. Ives had the benefit of skilled legal counsel, judges, a jury of sorts, and at least some good will from his fellow settlers. But the trial would take place under the auspices of an armed force that answered to unnamed men who believed that Ives was guilty and would be a danger to public order and common security as long as he lived.[13]

Bagg gave the opening argument for the prosecution, an indication that Sanders may not have trusted himself to make an easy connection with the masses of miners. The men assembled there that day, Bagg said, had willingly isolated themselves from civilization and survived immense hardship in the hope of making their fortunes. They now had a chance to rid themselves of a menace who meant to steal the fruits of their labors. They could make the countryside safe again, and they had a duty to do so. Ives's lawyers followed with objections that would seem familiar, and for the most part perfectly valid, to observers in a modern American courtroom. They had not been given adequate time to prepare a defense, to find and interview witnesses and examine evidence, and were operating in a climate corrupted by the public display of the victim's mutilated body. Under current law, they almost certainly would have been granted a continuance and possibly also a change of venue. But at the time, their motions were loudly shouted down by the crowd.[14]

The first witness called was Palmer, the discoverer of Tiebolt's body. He spoke in a clear, confident voice, describing his surprise at finding a corpse concealed in the bushes by the river and the subsequent refusal of Franck and Hilderman to help him. The story was familiar by now to the spectators and did not directly advance the case against Ives as the killer. But Palmer's testimony had an important psychological effect. It underscored the point that a criminal trial was underway and that the participants were acting with the utmost seriousness. It emboldened several men to come forward and speak in confidence to Sanders and Bagg, implicating Ives in the recent trailside holdups that had terrified the whole community. According to Sanders, drivers and passengers on the stagecoach route between Bannack and Alder Gulch approached him and accused Ives of involvement in a host of robberies and murders, including some that had not previously been reported. By one chilling account, Ives in recent days had gunned down an itinerant thief suspected of informing on him, leaving the unknown man's body to be buried beside the trail near the Cold Spring way station.[15]

Trial had begun late in the day, and Judge Byam adjourned the proceedings shortly after dark, to resume at nine o'clock the next morning. As they talked afterward, Sanders and Bagg realized they had a problem. Much as they believed Ives to be guilty, their legal case against him was weak. It would rely almost entirely on the testimony of a very unsympathetic character, John Franck, who had turned accuser to save his own skin. There were no other eyewitnesses. No physical evidence linked Ives to the crime scene. The same sense of urgency that handicapped the preparations of the defense applied to the prosecution as well. No coroner's inquest had been held. No medical examination of the body had been performed that might have yielded clues about the circumstances of the murder. There was no smoking gun, literal or figurative. On the other hand, Sanders was more certain than ever that Ives had taken part in numerous highway robberies and other acts of violence, now that so many victims had spoken to him. Ives was not standing trial for these other crimes, but if the crowd could be convinced that he had committed them, he might well be convicted.

One weakness of a people's court was that it combined the duties of two bodies that ordinarily acted separately: the grand jury and the trial jury. In a courthouse back east, the case against Ives might have been developed at leisure, with a grand jury meeting in secret and gathering testimony and evidence that established grounds for an indictment charging him with one or more crimes. Then, at trial, a petit jury of twelve would hear the evidence in open court and decide if Ives was guilty beyond a reasonable doubt. With these functions compressed by time and circumstance, the crowd gathered around the wagons in Nevada City would have to act as a hybrid—or so Sanders calculated. He would make his case against Ives as a dangerous criminal at large, not just as the murderer of Nicholas Tiebolt.

As Sanders feared, "Long John" Franck did not inspire warm feelings among the settlers. "He was one of the worst-looking men I have ever seen," an observer commented succinctly. But as the trial resumed on the morning of Sunday, December 20, 1863, Franck gave a vivid account of the events leading to Tiebolt's death. The young man had arrived in early December to collect two mules pastured on Franck's ranch. In making payment, he had opened a buckskin purse that revealed the gleam of hundreds of dollars in gold dust. Ives, who was visiting at the time, along with Tex Crowell and Aleck Carter, had watched the transaction with avid interest. As the young man rode off, Ives remarked ominously that it seemed a shame to let all that money get away, and two fine, silky-haired mules as well.[16]

According to Franck, Ives tossed a coin to determine who would pursue the young man and the mules. The lot fell to Ives, who quickly mounted his horse, checked his revolver, and rode off at a gallop. A few minutes later, he returned with the mules and the gold. It had not seemed right to shoot the young man in the back, Ives said, so he had called to him and shot him in the forehead after he turned around.

The cross-examination was as withering as expected. As Sanders put it in his memoirs, Franck "came in for the seven vials of the lawyers' wrath," vilified as a stool pigeon who would "peach on his pals" to save himself from hanging. By his own admission, Franck was an accomplice in the crime, and Ives's lawyers made a strong argument that he deserved to be executed, whether Ives was convicted or not. Had the testimony of Franck concluded the prosecution's case, it is hard to say what might have happened.[17]

Unlike a conventional trial, however, the proceedings in Nevada City did not turn wholly on the witnesses in the dock. The men who approached Sanders and Bagg and accused Ives of various crimes spoke to others as well, and soon the crowd was abuzz with rumor and gossip. Men who had encountered Ives in one hostile setting or another exchanged stories, and those stories were repeated among the observers in the crowd. For the first time, the full scope of the ongoing crime wave became clear to the general population of the mining camps, and it seemed plain that Ives was involved. One piece of physical evidence in particular pointed a damning finger at Ives in connection with the robbery of Leroy South-mayd. The posse that arrested Ives had discovered and confiscated a sub-stantial cache of weapons in the hut, including a revolver that Southmayd identified as having been taken from him. Lending support to his account, a miner named Amos Hall came forward and produced a ledger book with the gun's serial number recorded in it. He had sold the gun to South-mayd, he said, and the ledger was proof.[18]

The legal soundness of the cloud of accusation brought against Ives remains a matter of dispute. Because the trial transcript was lost, it is impossible to know how many, if any, of his putative victims actually climbed onto the witness wagon to give sworn testimony. The answer appears to be, not many. According to Sanders, "it was thought prudent to excuse them from testifying, because of their necessary exposure to the vengeance of Ives and his partners in crime"—an explanation that may ring a bit hollow, given the strength of numbers displayed by the dozens of armed guards who surrounded the makeshift courtroom. Several accounts of the trial make mention of the conspicuous departure of some of Ives's closest associates, among them Crowell and Carter, as the focus of the proceedings began to widen and appeared likely to ensnare them as well. The handful of sympathizers who had given vocal support to Ives in the early going fell notably silent on Sunday morning, intimidated by the mood of the crowd and the direction the trial was taking.[19]

Still, the climate of fear engendered by the violence of recent weeks did not dissipate easily. One of the miners serving as an armed guard during the trial, George Lovell, recalled overhearing a conversation in a gambling house on the first afternoon of the proceedings "that left no doubt as to the guilt of the parties on trial" and persuaded him that "they had many accomplices and sympathizers, who were organizing to rescue their friends." The fact that some of Ives's friends had fled the immediate vicinity of the trial did not mean they were gone for good, only that they might be out there on the trails somewhere, regrouping.[20]

Not surprisingly, Ives's lawyers objected loudly to what they considered a kangaroo court veering away from a specific criminal charge into a wider inquiry. And by modern standards, at least, they had a point. Hearsay evidence, unsworn statements, vague accounts of collateral crime, all made their way into the stew of information being considered by the jury of the whole. Even at the time, the merits of the case troubled some of the participants. The defense lawyers called two witnesses who attempted to provide an alibi for Ives, but their strategy was undone by the very uncertainty of the date of Tiebolt's murder. "There was an instinctive and unerring conviction that the worst man in the community was on trial," Thomas Dimsdale, the famous chronicler of the vigilante era, wrote two years later, "but it was hard work, after all the proof and all this feeling, to convict him."[21]

Ives elected not to testify in his own behalf, and at the finish of the second day's session, Judge Byam adjourned court and set closing arguments to begin in the morning. Sanders returned to Virginia City, where he was staying with a friend, to begin crafting his statement. The text has been lost, but Sanders captured the essence of his appeal quite eloquently in his memoirs. "It was apparent from the opening of the trial," he wrote, "that law and order, or *order without law* [emphasis added], had locked horns with crime, and that it was to be a fight to the finish." He would plead with every ounce of persuasion for a guilty verdict, and then, if he got it, Sanders intended to demand the immediate execution of Ives, right on the spot, with no further time or avenue for appeal. "The blood of too many desperate characters was up," he explained, "and it seemed [vital] to everybody connected with the prosecution that a vengeance so swift and so stern should follow his conviction as to cause it to be known that henceforth peaceable people would be in possession of their own."[22]

As he worked on his remarks that Sunday night, Sanders was interrupted by his host, a merchant named Nicholas Wall, who summoned him to an urgent meeting. Arriving in the back room of Nye & Kenna's dry-goods store in Virginia City, Sanders found a small group of men who shared his concern about the outcome of the trial and the challenge of enforcing a verdict. The participants included Wall, John Nye, Alvin Brookie, and a man with the odd name of Paris Pfouts. At one time or another in recent days, Sanders had spoken with all of the men in general terms about the possible need for a vigilance committee to impose order in the gold camps and on the trails that led in and out of them. That talk now turned specific. If Ives was found guilty the next day, as seemed likely in spite of the gaps in the case against him, it was imperative to avoid the sort of sloppy, inconclusive ending that had undone the people's trials of earlier days. Did anyone really want to give Ives and his lawyers a chance to plead for mercy or launch some endless round of appeals? Could the settlers of Alder Gulch afford another Dillingham case, with cold-blooded murderers set free to ride away and continue their depredations at will? The answer, they agreed, was a resounding no.

The armed men standing guard at Ives's trial were operating under the command of James Williams, who in turn answered to an informal group headed by John Lott, the Nevada City storekeeper, and "Old Man" Clark, the miner who had hired Tiebolt for his fatal errand and pressed the search for his killers after the body was discovered. Sanders and his companions now moved to give the loose-knit organization a sturdier foundation. The time had come, they agreed, for the creation of a formal vigilance committee, complete with officers, rules of self-regulation, and a set of objectives. If Ives was found guilty, they agreed, they would accept Sanders' call for his immediate execution, carry out the sentence, and then act to find and root out the rest of his accomplices and any other wrongdoers who threatened the common good. The outcome of the trial would not rest on the relatively feeble shoulders of two miners' court judges but on an armed body capable of imposing its will, no matter what form of resistance might burst forth.

The most striking thing about this small cell of self-appointed guardians was its diversity. Various historians have argued—mistakenly—that the men who organized the vigilance committee in Alder Gulch were united by common bond as Masons, Republicans, Union sympathizers, or membership in the merchant class. This was not so. Paris Pfouts, chosen as president of the group, was a slightly baleful-looking man, bearded and balding, who had worked in a general store and a newspaper office before joining the California and Colorado gold rushes as a miner and later as a merchant and inveterate gambler. He was a native of Ohio, the adoptive state of

Sidney Edgerton and Wilbur Sanders, but unlike those two proud abolitionists, Pfouts aligned himself with the Copperheads and embraced the
cause of the Confederacy. And there were other differences. Pfouts and
Sanders were Masons, but Wall and Brookie were not. Sanders was a
lawyer, not a merchant.

It might be simpler to characterize the men who met in Nye & Kenna's
Store that Sunday night as the "establishment" of the gold camps, to use
a modern locution, since they seemed to have an interest in protecting the
established order. But that notion is flimsy as well. In one important
respect, at least, Sanders and other supporters of independent territorial
status stood to gain from a *lack* of order, since crime and chaos would
underscore the need for accessible, functioning governance. Nor were they
simply men of wealth protecting themselves from the have-nots. They had
not been victims of highway robbery themselves and likely never would be,
so long as they did not plan to travel east with large stashes of gold dust.
Sanders found himself in jeopardy at the hands of the rough element not
because of his riches or social position but because he had volunteered to
prosecute one of its leaders.[23]

What joined these men in common purpose seems to have been a mix
of courage, duty, and also a large dose of skepticism about the ability of a
frontier democracy to police itself. They were fully conversant with the
activities of the San Francisco vigilance committee of 1856 and greatly
admired that movement's leader, William Coleman, for his success in dis-
mantling a corrupt but duly elected City Hall machine. San Francisco
had been divided by class, political party, ethnicity, and even religion, in a
way that the Montana gold camps were not, but at bottom the vigilance
committees in both places were rooted in the confidence of a core group
of powerful men that they knew better than others how to run things.

The accuracy of that belief was about to be tested.

Henry Plummer, who had watched the activities of the California vigilantes with alarm and distaste seven years earlier, viewed the trial in
Nevada City as an illegitimate exercise that would undercut his authority
as sheriff and lead to vigilantism. When word reached him that Ives had
been arrested and faced a charge of murder, Plummer told his friends and
family, the Vails, that he dared not leave Bannack. He would not travel the
seventy miles to Alder Gulch to assert his authority and take custody of
Ives. He would not interfere in any way. Instead, he would post sentries
around Bannack and wait to see if they planned to come next for him.[24]

CHAPTER ELEVEN

"Men, Do Your Duty"

Wilbur Sanders was a nervous wreck. Few lawyers sleep well the night before a closing argument, and Sanders faced the challenge of rallying a mass jury to convict one of the most dangerous men in the Rocky Mountains, an alleged killer capable of inflicting violent retribution if acquitted and released.

It could be argued, of course, that the defendant, George Ives, confronted the greater jeopardy, since he might well be executed if the settlers of Alder Gulch agreed on his guilt. But Ives maintained the same tranquil, unruffled manner that had marked his conduct since his capture three days earlier. He exuded an aura of confidence, as if conviction were the least likely thing imaginable. And in truth, Sanders had not by any means built an airtight case. Based on the preponderance of evidence, to borrow a standard used in modern civil cases, most observers could be satisfied that Ives was a bully, an armed robber, and probably a murderer. Yet those accusations had not been proven beyond a reasonable doubt. The specific charge against Ives, that he had killed the young German emigrant, Nicholas Tiebolt, lacked hard evidence. Stronger cases had unraveled in the past in the gold camps, leaving the guilty parties unpunished and at large. Sanders had every reason to feel jittery.[1]

Early on the morning of Monday, December 21, 1863, the trial's third day, Sanders made the two-mile trip down Alder Gulch from his friend Nicholas Wall's house in Virginia City to Nevada City, where he found several hundred miners already in place, surrounding the wagons that formed the makeshift courtroom. Dozens of men sat on the dirt roofs of nearby buildings, looking down on the scene, giving it the appearance of an outdoor amphitheater. As Sanders and the defense lawyers began their summations, it became clear that the crowd's patience had begun to wear thin. The day was warm enough to permit mining, and a voice from the crowd barked out a demand that the proceedings end by 3 P.M. Judge Don Byam was not happy with the peremptory deadline but gave his assent after a majority in the crowd yelled out their approval.[2]

Marshaling his key points, Sanders argued that Ives had killed Tiebolt, that he had committed other murders "of equal cruelty," that he had been "the leading actor" in the armed robberies of "Bummer Dan" McFadden and Leroy Southmayd, that he was a stagecoach robber by profession, and finally that he "belonged to the criminal classes, and that his appetite for blood had grown until it became a consuming passion." This last point, far too nebulous for admission in a modern courtroom, was actually the crux of the prosecution's case, summing up the prevailing view that Ives had slipped over the line from mean drunk to genuine menace, no matter how much the gentleman he seemed to be, sitting quietly in the wagon.[3]

Opposing counsel did their best to exploit the holes in Sanders' case. In his memoir of the trial, Sanders credited James M. Thurmond in particular with an effective rebuttal that earned a positive, audible response from many of those listening. Another of Ives's lawyers, John Ritchie, echoing the themes heard in earlier people's trials, argued that his client was "a little wild," perhaps, but a gentleman nonetheless and a friend to many of those in the audience. The circumstances of Tiebolt's death were far from clear, Ritchie added, and executing Ives would not bring the young man back to life.[4]

The defense lawyers did not confine themselves solely to attacks on the prosecution's case. They targeted Sanders personally as well, calculating that his stiff, formal manner would not win many converts. They made a point of his politics, sarcastically addressing him as "the gentleman from Oberlin," the college near his home in Ohio that was nationally renowned for its embrace of abolition and integration. A majority of the crowd—as many as four-fifths, by Sanders' nervous calculation—seemed to be in sympathy with the Southern cause, or at least hostile to the notion of racial equality. Sanders' co-counsel, Charles Bagg, took little role in the closing arguments, but his presence, as a Democrat and well-known Confederate sympathizer, helped balance the equation and soothe some of the friction.[5]

Still, the attacks took their toll on Sanders' equanimity. The lawyers bickered on past the appointed hour and it was dusk when Judges Byam and Wilson instructed the advisory jury of twenty-four to adjourn to an unfinished log building nearby and begin their deliberations. The jury of the whole would render the final verdict, but the smaller jury would have the first word. Sanders was not at all sure what its members would say, and he reached into the deep side pockets of his greatcoat several times to reassure himself that his two Colt police revolvers were there and ready if needed.

The jury of twenty-four returned in less than a half-hour. They reached a swift verdict, but they were not unanimous. One man, Henry Spivey, declined to vote for conviction, explaining that he could not agree Ives had been proven guilty beyond a reasonable doubt of killing Tiebolt. Ives certainly appeared to be a stagecoach robber, Spivey said, but he did not believe a criminal case had been brought and made against Ives on that specific charge. Hearing the divided verdict, the crowd buzzed with excitement and curiosity. This was exactly the sort of unexpected wrinkle that had stirred confusion and undone convictions in previous trials, and Sanders recognized the need to act quickly, before the idea took hold that a hung jury had created a mistrial.[6]

On his feet instantly, Sanders declared that the advisory jury had recommended conviction and moved that the jury of the whole adopt the finding and make it their verdict. Judge Byam accepted the motion before the defense lawyers could raise an objection, and moments later by loud assent the crowd found Ives guilty. More of a voice vote than a formal verdict, the will of the crowd nonetheless was plain. Pressing his advantage, Sanders next asked the jury of the whole to pass sentence on Ives—that he be hanged by the neck until dead. Judge Byam ordered a vote on the sentence, and again the crowd voted loudly in favor of the motion. In the relative blink of an eye, Ives found himself condemned to death. Sanders then moved the court to carry out the sentence immediately, and Judge Byam ordered the two mining district sheriffs, Robert Hereford and Adriel Davis, to find a suitable spot in town to rig a gallows and carry out the execution.[7]

The swift turn of events left Ives and his defenders dazed. One of his lawyers jumped up to demand that Ives's accuser, "Long John" Franck, be executed as well, a suggestion that earned shouts of agreement from the handful of Ives's friends and supporters in the crowd. But Ives recognized that having a companion on the gallows was not a useful outcome, and he gathered his composure in the next few moments for an attempt at saving himself. Watched closely by James Williams and his dozens of armed guards, Ives rose to his feet and moved slowly toward the wagon where Sanders was standing. Reaching Sanders' side, Ives slowly extended his hand to him, touched his sleeve, and pulled himself up onto the bench beside the prosecutor. "If there was any tremor in his voice, or tremulousness in his person, I did not detect it," Sanders wrote later, "and the great crowd, always muttering something, was hushed into profound silence."

By now nightfall was complete, the scene lit by bonfire, torch, and moonlight. Summoning his powers of persuasion, Ives spoke in a low, unhurried voice. "Colonel," he said to Sanders,

> I am a gentleman, and I believe you are, and I want to ask a favor which you alone can grant. If our places were changed, I know I would grant it to you, and I believe you will to me. I have been pretty wild away from home, but I have a mother and sisters in the States, and I want you to get this execution put off till tomorrow morning. I will give you my word and honor as a gentleman that I will not undertake to escape, nor permit my friends to try to change this matter.[8]

Ives's simple, eloquent plea had a profound impact on the crowd, and Sanders recognized that it would be very difficult to refuse the request, couched as it was in such seemingly reasonable terms. Rarely at a loss for words, Sanders fell quiet, wondering if postponement would open the way for some form of sloppy clemency, as it had in the past. Then, in the stillness of the moment, one of the hundreds of men surrounding the wagons broke the silence and launched himself into Montana history. John Xavier Beidler, known to one and all by his middle initial, "X," was an energetic little plug of a man, shorter than his rifle at five-foot-three, a sometime miner and merchant who had signaled his allegiance to the forces of order by digging the unused graves of the men who killed D. H. Dillingham the previous summer. Having volunteered his services as a guard during Ives's trial, Beidler was watching closely from an adjacent rooftop when the defendant asked for a day's mercy, and he made plain his

John "X" Beidler, who shouted, "Ask him how long he gave the Dutchman!" Courtesy of the Montana Historical Society.

lack of sympathy. "Sanders!" Beidler shouted into the night air. "Ask him how long he gave the Dutchman!"[9]

This loud, irreverent reminder of Ives's cruelty in killing the Deutsch boy echoed off the storefronts and over the crowd, triggering another shift in sentiment. Now the voices of the chorus growled with renewed calls for hanging Ives and avenging Tiebolt's death. Sanders had been pondering how best to refuse Ives's request "and yet satisfy the sense of propriety of the miners" when Beidler's question rescued him. "I have to confess," Sanders wrote later, "that X Beidler's remark lifted a considerable load from my mind. I replied to Ives, 'You should have been thinking of this matter before. Get down there, [and] maybe you can write a short letter to your folks before the sheriff returns for you.'" According to Sanders, Ives accepted his directive meekly: "He let go of my hand without response, jumped out of the wagon, sat down by the fire where some of his counsel were, and was furnished with a sheet of paper and a pencil, and proceeded to commence a letter to his mother."

Ives maintained his poise and seemed "imperturbable," in the word of one observer. But the same could not be said for Sanders or Ives's lawyers, who now turned on each other with a fresh level of ferocity. Without displaying the least hint of compassion or delicacy, Sanders made another motion to the court, that Ives's property be seized and used to pay the expenses of the trial, including the board of the guards, defendants, and witnesses, with the remainder to be paid to Ives's mother and family. John Ritchie, the most impassioned of Ives's lawyers, leapt angrily to his feet and objected that it was "an outrage" to execute a man—to murder him—and at the same time make him pay board for those who carried out the killing. Sanders, still agitated and utterly lacking in tact, answered hotly that it was standard practice to assess court costs against a convicted felon, adding that if Ritchie did not understand this simple principle he belonged in a law school rather than a law office.[10]

In his memoir, Sanders professed not to understand why this insult provoked Ritchie to such fury. Yet it is plain that Sanders knew he had crossed the line. As Ritchie stepped toward him, fists balled, Sanders nervously dug his hands into the pockets of his greatcoat, fingering the two Colt revolvers he was carrying. In his jittery state, Sanders accidentally touched the trigger of one of the pistols, sending a shot ripping through the fabric of his coat and into the ground next to his foot, badly startling himself and all those around him. Ritchie and some of Ives's other lawyers believed for a tense moment that Sanders had opened fire on them. Ritchie rushed forward and grabbed Sanders by the coat, and the two men were about to begin pummeling each other when James Williams and a couple of his guards pulled them apart and restored order. Sanders insisted in later years that he had test-fired his revolver deliberately, with no great injury done to anyone or anything other than the lining of his coat, but in truth he seems to have succumbed to the tensions of the moment to such a degree that he very nearly shot himself in the foot.

In any case, the role of the lawyers in the Ives affair had drawn to a close, and other actors now moved to carry out the sentence of the people's court. The two sheriffs, Hereford and Davis, returned to the judges' wagon after a half-hour and reported that they were unable to find a suitable gallows. Some in the crowd answered impatiently that any venue would do, and moments later a forty-foot log was carried inside an unfinished building across the street and wedged against a wall so that its tip rose at an angle above a crossbeam, high into the night air. A rope was tied to the end of the log with a noose attached, and a dry goods box was placed beneath it. Ives had dictated only a few words of the letter to his family when friends interrupted him by breaching the cordon of guards to touch his shoulder and bid him farewell. Some were weeping, though Ives was not. William Pemberton, the young lawyer acting as court reporter, said Ives spoke to him briefly and regretted that he could not cut his throat or poison himself, to avoid the shame of being hanged. Pemberton, who had begun the trial doubting Ives's guilt, was now persuaded otherwise.[11]

At the direction of Judge Byam, the guards led Ives a few paces from his spot at the makeshift defense table to the place of execution. He was lifted onto the box and the noose was placed around his neck. The crowd grew more excited, as the moment of execution grew near, exchanging cries of "Hang him!" with an occasional plea for postponement or mercy or for the execution of Franck as an equally guilty party. At one point, some of Ives's friends rushed toward the nearby store where Franck was being held, meaning to seize him and hang him, but they were repulsed by the armed guard. At last Ives stood still and the crowd quieted. Judge Byam asked Ives if he had any final words. In a steady voice, Ives replied, "I am innocent of this crime." Then he added, "Aleck Carter killed the Dutchman." He asked to speak to Franck, but Judge Byam refused his request, fearing it might lead to an attempt at escape.[12]

A voice called out, "Men, do your duty," and with that the box was kicked out from under Ives's feet. He fell hard and the noose cracked his neck, killing him almost instantly. Judge Byam waited a minute and then stepped to Ives's side and touched him. "His neck is broken," Byam announced. "He is dead." In later years, several men claimed to have given the order, "Men, do your duty," a phrase that earned a prominent place in Montana folklore as the vigilante motto, but no one can say for sure. Most likely, it was James Williams, the captain of the guard. Similarly, a number of men claimed to have kicked the box, and their identity, too, is uncertain. It may be most accurate to say that the crowd as a whole carried out the execution, since there is no dispute about the will of the vast majority of men who attended the trial and rendered their verdict.[13]

Some historians have argued that hanging Ives was a miscarriage of justice, since the prosecution failed to prove its case against him beyond a reasonable doubt. They have a point, certainly, if the standard at hand was the test applied by juries in courtrooms enjoying the full trappings and authority of the American criminal justice system. But, as we have seen, those elements were most emphatically absent in Alder Gulch in December of 1863, and what to do about George Ives could not easily be postponed until sturdier, more legitimate procedures presented themselves. Perhaps, given the impossibility of conducting a trial fully cloaked with the protections of due process, it might have been fairer to banish Ives, though the threat he posed by remaining at large is difficult to ignore. No one can know what would have resulted if Ives had lived another day, another week, another year.[14]

For his part, Sanders did not have much doubt that he would have been a target of violence had Ives survived. Sanders left Nevada City immediately after the execution and returned to Virginia City, where he took refuge in the store operated by his friend John Creighton. Later that night, a man named Harvey Meade entered the store, armed with two revolvers, and began abusing Sanders verbally, cursing him and accusing him of murdering Ives. Sanders slipped his hand into the pocket of his greatcoat and one of his friends, Dr. J. P. Maupin, reached for a pick handle behind the store's counter. Before any fighting took place, however, Creighton grabbed Meade by the arm and succeeded in hustling him out of the room. For the remainder of the time he spent in Alder Gulch, Sanders went about in public guarded by four armed men. His haughty manner had not endeared Sanders to the other settlers and the participants in the trial, but he would be respected to the end of his days for the courage he demonstrated in doing a job and carrying out a commitment that had scared him half to death.[15]

The most intriguing aspect of Ives's final moments was the accusation he leveled against Aleck Carter as the actual killer of young Tiebolt. Up to that instant, Ives and his lawyers had insisted vehemently that "Long John" Franck committed the murder and was framing Ives to save himself. There seemed no evident reason for Ives to recant and invent a "deathbed" indictment of a friend except to set the record straight, and quite a few observers in the crowd reached the conclusion that he must be telling the truth. Carter was well known as a member of Ives's inner circle. He had been in the hut when Ives was captured, along with the cache of weapons. His name had come up repeatedly in the welter of sidebar accounts of various armed robberies. And, most conspicuously, he had fled the area during the trial.

Had he not chosen to brand Carter as a murderer, Ives's hanging might have closed the book on the death of young Tiebolt. Now, however, the men who had prosecuted Ives, and who had decided in private that vigilante justice was their only recourse in the fight against crime, calculated that they had more work to do. A great deal of confusion has surrounded the founding of the famous vigilantes of Montana, which is hardly surprising, given that they were operating extralegally and secretly in a very dangerous, volatile atmosphere. But a thorough examination of memoirs, diaries, letters, and other documents from the era reveals a fresh and relatively simple conclusion. *Two* vigilance committees were born from Ives's trial, not one, as most historians have mistakenly assumed. One committee originated from the meeting that Sanders had on the second night of the trial in Virginia City with Nick Wall, John Nye, Alvin Brookie, and Paris Pfouts. Modeling themselves on the widely heralded vigilance committees of San Francisco, these men recruited others and formed what might be called the board of directors of the vigilance movement. A second, separate vigilante group grew out of the startling final accusation from the lips of George Ives. Persuaded that Carter and perhaps others in Ives's circle were complicit in the murder of Tiebolt, John Lott and William Clark took steps to revive the posse that had captured

Ives, and James Williams made plans to lead its members in pursuit of the accomplices.[16]

Ives's body was left dangling from the noose for about an hour, then cut down and placed on a bench in a wheelbarrow shop for the night. In the morning, friends were allowed to take the body for burial. The morning of Tuesday, December 22, 1863, found the principals of the Ives trial back in place in their makeshift courtroom on the streets of Nevada City, assembled to dispose of the cases of George Hilderman and "Long John" Franck. Having concluded that Hilderman was "a weak, foolish man," lacking the sense to know right from wrong or even to have been fully aware of the criminal activity around him, Sanders chose not to prosecute him but instead to have him banished. H. P. A. Smith, the grandiloquent lawyer who had remained relatively quiet during Ives's trial, took the lead in defending Hilderman, and raised a subtle but important point. As demonstrated by those who had come forward to whisper accusations against Ives during the course of his trial, it seemed many men had knowledge of criminal activity on the trails between the gold camps that they had not previously reported for fear of reprisal. Hilderman, he argued, fell into the same category. Hilderman's failure to disclose the murder of young Tiebolt was not evidence of complicity but rather of fear that Ives would kill him for telling. To illustrate the point with a more compelling example, Smith called Dr. Jerome Glick to the stand. Glick, the surgeon who had saved Henry Plummer's arm after he was shot by Hank Crawford, admitted that on occasion in recent weeks he had ministered to men he believed had been injured or wounded while committing robberies. He had kept silent about his suspicions, he said, because he was frightened of the consequences of revealing them publicly, and in this he was no different from victims who declined to identify their attackers for the same reason.[17]

Hilderman asked to speak to the court and was allowed to do so. He had no means to travel, he said, and nowhere to go. He asked to be allowed to stay. Unmoved by the plea, a miner yelled that he could go to hell. Sanders then moved to impose banishment. Showing that he had not leavened his hard edge, he asked the court to allow anyone to shoot Hilderman on sight if he stayed in the gold camps east of the Bitterroot Mountains after New Year's Day. The crowd assented, as it had in the verdict and judgment against Ives, and the judges gave Hilderman ten days to arrange his departure. Franck, having fulfilled his bargain to turn state's witness, was released and allowed to go free.[18]

To most of the miners, merchants, and other settlers of Alder Gulch, the great flaw of the Ives trial was not its failure to reach the standard of reasonable doubt in convicting the defendant and executing him, nor any other shortcoming in the procedural aspect of the affair, but rather the amount of time and trouble it occasioned. As the vigilantes' ardent apologist, Thomas Dimsdale, explained in the series of newspaper articles he wrote about their activities shortly afterward, "If every Road Agent cost as much labor, time, and money for his conviction [as Ives], the efforts of the citizens . . . would have failed altogether. Some shorter, surer, and at least equally equitable method of procedure [had] to be found."[19]

So it was, on the next day, Wednesday, December 23, 1863, that John Lott, the Nevada City storekeeper who had helped form the original Ives posse and who, along with his brother Mortimer, had persuaded Sanders to act as prosecutor, put his quill pen to paper and drew up a remarkable document that served as an oath of office for pursuers of Aleck Carter:

> We the undersigned uniting ourselves in a party for the laudable purpos of arresting thievs & murderers & recovering stollen property do pledge ourselves upon our sacred honor each to all others & solemnly swear that we will reveal no secrets, violate no laws of right & never desert each other or our standard of justice so help us God as witness our hand & seal this 23 of December AD 1863.[20]

Starting with James Williams, two dozen men signed the hastily written compact, including "Old Man" Clark, William Palmer, Elkanah Morse, Tom Baume, and other veterans of the first Ives posse. The most striking thing about the document, which survives in the archives of the Montana Historical Society in Helena, is its strained but obviously sincere effort to invest the undertaking with as many expressions of legitimacy as the author could invent (and misspell) on the spur of the moment. His protestations might have had a slightly defensive ring, as if advertising the absence of genuine instruments of justice, but the point is the men cared enough to sign an oath of honor. Critics of the Montana vigilantes have portrayed them as a lynch mob emboldened to scourge the community of various

John S. Lott, who wrote the vigilante oath and later gave it to the Montana Historical Society. Courtesy of the Montana Historical Society.

ne'er-do-wells without the formality of indictment and trial. But the men who swore the oath of December 23, 1863, believed in the rightness of their cause enough to proclaim it in writing, affix their signatures, and ask the help of God. Real lynch mobs tend not to observe such niceties.

The members of Williams's posse meant to conduct a search for Aleck Carter and other possible accomplices in the killing of Tiebolt. To that end, they took "Long John" Franck with them on their journey to give evidence against anyone he recognized as a participant in the affair. The group saddled their horses, took care to dress more warmly than they had on their miserable first expedition, and set off in the direction of Cottonwood, a small settlement about a hundred miles to the north near the present city of Deer Lodge, where they guessed Carter might have fled. Making slow progress, the group spent its first night at a crossing of the Big Hole River and the second, Christmas Eve, less than halfway to its destination. On Christmas Day, they encountered a lone rider coming toward them on the trail. They recognized him as Erastus "Red" Yeager, the bartender and handyman from the Rattlesnake Ranch, and asked him if he had any knowledge of the whereabouts of Aleck Carter and his crowd. Yeager responded that he had just seen Carter in Cottonwood, "lying drunk," having been expelled from a dance at a saloon the night before. Grateful for the information, and having no reason to doubt or detain him, the group sent Yeager on his way and stepped up their pace, hurrying to reach the settlement and find the fugitive.[21]

Meanwhile, the vigilante elders who remained behind in Alder Gulch were giving closer thought to the issues raised by the Ives trial. The killing of Tiebolt, they concluded, was not some isolated, random act of violence, but part of a pattern of criminal activity that now seemed widespread and very possibly coordinated. In the days after Ives's execution, the original group of leaders who had met with Sanders in Nye & Kenna's Store in Virginia City expanded their efforts. Specifically, they joined cause with John Lott in Nevada City and held an organizational meeting to set guidelines to define and govern their conduct. The result was the adoption of a full, formal—and properly spelled—set of regulations and by-laws that created a vigilance committee, provided for the selection of its officers, and outlined its mission. It would investigate any and all serious crimes and punish those deemed guilty. It would operate in secret. There would be no means of appealing its decisions. And its judgment would be severe. "The only punishment that shall be inflicted by this Committee," the document added, using capital letters for emphasis, "is DEATH."[22]

CHAPTER TWELVE

The Vigilantes

The way Paris Pfouts liked to tell the story, he got elected president of the Montana vigilance committee because he happened to be absent from the meeting when the vote took place and had no chance to decline the honor. Actually, he was a good choice for the job, far better suited to the task at hand than Wilbur Sanders, the prosecutor in the Tiebolt murder case and a co-founder of the committee. The diversity of the vigilante leaders—by region, religion, profession, politics, and social affiliation—extended to their personal characteristics as well. Sanders brought a harsh, wintry manner to the business of imposing order on the gold camps, and while it might have seemed entirely appropriate for a band of self-appointed executioners to look and act severe, the truth was that the committee of vigilance represented a form of government, and Paris Pfouts was a natural-born politician.[1]

Pfouts's family made its way across the Atlantic from the German duchy of Saxe-Coburg in the eighteenth century when his great-grandfather, an aristocrat who spelled the name von Pfautz, went broke and a bit mad after a lifelong fling with alchemy, exhausting the family fortune and his wits as well trying to spin gold out of base metals. "At all hours of the day and night he might be seen poring over some old volume," Paris Pfouts wrote in his memoirs, "or sweltering in heat by a blazing furnace watching his various compounds consumed by the fire, as each new theory and experiment in its turn proved fallacious and unavailing." Packing up his wife and four sons, von Pfautz fled the mockery of his friends and neighbors and settled in the New World, buying a large tract of land in Lancaster County, Pennsylvania, with the remains of his wealth.[2]

The alchemist's sons proved quick converts to American farm life, working the land, and they took to American democratic values as well, dropping the "von" from the family name and joining the rebellion against English rule. Gradually the family name was modified to Pfouts. Paris Pfouts's grandfather, George, married twice and had a son, George, Jr., as his only child by his second wife. Around the beginning of the nineteenth century, George Pfouts moved the family to northeast Ohio, and it was there the younger Pfouts grew to adulthood and became a merchant, ferrying dry goods from the East over the Allegheny Mountains to New Philadelphia, the settlement nearest the family farm.

In his memoirs, Paris Pfouts draws a detailed portrait of his father, George Pfouts, Jr., as a restless, energetic man, a natural athlete, skilled rider, hunter, and a seeker of wisdom in spiritual as well as business affairs, given to shifting gears frequently on both fronts. At age twenty-six he married a girl just turned sixteen, "the belle of the neighborhood," and proved prolific as a family man, too, fathering ten children over the next two decades. Paris, his fourth child and first son, was born on January 9, 1829, and took his middle name, Swazy, from one of the itinerant Methodist ministers who briefly converted his father while staying with the family.

After several changes of profession and moves among various small towns in Ohio, George Pfouts, Jr., took up the study of law and opened a practice as a notary public. Still active in politics, he was appointed postmaster of Mount Eaton, Ohio, in 1842 during the presidency of John Tyler. The next year, in 1843, he packed up the family for a fresh start and moved to Oregon, Missouri, just above St. Joseph in the untamed northwest corner of the state, near its border with Kansas and Nebraska. He farmed and raised cattle and also meant to resume his dry goods business. But he succumbed to a recurrent bout of bilious colic and the side effects of its supposed cure, a powerful dose of opiates, and died on June 24, 1845, his fifty-first birthday.[3]

Paris Pfouts was sixteen years old when his father died, just old enough to watch in frustration as his mother tried in vain to collect her late husband's various debts and maintain the value of his estate. Before long, Mrs. Pfouts was forced to take in boarders to make ends meet, and she reluctantly concluded to send Paris back to Ohio to learn the craft of printing, with the idea that he might become a newspaperman and help support his siblings. After a few weeks helping to harvest the farm's meager crops, Pfouts left for the trip back to New Philadelphia to begin a two-year apprenticeship with an old family friend, Charles H. Mitchener, the editor and publisher of the *Ohio Democrat*. In his memoirs, Pfouts admits that he had been an indifferent student up to that point and a disappointment to his father, and he repeats the bleak assessment of his future by a family friend: "He told me that I was not a boy of great mental promise, that my talents were about of a grade which, if properly cultivated, would entitle me to a fair position in society."

Arriving in his former hometown with two suits and $30 to his name, Pfouts took room and board with the Mitchener family and decided to apply himself to his work and prove his detractors wrong. Within weeks, he made himself a favorite of his boss and was given a wide range of responsibilities in the pressroom. After having confined his reading largely to pulp novels, Pfouts took advantage of the Mitcheners' library and immersed himself in Gibbon, Macaulay, and other classic historians, making up for wasted time in the classroom. He learned proper grammar and speech from a volunteer tutor. In short order he was rewarded with fresh responsibilities for writing some of the newspaper's articles and editorials.[4]

At the end of two years, young Pfouts could take satisfaction in having made good use of his opportunity. Yet his position in society remained an unsettled question and something of a sore point with him. He seemed to think his father's standing in Ohio gave him entrée into the drawing rooms of New Philadelphia, and he bristled when Mitchener sold a half-interest in the newspaper to his wife's brother, a Main Line Philadelphian who considered the apprentices little more than servants and treated them accordingly. On one memorable occasion, Pfouts took offense when Mrs. Mitchener, who shared her brother's attitude toward the hired help, ordered him to do the weekly wash, telling him preemptorily, "Paris, as soon as you and the other boys are done with your dinner, take that tub and bring it back full of water." Apprentice printers were not ordinarily required to perform household chores, and as Pfouts told the story, he responded defiantly by kicking the tub out of the front door and into the street. He later soothed things over with the Mitcheners, but he had shown that he would not tolerate a slight.

Of further significance, Pfouts's sojourn in New Philadelphia solidified his politics as a pro-slavery Democrat. His two years working for the newspaper coincided with the deepening rift between North and South over the issue of extending slavery into the new territories obtained as the fruits of war with Mexico, and young Pfouts came down squarely on the side of slavery and the South. In his memoirs, Pfouts does not dwell at any length on the reasons for this allegiance, except to say that he believed the Constitution granted slaveowners a right to keep their property. It may be that his teenage years in Missouri, where pro-slavery sentiment was widespread, contributed to his views. In any case, he embraced a cause that would put him on the wrong side of history.[5]

With his period of indenture completed and no immediate prospects for better employment at hand, Pfouts bade the Mitcheners farewell and took the coach to Pittsburgh, hoping for an opportunity in a bigger city. But the lone printing job he could find was setting type for a low-end newspaper, the *Gazette,* at a pay scale of twelve and a half cents per thousand ems—or about a dollar a day. After six months of scrimping and saving, Pfouts decided to return to Ohio. His only opportunity to better his situation had been the chance to marry a young woman who was infatuated with him and who brought a dowry of a farm and $10,000 in the bank. To his credit, he declined to marry for money and instead returned to New Philadelphia, where he moved in with his older sister, Rebecca, and took work as a clerk in a dry goods store. In the summer of 1848, he returned to northwest Missouri to see his mother, and it was there that he heard of the fabulous discoveries of gold in California. "The more I heard the subject of the mines discussed," Pfouts wrote, "the stronger my desire became to go."[6]

Following the familiar pattern, Pfouts joined a small company of other men, borrowed a pony, and arrived in Placerville, California, on September 20, 1849, after a "monotonous" cross country trip of four and a half months. What he saw there made a vivid impression on him: "hundreds of idle men around us, some drunk, others playing cards, while not a few were sick and emaciated, and all were dirty and bore a beggarly appearance." He and his partners sold their wagons, teams, and other cargo and bought a fleet of three small boats to ferry goods up the Sacramento River to the gold camps at the south end of the Trinity Mountains. Like others before him, Pfouts found river travel much more difficult than anticipated, and trade more treacherous. He spent the winter of 1850 quartered in a two-room cabin on the Trinity River without many comforts. When the weather permitted, he turned to mining and finally had some luck, accumulating $600 in gold dust after two months of picking and panning on a bar along the Trinity River.[7]

For the next four years, Pfouts lived the full spectrum of experience on the gold camp frontier. He had success in mining, trading, raising cattle and pigs, and buying and selling land. He had failures as well, notably an inability to drink in moderation. "Hardly a day passed that I did not make a few dollars in some way or another," Pfouts wrote in his memoirs, "and hardly a night went by that I was not more or less intoxicated. I had contracted another bad practice, which was growing on me—playing cards. I just commenced playing for whiskey, then for little articles of clothing, and finally for small stakes of money." What appealed to him most, Pfouts said, "was to get in company with a few convivial fellows, drink whiskey, sing songs, and tell stories."[8]

Recognizing the danger of surrendering to these favored pastimes, Pfouts got a grip on himself in the spring of 1854 and decided to return home, visit his family, and mend his ways. He found his mother remarried to a man he admired, and he decided to settle nearby, in St. Joseph, where he bought a half-interest in the *Gazette,* a weekly newspaper, and took on the duties of editor and publisher. Much to his embarrassment, Pfouts discovered that he was now utterly tongue-tied around young women of refinement, feeling that his life on the frontier had rendered him too coarse for polite society. Gradually he regained his footing, and within a few weeks he had fallen in love with Harriett Cundiff, the raven-haired younger sister of his business partner. They were married the next spring, on May 5, 1855, just before her sixteenth birthday.[9]

At the same time he took a wife, Pfouts joined the Freemasons and began a rapid ascent through their ranks to the position of worshipful master of the St. Joseph lodge. Honoring the secrecy of Masonic tradition, Pfouts reveals little of his involvement with the society, but it is plain that he sought in his new friendships a way to fraternize with other men while avoiding the temptations of drinking and gambling. In the middle decades of the nineteenth century, when many Americans declared themselves deists and resisted church affiliation, Masonry offered middle-class men a chance to gather and ruminate on spiritual questions and do good works. Pfouts's election to his lodge's highest post in the relatively short span of five years gave evidence of his popularity. At the newspaper, meanwhile, he led a vigorous campaign of opposition to the Know-Nothing movement, finding its anti-Catholicism offensive to his notions of freedom of religious worship and association. He began a family and seemed to be settling into the respectable life he had always craved, but by his own admission his taste for gambling eventually got the better of him. His game was draw poker, he confided in his memoirs, and the habit "continued to grow on me, until every hour I could possibly command away from the office was passed in playing cards." He promised himself again and again that he would quit, but found he could not.[10]

The outbreak of the Civil War presented Pfouts with a dilemma. Union troops occupied St. Joseph and stopped him from publishing a newspaper that advocated secession and supported the Confederacy. With his business shuttered indefinitely, Pfouts had no means of supporting his family, at a time when his wife was pregnant with their third child. He considered joining the Rebel army but opted instead to return to the West, where he hoped to rebuild his fortunes. He arrived in Denver on a hot, dusty afternoon in July 1861 with $7.50 in his pocket, a fraction of the amount that had launched his apprenticeship fifteen years earlier.

In partnership with a friend, Pfouts opened a dry goods store, cleverly fudging his lack of inventory by filling the place with boxes that looked full. He prospered and was able to bring his family to join him the next year. He kept his baser appetites in check and stayed active in Masonry, rising to become master of the Denver lodge, the second time in a year he was elected to the top position of a chapter. Federal troops threatened to arrest him on several occasions for his political sympathies, but he managed to remain free. A final business reversal awaited him when he lost his investment in a cattle drive, and in September 1863 he decided to abandon Colorado for the gold camps of Montana. He arranged for a friend, Samuel Russell, to accompany his family back to Missouri and to send him a shipment of dry goods for sale in Alder Gulch.[11]

Pfouts's journey from Denver to Virginia City included a difficult moment at Fort Bridger, in southwest Wyoming, when federal troops detained him and demanded that he swear an oath of loyalty to the United States. He did so, despite his continued support for the Confederacy, but was deeply offended. "This was the first time in my life, and the only time," he wrote in his memoirs, "that I was ever compelled to swear allegiance to my own country. I did it very reluctantly, and with many mental reservations."[12]

On arrival in Virginia City, toward the end of September 1863, Pfouts took stock of his new home and did not care very much for what he saw.

Paris Pfouts, president of the vigilantes. Courtesy of the Montana Historical Society.

On his first Sunday in town, he attended a session of the miners' court presided over by Gaylord G. Bissell, the Connecticut-born doctor who had memorably refused to name the infant settlement after Varina Davis, the first lady of the Confederacy. It was not so much Bissell's staunch Unionism that bothered Pfouts as the methods he used in his court to parcel out justice. The case Pfouts observed involved one miner accusing another of stealing gold dust from him. The sheriff, J. B. "Buzz" Caven, reported that he had searched the accused and found no evidence to support the charge of larceny, and after lengthy arguments from the lawyers for the two sides Bissell dismissed the case. He then assessed court costs against the plaintiff and ordered the man's cabin and horse to be sold immediately at public auction to satisfy the debt. The horse, Pfouts added, was bought at a steep discount of its actual value by the sheriff himself.[13]

In their diaries and letters, many settlers complained of unfairness in the way fees were imposed on the parties in miners' courts and people's courts, but Pfouts seemed especially offended, and his reaction may explain why he joined cause in the vigilance committee with men he would not otherwise have considered friends and allies. He and Wilbur Sanders could not possibly have differed more in their devotion to opposing sides in the Civil War and in their underlying beliefs about slavery and politics, yet they found common ground in concluding that the instruments of frontier justice were so fundamentally flawed that taking the law into their own hands was the only answer. They shared a commitment to Masonry and may have found a path of mutual trust in those ties, but in many other respects Pfouts's background gave him a closer bond to Henry Plummer—loss of a father as a teenager, resultant economic dislocation, the call to California, a hankering for liquor and cards, a streak of social ambition, an interest in politics, and a proven ability to win the votes of other men for offices of trust. The one crucial difference, of course, was that Pfouts avoided the violent encounters that marred Plummer's career.

What, if anything, did Pfouts think about the sheriff of Bannack? Until the trial of George Ives, it appears, Pfouts had never met Plummer and gave no indication that he shared any of the dark suspicions of Plummer harbored by Samuel Hauser, Nathaniel Langford, Francis Thompson, the victims of various stagecoach holdups, and others, including the family of Sidney Edgerton, the appointed but still unsworn chief justice of Idaho Territory. Pfouts had been a late arrival in Virginia City. He bought a sixteen-by-thirty-two-foot log cabin with a dirt roof that fronted Wallace Street, fixed it up, and with the arrival of his shipment of dry goods in late November 1863 opened his shop for business. He had no immediate plans to send his profits back east or to return there himself, and thus did not have reason to fear becoming a target of the robberies taking place on the trails between Bannack and Alder Gulch and out of the territory. Still, Pfouts insists in his memoirs that he was alarmed by the crime wave, outraged by the murder of Tiebolt, and determined to take a hand in "adopting some measures of redress . . . which would render life and property more secure."[14]

During the course of the Ives trial, Pfouts wrote later, he and Sanders urged "immediate and decisive action," though he does not specify the objectives they had in mind. The best guess is that he and Sanders considered detaining Ives's associates, including Aleck Carter, when their names were raised as accomplices in Tiebolt's murder. But the Vigilance Committee was not formally organized for another "three or four days," Pfouts wrote, until about fifty men had volunteered to join its ranks. Several meetings ensued, including one at a distinctively painted "blue house" belonging to Jeremiah M. Fox where some of the veterans of the 1856 San Francisco vigilance committee helped write the by-laws to govern the committee's actions. It was at a meeting Pfouts missed that he was elected president of the committee, and he claims in his memoirs that he demurred at first but finally agreed to serve after the "urgent persuasion" of the other leaders. In the same election, James Williams was named executive officer of the vigilantes, and John Lott was chosen to be secretary and treasurer.[15]

In the coming days, Pfouts said, more than a thousand men joined the vigilance movement, and he organized them into various companies and chose lieutenants and captains to lead them. It strikes a modern observer as more than a little strange that Pfouts could have enjoyed such a swift and thorough success in recruiting these forces. It was "perfectly wonderful to me," Pfouts wrote later, that so many men took the vigilante oath and joined the ranks, until "it was difficult to find . . . a good man who was not a vigilante." If, as all of the defenders of the vigilantes insist, the gold camps were infested with vast numbers of lawless hoodlums, it could not have been nearly so easy to assemble a force of overwhelming magnitude that included nearly every settler in the area. The size and strength of the criminal element simply has to have been exaggerated, though that does not mean the fear of crime was any less genuine than the settlers recalled.[16]

In any case, the Vigilance Committee took no immediate steps to capture or kill anyone. Instead, its leaders waited to learn the results of James Williams's expedition to Cottonwood to capture Aleck Carter. In Bannack, Henry Plummer viewed the doings in Alder Gulch with extreme alarm. The vigilance committee, he warned everyone who would listen, meant to impose its authority on the settlers of Bannack and would hang anyone who stood in the way. Plummer said he expected to be a target, along with his deputies Ned Ray and Buck Stinson, and he added that the leading citizens of the town might be in peril as well, including his patron,

George Chrisman, the storekeeper and county commissioner. Plummer's demeanor seems to have been persuasive, as several Bannack residents came to share his concern that the vigilantes represented a threat to them. On December 27, 1863, the Sunday after Christmas, Plummer signed a power of attorney authorizing Chrisman to act on his behalf in collecting a debt of $3,500 he was owed on the sale of a half-interest in a mining claim on the Dakota Lode—evidence that Plummer feared the vigilantes' intentions toward him and anticipated the likelihood of having to flee.[17]

On that same Sunday, Mary Edgerton wrote her family back home that her husband, Sidney, hoped to be able to leave for Washington sometime during the next week. "It is not safe now for men to travel alone if they have much money with them," she explained. "There are too many highway robbers." But a vigilance committee was at work, she added, clearing away the criminals. One had been hanged and the committee "likely will hang others, so it will be rather safer now . . . " The committee's intentions plainly were no secret to the chief justice and his wife.[18]

For all the confusion, distrust, and fear that gripped the Montana gold camps in this period, the situation actually seems to have been fairly clear-cut. Armed robbers had been holding up stagecoaches and a brutal murder had been committed. A strong case had been made against a suspect in the murder case and he had been executed. He was believed to have accomplices and a posse was pursuing them. Other robbers were suspected as well. A private army was gathering to find them, judge them, and execute them, making the trails safe for commerce with family, friends, and business associates back east. Or was it that simple?

James Williams led his men into Cottonwood on the afternoon of Saturday, December 26, 1863, the day after Christmas, and discovered that Aleck Carter had fled along with his friends. Though his posse had prepared more carefully this time, the trip proved to be almost as grueling as the hunt for George Ives. One night on the trail, the group had encountered an Indian, who sold them venison and rabbit. Charles Beehrer, a strapping young brewer who volunteered to pay for the meat, advised his fellow riders to cook it carefully and thoroughly before eating it. But they did not, and most of the posse spent a sleepless night on the trail desperately sick to their stomachs.[19]

After missing their prey, the men spent two nights in Cottonwood at a small hotel run by two Mexicans, resting and allowing their horses and mules to recuperate as well. They decided against pursuing Carter into the wilds of the Rocky Mountains beyond Cottonwood, and on Monday, December 28, 1863, deeply frustrated at the failure of their mission, they regrouped for the ride back to Virginia City. Williams could not help wondering if Carter had received a warning from someone that the posse was on its way. Why else ride off into the wilderness in the midst of winter—and with a hangover at that? The more he thought about it, the more Williams came to suspect that "Red" Yeager had lied to him. What had Yeager been doing in Cottonwood? Had he gone there to find Carter? Had he delivered the warning himself?

Just how quickly the cloud of accusation coalesced around Yeager is difficult to say. But in addition to the faulty information he gave them about Carter's whereabouts, the men of the posse had two other issues to consider. Yeager had arrived in their midst three months earlier in company with "Doc" Howard and others who were branded as "cut-throats and robbers" by Henry Plummer and who were now fugitives suspected of the murder of Lloyd Magruder. And Yeager had gone to work as a bartender and handyman at the Rattlesnake Ranch, a venue believed to have harbored some of the armed robbers active on the trail from Bannack to Alder Gulch. In the weeks after the bizarre *Rashomon* night of November 14, 1863, when Yeager had attended to Wilbur Sanders and Jack Gallagher and other wayfarers at the ranch, its proprietors, Frank Parish and Bill Bunton, had abandoned it and moved away. What had Yeager been doing since then?

On the trip home, the weather turned arctic, as it can sometimes in Montana. The temperature plummeted, the winds picked up, and it began to snow. Visibility grew dim. The horses and mules had to pick their way through eighteen inches of fresh powder and drifts two and three times higher. When the posse stopped to make camp, the animals struggled to paw their way down through the snow to find grass to eat. The men lacked adequate blankets and robes and were too cold to sleep comfortably at night. At one point the temperature reached thirty-three degrees below zero. "I never saw such weather," Williams told an interviewer years afterward, "nothing like it." For three days, the posse pressed southward in wretched conditions, growing hungrier and colder and more miserable with each passing mile.[20]

Eventually, the riders spotted the landmark Beaverhead Rock and regained their bearings. They made camp nearby, but as if to test their limits, the weather turned even worse. A full blizzard began, and the men could not find adequate firewood to create warmth. They subsisted on cold bacon and stale bread. The horses and mules were turned loose to forage, and scattered in the howling wind. It was during this period of intense suffering, Williams confided later, that he came to believe Yeager was responsible for leading him and his men on a wild goose chase of biblical proportion.[21]

On New Year's Eve, the final day of 1863, the storm finally abated, allowing Williams and his men to gather their stock, saddle up, and continue their journey home. When they reached the familiar trail that led from Alder Gulch to Bannack, Williams decided to press on toward Rattlesnake Ranch and try to find Yeager. Soon they met "X" Beidler coming in the opposite direction and learned that the diminutive guard from the Ives trial—the one who had yelled, "Ask him how long he gave the Dutchman!"—had some vital information to impart. On the day after Ives was hanged, Beidler had departed Nevada City to help search for an overdue wagon train believed to be disabled somewhere on the road from Salt Lake City to the Alder Gulch mines. He had wandered through the same harsh conditions as the Williams posse. "As cold a night as I ever camped out in my life," he wrote later in his memoirs. "[I] danced around a green willow fire all night to the music of the coyotes . . . " After helping to rescue the freighters, he started back for Nevada City and ran into a succession of notables.[22]

First, Beidler related, he encountered "Dutch John" Wagner, who was in wretched condition and suffering from frostbite. Unaware that Wagner was a suspect in the Moody wagon train robbery, and that he had been wounded in the shoulder by a gunshot during the episode, Beidler made no attempt to arrest or detain Wagner. Instead, Beidler ministered to Wagner's frozen extremities, bathing his hands and feet in warm water. In later years, Beidler served as a deputy sheriff and deputy federal marshal and fancied himself something of a detective, but he was utterly oblivious to the signs that Wagner might be a fugitive. Even after Wagner "acted very uneasy" and asked too many questions about the Ives trial and the search for the Moody robbers, Beidler allowed him to go on his way. A day later, when he passed a wagon train headed south to Salt Lake City, Beidler learned from its passengers that Wagner was a wanted man. By then it was too late to capture him.[23]

Next, Beidler said, he had returned to Bannack, where he stopped in Durant's saloon for a drink and a game of billiards and was warned that Sheriff Plummer's two deputies, Buck Stinson and Ned Ray, were looking for him. He met the two men in town and had a tense, wary exchange of pleasantries, then encountered them again the next night at Rattlesnake Ranch, which remained available as a refuge for travelers after its owners vacated it. Stinson and Ray had pestered Beidler with questions about the vigilantes and their intentions, giving Beidler the impression they were desperately afraid a company of the Vigilance Committee must be on its way to look for them. Stinson was widely considered culpable in the shooting death of D. H. Dillingham, and both deputies were suspect for their odd conduct in the aftermath of the robbery of Leroy Southmayd. During the night they spent at Rattlesnake Ranch, Beidler said, Stinson and Ray barricaded the door with a heavy table and threatened to hold him hostage if the vigilantes came for them. Stinson had not forgotten that Beidler dug his grave after the Dillingham affair, and Beidler spent a sleepless night worried about reprisals. Stinson and Ray were visibly nervous as well, up several times in the night to see if riders were approaching.[24]

Beidler left the ranch in the morning, anxious to get away from Stinson and Ray and return to Alder Gulch. He was relieved to encounter the Williams posse, and he urged them to pursue Stinson and Ray. But Williams had only one target in mind—Yeager. He asked if Beidler had seen him. No, Beidler replied, but he thought Yeager might be somewhere in the vicinity of Rattlesnake Ranch, because Stinson and Ray had mentioned his name.

With this fresh scent of his prey, Williams organized a small company of eight men to accompany him to Rattlesnake Ranch. The rest of the posse was sent to Dempsey's ranch, on the road back to Alder Gulch, and told to wait there. On New Year's Day, 1864, a Friday, Williams and his band of riders headed southwest in the direction of Bannack. They stopped around midnight at Stone's ranch for fresh horses and continued their journey without pausing for sleep. In the afternoon of the next day, they arrived at Rattlesnake Ranch and Williams pounded on the front door. Stinson opened the door, pistol in hand, and lowered it after surveying the forces arrayed before him. To the surprise of Stinson and Ray, Williams said he was not after them but wanted "Red" Yeager for questioning. They replied that he was staying in a small lodge several hundred yards up Rattlesnake Creek. Given their leave, Stinson and Ray saddled up quickly, fled the ranch, and rode back to Bannack.

Williams now led his men up the banks of the creek to a hut where they dismounted, guns drawn, and surrounded the little structure. Williams pushed aside the door flap and called inside, "It's mighty cold! Won't you let a fellow warm himself?" Yeager invited him to come inside and surrendered without protest when Williams told him he was under arrest.[25]

Given the late hour, Williams decided to spend the night at Rattlesnake Ranch, where he and his men and their captive had the premises to themselves. According to Williams, Yeager conducted himself with a good deal of composure. He was told only that he would be taken to Virginia City for questioning, but he sensed he was in dire jeopardy and seemed resigned to whatever outcome awaited him. In the morning, the party mounted up for the ride back to Dempsey's ranch to reunite with the main posse and continue on to Alder Gulch. Along the way, Williams gave his companions a moment of comic relief when his mule stumbled on the frozen trail, pitched forward, completed two full somersaults, and came to rest in deep snow without injury to man or animal.[26]

On arrival at Dempsey's, matters took a more serious turn. The bartender at Dempsey's, it happened, was George Brown, an itinerant ranch hand who had made the mistake of appearing as a witness for the defense during Ives's trial. Brown's attempt to provide an alibi for Ives had proved unavailing, since no time of death for the victim was ever established, but fairly or not his testimony placed him in a suspicious light as the search for Ives's accomplices picked up momentum. The presence of Yeager and Brown under one roof produced a major break in solving the crime wave of recent weeks. Under intense questioning from Williams and others in the posse, Yeager broke down and admitted that he had warned Aleck Carter to flee Cottonwood. Indeed, Yeager said, he had carried a written message that said, "Get up and dust, and lie low for black ducks," a warning that vigilantes were on their way. And, Yeager added, it was Brown who had written the message.[27]

Yeager's confession had a predictably keen effect on his pursuers. Here was proof that their wretched fool's errand to Cottonwood had been inflicted on them by a pair of Ives's cronies, and some of them began agitating for the immediate execution of both. Given their suffering, the desire for vengeance was understandable, but a nagging question intruded. Had either man committed a capital felony? Was it a crime deserving of the death penalty to have written a warning to Ives's alleged accomplices that a posse was after them? To have delivered that message? To have lied about it? The apparent simplicity of the situation came unglued rather quickly when the vigilantes confronted a pair of minor criminals whose actual degree of association with genuine killers and robbers could not be established.

Determined to let his men decide the outcome in a democratic fashion, Williams invited the members of the posse to walk outside Dempsey's ranch and join him on the bridge over the Stinking Water River. "Now, boys," he said, "you have heard all about this matter, and I want you to vote according to your consciences. If you think they ought to suffer punishment, say so. If you think they ought to go free, vote for it." All those who favored hanging, Williams said, should step to the right side of the bridge. Williams then stepped to the right, signaling his preference. Soon most of the men joined him, sealing the fate of Yeager and Brown.[28]

But then an unsettling thing happened. One of the men made plain his discomfort with the verdict by announcing that he planned to leave and not take part in the executions. According to Thomas Dimsdale, the vigilantes' first chronicler and great defender, several of the members of the posse responded by leveling their shotguns at their comrade and cocking the hammers. This moment of dissent in the ranks, quelled by force of arms, gives the first tangible evidence that the vigilantes would have a trickier challenge than anticipated in administering justice. In fact, it appears that Williams was unsettled by the episode, because he ordered Yeager and Brown to be kept in custody and taken to Virginia City, presumably to face a tribunal organized by Pfouts and Sanders and the leaders of the Vigilance Committee. Acting on Williams's orders, a vanguard of seven riders took the two prisoners and left Dempsey's for Laurin's ranch, the next station on the trail to Alder Gulch.[29]

Had Williams been satisfied with the vote on the bridge and convinced that Yeager and Brown deserved hanging, presumably he would have acted to carry out the executions on the spot. That he did not suggests uncertainty. And what happened next stirred even more confusion, triggering a debate that echoes to this day. Leaving Dempsey's with the main body of the posse, Williams arrived at Laurin's about two hours later, around dusk, and found the prisoners secured for the night. Exhausted, he lay down for a brief nap and was soon sound asleep. At ten o'clock that night, just a few hours later, Williams was awakened and summoned to the ranch's main room. There he found the other members of his posse, who had been discussing the danger of conveying the two prisoners any farther along a trail that had sprung so many ambushes in recent months. The brief for executing Yeager and Brown had been renewed while Williams slept, and the men expressed a fresh desire to hang the accused without further delay. Williams accepted their decision in spite of his misgivings. He wakened Yeager and Brown and before he could say a word, Yeager spoke. "I know I am going to die," he said with resignation. "I am going to be hanged."

Nodding assent, Williams replied, "It's pretty rough."

Yeager spoke again. "It is pretty rough," he said, "but I merited this years ago. What I wanted to say is that I know all about the gang, and there are men in it that deserve this more than I do. But I should die happy if I could see them hanged or know that it would be done." According to Dimsdale, one of the posse responded, "You know, Red, men have been shot down in broad daylight—not for the money, or even for hatred, but for luck, and it must be put a stop to." It would be best, the vigilantes said, for Yeager to tell everything he knew about the criminal enterprises in the area, and he agreed to do so.[30]

Yeager had grown up in modest comfort on a farm in eastern Iowa, just south of Cedar Rapids on the Cedar River, where his father raised crops and livestock and also practiced law. "Red," as he was known for the color of his hair, left home at age seventeen, shortly after his mother died giving birth to her tenth child, and moved to Washington Territory with an older brother. He became a freighter and later followed the call of the gold discoveries in the Rocky Mountains, eventually joining the party led by "Doc" Howard that crossed the Bitterroots from Idaho to Montana. Separated from the disciplines of family and home, he gave in to the lure of rough company. He might have died in oblivion, save that James and Granville Stuart knew him from their time in Iowa and remembered seeing him study as a young boy in the little schoolhouse in the settlement of West Liberty. They were surprised when they learned the extent of his fall from grace.[31]

According to Dimsdale, who published his chronicle of the events in the form of a newspaper serial a year and a half later, Yeager made a full and damning confession and provided a list of the alleged members of a tightly knit organization of highway robbers. The leader was Henry Plum-

Thomas Dimsdale, chronicler and defender of the vigilantes. Courtesy of the Montana Historical Society.

mer, he said, and the second-in-command was Bill Bunton, the half-owner of the Rattlesnake Ranch. Bunton's partner, Frank Parish, was part of the criminal enterprise, as were two dozen other men, some whose names were familiar—Cyrus Skinner, the saloonkeeper at the Elkhorn, George Ives, and Plummer's deputies, Stinson and Ray—while others were obscure and some known simply by alias, including one "Mexican Frank." Yeager said the men associated with "Doc" Howard were also involved. As Yeager recited the names of the conspirators, Williams had a member of the posse write them down. Then, most remarkably, Yeager volunteered that the group used a secret phrase for identity—"I am innocent"—and recognized each other by use of a special "sailor's knot" on their neckties and by shaving their mustaches and goatees in a unique pattern.[32]

These last details, so compellingly specific at first glance, have provided historians with an insurmountable challenge in the decades since Dimsdale's account first appeared in print. They simply do not ring true. Why would the members of a small band of highwaymen have used special signs to recognize each other? Why would they have advertised common cause by the use of distinctive facial hair or neckwear or any other signal? Why would they have had a password? And if they did, why would it be the odd phrase, "I am innocent"? In recent years, many a thoughtful observer has been moved to ask if "Red" Yeager actually spilled the beans on a genuine criminal operation and offered up the minutiae of their code of behavior, or if something quite different—something much less explicit and damning—actually occurred on that night.

As it happened, Williams decided immediately after hearing Yeager's confession to proceed with his execution and Brown's. The two were taken out behind Laurin's ranch to the banks of the Stinking Water River and hanged side by side from a tree. Hand-lettered signs were pinned to the back of each man: "Red! Road Agent and Messenger." "Brown! Corresponding Secretary." The bodies were left dangling for several days, then taken down and buried.[33]

The shaky authenticity of Yeager's purported confession was magnified by the posse's rush to inflict capital punishment. Had Yeager provided detailed evidence against the members of a crime ring, his testimony would have been of incalculable value to the leaders of the Vigilance Committee starting their work in Alder Gulch. Their duty to "try all criminals that shall be arrested" and render justice, sworn in their by-laws, could only have been aided by evidence from a member of the cabal. The fact that no written list of the names of the accused has been found, when other key documents of the Vigilance Committee were faithfully preserved, gives further concern that Yeager did not provide the information Dimsdale later claimed.

On the other hand, it does not seem nearly so improbable to conclude that Yeager gave some kind of confession to Williams that night, satisfying the posse that Yeager and Brown had acted to warn Aleck Carter to flee and that they had done so in cahoots with some form of organized criminal gang. As an employee of the Rattlesnake Ranch, a vital way station, Yeager had been in a position to know at least some information about the affairs of the men who owned and frequented the place. He spoke with particular venom about Bill Bunton, his former boss, saying it was Bunton who had lured him into criminal activity, first in the gold camps west of the Bitterroots and later at the ranch. Whatever the reason for their final falling out, Yeager leveled a "deathbed" accusation against Bunton that carried the same ring of truth that characterized Ives's indictment of Carter.[34]

Until the night of Yeager's confession, the members of the posse and the leaders of the Vigilance Committee had taken no steps to capture, judge, or punish any of the figures they broadly suspected of criminal activity. The posse was in pursuit of one man, Carter, and had pointedly ignored the opportunity to take Plummer's deputies, Stinson and Ray, into custody when they had the chance a day earlier. Beidler, who fancied himself a man hunter, had let "Dutch John" Wagner slip away and had even given him first aid. The Vigilance Committee had compiled no list of wanted men and had taken no steps to enforce order. But that was about to change. In whatever form it actually occurred, Yeager's confession made a vivid, persuasive impression—and we know this to be so because the mission of the vigilantes changed in a fundamental way after he uttered it.

CHAPTER THIRTEEN

"Red" Yeager's List

With their quarry still dangling from a tree behind Laurin's ranch, James Williams and his posse began the ride back to Alder Gulch to report on their mission. Arriving at Nevada City on Tuesday, January 5, 1864, Williams went into the Lott brothers' store and told John Lott about the executions of "Red" Yeager and George Brown. The significant news, from Lott's perspective as an officer of the Vigilance Committee, was that Yeager had disclosed the names of men allegedly involved in the string of stagecoach robberies and violent encounters that had convulsed the mining camps for the past several weeks. Lott and Williams hurried along to Virginia City, two miles up the gulch, to share the information with Paris Pfouts, the committee's president.[1]

Two full weeks had elapsed since the hanging of George Ives, and the Vigilance Committee had yet to take any steps toward imposing its brand of extralegal justice on the towns of Alder Gulch or Bannack. The committee's by-laws called for an executive committee of seventeen, led by Pfouts, to act on behalf of the larger committee whose membership now numbered in the hundreds. The executive committee was charged with conducting a review of criminal acts and deciding the fate of those believed responsible. No provision was made for public trial, nor did defendants enjoy any of the rights given in a modern court of law, including the right to face one's accusers. The executive committee intended to act as a secret tribunal.[2]

With Yeager's confession in hand, Pfouts and the other members of the executive committee worked to sort through the criminal incidents of recent weeks and figure out who was responsible. Aleck Carter remained at large, accused as an accomplice in the death of Nicholas Tiebolt. "Dutch John" Wagner and Steve Marshland were wanted for the botched robbery of the Moody wagon train that left both men wounded. Bill Bunton and Frank Parish, the owners of the Rattlesnake Ranch, stood accused of complicity in the "Bummer Dan" McFadden robbery. "Doc" Howard and his gang were the subjects of a manhunt in the Far West for the presumed murder of Lloyd Magruder. But the most pressing issue by far was the role of Henry Plummer, the sheriff of Bannack, in the robbery of Leroy Southmayd. Plummer's deputies, Buck Stinson and Ned Ray, had acted very suspiciously in shadowing Southmayd after the incident, and now Yeager had accused Plummer himself of masterminding that robbery and others.

As we have seen, suspicion of Plummer was a gradually unfolding thing, as one settler after another found cause to wonder if the elected lawman of Bannack was using his position to spy on those planning to travel with large caches of gold dust and then sending agents to ambush them and rob them along the trails out of the territory. Francis Thompson, the banker who had befriended Plummer and served in his wedding to Electa Bryan, still lived under the same roof with Plummer and continued to find him "pleasant and agreeable," in Thompson's phrase, even as he grew more and more convinced that his friend might be a criminal. Something of a last straw for Thompson occurred on New Year's Day, 1864, when Plummer came into his dry goods store on the main street of Bannack. Three young women, one of them the daughter of Sidney Edgerton, the territorial chief justice, were shopping and chatting with Thompson when the sheriff entered and greeted them cordially. Moments later, a driver from the Oliver & Company stagecoach line walked into the store. "Immediately," Thompson recounted, "both men began to fumble for their arms, and I saw there was going to be trouble." Thompson said he could not ascertain the cause of the difficulty, but the Oliver stage had been the target in the Southmayd robbery, and Oliver's drivers were leery of Plummer.[3]

As Plummer and the driver moved toward each other, Thompson wrote later, "both began cursing and the young ladies fled shrieking to the street. I ran between the two men facing Plummer and put my two hands against his shoulders[,] which hindered him from quickly getting at his heavy sheath knife." The other man fumbled for a pistol but could not pull it free.

Thompson pushed Plummer toward the back of the store, "where he made a lunge by my face with his knife, but was unable to reach his victim." With that, Thompson shoved Plummer out the back door and slammed it shut. The driver escaped out the front door and hurried out of town.

"If I ever understood the quarrel between the two men I do not recall it," Thompson added, "but Plummer afterward apologized for beginning a quarrel in my store, and more especially when ladies were present, but said I saved the rascal's life." It was the only time, Thompson said, that he personally witnessed the violent side of Plummer's nature. He might have concluded that Plummer was under intense strain, knowing that a posse was searching for accomplices in the Tiebolt killing while a Vigilance Committee was getting organized in Alder Gulch. How else to explain Plummer's rage, unprovoked and unleashed in the presence of prominent young women and a close friend still clinging to the hope that Plummer was not what he seemed?

With the arrival of the Williams posse back in Virginia City, the Vigilance Committee concluded that its jurisdiction must be extended to Bannack, where Stinson, Ray, and Plummer would have to answer for their crimes. Other suspected criminals would be addressed in due course, but the top priority now was the sheriff of Bannack, freshly accused by Yeager. In tying Plummer and Bunton together as leaders of the criminal gang, Yeager broadened the focus of the inquiry involving the sheriff beyond the Southmayd robbery to include the "Bummer Dan" McFadden affair and other incidents. If Plummer was in league with Bunton—and if, as Thompson came to believe, Plummer was a secret part-owner of the Rattlesnake Ranch—then there was powerful new evidence implicating him. "After acquiring a full knowledge of these facts, from confessions of members of the band and other sources," Pfouts wrote later, "the Executive Committee decided that parties should be sent from Virginia City to Bannack City," to arrest and execute members of the gang, "the sheriff, Henry Plummer, being one of the number." On the morning of Friday, January 8, 1864, John Lott and three other men left Alder Gulch for the seventy-mile trip to Bannack. They intended to recruit members there and try to convince them that Plummer and his deputies deserved to be hanged.[4]

For all the well-established suspicion and hostility that had come to surround Plummer, Lott's small committee nonetheless faced a ticklish task. Most of Plummer's detractors lived in Alder Gulch, and those who lived in Bannack had rarely expressed their beliefs publicly. True, Francis Thompson and Sidney Edgerton had blurted out their growing conviction that Plummer was behind the rash of crimes, but that accusation had taken place in a private conversation. Nathaniel Langford believed Plummer had tried to rob him, but Langford had gone east and his travails were unknown to the friends he left behind. Henry Tilden, the young member of the Edgerton party who claimed he was accosted by Plummer one night in November 1863, had kept the story to himself at the Edgerton family's insistence. In public, at least, the people of Bannack paid respect to Plummer and treated him with deference as the town's lawman. He still enjoyed the support of George Chrisman, the county commissioner, and other leading citizens. To bring a majority of Bannack's residents into open condemnation of their sheriff would be difficult and potentially dangerous.

Complicating matters, "Dutch John" Wagner managed to get captured at this exact moment, muddling the duties of the Vigilance Committee. After encountering "X" Beidler on the trail, a weak and injured Wagner had continued on his way south, hoping to reach Salt Lake City before the members of the Moody wagon train tracked him down and confirmed that he was the man they had wounded during the attempted robbery. Because of the harsh weather, Wagner was forced to stick close to the trail, where he passed several parties of travelers. Eventually, he was recognized by a freighter named Neil Howie, who disarmed him and put him under arrest.

For those dissatisfied with the verdicts reached by the various people's courts that had acted to date, the examination of "Dutch John" Wagner came very close to meeting the strict standard of guilt beyond a reasonable doubt. After Howie detained him, Wagner was brought into the circle of a campfire built by a large party of freighters, where he was stripped of his shirt and found to have been wounded in the same spot on the shoulder as the robber repulsed by the Moody wagon train. Under close questioning, Wagner swore that the wound had occurred innocently, when he fell asleep by a fire of his own making and rolled into it, setting his clothes ablaze and igniting a cap and ball from his own pistol. The freighters, scoffing at his account, promptly conducted an experiment. They fixed a cap onto a stick, held it in the hot flames at the center of their campfire, and demonstrated that a man would be burned to cinders before a cap exploded from the heat. Wagner did not bear any signs of having suffered burns. For good measure, the freighters also determined that a pistol discharged from a holster at Wagner's side could not have wounded him at the angle of his injury.[5]

Rather than execute him on the spot, Wagner's captors decided to return him to Bannack to face further interrogation and disposition by the authorities there. Howie, who would prove his fitness as a lawman in coming years as sheriff of Virginia City and as federal marshal of Montana Territory, took on the job of escorting Wagner to the gold camp. Another freighter, John Fetherstun, agreed to act as Howie's deputy. The two guarded their prisoner closely for three days and nights on the trail, finally arriving at Horse Prairie, twelve miles south of Bannack, on the afternoon of Saturday, January 9, 1864. Leaving Fetherstun behind with the prisoner, Howie rode ahead to reconnoiter and determine who was in charge and whether it was safe to proceed into town. He feared Wagner might have associates eager to free him.

Entering Bannack, Howie soon encountered Sheriff Plummer and informed him of Wagner's capture. According to Howie, Plummer offered to take Wagner into custody and conduct a trial on the charge of attempted robbery of Moody's stagecoach. "This new way our people have of hanging men without law or evidence isn't exactly the thing," Howie quoted the sheriff as saying. "It's time a stop was put to it." Not trusting Plummer, Howie declined to turn over his prisoner and said he would maintain custody until a people's tribunal determined what to do with him. Plummer was unhappy with his answer, Howie said, but did not press the point.[6]

At about the same time Plummer and Howie were engaged in debate, John Lott and his three colleagues arrived on the outskirts of Bannack, completing their trip from Alder Gulch. They looked up Wilbur Sanders, one of the founders of the Vigilance Committee, and other leading citizens they believed they could trust, including Plummer's patron, shopkeeper George Chrisman. In the late afternoon, a group of about two dozen men crowded into a miner's cabin and listened as Lott described the evidence against Plummer and his deputies, Stinson and Ray, culminating with the accusations leveled by "Red" Yeager. The sheriff and his deputies were road agents, Lott said, and the Vigilance Committee proposed that they be executed. For Chrisman and many of the other leaders of Bannack, the charges against Plummer came as a shock. No one was unaware of the suspicions of Plummer that had been gathering like a caustic, alkaloid cloud over the past weeks, but the idea that the sheriff actually commanded a crime ring was new to them and did not seem entirely credible. Even

Neil Howie, left, and John Fetherstun, who arrested "Dutch John" Wagner and brought him to Bannack. Courtesy of the Montana Historical Society.

though Sanders lent his support to the effort, the Bannack leaders balked at the suggestion of convicting and hanging the sheriff. As darkness fell, the men remained at an impasse, troubled and unsure what to do next.[7]

Meanwhile, Fetherstun had grown anxious about remaining alone in the field with Wagner. For all his injuries, Wagner was a powerful man, a shade over six feet tall and stoutly built. Fetherstun thought Wagner was watching him a little too closely, angling for an opening to snatch a gun and escape. He decided to bring his prisoner into town and took him to Durant's saloon, one of Bannack's central meeting places, hoping to find Howie there. While Fetherstun and Wagner were waiting at Durant's, Plummer's two deputies, Stinson and Ray, came into the saloon and spoke to them, making Fetherstun extremely uncomfortable. Within a matter of minutes, more than a dozen men entered Durant's and seemed to be taking an inordinate amount of interest in his prisoner, agitating Fetherstun to the extent that he considered drawing his pistol and taking his chances. The critical moment passed when one of the men announced that the group intended to take custody of Wagner, and Fetherstun allowed them to do so, seeing he was outnumbered. What Fetherstun did not know was that the men who came in after Stinson and Ray and took his prisoner were the same leaders who had been called together by John Lott within the past hour and who were still in a quandary over Sheriff Plummer. They had heard of Wagner's capture and they meant to interrogate him and try to find out if he knew anything about the sheriff's activities.[8]

Leaving Durant's a few minutes after his prisoner was taken, Fetherstun followed the group to the small cabin where they had met earlier, and it was there that he learned he was dealing with a Vigilance Committee in the making, one that shared his suspicions of Stinson and Ray. Neil Howie arrived at the cabin moments later and he, too, learned the actual situation. The vigilantes, satisfied that Howie and Fetherstun were acting as bona fide lawmen, made them part of the enterprise, and together the vigilantes from Alder Gulch and the top men of Bannack conducted a close examination of Wagner.

The decision to execute Wagner was reached fairly quickly. His wound and bogus alibi gave his accusers adequate evidence to satisfy them that he was involved in the attempted robbery of the Moody stagecoach. He had been the dominant partner during the crime and had fired his pistols at the driver, missing only when his horse reared. By the standards of his inquisitors, he was guilty of attempted murder and thus deserving of hanging.

But they also wanted him to confirm that Plummer was his secret collaborator, and this Wagner declined to do. Despite intense questioning, Wagner stubbornly refused to implicate the sheriff in planning the assault on the Moody party. Writing an account of the episode a year and a half later in his newspaper, Thomas Dimsdale insisted that Wagner ultimately confessed and corroborated Yeager's list of conspirators, but this seems far-fetched. Had Wagner given convincing testimony seconding Yeager's accusations, the infant Vigilance Committee of Bannack would have had very little trouble concluding that Plummer was a criminal mastermind. Instead, the community leaders of Bannack continued to express sharp misgivings about Plummer's complicity and plainly were not ready, after hearing from Wagner, to reach a guilty verdict against the sheriff.[9]

As a measure of his frustration over the stalemate that lingered into the wee hours of Sunday morning, January 10, 1864, it is noteworthy that Wilbur Sanders toyed with the notion of taking matters into his own hands. With the Bannack vigilantes still hesitant to act, Sanders briefly considered a plot to assassinate Plummer. Talking over his plan with his uncle, Sidney Edgerton, the territorial chief justice, Sanders suggested "that someone warn Plummer of his danger, and when he went to the stable for his horse have men concealed there to kill him." According to Edgerton's daughter, Mattie, who overheard the conversation and reported it later in her memoirs, Sanders and her father decided that doing so would make them as guilty as the men they meant to bring to justice. "On due consideration," she wrote, "this seemed to appear more unlawful than previous hangings, and the idea was abandoned." But it stands as ample proof that matters were not resolved by the interrogation of Wagner.[10]

At some point during that night, Sanders and Edgerton decided to try one final avenue of appeal to the Bannack vigilantes. Assembling the group once again in the predawn hours, they brought forward their young associate, Tilden, to give his account of the night of November 14, 1863, when he said Plummer and two other men stopped him at gunpoint on the prairie south of Bannack and tried to rob him. It was a story the Edgerton family themselves had doubted at the time, and to this day it does not carry an especially convincing ring, yet after hearing this concluding piece of testimony the Bannack elders at last gave their consent to the hanging of the sheriff.[11]

◆ ◇ ◆

Martha "Mattie" Edgerton, the chief justice's daughter, who overheard plans to execute Henry Plummer. Courtesy of the Montana Historical Society.

Daylight broke on an arctic scene in Bannack. Temperatures in town had reached forty degrees below zero during the week, and some settlers reported mercury freezing in the bulbs of their thermometers. At the Vail family's cabin, Francis Thompson took his place at the breakfast table with a troubled conscience. He had been present during the deliberations of Bannack's newly constituted Vigilance Committee, and he knew that its members had finally acquiesced in the decision to execute Plummer, Stinson, and Ray. James Vail was absent on business that morning, but his wife, Martha Jane, prepared breakfast for the rest of the household, which included her two children, Thompson's young partner, Joseph Swift, and Henry Plummer.

Thompson alone knew the "terrible secret," as he called it, that Plummer would be captured and hanged later in the day, and he remembered that "an unusual silence seemed to brood over the little settlement at Bannack." In his memoirs, Thompson reverts to the third person in describing himself, a sign that after many years he remained unsettled by the episode and the choice he confronted between "love for an individual and stern duty to the whole community." The temptation to warn Plummer and help him escape "struggled for mastery . . . in the bosom of that person," Thompson wrote, but in the end he opted to remain silent. He admitted that he never had been able to decide in his own mind if he acted out of "patriotism" and a duty to the larger community, or simply out of "prudence" and the fear that he might be ruined socially and politically if he intervened on Plummer's behalf.[12]

Whatever the case, Thompson excused himself after eating and hastened to his store, where he built a fire. Edgerton came to visit him and the two warmed themselves by the flames and chatted. At one point during the morning, Stinson glanced in the window, and later his fellow deputy, Ray, came into the store and made small talk. "It was very evident," Thompson wrote, "that these men were very nervous and anxious to know what was taking place." Plummer had been feeling ill for several days, Thompson added, and spent that Sunday indoors at the Vail cabin, resting.[13]

While some of the leaders of the Vigilance Committee got a few hours of sleep just before dawn, others were busy recruiting among the miners and merchants of the town. The task proved slow going, but by noon on Sunday, January 10, 1864, Sanders and Lott had sworn in several dozen men as vigilantes. George Chrisman and other town fathers let it be known that they did not oppose the campaign. During the afternoon, small parties went to the stables and removed horses belonging to Plummer and his two deputies, cutting off their means of escape.[14]

As dusk approached, Thompson left his store and headed for the Edgerton family's house beside the footbridge over Grasshopper Creek that led to the main area of miners' bungalows on Yankee Flats. Thompson was one of a small group who had begun holding Sunday worship services in a room in the back of Oliver's stagecoach office, and he participated in a weekly choir rehearsal on Sunday evenings with four female members of the Edgerton clan: Edgerton's wife Mary, daughter Mattie, niece Lucia

Darling, and Wilbur Sanders' wife Hattie. On arriving, Thompson learned that plans to go to the Sanders cabin for choir practice had been canceled. "Girls," he recalled Mary Edgerton saying in a sharp voice, "you will not go to Yankee Flats this evening!"[15]

The reason became clear moments later, Thompson reported, when he and the Edgerton household heard the muffled stomping of men's boots as a party of fifty to seventy-five armed men crossed the bridge headed for Yankee Flats. Sanders' cabin was very close to Vail's, and Thompson understood that choir rehearsal had been called off because the men were about to surround the Vail cabin and seize Plummer. Once across the bridge, the vanguard split in two. One detachment headed for a cabin where Stinson was staying and captured him without incident. The other formed a circle around the Vail cabin, and its leader—a "well known citizen," according to Thompson, but otherwise unidentified—knocked on the door. Martha Jane Vail answered and the man rushed past her to find Plummer lying on a sofa. It was Plummer's habit, Thompson said, to go armed at all times, even at home, with a heavy knife and pistol, but he had removed his weapons that evening and placed them on a chair because he felt ill. He was captured without resistance. As Plummer left he tried to soothe and reassure his sister-in-law, Mrs. Vail, that nothing was amiss. According to Thompson, he told her "he was needed to do something about Dutch John." Once outside the cabin, he was surrounded by guards and his hands were bound.

As they began the short march to the bridge, Plummer balked and called out for Wilbur Sanders in his cabin nearby. The cabin was dark, but Plummer pressed toward its front door and his guard hesitated for a moment and failed to restrain him. As Plummer approached, Sanders appeared in the doorway. He had not wished to confront Plummer or speak to him, but now he had no choice. Addressing Plummer's guard, Sanders barked out a military command, "Company! Forward march!"

Plummer objected, saying, "You men know us better than this!"

Sanders now spoke directly to Plummer. "It is useless for you to beg for your life," he said in a flat tone. "[The] affair is settled and cannot be altered. You are to be hanged. You cannot feel harder about it than I do, but I cannot help it if I could."[16]

Crossing the bridge into town, the men escorting Plummer and Stinson joined another party that had taken Ned Ray at a saloon, where he was passed out on a gaming table. The group now headed for the gallows on the edge of town where Plummer had carried out the execution of Peter Horen the previous August. Along the way, Plummer argued urgently for his life. He was innocent, he insisted, and deserved a trial before facing summary execution. If his captors preferred, he would leave the country forever, or they could chain him up as long as they cared. Seeing that they meant to carry out the execution, he asked for some time to arrange his business affairs and to speak a final time to his sister-in-law. All of these pleadings were ignored.

As the mass of men reached the foot of the gallows, Plummer briefly lost his composure. A young man who had befriended him came hurtling into the middle of the circle and embraced Plummer, crying and begging for him to be spared. As the young man was forcibly removed, Plummer again implored his captors not to hang him. He prayed for his life and a chance to see his wife again.[17]

The commander of the combined guard, John Lott, called for Ned Ray to be brought forward. Ray had revived and was cursing his captors, while his mistress, one Madam Hall, wept and agitated at the periphery of the crowd where the guard prevented her from rushing to Ray's side. The hangings that had taken place so far had been carried out with harsh efficiency, but not so with Ray. Guards placed a noose around his neck, lifted him as high as they could, and then dropped him. In the split second he was falling, he managed to reach up and stick his hand inside the noose, so that his neck did not break on impact. Instead, he dangled in the frigid night air, strangling, his contorted face illuminated by torchlight and his desperate gasps for breath silencing all other sounds. It took him several minutes to die.[18]

Stinson was hanged next, cleanly, and then it was Plummer's turn. "During this time Plummer became awfully alarmed," one of the guards, E. J. Porter, recalled, "and was walking around inside the circle formed by the vigilantes, begging those among them whom he knew to help him and imploring them to let him off, promising that if they did so he would leave the country." Seeing his friend and patron, George Chrisman, in the crowd, Plummer urged him to intervene, but Chrisman replied sternly, "No, Henry, we can't do anything for you."[19]

According to Thompson, Stinson offered to confess just before he died, and Plummer stopped him, saying bitterly, "We've done enough already to send us all to hell." Plummer asked for a "good drop," mouthed a prayer, and died instantly. But Thompson was not an eyewitness to the execution.

He had remained at the Edgertons' house, not wishing to see his friend die, and was still there when Martha Jane Vail came racing to the door in tears, calling for Thompson's help. Mary Edgerton and Thompson both worked to try to calm her down, and Thompson deliberately lied to her, saying that Plummer had been summoned on business involving "Dutch John" Wagner and was not in jeopardy. "I told her anything which I thought would allay her excitement," Thompson confessed in his memoirs, and he escorted her back home. Thompson then returned to the Edgertons' house. An hour later, a man appeared outside the door and informed Thompson simply, "It is all over." Calling it the "hardest trial of my life," he went to Mrs. Vail's cabin and told her what had actually happened. She cried out and fell to the floor in a dead faint.[20]

Dimsdale, the first chronicler of the vigilante period, insisted that Plummer "confessed his numerous crimes and murders" before dying. But the record suggests otherwise—that Henry Plummer maintained his innocence to the very end, dying with his dignity intact and the complete truth about his involvement in the criminal activities of Montana a secret he would carry, literally, to his grave.[21]

Did Plummer deserve to die? That is a question students of history must answer for themselves, by their own tenets of justice. To suggest, as Dimsdale did a year later, that Plummer was an "oily and snake-like demon" caught "red-handed" is plainly to exaggerate for dramatic effect. To say, by contrast, that Plummer was "open-minded and gentle mannered, yet flamboyantly courageous," and a man who "assumed a leadership role in civilizing the mining frontier," as a latter-day biographer and apologist has written, seems equally unbalanced. By the time of his death, at the age of thirty-two, Plummer had killed five men by gunshot or blunt force. He had a violent streak. No reasonable person in the gold camps of Montana could be faulted for being frightened of him. His failure to enforce the law during a serious crime wave, especially when he had proven himself so adept at capturing fugitives in his earlier career, stands as a harsh indictment. His use of Stinson and Ray as deputies, one a killer and the other a convicted mule thief and prison escapee, incriminates him as well. It is hard to lament his death. No one could say for sure if Plummer was demonstrably guilty of a set of specific crimes. But that was not the real issue. The real issue was whether the men who executed him could have afforded to take more time to gather evidence and conduct a proceeding more closely resembling a conventional trial than the hasty, secret tribunal that took place in confusion over a sleepless night and ended in a hanging.[22]

The author would not care to point a condemning finger at the settlers of Alder Gulch and Bannack who considered Plummer a menace and feared for their well-being as long as he remained at large. The provocations of recent weeks certainly had risen to a level that justified the organization of a committee of public safety. The duty of that body was not to try Plummer by a standard of guilt beyond a reasonable doubt, but to examine the totality of facts in their possession and decide whether he ought to be executed as a matter of communal security. To use a modern analogy, the committee was acting more in the capacity of a military tribunal assessing the threat posed by an enemy of the state than a jury judging one of its peers. One may argue that the vigilantes overstepped their authority even by this latter, looser test of dispensing justice—but not, it seems, by much.

On the other hand, those who believe Plummer's executioners acted too hastily can point to what happened next as evidence of the infirmity of trying to impose justice through the instrument of public opinion. In their deliberations over the previous two days, the men from Alder Gulch and their counterparts from Bannack had discussed what to do about an unsavory character in town named José Pizanthia, known as "the Greaser," the ugly nickname used for many Mexicans in that era. No record survives of any specific crimes charged against Pizanthia, only that he was considered a "rough" and a general nuisance who once had smashed a window at Durant's saloon with his pistol butt. He lived in a cabin on a hillside above town, and on the morning of Monday, January 11, 1864, a few hours after Plummer, Ray, and Stinson were hanged, a delegation acting on behalf of the Vigilance Committee went to his door and shouted for him to surrender.[23]

In the frigid morning light, no sign of life was evident inside Pizanthia's tiny domicile. After a moment of silent waiting, two of the vigilantes, Smith Ball and George Copley, moved to the door, shoved it open, and stepped inside. Pizanthia, who was hiding in the dark interior, opened fire, hitting Copley in the chest and Ball in the hip. The two men staggered backward out of the cabin, each shouting "I'm shot!" Copley was mortally wounded, and a large crowd of bystanders quickly transformed themselves into a mob howling for Pizanthia's blood. A group of men raced to Sidney

Edgerton's house, knowing he kept the small howitzer from the Fisk expedition under his bed. With no objection from the chief justice, the men took the gun and carried it by hand several hundred feet to Pizanthia's cabin, where they propped it on a large wooden box and aimed its barrel squarely at the windowless side wall. Two shells fired through the house opened jagged holes but failed to detonate, and then a third shell was sent into the chimney, exploding and shattering it.[24]

Seeing no sign of life within the cabin, a corps of men armed with rifles moved toward the front door, which had fallen inward from the effects of the bombardment. On coming closer, they could see Pizanthia's boots sticking out from under the door. Two of them lifted the door, two or three others pinioned Pizanthia's legs, and Smith Ball, whose wounded hip had been bandaged by now, emptied all six shots from his revolver into the body of the injured man on the ground.

Not yet finished, the mob found a clothesline, tied it around Pizanthia's neck, and dragged him across the frozen yard to a pole, where his body was raised high in the air and left to dangle. The crowd opened fired and sent more than one hundred rounds into the corpse, until eventually they ran low on ammunition. "Every time a bullet struck the body," one witness recalled, Pizanthia's red and white plaid shirt "would pop out a little where it struck." Meanwhile, other men set Pizanthia's cabin on fire. Pizanthia's body was cut down from the pole and pitched onto the bonfire until flames blackened his flesh and eventually reduced him to embers. When they had cooled sufficiently, his ashes were combed meticulously to see if "the Greaser" had been carrying any gold dust when he died. He had not.[25]

Writing of this awful scene just over a year later, Dimsdale attempted to excuse its violent excesses as a mob action that spiraled out of control and went beyond the lethal but disciplined justice authorized and meted out by the vigilante leadership. Indeed, Dimsdale argued that the "wild and ungovernable passion" ignited during the killing of Pizanthia actually served to underscore the preferable methods of execution used by the vigilantes. "The truth is," Dimsdale wrote, "that the Vigilance Committee simply punished with death men unfit to live in any community, and that death was, usually, almost instantaneous, and only momentarily painful." Others were more candid. Pizanthia's body was subjected to "cowardly mutilation," in the words of one participant, George Lovell, who added, "I blush to know it was done by men of white blood and Americans." Lott and Sanders and the other vigilante leaders stood by passively, allowing Pizanthia to be destroyed without raising a whisper of protest.[26]

Most disturbing of all was the role played by Edgerton, the chief justice. When the mob came to his house to seize the cannon, he freely gave it up and went to the hillside to watch it being fired. Many years later, his daughter, Mattie, described the glacial pace of his realization that something wrong was happening. "When the order came to pull down the cabin and burn the body of the hanged Mexican," she wrote, her father "turned about and hurried home, remarking that it was no place to remain, for one in his official position." This belated expression of concern about the propriety of the situation, uttered only as the frenzy of violence toward Pizanthia reached its apex, cannot easily be excused. What had prevented Edgerton from declining to surrender the cannon? What scruple kept him from standing up to the mob and demanding that they cease and desist?[27]

Edgerton's refusal to take up his duties as a judge, born of his reluctance to act without taking the oath of office and later cemented by his desire to travel to Washington to lobby for creation of a new territory and appointment as its governor, was beginning to bear serious, disturbing consequences. What outcome of greater legitimacy might have occurred, one may fairly ask, if Edgerton had conducted himself from the moment of arrival as the instrument of federal authority in the portion of Idaho Territory east of the Bitterroot Mountains? Granted, he had no criminal code to enforce or administer, because Congress had failed to adopt any laws for Idaho Territory, even on a temporary basis. He had no bailiffs or other court personnel to assist him. No deputy federal marshal had been assigned in the region, after Plummer was blackballed. All the same, it seems more than likely that the settlers would have accepted Edgerton's authority. He was, after all, an appointee of the president of the United States, confirmed by the U.S. Senate. He could have overseen the inquiries that were made into the Tiebolt killing and other crimes and presided over the ensuing trials, investing them with a degree of legality the people's courts and the vigilantes plainly lacked.

These are hypothetical questions, of course, but they are more than a matter of mere guesswork. On the other side of the Rockies, the territorial government at Lewiston was functioning by now in a competent, orderly way that the mining camps of Bannack and Alder Gulch were not. Even as the blackened remains of poor Pizanthia cooled on the hillside, officials in Lewiston were handling a murder case in a manner that could and should have served as an example to the vigilantes of Montana.

CHAPTER FOURTEEN

Five Hanged Side by Side

The hunt for the suspected killers of Lloyd Magruder began when his friend, hotel owner Hill Beachy, was sworn in as a deputy sheriff and took off in pursuit of the four shadowy men who had passed through Lewiston, the capital of Idaho Territory, on their way west, leaving behind a horse and saddle that belonged to Magruder. A trader and politician, Magruder had disappeared on his return trip over the Bitterroot Mountains from the Alder Gulch gold camps after selling out a large supply of dry goods in October 1863. Beachy believed Magruder's companions had killed him for the gold dust he was carrying.

Beachy was not a formally trained lawman. One of his biographers likened him to Huckleberry Finn, a river rat who grew up on the Mississippi and ran away from home at age thirteen to serve as a cabin boy on steamships. Beachy lived for a time in New Orleans, baked bread and sold it to U.S. troops stationed on the Rio Grande during the Mexican-American War, returned to the river as a pilot, and eventually ended up in California during the gold rush. Like so many pioneers, he made his living as a merchant, not a miner, operating a succession of saloons and hotels. He gained a measure of experience dealing with criminals in the late 1850s when he agreed to house and guard prisoners in his hotel in Red Bluff, California. Slope-shouldered and powerfully built, Beachy commanded a good deal of respect by his physical bearing and was taken seriously by other men, even though he enjoyed playing practical jokes on them. (He once prowled the outskirts of town wearing a bear skin, giving a performance so convincing it triggered a full-scale bear hunt, which he joined with great amusement.) In 1858, he married an Irish immigrant, Margaret Early, in Marysville, California, and it was there he befriended Magruder.[1]

When gold was discovered in Idaho in 1862, Beachy and his wife moved to Lewiston and opened a hotel, the Luna House, whose roof proclaimed its name to the world in black landmark lettering. Magruder's career as a merchant in California had collapsed under the weight of bad debt, and Beachy persuaded him to pick up stakes and come along to Idaho. As a fellow Copperhead, Beachy encouraged Magruder to resume his involvement in politics and endorsed his bid for the post of territorial delegate. When Magruder left Idaho for the pack trip over the Bitterroots to Bannack and Virginia City, Beachy gave him an extra rifle to carry for protection. Magruder's failure to return on time filled Beachy with a sense of foreboding. By one account, he had a vivid dream of his friend meeting violent death at the hands of a man wielding an ax. As he set off after the suspects, Beachy felt a surge of dread about Magruder's fate, along with a sense of responsibility.[2]

Traveling west with all possible speed by coach, steamboat, rail, and portage, Beachy reached Portland, Oregon, just in time to learn that his prey had boarded a steamer, the *Sierra Nevada,* bound for San Francisco. Frustrated at having come so close, Beachy got on a stagecoach for the long, bumpy ride down the Willamette Valley to northern California. At Yreka, he found a telegraph office and sent a description of the four suspects to the San Francisco Police Department along with an urgent request for their arrest.

Arriving two days later in San Francisco, Beachy learned that his telegram had arrived too late, after the *Sierra Nevada* docked. But police Captain J. W. Lees had taken his message with the utmost seriousness and had tracked down the four fugitives and arrested them, two at a boarding house and the other pair at a hotel. They were behind bars in the San Francisco jail, Beachy was relieved to discover. Among other incriminating acts, they had deposited some $7,000 in gold dust at the San Francisco Mint and converted it into greenbacks.[3]

Confronting the men at last in their jail cell, Beachy learned that their leader, "Doc" Howard, was actually a man named David Renton, not a physician at all but an ex-convict who had served time in San Quentin,

Hill Beachy. Courtesy of the Montana Historical Society.

and whose experience there so closely paralleled Henry Plummer's as to be eerie. Renton, the son of a New York City businessman, had joined the gold rush to California, worked for a time at a stable as a horse doctor, and eventually settled in Sacramento as a laborer. There he was accused of robbery and, after two mistrials, was convicted and sentenced to five years at hard labor. At San Quentin, Renton was befriended by the prison doctor, Alfred Taliaferro, and given a privileged position as a medical orderly and trusty. Renton's wife and friends orchestrated a pardon campaign, and in August 1858, just a few months before Plummer arrived at the same place, Governor John Weller ordered Renton released on a strict promise to leave the state of California for good. He returned briefly to New York before resurfacing in Washington Territory under an alias.[4]

Another of the cellmates also counted San Quentin in his background. George Christopher Lower (or Lowrey, as his last name was variously rendered) was a stocky, blond, muscular man, a blacksmith by trade, who had joined the gold rush from his native Pennsylvania and settled in Shasta County, California. There he was convicted of grand larceny and sentenced to five years in prison. He entered San Quentin on October 24, 1857, and had served nearly three years when he escaped in August 1860. His time in prison overlapped Plummer's six months there, and it seems reasonable to assume that the two men knew each other. Plummer's memorable warning to Francis Thompson that he was in the company of "cut-throats and robbers" likely was prompted by his having recognized Lowrey as a fellow inmate from California.[5]

The third suspect in the San Francisco jail was a scruffy Cornishman named Billy Page, a sometime farmer, trapper, and mule-driver with a sullen manner and a bad limp. Alone among the four, Page had resisted arrest, refusing to submit until Captain Lees held a pistol against his side and threatened to use it. A good deal older than his companions, he seemed the most fearful and easily agitated.[6]

To Beachy's surprise, the fourth man in the quartet turned out to be an old acquaintance, James Romaine, a gambler known for his polished manners. Romaine had known Beachy and Magruder on friendly terms in Marysville, California, where he worked as a contractor and helped plaster the office walls of the newspaper Magruder partly owned. Romaine had been in school with Beachy's wife, Maggie, who recalled him as a decent sort from a good family. In recent years, Romaine had pursued the gambler's life, at one point operating a pool game in a beer hall in Oregon, before joining the exodus to the gold camps. When Magruder encountered Romaine in Bannack, he evidently trusted him enough to sign him on as a helper, along with Romaine's companions.[7]

By the time Beachy presented himself at the jail, the four suspects had hired a lawyer and were planning to fight extradition back to Idaho. They filed a writ challenging Beachy's right to take prisoners from a state to a territory, and their lawyer argued that the suspects faced the threat of lynching at the hands of a mob in Lewiston. Since no body had been found, the lawyer added, there was no evidence that Magruder had been murdered or that any crime had taken place. No witness had identified the four men as members of Magruder's party. These objections were more than mere boilerplate, and Beachy found himself forced to hire a lawyer of his own to argue his case in court. Newspapers in Oregon and California got wind of Beachy's mission and one, the *Portland Oregonian,* pointedly raised the specter of a "necktie party" awaiting the four suspects if they returned to the Idaho gold camps. Three men believed guilty of trailside robbery had been hanged by vigilantes in Lewiston in 1862, and the ability of freshly settled frontier towns to mete out proper justice was a matter of open skepticism. It is a testament to Beachy's doggedness and credibility that he managed to talk California Governor Leland Stanford into signing the extradition papers. Beachy also won every point in court, based in large part on his solemn oath that he would protect his prisoners from lynching and guarantee them a fair trial.[8]

In late November 1863, with all legal and political impediments removed—and after a final attempt by Renton to bribe his way out of jail had failed—Beachy set off from San Francisco aboard the steamer *Pacific* with the four suspects snugly shackled in the ship's brig. The trip back to Lewiston would be a long one, by ocean, river, and coach, and Beachy was grateful for the protection of a small contingent of federal soldiers on one leg of the journey up the Columbia River. He finally reached Lewiston in early December and drew a crowd of excited onlookers as he marched his prisoners from the Snake River landing several blocks to his hotel, the Luna House, which served as the town jail, where he gave them into the custody of Sheriff Fisk of Nez Perce County. On examination, the sheriff discovered that Renton had been busy trying to saw through his chains with a file, information that might have inflamed the crowd to attempt summary punishment had not Fisk and Beachy both urged restraint with all the persuasion they could muster. Speaking from the front steps of the Luna House, Beachy explained that he had given his word the men would receive a fair trial. His reputation was on the line, he warned, and so was the town's. A few days later, adopting a confident tone that may or may not have been fully justified, the editors of the *Golden Age* assured their readers, "We have not heard a single expression that would tend to excite mob violence."[9]

At the very time Nicholas Tiebolt's murder was triggering the formation of a posse and people's court in Alder Gulch, authorities in Lewiston began their interrogation of the four men suspected of killing Lloyd Magruder. One advantage the Idaho lawmen enjoyed, ironically, was the absence of a corpse. Magruder was dead, by all reckoning, but his body had not been discovered and put on display on the main street of town, as Tiebolt's had, inciting men to revulsion and anger and the impulse to take quick vengeance. In Lewiston, Sheriff Fisk and the prosecuting attorneys had the luxury of time to question the suspects and probe their weak spots. In due course, they were able to gain a confession from Billy Page and turn him state's witness in exchange for his freedom.[10]

Page had quite a lurid tale to tell. After working for several years in California and the Rocky Mountains as a mule driver and day laborer, Page had joined a party of travelers led by "Doc" Howard as it crossed the Bitterroots from Idaho into Montana—the same party that had picked up Francis Thompson along the way and arrived in Bannack on the last day of August 1863. Magruder had come through Bannack soon afterward, and Page met him in the Elkhorn, Cyrus Skinner's bar. Howard, Lowrey, and Romaine had gone to work as clerks for Magruder in Virginia City, helping him sell his inventory. They planned to travel with him on his return trip to Idaho and invited Page to join them. Four other men completed the party: Charley Allen, Magruder's chief packer, and three strangers—William Phillips and Horace and Robert Chalmers, brothers from Missouri—who were headed to Idaho and wanted the protection of numbers. On October 5, 1863, accompanied by forty mules, the group of nine left Bannack for the arduous trip over the Bitterroots via the Nez Perce Pass.

On the fourth day out, Page claimed, the man he knew as "Doc" Howard took him aside and confided that he and Lowrey and Romaine planned to steal Magruder's gold dust. They also meant to kill Magruder and the other members of the party to cover up the crime. Page agreed to participate and was assigned to sleep in the same tent with Phillips and shoot him if he awakened and tried to resist. Nothing happened that evening, Page said, because the sentry pairings were unfavorable. But the next night, October 10, 1863, Lowrey and Magruder drew the first watch and left together to patrol the periphery of the camp. According to Page, Magruder carried a rifle and Lowrey an ax to cut firewood as the two men climbed up a steep hillside on their way to the pasture where the mules were kept. The rest of the party retired for the evening, Charley Allen in a tent and the others in blankets and hides on the ground. Some hours later, Page said, Lowrey slipped quietly back into the campsite—without Magruder. Lowery had surprised Magruder from behind in the inky darkness of the mountain forest and shattered his skull with the ax, killing him instantly. Now Lowrey, Howard, and Romaine took off their boots and moved silently through the camp, killing the Chalmers brothers and Phillips with powerful blows of the ax, then finishing the awful job with a shotgun blast that nearly decapitated Allen in his tent. Page swore he took no direct hand in the "dirty work," as he termed it. He was so scared by the turn of events he was shaking, he recalled, and Howard calmed him, saying, "Billy, Billy, you're all a-tremble. Now don't be frightened."[11]

The rest of the night was given to a series of grisly chores, Page said, as the killers searched their victims' belongings for gold dust and weapons, burned their clothes and extra supplies, pitched their bodies into ravines, scattered various other pieces of evidence, and organized a smaller pack train for their escape. They did their work in moccasins, hoping the tracks would make Indians appear to be the culprits. At first light, when they departed, Page said, the mules they meant to leave behind followed instinctively and had to be slaughtered, completing one of the bloodiest, deadliest crimes in western history.

Why was Page spared in this carnage? He may have been a more active accomplice than he admitted in his confession, or the others may have realized they would have to rely on his skills as a mule handler and his knowledge of the terrain as they left the trail to avoid by-passers. Already a handful of small parties had encountered them, and there would be witnesses who could testify that the nine men had been traveling together. Whatever the case, Page was given a full share of the gold dust taken in the robbery, which totaled some $12,000. He led the others through the trackless wilderness for a week until they emerged at Lewiston, where they bought tickets on the stagecoach out of town, arousing the suspicions of Hill Beachy, whose nightmare about Magruder's death by ax blow proved prescient indeed.

As they questioned Page over and over again, probing for inconsistencies, Sheriff Fisk and prosecutor Enos F. Grey came to believe they had a strong case. Not only would Page provide eyewitness testimony, there was physical evidence as well—Magruder's horse and saddle that the men had left in the remote pasturage when they passed through Lewiston, and also a small cache of abandoned gear that Page told them where to find on Cottonwood Creek. Several witnesses placed the nine men together on the Nez Perce Trail in the days before the crime, and other witnesses would say they had recognized the four suspects in Lewiston on the night they arrived to take the stagecoach. The most incriminating evidence, the murder scene itself, with its corpses and their charred and scattered belongings, would remain inaccessible until the warmth of spring melted the snowpack and investigators could get there. Still, the prospects of conviction seemed promising, and Grey was ready to proceed to trial.[12]

Lewiston enjoyed a number of advantages that the settlements to the east of the Bitterroots did not. The town had telegraph service, an army post nearby at Fort Lapwai, a newspaper, and was reachable year-round by river and road. On December 7, 1863, around the time Beachy returned with his prisoners, the territorial legislature convened, gathering many of the region's leading citizens under one roof. Unlike Bannack and Alder Gulch, Lewiston had some of the instruments of territorial government in place. Men of respect, among them Beachy, Sheriff Fisk, and prosecutor Grey, had pledged a fair trial for the suspects and meant to carry out their promise.

Yet there were problems as well. Acting in haste, Congress had neglected to provide a civil or criminal code for interim use until the territorial legislature could enact laws and establish a court system. Ordinarily, when a new territory was created, it was carved from an existing territory and automatically carried with it the laws of its parent. But Idaho had been cobbled together from parts of Washington, Dakota, Utah, and Nebraska territories, and as a result, legally speaking, it was an orphan with no law codes to inherit. This was not some purely hypothetical point. The defendants had hired a brace of lawyers who argued that the criminal proceedings against their clients were taking place in a jurisdiction, Nez Perce County, that had been established as part of Washington Territory and now no longer existed. And, they said, their clients were being charged with the violation of laws that did not exist.

Unsure exactly how to cope with this challenge to its ability to keep the peace and prosecute criminals, the Idaho legislature took the expedient step of adopting a simple two-paragraph act that said English common law would be the basis for all legal proceedings in the territory, commencing with passage of the measure on January 4, 1864. Accordingly, over the objections of defense counsel, a grand jury was convened and returned murder indictments against Renton, Lowrey, and Romaine.[13]

With the territory's chief justice, Sidney Edgerton, stuck on the eastern side of the Bitterroots for the duration of winter, the job of presiding over the trial fell to an associate justice, Samuel Parks, who made plain his respect for Edgerton's "high moral and official character, and his experience," while adding that it was necessary to carry on without him. The defendants were arraigned on January 10, 1864, the same day Henry Plummer and his two deputies were marched to summary execution in Bannack, and trial commenced a week later. A transcript of sorts was made by court reporter Charles Frush (whose penmanship "defies deciphering," in the lament of one historian) that nonetheless managed to capture the damning essence of Billy Page's testimony against his partners in crime. In convincing detail, Page described the night of the murders, and how "all the dirty work was done," culminating with Renton's boast about his skill in executing Charley Allen by blasting off half his skull when a lesser shooter might have hit him in the shoulder. As Page described this last exchange, Sheriff Fisk recalled years later, Renton glared at him across the courtroom with an expression of savage anger.[14]

Additional incriminating testimony was given by L. O. Holt, who had traveled with Magruder from Idaho to Alder Gulch but was fortunate enough not to have joined the return party. Holt was able to identify some of the mules the defendants had brought with them to Lewiston and also a piece of cloth Magruder had used to bundle up his gold dust that was recovered from the mint in San Francisco. Coupled with the other physical evidence that had been recovered, the case against the defendants was overwhelming, and the jury deliberated only briefly before returning a guilty verdict against all three, on January 23, 1864. The jury recommended the death penalty and Justice Parks set their executions for March 4.[15]

In imposing sentence, Parks took pains to invest the moment with the seriousness and decorum he believed it deserved. Pulling a written text from his coat pocket, he chastised Renton, Romaine, and Lowrey for wasting their opportunities and becoming "degraded and abandoned outcasts, universally regarded as the implacable enemies of humanity." He talked of their descent from gambling to petty crime, and from robbery to murder. They had tried to conceal the evidence of their killing spree, he continued, "but like the blood of Abel it cried to God against you and the cry was heard and answered." Some might expect to get away with crime in a region so rugged and remote, the judge added, but the trial and its outcome would "let them know that the reign of law and order has commenced."[16]

Some skeptics believed Justice Parks was inspired in his oratory by the presence of several newspaper reporters who were covering the trial and publicizing the eloquence of some of its participants, but he seems to have been moved as well by a genuine desire to invest the proceedings with weight and legitimacy. "You have had a fair trial and been legally convicted," he admonished the defendants, "and your punishment will be just."

In one respect, at least, this assertion of authority rang hollow, since it was based on the legislature's embrace of English common law, which might not pass muster upon review by the federal appellate courts or by Congress. Indeed, the defendants' lawyers filed an appeal arguing that it was improper to try them *ex post facto,* using common law or any other law that was adopted after the alleged crime had been committed. In a nation founded on strict adherence to the rule of law, the issue carried some resonance. But it also mattered that the men who brought the Magruder killers to justice had behaved with a high level of scrupulousness, adopting and following procedures that gave the defendants their day in court. Compared with the mob frenzy that claimed the life of José Pizanthia, the arrest, trial, and conviction of Renton and his crew strike a modern observer as remarkably fair under the circumstances. Had Plummer conducted himself as Hill Beachy did, Bannack and Alder Gulch might not have had to resort to vigilante justice. And Plummer himself might not have been a target of it.

If the vigilantes on the east side of the Bitterroots were embarrassed by the annihilation of José Pizanthia, they gave no indication. On the same day the Mexican was shot, hanged, and incinerated, the committee turned its attention to "Dutch John" Wagner, who had remained in custody since arriving in Bannack. Wagner's guilt was established by the gunshot wound he received in his shoulder during the attempted robbery of the Moody wagon train, and the vigilantes reached a unanimous decision to hang him. Even so, some of them expressed regret at the outcome because Wagner had conducted himself with considerable dignity during the interrogation. Mattie Edgerton got the impression from her father, the chief justice, that Wagner had been promised his life in exchange for a confession, and if so the vigilantes' regret might have included an element of remorse for misleading him. When he was told that he must die, Wagner at first was shocked, according to Thomas Dimsdale, the vigilantes' chronicler, and "begged hard for his life, praying them to cut off his arms and his legs, and then to let him go."[17]

His plea denied, Wagner regained his composure and asked to send a letter of farewell to his mother. With his frostbitten fingers wrapped in rags, he dictated a message in German to a countryman who tried to take down his words. But the fellow did a poor job, and Wagner eventually unwrapped his blackened hands and laboriously wrote the letter himself, admitting his complicity in the robbery. He was then taken to an unfinished building where the stiff, lifeless body of Plummer lay on a workbench. Stinson's body was on the floor, while Ray's had been recovered by his mistress and taken for burial. Francis Thompson, Plummer's roommate and friend, had received "quite a little sum of money" from him for safekeeping in recent days, and he arranged to spend $42.50 for a coffin and the costs of interment, and then sent the rest to the sheriff's widow, Electa Bryan Plummer, in Iowa.[18]

Wagner asked for a moment to pray, while a rope was thrown over a crossbeam in the building and a barrel was placed beneath it. He had never seen a man hanged, Wagner said, and he asked how long it would take to die. "Not long," one of his executioners replied. The noose was put around his neck, the barrel kicked away, and in minutes Wagner was dead.[19]

Their work in Bannack completed, the vigilantes rode back to Alder Gulch to decide what further action they ought to take. According to Dimsdale, the lives of the leaders of the Vigilance Committee were in extreme jeopardy, because a group of "desperadoes" remained at large and wanted vengeance for their friends who had been hanged. "Every man who had taken part in the pursuit of the criminals . . . was marked for slaughter," Dimsdale wrote, "and nothing remained but to carry out the good work so auspiciously begun." Actually, there is no evidence of any organized resistance to the vigilantes after the first round of executions, and it seems more accurate to say that they agreed to continue arresting and hanging the men they suspected of being highwaymen or dangers to the community. To that end, Paris Pfouts and his executive committee met in private in Virginia City on the night of Wednesday, January 13, 1863, and drew up a list of six men they meant to put to death.[20]

Some of the names on the list were familiar, their fates determined by crimes they had committed in the recent past. Jack Gallagher and Hayes Lyons were targeted for their participation in the cold-blooded murder of D. H. Dillingham on the main street of Virginia City the previous June, the same act that doomed Buck Stinson. Frank Parish, the co-owner of the Rattlesnake Ranch, stood accused by his ex-bartender, "Red" Yeager, of participating in stagecoach robberies along with the ranch's other principals. "Club-foot George" Lane, the cobbler who worked in Dance and Stuart's store, was included on the list for a more nebulous reason—the belief that he had acted as a spy for Henry Plummer, eavesdropping on customers and passing along information about their travel plans, and because he had ridden to Bannack to warn Plummer after the arrest of George Ives. According to their by-laws, the vigilantes did not mete out punishment for crimes committed in other venues, but occasionally they ignored their own rules. Lane had been accused of stealing horses in Washington Territory, and those charges were counted against him as well.

The fifth man marked for execution by the vigilantes had perpetrated no known crimes in the Montana gold camps, but his past was so appalling that it seems accurate to say he was condemned on general principle. Boone Helm had killed a friend in his native Missouri with a knife in a fit of drunken meanness, had killed another man in a bar fight in California, and most infamously had survived a horrific, snowbound winter in the Sierra Nevada mountains by means of cannibalism, which he freely admitted and occasionally bragged about. As Dimsdale put it, "Helm was the most hardened, cool, and deliberate scoundrel of the whole band, and murder was a mere pastime to him." Nathaniel Langford, another chronicler of the period, called Helm "one of those hideous monsters of depravity whom neither precept nor example could have saved from a life of crime." His very existence seemed to frighten the vigilantes to the point they were determined to eliminate him. The sixth and final man on the list, William Hunter, was accused vaguely of having robbed an unnamed Mormon miner on the road to Salt Lake City. Hunter escaped from Virginia City on the same night the vigilantes sentenced him to death, quite possibly because some of them disagreed with the decision and tipped him off. In his memoirs, Pfouts claims that around this time a man named Harrison "fired off his pistol and swore he would kill me and others," but it proved an empty threat and Harrison was not targeted by the committee.[21]

First light on Thursday, January 14, 1864, found scores of armed men posted on the hillsides around Virginia City, acting as pickets to prevent anyone from leaving. According to a diary entry made that day by miner John Grannis, he and others were "obeying a notice of the vigilance committee" that directed them to surround the town. The extreme cold snap of recent days had broken, and the morning was mild under a partly cloudy sky. At ten o'clock, the executive officer of the committee, James Williams, gathered a large force at the foot of Wallace Street and dispatched them to find and arrest the wanted men. "I saw them march in perfect order up the street a hundred yards or so, halt and receive some orders, and disperse in squads," settler Chauncey Barbour recalled. One of the units, led by William "Old Man" Clark, entered a saloon called the California Exchange and emerged moments later with Jack Gallagher in custody. Frank Parish was taken in a store, George Lane at his cobbler's bench, Boone Helm in the street in front of a hotel, and Hayes Lyons in a cabin above town, cooking breakfast. None of them resisted arrest, a phenomenon Clark dismissed as showing they were cowards when sober. Fortunately for the vigilantes, Helm was suffering from a badly infected finger on his right hand and wore a sling when he was detained, or he might have tested Clark's notion.[22]

At gunpoint, the five captured men were brought before Pfouts and his committee in a store on Wallace Street and confronted with the findings against them. All professed innocence, and Helm earned a place in Montana legend by offering to swear on the Bible that he had done nothing wrong. Fascinated by what they considered a brazen display of apostasy, the vigilantes produced a copy of the Good Book, which Helm made a show of kissing. "I am as innocent as the babe unborn," he swore. "I never killed anyone, or robbed or defrauded any man." He then asked one of the members of the executive committee if he could speak with him in private. Taken into a smaller back room, Helm asked if there were any possible way he could escape execution. Told there was not, he confessed to the two earlier killings in Missouri and California and also admitted breaking out of jail in Oregon. But he insisted he had no association with Henry Plummer and no involvement in crime in the Montana gold camps. Pressed to admit anything he knew about the sheriff and his alleged criminal conspiracy, Helm answered, "Ask Jack Gallagher. He knows more than I do."[23]

According to Dimsdale, the vigilantes had arranged to place all of the captives within earshot of each other, and Helm's accusation provoked an angry, profane outburst from Gallagher, who was hidden behind a partition. The interrogation of the prisoners, meant to turn them against one another and provoke accusations and confessions, yielded mixed results. Parish admitted complicity in the recent crime wave, disclosing that he had participated in the holdup of the stagecoach carrying "Bummer Dan" McFadden. "Until his confession," Dimsdale wrote, "it was not known that he had any share in the robbery of the coach." And Lyons conceded his involvement in the killing of Dillingham. But in spite of Helm's allegations, Gallagher staunchly denied any wrongdoing, as did Lane. Whatever hopes the vigilantes held that the men would inform on each other or implicate Henry Plummer as their leader or give further information about recent crimes came basically to naught. At one point, according to Pfouts, two more men were arrested and brought before the tribunal, only to be released "because no positive proof implicated them in any of the depredations committed in the territory."[24]

The absence of fresh evidence against the five prisoners and their failure to give incriminating testimony against each other might have disappointed the members of the vigilantes' executive committee, but it did not in the least discourage them from proceeding with plans for a communal execution. In the late afternoon, the condemned men were led from the store, their arms pinioned behind them, into the middle of Wallace Street. Each of the accused was guarded by a pair of vigilantes armed with Colt navy revolvers, while a phalanx of other vigilantes stood four deep facing outward toward the crowd, ready to prevent any attempt at rescue. On his way out of the store, Gallagher briefly broke free, pulled a knife from his clothes, and tried to place it to his throat, meaning to kill himself rather than suffer the stigma of being hanged. But he was disarmed, and Helm warned him to get a grip and "not make a damned fool" of himself. "There's no use in being afraid to die," Helm said.

Giving the sharp order "March!" James Williams led the procession up Wallace Street toward the corner of Van Buren, where an unfinished building—Clayton & Hale's Drug Store, still standing today—would serve as the gallows. Five ropes had been pitched over the exposed main beam, and men were now fashioning nooses on the ends and placing barrels beneath them. As the marchers reached the Virginia Hotel, Williams stopped them for a moment to allow completion of the work up the street. George Lane, seeing his patron Walter B. Dance among the onlookers, cried out for help and begged him to intercede. Dance declined. "Your dealings with me have been upright," Dance told him, "but what you have done outside of that I do not know." Lane fell to his knees in prayer, Dance joined him, and Gallagher knelt as well. Hayes Lyons spotted "X" Beidler, the little man who had dug his grave once before, and for some reason asked him to walk by his side to the scaffold and keep him company.[25]

Helm alone seemed intent on treating the occasion with rude, stoic humor. After the interrogations, the others had asked for prayer or the chance to write a letter or settle their affairs; Helm asked for a shot of whiskey. Now, in the street, he cast a sidelong glance at the handsome U.S. cavalry coat Gallagher was wearing. "Jack!" he called out. "Give me your coat. You never gave me anything." Helm spoke to several men he recognized in the crowd, saying to one, "They've got me this time!" and to another, "They've got me sure!" Tiring of the sanctity of the farewells, he barked to the vigilantes, "I wish you'd stop this damned foolishness and take me on and hang me. I don't want to stand here all day in the cold."[26]

At length the scaffold was ready and the men and their guards entered the store. Williams surveyed the five ropes that stood side by side and ordered the condemned men to be lifted onto the barrels in order—Lane first, then Lyons, Gallagher, Helm, and Parish. The hats of the five were removed. Gallagher, having recovered a touch of bravado, now demanded a drink of whiskey as his final request, and some in the crowd agitated on his behalf until a shot glass of whiskey was brought to him and he gulped it down. After the nooses were fixed and adjusted, Williams gave his famous order, "Men, do your duty!" Before anyone could act, Lane jumped off his barrel by his own volition and fell nearly to the ground, his bad foot scratching the hard-packed dirt floor as the noose choked him. Seeing Lane's struggles, Gallagher shouted angrily at the executioners, "I hope forked lightning will strike every strangling son of a bitch of you," whereupon the box beneath him was kicked away and he fell, twisting and jerking.

The death throes of the first two men did nothing to discourage the defiance of Helm. "Kick away, old fellow," he called to Gallagher. "I'll be in hell with you in a minute." Then he shouted to the crowd, "Every man for his principles! Hurrah for Jeff Davis! Let 'er rip!" With the name of his beloved president of the Confederacy still echoing from his lips, Helm was dropped, dying quickly as the noose snapped his neck. Parish, who had remained quiet through the entire ordeal, asked that a handkerchief be tied over his head. This was done, and he, too, died cleanly. On the way to the gallows, Lyons had asked to say farewell to his mistress, a request the vigilantes denied, fearing the effects of tears and sentiment on the crowd. Now he simply asked that she be given his gold watch. And he asked that his body be taken down and given a decent burial. With these final words, Lyons joined the others.

For the next two hours, the five corpses dangled side by side on the scaffold. Rarely has any American community been treated to such a spectacle—a lynching choreographed with military precision in broad daylight

Virginia City, where five men were hanged side by side at the main intersection. Courtesy of the Montana Historical Society.

at the central intersection of the largest city in the region, carried out by men who felt no need to hide their faces. The defects of the death sentences imposed on the five men certainly are open for discussion. Lane had not committed a capital offense. Lyons was subjected to a form of double jeopardy, as was Gallagher. Helm had not engaged in any known criminal activity in Montana. As an accomplice in an armed robbery, Parish alone merited execution under the rules adopted by the Vigilance Committee. By modern standards of criminal justice, it is entirely possible that none of the five would have been convicted of any offense at all, let alone a crime justifying the death penalty.

Yet there was virtually no dissent over the outcome. Some historians have argued that the vigilante leaders intimidated their fellow settlers into silence and acquiescence when they might otherwise have objected to the severity of the punishment being inflicted. The record suggests otherwise. "All of them said they were innocent, but their guilt appeared well established," Granville Stuart wrote in his diary. In letters and journal entries written at the time, and in memoirs and oral histories written or dictated later, the settlers of Bannack and Alder Gulch express a nearly unanimous sense of relief that the vigilantes were acting to make the trails safe. On the day the five men were executed, miner James Morley confided in his diary, "Such wholesale hanging ought to rid the country of these desperadoes who have rendered traveling so dangerous." The next day, settler John Jones wrote his wife, Rebecca, in Missouri, "By the time the committee are done, people will be able to travel safely." The guilt or innocence of any given target of the vigilantes mattered far less to the settlers than their overriding concern about safety on the trails between the gold camps and from the camps back to "the States." The author has reviewed more than forty first-hand accounts of the period in question—several of them previously unpublished—and can find not a single criticism of the executions carried out by the vigilantes. As Alexander Toponce put it in his memoirs many years afterward, "I don't think they made a mistake in hanging anybody."[27]

For a miner who yearned to bring his wife out west to join him or a merchant who needed to pay off his creditors back home, for any man who had felt his flesh crawl with fear of assault or bullying, the vengeance exacted by the vigilantes was a cause for gratification. The men seized by the committee were not viewed as defendants to be charged with specific crimes and tried by rule of law, but as menaces to be expunged for the benefit of public order. Their executions were carried out publicly to make a point. "Far from the control of any organized government," Francis Thompson wrote, "the people felt compelled in their might to rise and show the gamblers, robbers, and murderers that they could no longer terrorize the people." As a matter of crowd psychology, the condemned men were lumped together as villains, with little distinction drawn between their degrees of culpability or the threat they actually posed to the community. Chauncey Barbour, an eyewitness to the hangings in Virginia City, later gave a vivid, merciless description of the vigilantes' prey: "broken-down gamblers and adventurers, gamblers of the high-toned and nip-cat sort, pioneer pelicans who had shed their tail feathers twenty years before and run all the camps, disbanded jail-birds, fugitives from justice, veterans in robbery and murder, cadets of the dime novel school, and the whole foul rookery, hunted from their roosts elsewhere . . . " To use a modern locution, the settlers dehumanized their targets, making it easier to justify putting them to death.[28]

The lone exception to this wholesale condemnation came from Alder Gulch's small coterie of defense lawyers. Two of the attorneys who had represented George Ives during his murder trial, James M. Thurmond and H. P. A. Smith, objected loudly to the executions of the five men. While their arguments were not recorded in writing, one can imagine the points they made about the secret tribunal—no jury of peers, no chance to confront one's accusers, no rules of evidence, no representation by counsel, and so on. The procedural flaws were obvious and abundant. Thurmond and Smith had begun agitating against extralegal justice with the execution of Ives and had been trying for several days to recruit an organized opposition to the Vigilance Committee. They did not get very far, but the vigilantes displayed little patience for criticism of their actions and responded by banishing both lawyers on the same afternoon as the mass hanging. "About dark," Granville Stuart recorded in his diary, "written notices were handed to H. P. A. Smith and J. M. Thurmond, lawyers of this place, telling them to leave not only the gulch but this part of Idaho Territory and never to return under penalty of death." According to Stuart, Smith responded by bursting into tears and weeping profusely. The less theatrical Thurmond remained dry-eyed. Both expressed bitter anger at their treatment.[29]

Had the two lawyers possessed a bit more diplomacy, they might have enjoyed a different fate. One of their colleagues, Alexander J. Davis, another of the defense lawyers in the Ives trial, shared their distaste for vigilante justice. He considered his invitation to join the Vigilance Committee a form of coercion and refused to become a member. When its leaders threatened to banish him, he summoned his courage and refused that course as well, announcing he would stay even at the risk of death. Davis was a man of unusual character. A native of Kentucky, he had grown up in a slaveholding family. On the eve of the Civil War, he freed his slaves as a matter of principle—and then joined the Confederacy because he believed in states' rights. Captured by Union forces, he gave his parole that he would fight no more and moved to the West.[30]

Rather than denounce them publicly and incur their wrath, "Aleck" Davis stood up to the vigilantes in a quiet, determined way and made his points with calm conviction. The committee had done what its leaders thought they must, Davis said, and that was that. He did not agree, but neither did he censure them. No one could undo the summary executions and he had no wish to try. But the vigilantes had won. They were in charge now. They had made their show of force and routed the ranks of whatever criminal ring might have existed. They had no effective opposition, and no one to fear. From now on, Davis insisted, those accused of crime should have the benefit of a people's court with the minimal protections that came with the presence of lawyers, juries, rules of procedure, and public scrutiny. The Ives trial had met those standards, Davis argued, but the secret tribunals that had led to the executions of the men in Bannack and Virginia City had not. They must not be repeated.

Remarkably, Davis not only convinced Pfouts and the rest of the vigilantes' executive committee that he was right, but got himself named judge of the people's court as well. Pfouts in particular seemed impressed with Davis's forthrightness, and the two men became fast friends. "After the execution of the five men on the fourteenth of January," Dimsdale wrote, "the vigilantes considered that their work was nearly ended. They had freed the country from highwaymen and murderers to a great extent, and they determined that in the absence of the regular civil authority they would establish a people's court, where all offenders should be tried by a judge and jury." Dimsdale's account fails to credit Davis with gaining this outcome almost singled-handedly, and it also glosses over the committee's insistence on finishing its mission by tracking down and punishing the fugitives who remained at large. Had the vigilantes concluded their activities with the executions of the five men in Virginia City on January 14, 1864, they might have secured a less controversial place in history and escaped the distinction of carrying out the deadliest campaign of vigilante justice ever prosecuted out in the United States. But they did not. They agreed to submit *future* cases of alleged criminal activity to Judge Davis for public trial, but in the meantime they intended to continue rounding up the men they held responsible for the crimes of recent weeks.[31]

There was now a sense of urgency about the vigilantes' mission, as if they faced a deadline and had to complete their task before Judge Davis inaugurated his people's court and insisted on trying the accused. From now on, if wanted men were captured and returned to Alder Gulch, there would be trials—expensive, time-consuming trials, with slippery, uncertain outcomes. But if the wanted men should be taken in the wild or in distant settlements far from Alder Gulch, then the vigilantes could impose justice in the field and free the territory of troublemakers once and for all. In sum, the agreement reached between Davis and the executive committee had a substantial loophole: the summary executions would end soon—but not immediately.

Completing their agenda that night, as the bodies of the five men still swung from the crossbeam, the executive committee organized a party of twenty-one riders who would leave at dawn in search of the remaining men targeted for death. The vigilantes still wanted Aleck Carter for the murder of Nicholas Tiebolt. They wanted "Dutch John" Wagner's partner, Steve Marshland, for the attempted robbery of Moody's wagon train. They wanted Bill Bunton, the co-owner of Rattlesnake Ranch, for the holdup of "Bummer Dan" McFadden. And they wanted other men named as criminal conspirators by "Red" Yeager, the bartender of Rattlesnake Ranch, when he confessed to James Williams.[32]

As a mark of the fresh haste spurring the committee, they did not wait for volunteers to fill the ranks of the search party. They drafted members and ordered them to go, and they ignored the protests of at least one settler who asked for time to arrange his business affairs before leaving. Conrad Kohrs, the future cattle baron of Montana, was living at the time in Summit, the highest and farthest of the mining camps of Alder Gulch, where he and a partner kept a herd. Kohrs told the leaders of the executive committee he was willing to go on the raid, but he owed money to a man in Deer Lodge and needed to make a quick trip home to fetch his cache of gold dust. They flatly refused and told him he must prepare to leave from Nevada City at once. According to his memoirs, Kohrs had to borrow $5,000 on the spot from two private bankers at a steep interest rate of 10 percent per month, "which looked almost like highway robbery." That Kohrs would use such a loaded phrase, writing many years after the fact, suggests how angry he remained about the incident and how unfairly he thought the vigilantes had treated him.[33]

It is a matter of some irony that the only surviving, written complaints about the vigilantes were lodged by men objecting to the costs associated with paying for their mission, rather than the mission itself. Kohrs was not alone in grousing about the attitude of the executive committee. His friend Johnny Grant, who had a ranch near Deer Lodge (which Kohrs later bought), recalled that the party of twenty-one "came to my place and they wanted to help themselves to my horses. I objected to having them help themselves. I told them they were as bad as the robbers." John Grannis, the miner, complained in his diary that he could not go prospecting because "the vigilance" had commandeered his pony for their venture. Under the auspices of their secretary, John Lott, the vigilantes instituted a "ferreting fund," raising money by subscription to pay the expenses of Captain Williams and "X" Beidler and other vigilantes, including the Lott brothers themselves, and these fees eventually created resentment, as did the expectation that all newcomers to Alder Gulch and Bannack would join the vigilance committee and support its work financially.[34]

The harshest criticism of the vigilantes came from the two men whose livelihoods were most severely impacted by them, the banished lawyers. Even as five dead men hung in the night air, Smith and Thurmond packed their belongings under duress and prepared to leave, swearing to get even. One of them, Thurmond, would cause the vigilantes serious trouble in days to come, and he would do so not because they had executed his client, Ives, nor because they had hanged five other men over his objections, but because they had put him out of work.

CHAPTER FIFTEEN

One Hundred and Two!

On Sunday, January 17, 1864, Mary Edgerton sat at the rough hewn dinner table in her cabin by Grasshopper Creek, dipped her quill pen in ink, and began a long letter to her family back in Tallmadge, Ohio. "The past week has been an eventful one here," she wrote with some understatement. Her husband, Sidney, the chief justice of Idaho Territory, had been planning to return east to Washington, D.C., via Tallmadge, for several weeks. But he had been delayed, first by the weather and then by the campaign the vigilantes waged to track down and execute the highwaymen who had made travel unsafe. "I hope the Committee will not have to hang any more [men] here for I do not like such excitement," she told her sisters and mother, "but I shall feel that Mr. Edgerton will go much more safely now, than he would have gone two weeks ago, for I have no doubt that they intended to rob him . . . "[1]

Written a week after the hanging of Sheriff Henry Plummer in Bannack and two days after the group execution of five men in Virginia City, Mary Edgerton's letter serves as a sort of affidavit, setting out in detail her version of the events that triggered the wave of violent retribution. She explained that some of the suspects had implicated others. "Their confession was that there was a regularly formed band of them and that the sheriff of this district was the captain." And, she said, the crimes committed by that organized ring were not limited to the specific incidents of robbery and killing that had become a matter of record. "During the past year," Mrs. Edgerton wrote, "they have committed about one hundred murders—and these murders had not been discovered by the people here. The victims were those who had made money and had started for the States. They were murdered and robbed and then their bodies, some of them, cut into pieces and put under the ice, others burned and others buried."

This wildly exaggerated claim of a hundred homicides merits examination. What inspired Mrs. Edgerton to inflate the number of deaths in the region by such magnitude? It is conceivable, of course, that she invented a figure meant to bolster the case in support of the vigilantes. Eight or ten killings, even fifteen, if one included the victims of the Magruder massacre, might not have sounded like a wave of slaughter adequate to excuse the number of executions carried out by the committee. Counting George Ives, thirteen men had been put to death by this point, more than the total executed by the two famous vigilance committees of San Francisco combined—more, in fact, than the total killed during any vigilance movement in American history, since the first so-called regulators inaugurated the use of extralegal justice in the back country of South Carolina in the 1760s. When Thomas Dimsdale wrote his series of newspaper articles about the vigilantes in the summer of 1865, he stated flatly, "By discoveries of the bodies of the victims, the confessions of the murderers before execution, and reliable information sent to the Committee, it was found that one hundred and two people had been certainly killed."[2]

One hundred and two! The use of such a precise figure has persuaded several generations of historians that it must be accurate, and most standard accounts of Montana's early days faithfully repeat the number, as do many scholarly studies of American vigilantism. Some writers have treated the number as a *minimum*, representing the "known" dead, while assuming that the actual casualty rate must have been even higher. And, as a result, the response of the vigilantes in hanging a large number of the accused perpetrators has seemed fully justified.[3]

Not surprisingly, perhaps, skeptics in recent years have disputed Dimsdale's figure and asked where he got it. The answer, it seems, is that Dimsdale got his figure where Mary Edgerton got hers—from a consensus reached around the time of the vigilante executions that the level of menace confronting the community was vastly greater than one could tell from the list of incidents in which a corpse had been recovered or some other tangible proof of a killing was in hand. Plainly, a defensive tone had taken hold, a perception that the bare facts alone might not be enough to convince the outside world that the vigilantes had acted with proper cause. One prominent revisionist has dismissed Dimsdale's book as "marred by propaganda prepared after the fact"—a harsh judgment, but one permitted by the utter unreliability of his count of victims.[4] Yet the "propaganda" did not begin with Dimsdale, and it was not the work of a professional writer setting out to whitewash the excesses of his friends and colleagues. It was in truth a far hazier thing, a collective belief that was part self-serving and part genuine hysteria. Just as settlers crossing the plains often exaggerated the danger posed by Indians, a form of mass delusion was at work—not some carefully calculated lie meant to exonerate the vigilantes for unwarranted and excessive killing, but the embrace of rumor and myth, leading to the extrapolation of several very real, very gruesome murders into a killing spree several times greater than it really was. Dread of ambush and violence in the gold camps east of the Bitterroots was no less real for an overstatement of the actual statistical risk.

Naturally, Mrs. Edgerton was echoing what her husband and others in her family, including Wilbur Sanders, had told her about the extent of the crimes committed by Henry Plummer and his band. Her men had good reason to exaggerate, both to justify the vigilante action taken to date and also to publicize the need for a new territory, the cause Edgerton was taking to Washington to press with President Lincoln and the Congress. Even so, it was an exaggeration she found entirely credible and one she passed along to her family as the simple truth. There is not the least hint of guile in her letter, no whiff of someone passing along a tall tale. It can be dangerous to attribute honesty to someone by reasoning that she would have told a better, more convincing lie if she had meant to deceive—but what else are we to make of Mrs. Edgerton's assertion that the hundred murders "had not been discovered by the people here"? By whom, then? It seems she believed that dozens upon dozens of travelers whose whereabouts were unknown, and whose families had sent letters of urgent inquiry to Bannack and Alder Gulch, had been ambushed and robbed and consigned to unmarked graves. And there were, undoubtedly, at least a few victims who fit this category, because thousands of prospectors and other itinerant settlers were crisscrossing the region, and some did meet anonymous death on the trails. Perhaps the notion of profligate death did not seem so far-fetched in a nation approaching the end of the third year of a civil war that had elevated mass casualties to a new and horrifying level.

The Edgertons' cabin in Bannack. Courtesy of the Montana Historical Society.

It is hard to see Mrs. Edgerton as much of a conniver after reading her letters. All through the intense cold snap that January she had hovered over her children at night, afraid they would catch cold or suffer frostbite. The cabin had two stoves, neither of which generated enough heat to cope with temperatures of forty below. "I never knew such cold weather or anything like it," she wrote her twin sister, Martha. "I was so afraid that the children would freeze their noses or ears in the night that [I] got up a number of times in the night to see that their heads were covered. Their beds would be covered with frost. I saw their breath freeze." And it was not just her four children—Mattie, Wright, Sidney, and Pauline—who concerned her. She was five months pregnant and would turn thirty-seven years old on January 21, and she had her own health and her unborn baby's to protect as well. Her husband was an ambitious man with personal reasons to hasten his trip east, but that ambition did not spring from a needy or demanding wife. In the privacy of her correspondence with her family, she breathed not a word of material want. She asked for thread and cloth, a sewing machine, preserved lemons and canned fruit, schoolbooks for the children, a small mirror. "In sending dry goods," she wrote, "don't send anything nice for I should never wear it here, but send things suitable for everyday wear." Knowing that her letters would be read aloud to the whole family in the parlor in Tallmadge, she took care to be discreet. "Now this next that I write don't read outloud to anyone," she cautioned her sister—and then asked her to send a chamber pot.[5]

Mrs. Edgerton believed that Sheriff Plummer and his henchmen had been plotting to waylay her husband on his way out of town, she told her sister, "for they were very anxious to know when he expected to leave here and how much company he would have, etc., etc." The execution of the men who might have carried out the plot did not greatly trouble her. "I think that there is no danger of his being robbed now," she wrote, and one could understand her sense of relief. For his part, Edgerton took advantage of the delay to complete his preparations for the trip. According to his daughter, Mattie, he thought the cause of creating a new territory would be furthered by a display of the wealth of the gold camps east of the Bitterroots, so he gathered a stockpile of gold nuggets and ingots and had them sewn inside the lining of his greatcoat and the sides of his valises. He told Mattie he would have to carry his own belongings at all times to avoid creating suspicion of his hefty cargo. Once in Washington, his daughter said, he planned to carry the gold directly onto the floors of the House and Senate chambers "to dazzle the eyes of [the] Congressmen" and "to give them some idea of the great mineral wealth of this section of the country."[6]

In addition to the gold, Edgerton carried $2,000 in cash, the fruits of a subscription among the wealthier merchants and miners who backed his campaign for a new territory and believed the purse could be of some usefulness in the corridors of power in the nation's capital. Thus laden, Edgerton finally left Bannack on the morning of Thursday, January 21, 1864, his wife's birthday, wearing a fisher fur cap to keep his head warm, leading a train of pack horses on the trail to Salt Lake City and from there east, on a mission of reverse alchemy, to turn gold into the base metal of political influence.[7]

The twenty-one men who rode off as a posse to complete the work of the Vigilance Committee did not have far to go before encountering their first target. A day after leaving Alder Gulch, as they passed into the Big Hole River valley on their way to Deer Lodge, they got word that Steve Marshland, the man wounded during the attempted robbery of the Moody wagon train, lay incapacitated in a cabin at a nearby ranch. A detail led by Thomas Pitt split off from the main posse and surrounded the cabin on the evening of January 16, 1864. After knocking on the door and getting no response, Pitt entered with his pistol drawn and found Marshland in bed in the dark, shuddering with the chills.[8]

Marshland had fared poorly after escaping the botched robbery with a gunshot wound to the chest. He had suffered severe frostbite during the harsh cold snap of early January and his lower legs and feet were now black with gangrene. Dimsdale makes a strained effort to portray Marshland as healthy enough to present a threat, but the truth is he could not defend himself and probably would have died of his injuries in a matter of days if left untreated. As it was, the vigilantes opened his shirt, found the evidence of his wound, and decided to hang him. After building a fire to warm themselves, they executed Marshland with a rope thrown over a corral log. Their custom of leaving the body to dangle had to be abandoned because the smell of decay from Marshland's legs attracted wolves, and he was buried that night.[9]

The notion that the vigilantes acted only to protect society from violent, dangerous criminals evaporated with the hanging of Marshland. Whether he could have survived being arrested and taken to Alder Gulch to face trial is a moot point, but his execution marked a new turn in the work of the vigilantes, an act of pure and simple vengeance undertaken against a helpless man. The vigilantes' executive committee had authorized the death penalty for the targets of the posse, and the sentences apparently were to be carried out regardless of the circumstances encountered at the time of arrest. Marshland was a felon, granted, but a pathetic one who posed no risk to public order. The mass hanging in Virginia City the day before had served the purpose of advertising the vigilantes' ascendancy. The truth of Lord Acton's maxim, that power tends to corrupt, was evident a day later.

(Marshland's death also provided a small but significant footnote about the challenge of identifying the vigilante leaders as their work became more secretive. In Dimsdale's account, the leader of the Marshland foray is described as "No. 84," and some historians assumed that the vigilantes had decided to go by membership numbers, much as the San Francisco Vigilance Committee of 1856 did in issuing public notices signed by "No. 33, Secretary." As it happened, though, "No. 84" was actually just a nickname. Thomas Pitt was an admirer of the abolitionist John Brown, whose knapsack, the song "John Brown's Body" reminds us, bore the number eighty-four. In his memoirs, Francis Thompson describes how Pitt liked to sing the song in a booming voice, rendering the number as "highty-four" in his English accent, and through the teasing of friends it became his moniker. As the flush of their victory wore off, the vigilantes grew guarded about discussing their activities and would not allow their real names to be used by Dimsdale and other chroniclers. But they did not go by numbers.)[10]

Rejoining the posse the next day, Pitt and his squadron continued their ride to Cottonwood, where Aleck Carter and the other wanted men were believed to be hiding out. Unlike the frigid, tormented journey of late December and early January, the second mission to the area moved at a fast clip, with two columns of riders mounted side by side, making sixty to seventy miles per day. The men endured hardship, refusing to light campfires or cook their meals for fear of giving away their position, but they did not suffer anything close to the misery they had earlier. Around four o'clock on the afternoon of Monday, January 18, 1864, they halted on the outskirts of Cottonwood, by the banks of Deer Lodge Creek, and sent a scouting party forward. The alleged second-in-command of Plummer's crime ring, Bill Bunton, had moved to Cottonwood in recent weeks and was running a saloon there. The advance party reported him holed up in a cabin behind the bar, and by nightfall the full company of twenty-one had arrived and surrounded the small complex.

James Williams, the captain of the vigilantes, banged on Bunton's door several times without getting a reply and then shouted for him by name. Bunton answered, demanding to know who was outside and what they wanted. At length a young man opened the door a crack and three of the vigilantes, led by the diminutive "X" Beidler, rushed in and attempted to seize the stoutly built Bunton. Beidler was thrown off and spun into a corner, but the other men succeeded in subduing Bunton and tying his hands behind him. They also arrested Tex Crowell, one of Bunton's friends and a suspected lookout in some of the recent robberies. The two were taken to a nearby cabin and held overnight.[11]

In the morning, after breakfast, Williams and other vigilante leaders conducted an interrogation of Bunton. Erastus "Red" Yeager, the cook at Rattlesnake Ranch, had identified Bunton as Plummer's top lieutenant and also provided details of several specific crimes Bunton had committed, including his involvement as a "pigeon" in the "Bummer Dan" McFadden robbery and some earlier episodes of cattle rustling on the western side of the Rockies. Yeager blamed his own predicament on Bunton's bad influence and made plain his animus toward him, giving strong evidence in the eyes of the vigilantes that Bunton was guilty. On a show of hands, they voted unanimously to hang him, even though he protested his innocence.

After the brief hearing, the vigilantes marched Bunton to a neighboring corral and fixed a noose on a crossbeam between two upright posts. Bunton insisted on taking a hand in his own execution and jumped to his death before the vigilantes could pull the plank from beneath him. As in other cases, the lack of a proper trial left Bunton's friends with a powerful protest against the outcome. One of the young men who worked for him, Dave Meiklejohn, went on to become a deputy federal marshal and insisted in later years that Bunton was wrongly accused. The vigilantes, he said, had acted like a mob and "looted" Bunton's cabin and saloon and "took over everything that Bunton had owned." In the aftermath of the hanging, the horrified wife of the corral owner had the posts cut down so they could never again serve such a purpose.[12]

As if to mitigate the merciless executions of Marshland and Bunton, the vigilantes adopted a surprisingly generous attitude toward Tex Crowell, deciding to release him for lack of evidence. Had they examined him more closely, Dimsdale swore, they would have found proof "that he was a highwayman and a common thief," but at the time they opted for leniency. Their decision can be interpreted as showing that the vigilantes did in fact weigh the evidence for and against some of the men they captured—and it can just as easily be used to ask why they voted to hang so many other men whose guilt seemed equally unproven. By their own by-laws, the vigilantes were authorized to arrest men they suspected of criminal acts "and then report the same with proof to the Chief who will thereupon call a meeting of the Executive Committee and the judgment of such Executive Committee shall be final." Apparently, Paris Pfouts and his seventeen-member executive committee had conducted tribunals "in absentia" for the men on the wanted list and had convicted them and sentenced them to death. But if Williams and his posse were simply carrying out orders, what reason was there for them to take a vote? By what authority were they acting as a jury? Why had they executed Marshland and Bunton but not Crowell? The moral and legal legitimacy of the Vigilance Committee, a delicate question, grew murkier.[13]

Carrying out their sweep of the small community at Cottonwood, the vigilantes discovered that their original target, Aleck Carter, had eluded them once again. He had fled along with some friends, reportedly in the direction of Hell Gate, the tiny settlement near the present-day city of Missoula, nearly a hundred miles downstream on the Clark Fork River, northwest toward the passes of the Bitterroot Mountains. Determined to finish the job this time, Williams ordered the posse to saddle up and give chase. As if to test the vigilantes anew, conditions turned harsh again, and the men had to force their horses through a snow cover two feet deep. Again the horses had to paw through the snow to forage, and again the men suffered from intense cold. At one point they attempted to cross a frozen creek and several riders broke through, sending man and beast alike tumbling into the inky, icy water. On another occasion a horse stepped into a badger hole, broke its leg, and had to be destroyed. The party spent one night at a ranch, grateful for fire, blankets, and warmth, and then resumed their glacial journey.

On the evening of Sunday, January 24, 1864, the vigilantes reached the outskirts of Hell Gate, the remote settlement where the Stuart brothers, Granville and James, once held office as county commissioner and sheriff, respectively, of Missoula County, a jurisdiction created by the lawmakers of Washington Territory. The area was now part of Idaho Territory, whose legislature in far-off Lewiston was just beginning to get organized and provide some of the tools of government for the vast region. On January 16, eight days earlier, the Idaho legislature had created ten counties east of the Bitterroots, but it would be some time before the news crossed the mountains. As far as Williams was concerned, the vigilantes remained a law unto themselves.

Wary of losing his prey again, Williams stopped short of Hell Gate and divided his command, sending one party ahead several miles along the Clark Fork River to cut off an avenue of escape to the west through the mountain passes on the Mullan Road. Another party of vigilantes rode at a gallop directly into Hell Gate, looking for Carter and his associates and also for Cyrus Skinner, the former owner of the Elkhorn saloon in Bannack, a friend of Plummer's and an escapee from San Quentin. "Red" Yeager had identified Skinner as a member of the sheriff's criminal conspiracy, a spy and robber and also a fence for stolen goods. In their haste, the men overshot Skinner's saloon, riding headlong past it before stopping and turning to wheel back, as Skinner watched in bemusement from the front door. The riders ordered him to throw up his hands and placed him under arrest. He put up no resistance, but his wife, Nelly, angrily mocked the vigilantes and asked sarcastically if they had learned their theatrics from a troupe of traveling actors who had once put on a show in Bannack.[14]

After seizing Skinner and binding his hands, the vigilantes entered the house next door and found their elusive quarry at last. Aleck Carter was lying half-drunk in bed and surrendered without putting up a fight. Coming slowly to his senses, he looked closely at the men who had captured him. He read the expressions on their faces and said warily, "This is tight papers, ain't it, boys?" According to Dimsdale, Carter listened as his captors recited the list of men they had executed to date and remarked, "All right, not an innocent man hung yet."

Skinner and Carter were taken to the settlement's general store, operated by merchants C. P. Higgins and Frank Worden, and questioned for several hours. Exactly what they confessed is a matter of conjecture, but the vigilantes learned that Carter had wounded another man, Johnny

Cooper, in a drunken dispute the day before. A slight young man with a knack for handling horses, Cooper had been planning to leave Hell Gate with Carter and a small herd when they started bickering and Carter pulled his pistol and shot Cooper three times. The vigilantes found Cooper lying in bed in a back room at Skinner's saloon and arrested him. He, too, was brought to Higgins & Worden's Store for interrogation.[15]

While Williams and the main posse were detaining Skinner, Carter, and Cooper and trying to sort out the cases against them and learn the particulars of the recent shooting affray, the advance party led by Thomas Pitt rode beyond Hell Gate and paid a call on a rancher named Barney O'Keefe, a colorful character who liked to be called "the Baron" and wore the uniform of a colonel in the Georgia militia. O'Keefe feared he might be a target of the vigilantes himself and asked nervously if they meant to arrest him. Pitt quickly assuaged his concerns. The vigilantes had heard that Bob Zachary was staying with O'Keefe, and Zachary was wanted for questioning in the robbery of Leroy Southmayd. Zachary had been lying low since that episode, as had another man identified by Southmayd as a participant, "Whiskey Bill" Graves. Graves, too, was reported to be holed up somewhere in the vicinity of Hell Gate, and the vigilantes were after him as well. Southmayd had not forgotten how Carter, Zachary, and Graves menaced him on the trail from Bannack to Alder Gulch, and how Plummer's two deputies, Stinson and Ray, had appeared to warn them off by singing at the top of their lungs. Southmayd's testimony had been crucial in convicting George Ives, and the same evidence implicated Zachary and Graves. As "Baron" O'Keefe quickly admitted, Zachary was indeed his guest—adding immediately that the vigilantes were welcome to him. Zachary was arrested in a bedroom of O'Keefe's ranch house and taken into custody to be returned to Hell Gate.[16]

The end of the vigilantes' mission was nearing, but the substantial number of wanted men who remained at large, combined with the harsh winter conditions and the remoteness of the region, contributed to a good deal of confusion about the exact chronology of events. In talking with O'Keefe, Pitt learned that an alleged road agent named George Shears was also in the area, staying at a nearby ranch. Precisely what crimes Shears might have committed remains a matter of utter mystery, as his name does not appear in any letters, diaries, or other documents of the period, nor in any subsequent memoirs or accounts. Apparently, he was a garden-variety horse thief because he freely made a confession to the vigilantes and, in effect, volunteered to be executed. "Taking a walk with [Pitt]," Dimsdale wrote, "he pointed out to him the stolen horses in the coral, and confessed his guilt, as a man would speak of the weather."

Confronted with such a complaisant offender, Pitt and the other members of the advance party decided there was no point in returning Shears to Hell Gate for further questioning. They informed him they planned to hang him on the spot. He made no objection, according to Pitt, but seemed "perfectly satisfied." He was taken to the barn, where a noose awaited him. Rather than place him on a box or plank, the vigilantes told him to climb the rungs of a ladder. He did so and then uttered a remark that entered Montana legend. "Gentlemen," he said, "I am not used to this business, never having been hung before. Shall I jump off or slide off?" Told to jump, he said, "All right, good-bye," and launched himself into eternity. His death was recorded late on the night of Sunday, January 24, 1864. That same night, William "Old Man" Clark, the veteran prospector whose search for the killers of Nicholas Tiebolt had triggered the trial of George Ives and the subsequent vigilance movement, split off from the vanguard and went riding south in search of "Whiskey Bill" Graves.[17]

After midnight, back at Hell Gate, Williams and the main body of vigilantes completed their questioning of the captives. Skinner and Carter were taken to the corral behind Higgins & Worden's Store and hanged, both men proclaiming their innocence to the very end. Confronted with Ives's final words accusing him of killing Tiebolt, Carter denied involvement and remained defiant, telling Williams, "If I had my hands free, you son of a bitch, I'd make you take that back." It appears that both men were doomed as much by their behavior in Hell Gate as by their previous misdeeds: Higgins and Worden kept a safe in their store, and they believed the men had designs on it and on the $65,000 in gold dust it held. Thus the executions of Carter and Skinner could be considered preventive as well as punitive. Similarly, Cooper was convicted largely on the complaint of his neighbors that he frightened them and stole from them by simple intimidation. He had been planning to marry a young woman in Hell Gate, the daughter of a French fur trader and an Indian mother, and the girl's father sealed his fate by complaining that he was a thief. Unable to walk because of the injuries inflicted on him by Carter, Cooper was brought by sleigh to the makeshift scaffold, where he followed Carter and Skinner into oblivion. At daybreak, Pitt and his party returned to Hell Gate with

Zachary, who also was hanged, becoming the fourth casualty of the day, January 25, 1864.[18]

The work of the vigilantes was almost over. "Old Man" Clark and his two companions rode south from Frenchtown into the Bitterroot River valley toward Fort Owen, searching for "Whiskey Bill" Graves. They found him two days later in the wild, snow-blind and unable to resist arrest. Clark demanded that Graves confess his crimes, but he, too, refused. Clark took him away from Fort Owen out of deference to the Indians camped there, who thought hanging was a barbaric practice and would have scattered in horror if the execution had taken place in their presence. Out on the trail, lacking the logs, walls, crossbeams and other facilities that had provided the tools for previous hangings, Clark fashioned a noose, tied it to a tree, mounted Graves on a horse underneath, and spurred him to his death. This last hanging, on January 26, 1864, brought to twenty-one the number of men executed by the Vigilance Committee.[19]

After disposing of the property of the dead men, Williams regrouped his party and prepared them for the ride back to Nevada City. "Tired and worn," Dimsdale recorded, "the command reached [home] and received the congratulations and thanks of all good men." He likened them to Joshua's army.[20]

How shall we judge the acts of the vigilantes? The safest answer seems to be, subjectively. Because of his charisma and mystique, and because he held an office of public trust and abused it, most of the historical debate has focused on Henry Plummer. As we have seen, the sheriff invites a full gamut of responses and characterizations, from sociopath to hero, with a broad middle ground reserved for those who accept the reasons for his death without the comfort of proof of his guilt beyond a reasonable doubt. The eight men hunted down and executed by the vigilantes between January 16 and January 26, 1864, did not meet modern standards of capital crime justifying the death penalty. But like earlier targets, they were an unsavory lot whose deaths are hard to mourn. Credible evidence existed that four of them—Marshland, Carter, Zachary, and Graves—had committed armed robbery, a felony that merited hanging under the vigilantes' rules and by general assent of the settlers. By shooting his friend, Cooper, in a drunken rage, Carter satisfied another test of the vigilantes' authority, the need to protect public safety. Yet that need was dwindling. In their latest foray, the vigilantes had hanged two badly injured men, along with others who seemed only to be trying to banish themselves from the area. The very difficulty of finding the wanted men suggested they posed little threat to the population centers of the mining camps at Bannack and Alder Gulch.

And there was another disturbing element. The vigilantes had acted in large part on the basis of information given to them by "Red" Yeager, who provided a list of men allegedly in league with Plummer in a tightly knit criminal conspiracy. Yet no such list survived. There seems little doubt that Yeager confessed to *something,* but the particulars—and the names of those he implicated—remain a matter of dispute. As described by Dimsdale in his newspaper series in 1865, for instance, Plummer's band included the men responsible for the massacre of Lloyd Magruder and his party in the Bitterroots the previous October. According to Dimsdale, the Magruder robbery was planned by Plummer in "council" with Cyrus Skinner, "who ingratiated himself into the favor of Page, Romaine, and others, so that Magruder thought his murderers were his friends, and went on his last journey without suspicion." But it is a matter of record that Plummer warned his friend, Francis Thompson, that "Doc" Howard and his party were "cut-throats and robbers," a warning he almost certainly would not have uttered if they had been his accomplices. In his extensive testimony after turning state's witness in the trial of the killers in Idaho, Billy Page failed to implicate Plummer or Skinner in Magruder's murder, and there is no other evidence to suggest that the perpetrators, who fled west to California, planned to share the proceeds of the crime with anyone back in Montana. It appears Skinner's only contact with Magruder's killers was to have served them a drink in his saloon. Just six days before his death, Skinner borrowed several hundred dollars from George Chrisman, the respected shopkeeper from Bannack, a transaction that would have made no sense if Skinner feared execution or Chrisman knew he was marked for it.[21]

Some skeptics have argued that Dimsdale made up the list he attributed to Yeager after the fact and simply placed on it everyone hanged by the vigilantes, thereby concocting an ex post facto validation for the executions. It is a plausible theory, but one weakened by Dimsdale's failure to do a thorough and complete job if deceit had been his purpose. As published by Dimsdale, Yeager's list contains the names of two men—Gad

Moore and Billy Terwilliger—who were not targeted by the vigilantes, and it excludes another, Jack Gallagher, who was one of the most prominent members of Plummer's circle. Another name on the list, "Mexican Frank," may or may not have referred to José Pizanthia, but if Dimsdale's purpose was to justify the most invidious of the executions, one imagines he would have gotten the name right. Absent discovery of the list itself, no certain conclusion about its authenticity seems possible.[22]

Still, the fragility of Yeager's evanescent list is more than a matter for parlor debate by historians. Even among a populace united in relief and gratitude that violence on the trails was being curtailed, the shortcuts taken by the vigilantes in imposing justice gradually aroused a small but vocal opposition. H. P. A. Smith, the lachrymose defense lawyer who was banished to Gallatin City, near the headwaters of the Missouri River, renewed his objections to the hangings and was sent away for good to Salt Lake City, where he joined his colleague James Thurmond in denouncing the vigilantes for taking the law into their own hands and targeting innocent men. Despite the isolation of Bannack and Alder Gulch, the vigilantes were not operating in a vacuum, and accounts of their activities began turning up in newspapers in California, Oregon, Colorado, Idaho, and Utah. The *Sacramento Union,* once Plummer's nemesis, ran an article on the hangings that quoted Plummer's associates as expressing "the greatest astonishment at the charge preferred against him—of being the chief of this organized band of fiends." The same newspaper questioned the case against George "Club-foot" Lane and wondered pointedly "whether the organization of robbers and murderers was as great as reported." The *Portland Oregonian* suggested that Williams's posse was in fact a band of bullies acting to keep other prospectors away from the rich diggings east of the Bitterroots, an accusation seconded by a newspaper in Idaho.[23]

Word of the hangings reached the East Coast as well, including the ears of some of Plummer's relatives, whose response to the news was significant. For years, historians have relied on an account in Nathaniel Langford's influential work, *Vigilante Days and Ways,* to describe a meeting in New York City in 1869 in which a brother and sister of Plummer's called upon Edwin Purple, a Bannack pioneer who had returned east, for information about the circumstances of their sibling's death. According to Langford, he accompanied Purple on his visit and found that Henry Plummer had written his family letters warning that he was in mortal danger at the hands of Southern sympathizers because of his loyalty to the Union in the Civil War. "They honestly believed," Langford wrote of the brother and sister, "that his loyalty and patriotism had cost him his life, and they mourned his loss not only as a brother, but as a martyr in the cause of his country." Langford said he and Purple had to argue urgently to dissuade the Plummers from a planned trip west to avenge their brother's death, and succeeded only after supplying a copy of Dimsdale's book detailing Plummer's criminal career. On learning the full truth about Plummer's villainy, Langford reported, the brother's voice was "broken by sobs and sighs," the sister was "prostrated with grief," and the two called off their journey.[24]

Those familiar with Langford's flair for the melodramatic have had their doubts about the accuracy of his version of this encounter, and thanks to a fresh discovery in the archives of Montana State University we now have the benefit of a more straightforward explanation. Charles Ohle, a pioneer merchant who left Virginia City for Missouri in the winter of 1864 and then traveled to New York City, wrote his friend and partner John S. "Jack" Mendenhall on March 24, 1864, saying, "I learn from the papers, and from letters I have seen from Bannack, that the 'ruffs' and thieves about the mines have been pretty well cleaned out and that parties can travel through the country now with some degree of safety." The "ringleaders," he added, seemed to have been wiped out. According to Ohle, Plummer's brother already had called on Purple at this point "and asked Ned if he knew what [Plummer] had been doing to deserve such a fate." Because it was "a very delicate matter," Ohle added, "Ned made it as smooth as possible [and] did not tell Plummer's brother why he had been hung." The sister, he said, continued to believe that Plummer's death "was for political purposes." Thus the meeting with Purple did not shed much light on the reasons the vigilantes had for executing Plummer, and probably reflects the same challenge Wilbur Sanders and others experienced in convincing the town fathers of Bannack that Plummer was the mastermind of the criminal ring. But Plummer's siblings did not take up their brother's cause, so far as is known, and there is no record of their pursuing any inquiry into his death. Indeed, their names are lost to history, and it may be that the man who met with Purple was not Plummer's brother at all, but rather his cousin, Horatio Nelson Plummer, the sea captain, who was the only member of Plummer's family known to be living in New York City at the time. In any case, the death of Henry Plummer did not become a cause célèbre in the East, the West, or even in his own family.[25]

During the same week that Williams and his posse were off in pursuit of the wanted men at Deer Lodge and Hell Gate, the weather in Montana improved enough to permit general travel, and hundreds of miners joined various "grand stampedes," as Granville Stuart called them, dashing off in all directions in pursuit of rumored new gold finds. Barney Hughes, one of the six discoverers of the Alder Gulch diggings, led a large group north and east into the Gallatin River valley and made camp there. Others headed to the Boulder River and Wisconsin Creek. Stuart recorded with satisfaction in his diary that business was good. "Horses are selling very high," he wrote. "Any 'plug' brings from eighty to one hundred dollars."[26]

Unhappily for the treasure seekers, no new deposits of consequence were found, but the brief gold rush of late January 1864 did have a significant side effect. With so many men out in the field, the hiding place of Bill Hunter was discovered, sending the vigilantes on a last foray after the man who escaped their death sentence during the mass hangings in Virginia City. Hunter had suffered during the cold snap and was holed up in a cabin in the Gallatin valley with two settlers who took mercy on him and gave him a refuge in their tiny back bedroom. With Williams and his party just returned from their difficult travels, a small, fresh posse of four men—led by Adriel Davis, the sheriff of the Junction mining district, and including John Lott, John Bagg, and Richard McLaren—set off to track Hunter and bring him to justice.

On the night of Tuesday, February 2, 1864, Davis's party arrived at the cabin in question and posed as exhausted prospectors eager for a night's lodging. They made no inquiries about the silent boarder in the back room, but in the morning they burst through the door and arrested him at gunpoint. According to Dimsdale, Hunter asked to be taken back to Virginia City to face the charges against him, and one of the vigilantes agreed and told him there was a horse outside for him to ride. This was a ruse, however, meant to get Hunter away from the cabin without arousing the suspicions and resistance of his hosts. Once they were a few miles distant from the cabin, the vigilantes stopped, took a vote, and decided to hang Hunter on the spot, over the objections of the posse member who had promised to convey him to Virginia City. Left dangling from a tree limb along the trail, Hunter was "the last of Henry Plummer's band," by Dimsdale's reckoning, the final target of the Vigilance Committee, executed late on the morning of February 3, 1864.[27]

Writing a benediction on their activities, Dimsdale praised the vigilantes for carrying out a "dreadful and disgusting duty" that brought order and tranquility to a violent region. He did not apologize for the lie they told Hunter, but he did choose an odd way of summing up their campaign. "The vigilantes," he wrote, "for the sake of their country, encountered popular dislike, the envenomed hatred of the bad, and the cold toleration of some of the unwise good." After enjoying almost universal support in their first days of operation, the vigilantes by the time of Hunter's death had managed to raise eyebrows both at home and abroad. Their conquest was so swift, so complete that in the space of one month they had exhausted their license to act at will.[28]

On February 7, 1864, the first Sunday after Hunter's death, the settlers of Alder Gulch took advantage of a cold, clear day to call a miners' meeting at Virginia City and enact a set of laws governing public decorum. Among other things, the participants in the town meeting voted to impose fines for littering, cursing, discharging firearms within the city limits, and frequenting houses of ill repute. As if to emphasize the widespread sense that evil had been defeated and a new order put in place, the settlers moved directly from vigilantism to the embrace of utopia, adopting a code of morals and manners based on the assumption that from now on people would begin behaving themselves (or if not, that enforcement somehow would take care of itself). The laws were to be administered by Alexander Davis, the attorney who had been selected to serve as judge of a new people's court after objecting to the summary justice dispensed by the vigilantes. In theory, at least, mob rule was now a thing of the past.

Not everyone shared the mood of triumph. Granville Stuart confided a note of skepticism in his diary, saying the ordinance against visiting brothels "is very foolish & will probably be a dead letter." As a practical matter, the gold camps of Montana were still a remote, virtually ungoverned province of Idaho Territory. The territorial legislature had only gotten around to adopting a code of civil and criminal laws on February 4, three days earlier. On February 6, James Fergus, the miner who so desperately missed his wife, was named commissioner of Madison County, the new jurisdiction that contained the mining districts of Alder Gulch, but it would be several days before travelers from Lewiston crossed the Bitterroots and brought him word of the appointment. Sidney Edgerton had yet to reach Washington to begin work on creating a new territory. The potential for mischief remained, largely undiminished.[29]

In his diary entry for Wednesday, February 24, 1864, Stuart wrote matter-of-factly, "Slade and Fairweather on a drunk today." The item was not exactly news. J. A. Slade, the legendary boss of the Overland stage, the man who carried the dried ears of a slain enemy in his pockets, and Bill Fairweather, the wild-eyed prospector who had held off a tribe of hostile Indians by waving a rattlesnake at them, were a pair of notorious, hell-raising drinkers, loud and unruly and, as it happened, tailor-made for a toot that would test the new civility around them in the days to come.

CHAPTER SIXTEEN

Slade of the Overland

Slade of the Overland! Here was a man to conjure with—legend of the Old West, larger-than-life figure, carrying those two dried and cured ears in his pockets, trophies taken from a nemesis who shot him five times but failed to kill him and paid the price. Thomas Dimsdale, the vigilantes' chronicler, wrote extensively about Slade, and Mark Twain appropriated the material for a tribute to Slade in *Roughing It*. Charles Dickens, on a visit to the United States, borrowed a friend's copy of Dimsdale, pronounced it one of the best books he had read, and said he, too, wanted to write about the vaunted vigilantes. Quite an irony, then, that of all the literary titans who tackled Slade, the one who captured him most vividly was little Molly Sheehan, the perceptive eleven-year-old whose sharp eye fell on all that surrounded her in the Montana gold camps.[1]

According to Dimsdale, J. A. Slade—the first initial stood for James, or John, or most likely Joseph, no one could agree—made his reputation as a boss on the Overland Trail, where he killed a corrupt stationmaster named Jules Reni and kept his ears as souvenirs. Slade came to Montana in 1863 in the same wagon train with James Williams, losing to him in a trailside election for captaincy of the mission. Settling in Virginia City, Slade worked as a freighter and earned a small fortune recovering cargo that was abandoned when the Missouri River remained too shallow for navigation. Slade and his wife, a black-haired beauty named Maria, settled on a creek on the Madison River and built a comfortable stone cabin where they might have enjoyed a life of quiet domesticity except for one thing: Slade was a drunk, and when he went on one of his fabled benders he turned into an absolute menace—an "ogre," in Twain's word. Sober, according to Twain, who met him briefly on a trip west, Slade was "so friendly and so gentle spoken that I warmed to him in spite of his awful history." Drunk, Slade liked to "take the town," as he called it—racing hell-bent up and down the street on his horse, hollering, shooting his pistol, riding into stores and saloons, upending furniture, breaking glasses, tossing gold scales into the street, and terrorizing all those he encountered. Molly Sheehan had the opportunity of witnessing one of these episodes one day while walking toward the meat market in Virginia City.

> I was alarmed [she wrote] by a clatter past me of horse's hoofs and the crack of pistol shots. A man galloping his horse recklessly down the street was firing a six-shooter in the air and whooping wildly. Suddenly he reared his horse back on its haunches, turned it sharply, and forced it through the swinging door of a saloon. I sidled into the first open doorway that I dared enter. "That's Slade," said the storekeeper, "on one of his sprees, shootin' up the town, scarin' women and children. That smart aleck orter be strung up." He led me out the back door and warned me to run home quickly and stay out of range of stray bullets. "He'll get his needin's yit," he threatened.[2]

Several settlers reported encounters with Slade that left them angry or frightened or both. Nathaniel Langford was running a lumberyard in Virginia City in the summer of 1863 when Slade rode up with a crew of men and began loading boards onto his wagon. When Langford asked about payment, Slade demanded the wood on credit. Langford refused and ordered the boards taken off. Slade ordered them back on. According to Langford, teamsters loaded and unloaded the wagon three times as he and Slade kept contradicting each other, their voices and tempers rising. The situation threatened to escalate out of control when one of Langford's friends intervened and guaranteed payment on Slade's behalf. Some days later, Langford said, he encountered Slade in a bar. Slade, who had satisfied the debt by then, clapped Langford on the shoulder, offered him a drink, and said affably, "Old fellow! You didn't think I was going to cheat you out of that lumber, did you?" Though that was precisely what Langford had feared, he let the matter drop.[3]

By most accounts, Slade supported the work of the vigilantes and joined their ranks as a member, though he did not ride on any of the missions that carried out the hangings. Members of the posse that tracked down and executed Bill Hunter recalled spending a night at Slade's cabin during their search, where they managed to lose $1,200 playing poker with Slade's wife.[4]

In the weeks after Hunter's death, as Alexander Davis assumed his duties as judge of the people's court and began to enforce the new code of ordinances requiring public decorum, Slade on two occasions was summoned before the bench to pay fines for drunken mischief. Some of his friends warned him that his antics had to cease. Though he had friends among the leaders of the Vigilance Committee, including the presiding officer, merchant Paris Pfouts, Slade risked banishment or worse at their hands if he continued to defy them and run riot in their town. The vigilantes had advertised their willingness to carry out summary judgment against men they considered a threat to public safety, even if the targets occasionally included men they knew and liked. On February 17, 1864, according to the diaries of John Grannis and James Morley, an unnamed man was hanged in Virginia City in retribution for killing a man a few days earlier. No details of the episode survived, but it appears to have taken place under the auspices of the people's court with the blessing of the vigilantes.[5]

Slade promised to repent and to pay for any damages he had caused, but he could not control his drinking and the violent behavior it unleashed. On the night of March 8, 1864, he and two friends went on a drunken spree and disrupted business at two of the brothels in Virginia City. One of the madams, a woman called Moll Featherlegs, brought charges against Slade, who responded by crafting and singing a wicked ditty about her alleged association with Pfouts and the newly chosen sheriff of the county, Jeremiah M. Fox, one of the founders of the Vigilance Committee. With this libel against two of the most powerful men in town, Slade exhausted much of the remaining good will toward him.[6]

The final affray occurred two days later, on the morning of March 10, 1864, when Slade's drinking buddy, Bill Fairweather, the pioneer miner who helped discover Alder Gulch, was arrested by Fox after a violent bender that had begun the night before. The sheriff hauled Fairweather before Judge Davis and was attempting to read a writ against him when Fairweather grabbed the paper from his hand and tore it into shreds. Slade arrived on the scene, drunk as well, and egged his friend on. As Judge Davis told the story, Fairweather shook himself free from Fox's grasp, pulled out his navy revolver, and began waving the weapon around the small courtroom, driving Fox from the scene. "Go in, Bill! I'm with you!" Slade shouted. Davis, a man of remarkable composure, rose from his makeshift bench and tried to calm the two men. "At this," Davis recalled, "Slade quieted down, said he was my friend, that he had always liked me, but that he didn't like this fellow Fox, the sheriff." Sensing that Slade and Fairweather were in mortal danger, Davis urged them to go home before the vigilantes took matters into their own hands.[7]

Soothed for the moment, Slade left the courtroom. But he was still very drunk and refused to go home. By now a good many miners and merchants had gathered in the main street of town, having heard about the defiant language and gunplay in Judge Davis's court. Fairweather took heed of the warnings and left town, but Slade did not. Confronted by armed and openly hostile men, Slade ducked into a store where Davis was talking with a friend, stepped to the judge's side, and pulled a derringer on him. Ranting, Slade yelled that the judge was his hostage and would come to harm if the mob did not leave him alone. Once again, Davis displayed stoic nerves in the face of danger. He did not believe Slade meant him genuine harm, he insisted later, but others who came into the store reacted very differently. One of them, a bystander named Bill Hunt, drew two revolvers and aimed them directly at Slade's head, telling him to put down his pistol or be killed.

Slade uncocked his derringer and again apologized to the judge. "He was that kind of man," Davis recalled, "saying he was only joking with me, didn't intend harming me, but that he liked me very much." Slade was disarmed at gunpoint, and Davis urged him to flee immediately because he was now in serious danger of being hanged. But it was too late. "The first thing I knew," Davis said, "there were poked into the doorway enough guns to fill it, and I saw three hundred or four hundred armed men in military style, and their leader, Captain Williams, came in, walked up to where Slade was talking to me, put his hand on his shoulder, and said, 'Slade, you are my prisoner.'"

Williams informed Slade that the vigilantes' executive committee had met and voted to hang him within the hour. Sobered at last by his predicament and Williams's icy pronouncement, Slade begged for his life.

Alexander Davis, judge of the people's court, who tried to spare Slade's life. Courtesy of the Montana Historical Society.

Davis interceded one last time on behalf of Slade, asking Williams to spare his life and offering to ride with Slade out of the region into banishment if that would satisfy the vigilantes. Williams answered that the committee's decision was final, adding that the community was too inflamed against Slade to let him go. Davis asked if he could address the crowd outside the store, and Williams told the judge he had every right to say whatever he pleased but might place himself in physical jeopardy if he tried to defend Slade.

Leaving the store, Davis spoke individually to several of the vigilante leaders and found that he could not sway them from their determination to hang Slade. "I went back and told Slade I could do nothing for him, and told him what had occurred," Davis recalled, "and he just kept begging and begging me, and got me so wrought up that I shed tears as freely as a child." Seeing how dire the situation had become, one of Slade's friends climbed on his horse and rode at a gallop to Slade's home to fetch his wife, Maria, with the hope that she might sway sentiment in her husband's favor. She was "possessed of considerable personal attractions," according to Thomas Dimsdale, the vigilante historian— "tall, well-formed, of graceful carriage, pleasing manners, and . . . an accomplished horsewoman." Told of her husband's predicament, she leapt into the saddle and began a desperate race to cover the twelve miles to Virginia City in time.[8]

His arms pinioned behind him, Slade was marched to a corral behind Pfouts & Russell's Store, where a crossbeam had been placed atop the fence posts and a noose attached. Friends told him his wife had been summoned, and he implored Williams and his men to let him live long enough see her one last time. By all accounts the Slades had a loving marriage, despite her enduring dismay over his drunken escapades.

Fearing the effect a weeping wife might have on the assembled crowd, Williams hastened to carry out the execution. Slade was hurried to the gallows, lifted onto a dry goods box, and the now-familiar order was given: "Men, do your duty." The box was kicked away and Slade fell hard, breaking his neck. His body was cut down quickly and taken to the Virginia Hotel and laid out in a dark room. Maria Slade arrived soon afterward and fell on the corpse in hysteria. "I found her sobbing and moaning," one observer remembered, "bowed over a stark form shrouded in a blanket." She asked bitterly why no one had had the decency to shoot her husband to spare him the ignominy of hanging.[9]

Young Molly Sheehan witnessed Slade's hanging—he wore fringed buckskin, she recalled, and was hatless—and she wrote later that she and her family were among many settlers in Alder Gulch who did not approve of the execution. Slade was a demon, granted, she said, but he had committed no capital crime and did not deserve to die. Another observer, George Lovell, argued that Slade's case exemplified the town's desperate need for a jail. Slade could not be governed when drunk, but he could have been locked up instead of killed. Dimsdale defended the execution of Slade as a "stern necessity," but other settlers found it very disquieting. The judge of the people's court, a man of uncommon physical courage and restraint, had begged the crowd to spare Slade's life and had been ignored. He would not be final authority in Virginia City and Alder Gulch, it seemed. The committee of vigilance would.[10]

As Sidney Edgerton, the chief justice of Idaho Territory, made his way east toward Washington, D.C., the apparatus of governance in the place he left behind remained twisted in a terrible knot. As a matter of federal law, the gold camps of southwest Montana were part of Idaho Territory and had been since that jurisdiction was created on March 3, 1863, a year earlier. Congress had failed to provide a code of civil and criminal laws for the new territory, an oversight corrected by the territorial legislature by the temporary adoption of English common law as the standard for conducting criminal trials and only later by passage of a criminal code. No appellate court or other authority had given its blessing to the stopgap measures.

After convening in December 1863, the Idaho legislature tried to bring a measure of order to the chaos by creating counties and appointing commissioners, sheriffs, probate judges, and other local officials, but most settlers in Alder Gulch and Bannack anticipated the creation of a new territory tailored especially for them and seemed content to wait for Congress to act. Edgerton reached Tallmadge, Ohio, his old home, on February 23, 1864, and hurried on toward Washington two days later, reaching the nation's capital around the first of March. There he found several familiar faces already convened to help with the lobbying effort. Samuel T. Hauser, Nathaniel Langford, Walter B. Dance, Francis Thompson, and other prominent men had completed the arduous trip from Bannack and Alder Gulch and were busy lining up support from their hometown congressmen.[11]

The first order of business was to demonstrate to Congress the wealth of the new gold discoveries. Edgerton and the others had arrived with dust and nuggets sewn into their coat linings and luggage, and they now carried their treasure onto the floor of the U.S. House of Representatives, where members crowded around to see the glitter. By far the biggest impression was made by Thompson, the erstwhile friend of Henry Plummer's, who brought a remarkable *objet* with him: a heavy ingot of pure gold that had been created when a crucible broke over a fire in Virginia City and dumped some $1,500 in gold dust into the flames below. "The gold ran down into the cinders, making when congealed a most beautiful spangle," Thompson related in his memoirs, adding that he was not a bit embarrassed to let the congressmen believe it had been discovered exactly that way, a giant jewel in the rough. Having endured a host of tribulations on his journey east—stripping off his clothes and swimming naked across two half-frozen streams on the way to Salt Lake City, spending a night sleeping in the wild under a foot and a half of snow, and riding the Overland stage route to St. Louis with two heavy dragoon pistols in his lap, fearing assault from Indians—Thompson was delighted when his nugget became "the center of attention" for several dozen House members and a few senators who wandered over from their chamber to have a look.[12]

Given the Union's need for gold reserves and tax revenues to support the war effort, sentiment in favor of creating a new territory was solid in both houses of Congress. To their chagrin, however, Edgerton and his friends discovered that James Ashley, the influential chairman of the House committee on territories, hoped to secure passage of a version of the same measure he had championed during the previous session, which would have placed Bannack and Alder Gulch in an interior mining territory along with the Salmon River and Boise Basin settlements in the lower part of the modern state of Idaho. It is an irony of interest perhaps only to today's residents of the upper Rocky Mountain West, but Ashley's plan, had it succeeded, would have created a very different map of the western United States: The eastern two-thirds of modern Montana would have become a territory called Idaho; the lower portion of modern Idaho (along with most of Wyoming) would have become a territory called Montana, and Washington Territory would have been expanded eastward to include the northern panhandle of modern Idaho and the northwest portion of modern Montana all the way to the Continental Divide—a flip-flop of tens of thousands of square miles of American real estate.[13]

In the event, Edgerton and crew found they had a powerful ally in William Wallace, the congressional delegate from Idaho Territory, who shared their desire to separate the diggings east and west of the Bitterroot Mountains. Wallace, who hoped to rid himself of a mostly Democratic constituency, endorsed a plan favored by Edgerton to make the boundary between the two territories the crest of the Bitterroot Mountains, agreeing that the settlements along the Clark Fork River all the way to the Mullan Pass should be part of the new territory. Thus the highest elected official in the mammoth, year-old territory of Idaho agreed with a plan that would reduce his realm to a much smaller jurisdiction with only a slender panhandle rising to the Canadian border. With the western visitors united in common purpose, Ashley agreed to withdraw his plan and substitute theirs, and on March 17, 1864, the bill creating Montana Territory reached the floor of the House of Representatives for debate. Ashley spoke in favor of the measure, saying, "Let a man . . . go westward, and, as the territories are now organized, he has to travel over six hundred miles before he reaches a point where he can have government protection."[14]

Edgerton and his supporters had canvassed the House and anticipated little if any opposition to the bill. Indeed, so confident were they of swift passage that the leaders of their delegation presented a letter that same day at the White House, signed by Langford, Hauser, C. M. Davis, Thomas Pitt, and James Stuart, asking President Abraham Lincoln to appoint Edgerton as governor of the new territory. On the House floor, they had a friendly congressman move to amend the bill to allow officers of Idaho Territory to serve as officers in the new territory without going through the time-consuming formality of nomination by the president and confirmation by the Senate.[15]

The propriety of Edgerton's haste to return to Bannack as governor, when he had declined to serve at all as a territorial judge, raised eyebrows on the House floor. His old mentor, Rufus Spalding, the congressman from Ohio, made a point of objecting to the creation of a second territory only one year after the birth of the first and asked why the expenses of governing a sparsely populated area should be doubled. Acting as Edgerton's proxy, Fernando C. Beaman of Michigan responded sharply that some 17,000 settlers east of the Bitterroots were effectively cut off from any governance at all. "I am informed by one of the judges of Idaho," Beaman added, quoting Edgerton directly, "that not long since, under order of a vigilance committee, the people hung twenty-one men."[16]

This open citation of the work of the vigilantes was significant. Had there been any genuine opposition to the acts of the committee, any widespread feeling that hanging the twenty-one men targeted for death was unjustified or even subject to second-guessing, Beaman certainly would not have broached the subject on the floor of Congress and credited Edgerton as his source. Even though some of the settlers back in Bannack and

Alder Gulch had begun to express reservations about the continued reliance on summary executions, and though a handful of newspapers in the West questioned the justification for some of the hangings, people in the East—as represented by their congressmen, at least—expressed no criticism whatsoever of the killings. Beaman's comment about the vigilante killings passed into the congressional record without a single comment in response.

The truth was that members of Congress did not take territorial matters very seriously. Worried about the implications of tampering with the prerogatives of the president and Senate in choosing territorial officials, the House voted down the amendment that would have permitted Edgerton to take office immediately. The members then indulged themselves in some fun over the name of the new jurisdiction. Ashley had long been enamored of the word "Montana," a derivation of Latin and Spanish origin that pleased his ear as a synonym for mountainous. He had tried to give the name to Idaho Territory the year before, but was outvoted by members who believed—mistakenly—that "Idaho" was an Indian word meaning "Gem of the Mountains." The delegation from Lewiston advocated calling the new jurisdiction east of the mountains Jefferson Territory, to honor the president responsible for acquiring the land, but Ashley, a Republican, insisted on Montana in committee and prevailed. Now, on the House floor, one of his Democratic colleagues from Ohio rose to make mischief at Ashley's expense. Samuel "Sunset" Cox, who perhaps had a right to speak about the subject of nicknames and their appropriateness, objected sharply to the name Montana. "I desire to say that I do not like the proposed name of the new territory," he observed with disdain. "I do not know whether it is Spanish, French, or English."[17]

As more than a few congressmen began chuckling, Ashley responded tersely, "It is a Spanish word, meaning mountainous." Ashley's obvious irritation goaded several other colleagues to torment him. One suggested Abyssinia for the new territory. Another offered Shoshone, an Indian word for snake, and with that the humor turned biting. "I believe it means Copperheads," Cox said, drawing laughter with his reference to antiwar Democrats. Perhaps, he added, they could name the place Douglas, honoring both Stephen Douglas and, for the benefit of the radical Republicans, the black abolitionist Frederick Douglass. Before the taunting got out of hand, the speaker gaveled order and the bill was adopted by voice vote, with Montana as the name. But the jokes about the name had sent up a sobering warning. No measure that came before Congress in the spring of 1864 could be divorced from the very earnest, life-and-death issues of the Civil War.

At the time Congress took up the Montana Territory bill, the Union victories of the previous autumn and winter had given the North hope that the conflict might be nearing an end. Even after stiffening Confederate resistance led to several battlefield reversals, including the awful bloodletting at the Battle of Cold Harbor in the first week of June 1864, members of Congress looked ahead to eventual surrender and the rules that would apply to readmission of the states of a defeated South. The word "Reconstruction" had entered the vocabulary and the outlines of a bitter conflict between moderates and radical Republicans had taken shape. Specifically, radical Republicans who hoped to force wholesale social change in the South took the position that the southern states would have to re-enter the Union as territories, subject to the broad rulemaking authority of Congress. President Lincoln, on the other hand, argued that because secession was an illegal act, the states of the Confederacy had never left the Union—making their re-entry a military matter and giving him, as commander-in-chief, the upper hand in recognizing new state governments loyal to the Union.[18]

The finer nuances of this power play between the executive and legislative branches could be technical and mind-numbing, but the point was that any matter involving territories—even the simple need for a new jurisdiction in the distant Rocky Mountains—most likely would be swept into fierce, partisan debate. When the House bill creating Montana Territory came up for action in the U.S. Senate on March 30, 1864, Senator Morton S. Wilkinson of Minnesota objected to a clause that restricted voting in the new jurisdiction to every free "white male inhabitant" and proposed an amendment giving the franchise instead to every "male citizen of the United States and those who have declared their intention to become such." In later debate, Wilkinson would insist that his purpose was not so much to give blacks the right to vote in the new territory, but rather to prevent noncitizens—French Canadian fur trappers, for instance, or possibly even Indians—from gaining access to the polling place.[19]

Senator Reverdy Johnson, a Democrat from Maryland and an unapologetic foe of voting rights for a race he considered inferior, refused to accept any benign explanation for Wilkinson's amendment. Its purpose, he insisted, was obviously to open the territorial franchise to black people, with potentially ruinous consequences. There were some four million men and women of African ancestry living in the United States at the time, Johnson estimated, most of them freshly emancipated ex-slaves unable to read or write. "They may go, for aught I know, in numbers to the proposed Territory," he warned, "and may get the whole control of the Territory." His colleagues, bemused at the improbable specter of great masses of freedmen stampeding across the country to stage a legal coup in the mountains of far-off Montana, did not respond to Johnson's rhetoric. Instead, seeing that further debate was inevitable, they laid the matter over to the next day.[20]

An agreement appears to have been reached off the Senate floor, because Wilkinson's amendment came up the next day and was approved without debate on a 22-to-17 vote, with the chamber's radical Republicans in the majority. A minor amendment dealing with surveying the new territory occupied a few minutes, and then Charles Sumner rose to raise a by-now familiar question. "The name of this new territory—Montana—strikes me as peculiar," Sumner complained, adding that it sounded as if it had been "borrowed from some novel." A colleague blithely assured him that the name was "pure Latin" and appeared in the works of Livy. Sumner then asked if a "good Indian name" might be substituted, only to drop the matter when he was invited to suggest one and proved not to know one. So the name Montana stuck. But the sight of Sumner on his feet—Sumner the abolitionist whose fiery, angry rhetoric against slavery had provoked a hot-tempered congressman from South Carolina to cane him nearly to death on the floor of the Senate in 1856—triggered a fresh outpouring of passion on the subject of blacks and the vote.

Soon Reverdy Johnson was back on his feet, declaiming at length on the *Dred Scott* case and the refusal of the Supreme Court to say that a Negro could be considered a citizen of the United States. Sumner answered that the decision had "disgraced" the Court and was not, in his opinion, the law of the land. Johnson replied with withering scorn that Sumner lacked the standing "to be able to pronounce *ex cathedra* against a decision" of the nation's highest court. Just as it seemed the whole swollen, insoluble conflict would be revived and reargued in its entirety, a Senate floor leader called for the vote, and in the interest of saving time and advancing the legislative calendar, the Senate voted 29-to-8 in favor of the bill creating Montana Territory.[21]

Had the Senate seen fit to approve the bill as it arrived from the House, the legislation would have gone immediately to President Lincoln for his signature, which he had promised to give. But the Wilkinson amendment, by altering the language governing who could and could not vote in the new territory, meant that the two houses had adopted differing versions of the measure, and those differences would have to be reconciled in a conference committee and then the chambers would have to vote again on a final draft. For Edgerton, the prospect of further delay brought on a feeling of near anguish. He can be faulted for excessive ambition in leaving Bannack to lobby for the creation of a territory he hoped to be appointed to lead. But he was also a husband whose wife was in the late stages of pregnancy, and his yearning to return to her side is understandable. He had no control over the timetable, no way of knowing when the leaders of Congress—operating in an election year, in wartime, with an almost endless list of major issues stacked before them—would find a chance to return to the lesser challenge of putting boundaries around a piece of sparsely populated land in the West. Or if they would at all.

For nearly three weeks, as Edgerton and his allies looked on in frustration, the slow, elaborate grind of parliamentary machinery held the Montana bill in its gears, with each house of Congress insisting on its position. At length, on April 18, 1864, William Wallace, Idaho's elected delegate, asked the House to appoint another conference committee for a final try at compromise. The House agreed, and the next day the Senate took up the measure.

Senator John Sherman, Republican of Ohio and the brother of General William Tecumseh Sherman, who was at that moment poised to begin his decisive march through Georgia, took the first swipe at finding common ground. The Wilkinson amendment, he argued, was of "comparatively little consequence" because few if any black men lived within the proposed borders of Montana. Had that been the only issue, he said, he would have moved to agree with the House position. But by giving the vote to "inhabitants," Sherman continued, the House version would open the vote to noncitizens. "Canadians might come over and vote," he said, calling such a prospect "objectionable." He urged the two sides to compromise on language that would restrict voting to citizens of the United States and at the same time "entirely avoid this controversy about Negro suffrage." Senator James R. Doolittle, a Wisconsin Republican, lent his support to

Sherman. The Senate's amendment, he insisted, was "the merest abstraction in the world. There is not a Negro in [Montana] Territory, and probably will not be for years. It has no practical bearing or effect."[22]

Sherman and Doolittle were giving voice to a widely held belief among moderate Republicans that the mere mention of voting rights for blacks could divide their party in the upcoming election and deprive Lincoln of a second term. The relatively liberal states of New England permitted blacks to vote, but Republicans in other states with larger black populations bitterly opposed the idea. Blacks were barred from voting in New Jersey, Pennsylvania, Ohio, Illinois, Wisconsin, Minnesota, and other northern states. New York would allow a black man the ballot—but only if he could demonstrate a net worth of $250 or more. An effort to give the franchise to blacks in the federally administered District of Columbia was pending, and moderates feared the Montana bill would turn into a dress rehearsal of a divisive showdown on that measure.

Listening to these expressions of practical concern, sprinkled with the occasional disparagement of blacks as a race, other senators heard the dismal screech of expediency and reacted accordingly. One did not have to be a fire-breathing abolitionist to feel a flush of indignation at any act of Congress, no matter how limited its application, that would deny the vote to black men who even at that moment were taking up arms and risking their lives, fighting to preserve the Union. John P. Hale, a Free-Soil Republican from New Hampshire, jumped to his feet and objected to the clinical dismissal of Negro suffrage in Montana as a meaningless abstraction. No territory, he insisted, should be brought to life scarred with an "absurd and barbaric prejudice" against men of color.

As it became clear that several senators meant to be heard on the subject, and that some of them intended to be heard at length, the Senate postponed the bill for a day. On April 20, 1864, Senator Wilkinson delivered a passionate defense of his amendment. It was meant to prevent foreigners from voting in the first election in Montana, he said, but he endorsed the bill's symbolic purpose as well. "I am opposed," he said, "to being governed any longer by that pro-slavery prejudice that has ruled in the Congress of the United States for more than thirty years, and is today exerting an influence over the minds of many of our Republican members which it ought not to exert."[23]

Had Wilkinson stopped at this point, the internal politics of Montana might have taken a slightly different turn in days to come, but the senator from Minnesota was plainly angry, and he told his colleagues he rejected the notion that no black people were living in the new territory. "There *are* some Negroes there," he thundered. "I wish to state that I called upon a friend of mine who had moved into Montana from St. Paul, Minnesota, and I asked him that question. He replied that there were Negroes there; that one of the most respectable men in the Territory was a Negro worth over fifty thousand dollars." The friend who provided this surprising information, Wilkinson added, was Nathaniel Langford.

As a matter of practical politics, Wilkinson's speech added a serious complication to the challenge of passing the Montana bill. Now the issue of black voting no longer could be treated as an empty abstraction. Real black men, it seemed, would be casting real votes. Senators who opposed black suffrage could conjure up the vivid mental image of a successful black prospector who had hit a big claim and would be carrying a buckskin poke with $50,000 in gold dust stretching its seams as he went swaggering to the polling place to cast his first vote in the new territory. Whatever its original intent, Langford's aside to his home state senator had entered the congressional record and would be an impediment to the cause he and the other members of the Montana delegation held dear. Just as Edgerton hoped to win appointment as governor of the new territory, Langford too had aspirations for federal office, as surveyor general or tax collector or some other position, and his own words now threatened to undo his ambitions.

It did not take Langford very long to recognize the damage he had done to himself and his friends. He was sitting in the Senate gallery listening when his friend, Senator Wilkinson, quoted him to such devastating effect. Acting quickly, Langford sent his calling card onto the floor of the Senate asking for a meeting with Senator Doolittle, the Wisconsin Republican who had declared himself a champion of the principle Wilkinson detested—that the black franchise in Montana must be sacrificed.

With other issues crowding the agenda, the Senate again postponed action on the Montana bill, this time until the morning of Monday, April 25, 1864, when Doolittle took the floor for a final try at compromise. In a speech that would stretch over two hours, Doolittle began by insisting that the creation of Montana could not and must not become a referendum on black suffrage, lest the presidency be lost in the fall. Making swift work of the problem Langford had created, Doolittle said he had talked with the young man from Montana and learned that in fact the wealthy black prospector "*is dead,* and now there is not one single person of African descent in the proposed territory of Montana [emphasis added]." The cameo appearance of this phantom black prospector and his convenient, unelaborated demise a short time later may tickle a modern observer's funny bone—except, of course, that there was nothing amusing about the larger issues involved. Senator Wilkinson did not appreciate having been misled and sabotaged. What he found especially galling was that Edgerton, the leader of the Montana delegation, a man who held himself up as an abolitionist and defender of equal rights for all men, apparently was complicit in the turnabout and seemed to be willing to jettison his ideals for the sake of personal interest and advancement. And so Wilkinson became an implacable enemy of Sidney Edgerton.[24]

The disappearance of the rich black miner was forgotten quickly in the Senate chamber as Doolittle continued his stem-winder. At one point he demanded to know if Negro suffrage should be allowed to determine the outcome of the fall elections, and the gallery erupted in cries of "Never! Never!" until the presiding officer restored order with his gavel. A little later Doolittle grew confused and discomfited as he saw several of his colleagues rise and leave the chamber, until Sumner interrupted with satisfaction to explain that General Ambrose Burnside was outside marching past the Capitol at that very moment at the head of an army of ten thousand freedmen going south across the Potomac to join the fight against the Confederacy. Sumner arranged a half-hour recess so that everyone could rush out to see the glorious sight—black men in Union blue— the very embodiment of the point he and others had argued so long and so passionately.[25]

Wilkinson had the final word. Carried away a bit by the passions of the hour, he warned that abandonment of his amendment would open the vote in Montana to "Englishmen, Frenchmen, Germans, Chinamen, traders, men from the rebellious states, men from anywhere, holding any creed, any faith, monarchists, haters of republican liberty—*everybody!*" Nearing exhaustion by now, the Senate voted to appoint another conference committee and negotiate again with the House.

It would take another month of negotiation, another month of frustration for all concerned, but the seeds of compromise had been planted, and on May 18, 1864, the conferees reported out a bill that gave the vote in Montana to the very same class of citizens enfranchised in the act adopted a year earlier creating Idaho Territory—white men. The House, which had favored the restriction in the first place, quickly approved the bill. On May 20, 1864, over the continued objections of Sumner and other radical Republicans, the Senate followed suit. Senator Hale of New Hampshire grumbled that defeating the bill would injure no one save "disappointed candidates for office" in the new territory, but in the end the legitimate need for government in the gold camps of Montana prevailed, and the bill was approved.[26]

On May 26, 1864, President Lincoln signed it into law.[27]

CHAPTER SEVENTEEN

"The Wounded Man Recovered"

Before leaving Washington to return to his wife and family, Sidney Edgerton went to the White House for a meeting with President Abraham Lincoln. Edgerton hoped to be appointed governor of the new Montana Territory, and protocol dictated that he ask the favor in person, looking the president in the eye. Given the heat of the debate in Congress, Edgerton was not surprised to learn that some voices had been raised against him. He had heard that one senator in particular went so far as to lodge a formal protest against his nomination, and he asked Lincoln if it were so. Yes, the president said, it was. No names were mentioned, but Lincoln had a letter on his desk from Morton Wilkinson, the Republican senator from Minnesota whose amendment on black suffrage had been defeated, chastising Edgerton for leaving his post as chief justice of Idaho Territory to lobby in Washington. The people of Idaho, Wilkinson complained, "being left without courts, have without law Arrested and hung over twenty persons Supposed to be guilty of Crimes."[1]

Wilkinson's criticism was prompted more by personal animus toward Edgerton than any genuine worry over a shortage of due process for the targets of the vigilantes, but it nonetheless carried a sting. Edgerton had been away from Bannack for more than three months. He had never held court there. Putting the best face on things, he told the president he knew he had picked up political baggage during the floor fight and said he would understand if Lincoln decided to choose another man as governor.

In spite of his dour appearance, Edgerton had a sense of humor, and he knew the president welcomed the chance for a laugh in the grim days of managing war. He asked if Lincoln remembered the story of their friend Dosheimer, a minor political figure in upstate New York. The name sounded familiar, the president said, urging Edgerton to continue. "Dosheimer," Edgerton reminded the president, "attended a convention at Utica hoping to obtain the nomination as canal commissioner. He was defeated, and rising from his seat, said, 'Shentlemen, I goes back to Puffalo and keeps tavern like hell!'" Lincoln guffawed. Should he fail to gain the appointment as territorial governor, Edgerton said with forced cheer, he would return to his home and family and attend to business like Dosheimer. The president thanked Edgerton for coming by and showed him to the door, saying he would have to think the matter over.

Edgerton hastened to pack his bags and begin his journey back to Bannack, not knowing if the job he coveted would be his when he got there. Nor did he have any way of knowing that he had just become a father for the fifth time. On May 23, 1864, Mary Edgerton gave birth to a healthy baby girl and christened her Idaho, unaware that the name would become outdated three days later with the creation of Montana Territory. In the spring of 1864, most cities in the United States had telegraph service and enjoyed the luxury of swift communication. But the lines had yet to reach over the passes of the Rockies into Montana, and letters to and from the gold camps took a month or more to arrive, depending on the weather. When he got to Tallmadge, Ohio, on June 4, 1864, Edgerton found a small stack of letters from his wife wondering why she had not heard from him and giving him so many lists of things to bring he despaired of fitting them into a single trunk. In her last letter, dated April 27, 1864, Mary Edgerton told her sister she was "very much disappointed not to hear from Mr. Edgerton last mail, but I hope that the reason was that he is on his way home. I shall look for him every week until he comes, and hope that I shall not have to look very long . . ."[2]

The Edgertons were not the only couple eager for a reunion. Francis Thompson left Washington for New York, where he met with investors, and then returned to his hometown of Greenfield, Massachusetts, to propose to his longtime sweetheart. She accepted, but much to his regret declined to accompany him west. Postponing the marriage indefinitely, he bade her reluctant farewell and departed instead with her younger brother as his new business partner. In St. Louis, Thompson invested in a steam-powered sawmill, which he had disassembled and packed for shipment to Montana via the Missouri River, along with a cargo of general merchandise to sell.[3]

In Montana, James Fergus, the Scot miner who pined to see his wife, Pamelia, finally got his wish. As instructed, she liquidated their holdings in Minnesota and brought the family by wagon train to Alder Gulch, carrying a full inventory of kitchen utensils, household tools, and foodstuffs. Fergus sent her $750 in gold dust at Omaha, where she went on a shopping spree for fabrics, ribbon, pins, socks, hose, combs, shoes, and shoestrings. Not long after her arrival, she cooked him dinner, and when he made the mistake of criticizing her for putting too much salt in the food she responded by dressing him down with a sharp tongue—evidence not so much of erosion in their affection as of the inevitable tension that occurs when two competent people of strong, independent will have to learn anew how to share command. Fergus held several positions of responsibility in Virginia City at various times—deputy recorder, mining district president, county commissioner, elections supervisor—yet nothing he achieved surpassed his wife's accomplishment in feeding and clothing her family as a single parent and fetching them safely halfway across the continent.[4]

With the spring thaw, life resumed its hectic pace in Bannack and Alder Gulch. "'Biz' begins to look up a little, mainly of the miners beginning to work again," Granville Stuart recorded in his diary. Mary Edgerton noted the arrival of thirty new settlers from Salt Lake City in the second week of March 1864 and predicted many more to come. Some of the new mining claims looked very promising, she reported, including one in which she and her husband owned a share. The hanging of J. A. Slade seemed to have a sobering influence on the townspeople, and for a time, at least, the streets were quiet. But the outcome of the Slade affair had the effect of discouraging Alexander Davis from serving any longer as judge of the people's court, and his informal institution promptly withered and disappeared. The Vigilance Committee remained intact, ready to act as needed while the new territorial government got organized. In Lewiston, the capital of Idaho Territory, the men convicted of murdering Lloyd Magruder and his party were executed, and later Billy Page, the state's chief witness, led a small group to the crime scene in the wilds of the Bitterroot Mountains, where the victims' remains gave silent testimony that the verdict and sentence had been justified.[5]

On June 14, 1864, around an hour before midnight, the stillness in Nevada City was shattered by the sound of two rapid gunshots. James

James Fergus and his beloved wife, Pamelia, reunited at last. Courtesy of the Montana Historical Society.

Williams, the executive officer of the vigilantes, heard the sharp reports as he lay in bed trying to fall asleep, and he wondered if some fresh capital crime had been committed that would require him to act. Moments later a friend roused him, saying a man had been shot. Williams organized a company of a dozen associates to investigate the incident. The wounded man, an Irish miner named Murphy, had been shot through the tiny window of his cabin and then a second time from the doorway. He was badly hurt but conscious and identified his assailant as a saloonkeeper named James Brady, with whom he had been feuding.[6]

Williams went to Brady's saloon, where bystanders had taken custody of a friend of Brady's named Jem Kelly, saying he was an accomplice in the crime. According to witnesses, Brady had been tending bar when he saw his enemy, Murphy, walk past in the street outside. Brady handed over his bartending duties to Kelly, borrowed a pistol from him, then went to Murphy's cabin and shot inside, trying to kill him. Afterward, drunk and dazed, Brady fled from Nevada City to Virginia City, hurling the gun into the brush along the way. Williams and his posse captured Brady shortly after midnight and returned him to Nevada City for trial by the Vigilance Committee.[7]

In the morning, Paris Pfouts convened about fifty vigilante leaders in Adelphia Hall and took testimony. Brady admitted firing the shots, and the gun he threw away was recovered and placed in evidence. Several doctors said they expected Murphy to die of his injuries, and the committee duly sentenced Brady to be executed. His accomplice, Kelly, was ordered to receive fifty lashes. Following a familiar pattern, Brady put his affairs in order—using the young lawyer William Pemberton, the court reporter in the Ives case, to prepare the papers—and wrote a letter to his daughter confessing his sins and asking her to pray for his soul. At four o'clock in the afternoon, escorted by two hundred armed men, Brady was taken a half-mile east of the town, to a gallows fashioned out of a butcher's hoist, and hanged.[8]

The problem with this latest act of the vigilantes became evident in ensuing days when Murphy, a man of durable constitution, refused to succumb to his wounds. As he recovered, he became a walking advertisement that Pfouts and his committee had acted in haste and without adequate justification. True, other targets of the vigilantes had been executed for lesser crimes than murder, and those executions had been approved by a vast majority of the community. But this case was different. In his newspaper series on the vigilantes written a year later, Thomas Dimsdale argued that Brady's execution was justified because his intent was to kill. "Now," Dimsdale wrote, "we have always held that a man who fires at another, deliberately and with malice [aforethought], inflicting upon him a wound of any kind, is as much a murderer as if the shot had proved instantly fatal."

Though this line of thought might qualify as legitimate drawing-room philosophy, it is plainly contrary to the law, then and now, which does not permit a conviction for murder if the victim lives. In sum, Brady was executed for a crime he did not commit. Hinting at widespread opposition to Brady's hanging, Dimsdale wrote, "Brady was an honest man, and had never before ventured into the path of crime. Many felt sorry for his fate."[9]

For a later generation of revisionist historians, the Brady case marked a turning point when the justification for vigilante action ran completely out of steam. J. W. Smurr, a professor at Montana State University who took the brave step of becoming the first prominent historian to attack the legitimacy and integrity of the vigilantes, in an article published in 1958 in *Montana: The Magazine of Western History*, took particular note of the Brady hanging. "The most cynical passage I have ever seen in a book of Western literature," Smurr wrote with scalding anger, was an account of the Brady case that concluded: "Somewhat to the chagrin of the Vigilantes the wounded man eventually recovered."[10]

Around June 20, 1864, five days after Brady's execution, Sidney Edgerton reached Salt Lake City and received a telegram from the White House informing him that President Lincoln had appointed him governor of Montana. His dream fulfilled, he joined a wagon train for the difficult trip north from Utah over Monida Pass to his new jurisdiction. As a mark of the prestige and deference enjoyed by a freshly minted territorial governor, Edgerton found that he could not talk the freighters into taking him to his home at Bannack. Opting instead to go directly to the richer and more populous camps of Alder Gulch, they deposited Edgerton and his trunk at a fork in the road sixty miles from his destination. He was forced to buy a horse, saddle, and bridle and ride to Bannack by himself, leaving his trunk behind. Much to the surprise and joy of his family, he returned to them at last, unannounced and exhausted, late on the afternoon of Friday, July 1, 1864. He saw his baby girl for the first time and wrote his sister-in-law in Ohio that she was "a wonderful child, weighs twelve and a half pounds, has blue eyes . . . and is said to be good-looking."[11]

Edgerton had come a long way from the nation's capital, but the political webs that had held him there for three months and nearly undid his ambitions were present as well in the remote foothills of the Rocky

Mountains. On the Fourth of July, Edgerton and his nephew, Wilbur Sanders, raised the flag, fired the howitzer, and made patriotic speeches in support of the Union, much to the disgust of the Southern sympathizers in the area. Exaggerating their hostility, though perhaps not by much, settler George Lovell said he saw dozens of armed men on Main Street in Bannack that day, shouting for Jeff Davis and the Confederate cause. Edgerton's daughter, Mattie, claimed that "drunken horsemen" galloping by her house and seeing the flag "often fired random shots at the red, white, and blue target while hurrahing lustily for Jeff Davis."[12]

Thanks to the act signed by the president, Montana was now a legal entity, with borders and a budget and a set of laws inherited from Idaho. But the counties east of the Bitterroots recently created by the Idaho legislature had ceased to exist at the moment Montana was born, and all of their office-holders were automatically terminated. The president's choice for territorial secretary, the Reverend Henry Torsey, president of Wesleyan Seminary in Maine and a friend of Vice President Hannibal Hamlin's, declined the position owing to poor health. Samuel T. Hauser, who had petitioned the president for the job, was spurned because he belonged to the Democratic Party, and for months to come the position would remain empty. The three justices of the territorial Supreme Court had yet to be chosen. Nathaniel Langford, whose invention and quick renunciation of a rich Negro prospector had sown mischief during congressional debate, was denied his wish of becoming surveyor general but would be rewarded—if that is the right word—later in the summer with appointment as the territory's tax collector. All other positions remained unfilled. For the moment, at least, the lone member of Montana's government was Edgerton.[13]

Meanwhile, the pace of settlement continued to quicken. Gold was discovered at Last Chance Gulch on July 17, 1864, giving birth to the town of Helena. Other valuable deposits were found thirty miles east of there at Confederate Gulch and to the west at Butte, where copper would be king one day. Wagon trains poured into Montana from every direction, swelling the population of the towns along Alder Gulch. The digging became more sophisticated—and dangerous—as miners excavated in the hills and built shafts to reach bedrock. In April 1864, two prospectors in the Highland district were caught in a cave-in and one of them was killed. Stamp mills—huge industrial pile drivers that could pound tons of gravel into rubble for the sluices—arrived from the east and were put in operation.[14]

As he showed by refusing to serve as a judge without the oath of office, Edgerton was a stickler for form, and he declined to take any actions as governor until he received his written commission from the president, which arrived on July 30, 1864. Even then, Edgerton hesitated to announce his choice for the territorial capital. Bannack, where he made his home, had been surpassed quickly in population by Virginia City, and the towns of Alder Gulch combined now held more than two-thirds of the settlers in the territory. Wilbur Sanders, Edgerton's nephew, had picked up stakes and moved his family to Virginia City. But Edgerton did not wish to follow. He had several mining claims in Bannack and also enjoyed the political support of the large community of Minnesotans and other Union loyalists who lived in Yankee Flats just across the creek from his house. Mary Edgerton did not relish the thought of moving her household the seventy miles from Bannack to Alder Gulch, as she wrote her mother, "for it is so much work to move, even if we have but little to move."[15]

Still, Edgerton realized that he needed to make a formal visit to Alder Gulch. On the evening of Friday, August 19, 1864, he was treated to a "serenade" of band music on Wallace Street and welcomed at a rally by the city fathers of Virginia City. According to the *Montana Post*, a four-page weekly newspaper that inaugurated publication eight days later, Edgerton made a favorable impression. "He remarked that the growth of our beautiful city appeared the work of magic," publisher John Buchanan wrote. Edgerton called Montana the "Switzerland of America" and predicted that its climate, scenery, and "vast richness" of resources would assure a continued flow of settlement. Referring only obliquely to the work of the vigilantes, Edgerton called for the rule of law, and, according to the *Post*, "pledged his word that the laws should be executed."[16]

In the aftermath of Edgerton's visit, someone printed up a poster and tacked copies of it around town warning against the careless use of firearms and threatening "summary punishment" for those violating public order. It was signed by the Vigilance Committee and the editors of the *Post* treated it as genuine. "From what our community knows of this Committee," they reported, "they know it is not a 'myth,' but what is written will be executed." The poster appears to have been intended as a rebuke to Edgerton, or at least as a reminder that whatever order existed in the territory had been the doing of the vigilantes and not the governor. But the exchange was overtaken almost immediately by a serious crime and a violent response by the vigilantes that left no doubt whatsoever about their intentions.[17]

On Sunday, August 21, 1864, just two days after Edgerton's visit to Virginia City, a pack of highway robbers ambushed the stagecoach headed from Alder Gulch to Salt Lake City at a remote spot along the Portneuf River canyon near the present-day city of Pocatello, Idaho. The passengers—Jack Hughes, Howard Norris, E. L. Stanley, and Charles Bessor—reported the loss of an estimated $27,000. When word of the incident reached Nevada City a few days later, James Williams organized a posse of twenty riders and took off in search of the culprits. The expenses of these missions had become substantial, and the vigilantes' executive committee continued to collect subscriptions in the so-called "ferreting fund" to help defray the costs. Records of the fund kept by John Lott, a founder of the Vigilance Committee, show a broad base of support for the posse's work, mostly among the merchant class. One surviving receipt indicates that Paris Pfouts, the president of the executive committee, authorized a bank draft of more than $1,000 to repay Williams and his men. One chilling entry in Lott's ledger shows the payment of $5 "for rope"—presumably the rope used in hangings.[18]

Continuing his record of operating in bad weather, Williams departed on the morning of Sunday, August 28, 1864, and led his men south through three consecutive days of heavy rains until they reached the Snake River and found dry lodging in a haystack at a ranch. For the next several days, they rode back and forth among the camps in the area, pressing inquiries about the robbery. A freighter they knew reported that Jem Kelly, the man given fifty lashes in the Murphy shooting, had been involved in several instances of petty crime in the region in recent days, and they set out to find him. They soon learned that a company of prospectors from California had taken Kelly into custody, suspecting him of stealing a horse, and were holding him at their camp at the Snake River ferry.

"A trial was called," Dimsdale reported later, "and the evidence being heard, Kelly was unanimously condemned to death" for the Portneuf Canyon robbery. The vigilantes' chronicler did not elaborate on the evidence against Kelly, only that he accepted the sentence and was hanged on September 5, 1864, from the end of a plank wedged in the notch of a Balm of Gilead tree. Conspicuously absent from Dimsdale's account is any discussion of the fact that the posse had hunted down and executed a man outside the borders of Montana Territory. Since they were operating extralegally anyway, the formalities of jurisdiction probably mattered little to Williams and his men. Until the creation of Montana Territory three months earlier, they had been active in Idaho Territory, and it was Idaho Territory where they hanged Kelly. But the boldness of their strike did not go unnoticed in neighboring cities. The vigilantes of Montana were gaining a reputation.[19]

According to Dimsdale, Kelly's execution took place in the presence of a small band of Shoshone Indians, whose customs did not include such barbarities as hanging and who became physically ill at the sight of a man dangling dead from a tree. The vigilantes laughed at the Indians retching on the ground, but from the vantage point of a later day their horror and nausea does not seem particularly amusing.[20]

Governor Edgerton's private opinion of the vigilantes must remain a matter of speculation, since he did not record his thoughts on their activities. From his actions, however, we may infer that he regarded them warily, as a political force to be treated with respect and also a degree of fear. Certainly he felt no kinship with Paris Pfouts, the antiwar Democrat who served as president of the committee. On arriving in Montana, Edgerton commissioned a census and found he now served nearly 16,000 constituents, about 11,500 of them in Virginia City and the other towns of Alder Gulch. He decided to leave the latter settlements intact within Madison County, the local government created by the Idaho legislature, and he gave a strong vote of confidence to the men already serving in leadership positions in the county—some of them vigilantes and some not.

Signaling that he intended to support a system of local law enforcement and courts, Edgerton named Neil Howie, the intrepid freighter who had captured "Dutch John" Wagner, as sheriff, and gave the post of justice of the peace to Gaylord G. Bissell, the long-serving judge of the miners' court at Virginia City. Edgerton also reappointed James Fergus as a county commissioner and may well have intended sending a pointed message by doing so. On September 10, 1864, responding to the Vigilance Committee's posted notice of recent days and also to the hanging of Jem Kelly, Fergus wrote a remarkably frank open letter to the vigilantes warning them to disband.[21]

In the beginning, Fergus said, the vigilantes had been justified in their actions. "I for one," he wrote, "am willing to admit that circumstances may arise when for the benefit of the community at large good men may be compelled to disregard the laws and the rights of the citizens for the time being and deal out swift and certain punishments on the offenders. Such I believe was the case last winter. Our roads were infested by High-waymen beyond the reach of our laws. Our own safety required they be eliminated." However, Fergus added sharply, vigilante justice was a very dangerous tool. "American citizens claim the right to be tried by the laws of their country, in open court and by a jury of their countrymen," he wrote, "and the power that deprives them of that right is a tyrant and a usurper, be it one or many. . . ."[22]

As we have seen, Fergus was a man of strict moral purpose. Having endured physical beatings from his father rather than profess a faith he did not honestly share in the teachings of the Presbyterian Church, Fergus did not shrink lightly from obligation. Still, it took a great deal of courage to stand up to the vigilantes and condemn them in public, using the loaded words "tyrant" and "usurper" as he did. Fergus believed strongly in the tendency of power to corrupt. "If one man or body of men set the laws aside," he admonished the vigilantes, "another man or body of men can choose the same right."

It is a testament to the respect Fergus commanded that he suffered no direct rebuke or punishment for his apostasy. Other critics of the vigi-lantes had been banished or worse. Instead, like Alexander Davis, the short-term judge of the people's court, Fergus was simply ignored. His let-ter may have proven a touch too strong for Edgerton, who in coming days appointed John Lott to the post of territorial auditor, well aware that Lott was a founder of the Vigilance Committee and served as its treasurer. Neil Howie, the new sheriff, appointed the well-known vigilante "X" Beidler as his deputy. These choices may have been meant to placate the leaders of the Vigilance Committee in the aftermath of Fergus's broadside. But the truth was the vigilantes did not depend one way or the other on the suf-ferance of the governor for their existence, a point they made with stark eloquence by disregarding him entirely and going about their business as usual.[23]

Williams and his men returned to Alder Gulch and resumed their daily lives, unmolested in any way by the newly appointed territorial officials. The *Montana Post* changed hands after a single issue, bought by D. W. Tilton and his partners and now to be edited by Thomas Dimsdale, the consumptive English schoolteacher who in coming months would help turn the vigilantes into legend. Though he was "small, delicate-looking, and gentle," according to the ever-observant Molly Sheehan, Dimsdale proved ferocious in support of the Vigilance Committee. As noted in the pages of his newspaper, Virginia City was now a proud, burgeoning community that boasted a bookstore, stationer's shop, confectionary and bakery, lumberyards, a drug emporium, meat market, photographic gallery, boot shop, reading room, dry goods stores, and shaving and hairdressing salons. It was also a place with a continuing appetite for summary justice.[24]

A miner named James Redmond reported in early September that he had been robbed of $700 in gold dust by his cabin mate, John "the Hat" Dolan, who convincingly denied any knowledge of the crime for several days but then bolted town suddenly in the direction of Salt Lake City. Dolan's disappearance persuaded the Vigilance Committee that he was the culprit in the theft, and they hired a man named John McGrath to track him down and bring him back for trial. The use of a private detective marked a new level of sophistication for the vigilantes, as did their assumption, in effect, of the powers of extradition. Making inquiries in Salt Lake City, McGrath learned that his prey had assumed an alias, John Coyle, and moved to Springville, a settlement south of the Mormon capital. Finding Dolan there a day later, McGrath attempted to arrest him, only to be blocked by a local marshal who asserted that McGrath had no legal standing to detain anyone in Utah Territory and in any case carried no arrest warrant, formal charges, or other papers. Refusing to give up, McGrath and a few allies abducted Dolan hours later and spirited him away, arriving in Nevada City on September 16, 1864.

The next morning, a Saturday, the executive committee of the vigilantes met once again in closed council and conducted a "patient and lengthened trial," in Dimsdale's words, before finding Dolan guilty and sentencing him to death. Some on the committee suspected that Dolan might have been involved with Jem Kelly in planning the Portneuf Canyon robbery, but no evidence was furnished and he was not convicted of that crime. According to Dimsdale and other accounts, Dolan admitted the theft from his cabin mate, explained that he was drunk at the time, and offered to make restitution if his life were spared. The committee refused.[25]

At nightfall, James Williams assembled a command of some two hundred vigilantes, who arrived in Nevada City from Highland, Pine Grove,

Virginia City, Junction, and other settlements up and down Alder Gulch. Dolan was being held in the ballroom of the Jackson House hotel, and the company formed an avenue of armed sentinels on either side of the door to accompany the condemned man to the gallows east of town. A crowd of several thousand, perhaps as many as half the area's settlers, jammed the street outside Jackson House and pressed close as Dolan emerged, arms pinioned behind him, in the middle of a heavily armed guard. A small but insistent contingent of onlookers reacted to the sight of Dolan by objecting loudly to the proceedings, calling his hanging gross excess.

Dimsdale dismissed these protesters as Dolan's "companions in crime and sympathizers," but the truth is many people believed the vigilantes had finally gone too far. In an account written later, settler L. A. Fenner described a "little knot of men" who bravely stood their ground in the path of the vigilantes and challenged their authority. Reading between the lines of Dimsdale's version of events, it is plain that Captain Williams and his men reacted fearfully and desperately to this gesture of defiance and aimed their weapons pointblank at the ranks of the crowd that surrounded them, holding any would-be rescuers at bay. Arriving at the gallows, Williams addressed the crowd directly. "It has been said that you will rescue the prisoner," he yelled, commanding silence in the chilly darkness. "Don't try it, for fear of the consequences. What is to be done has been deliberately weighed and determined, and nothing shall prevent the execution."[26]

Dolan was permitted to speak his final words. In a calm voice, he admitted the theft, said he was drunk at the time, offered restitution again, and reminded the onlookers that he had never been accused or convicted of any other crime. His stoic demeanor incited a fresh wave of excitement and calls for his life to be spared. The vigilantes hanged him anyway, and Dimsdale's account of what followed has the ring of accuracy: "The dull sound of the drop was followed, or rather accompanied, by the stern order to the crowd, repeated by one hundred voices, 'Fall back!' The glancing barrels and clicking locks of five hundred revolvers, as they came to the present, sounded their deadly warning, and the crowd, suddenly seized with a wild panic, fled, shrieking in mad terror, and rolling in heaps over one another."[27]

A wagon and mule team were parked just behind the circle of the crowd, and the retreating stampede crashed over them, creating a writhing pile of men and upturned animals amid broken timbers and bent wheels. Remarkably, no one was killed or badly injured. The vigilantes did not fire on the crowd, and after a time order was restored. According to Dimsdale, a "gentleman of Nevada [City]"—probably John or Mortimer Lott—then stepped forward and delivered a short, pointed speech in defense of what had happened. Such examples were necessary, he insisted, and nothing short of severe, summary punishment would prevent a return to the days when no man's life or gold were secure. Hearing this harsh kernel from a man they admired, the onlookers grudgingly dispersed and the vigilantes marched away.[28]

Giving the affair a benediction that explains why later historians have branded him an apologist, Dimsdale wrote, "There was a solemnity and decorum about the proceedings of the Vigilantes that all admired." Actually, the Vigilance Committee could now add kidnapping to its list of methods. Its leaders had acted in defiance of territorial officials in Utah and Montana, and they had just incited an open rebellion that had to be put down at gunpoint, resulting in a moment of chaos that came very close to fatal mayhem. In the debate over the question of when the vigilantes finally crossed the line, the author is willing to defer to J. W. Smurr and his angry assessment of the Brady execution. Yet it seems the hanging of John "the Hat" Dolan also deserves special mention for the totality of its violation of the principles that had guided the vigilantes in their early days—just nine months earlier.[29]

The passions aroused by a lynching could dissipate with remarkable suddenness, as proved to be the case with Dolan. The very next morning after his hanging, hundreds of settlers gathered at a makeshift corral above Virginia City and laid bets on the outcome of a prize fight between Joe Riley and Tom Foster. Sundays were set aside for chores, letter-writing, and also popular amusements, and the pages of the *Montana Post* duly recorded Riley's victory and his claim on the purse of $750 in gold dust. The following week a bullfight was staged in Virginia City, amid grumbling from several bettors that the bulls were old and feeble.[30]

At his home beside Grasshopper Creek in Bannack, Governor Edgerton busied himself with the grubby task of scraping the protective coating of mud off the roof and walls and replacing it with lime. "We are now in the midst of the dirtiest kind of work," Mary Edgerton wrote her mother on September 18, 1864, referring to the housework and not to the hanging of Dolan the evening before. Edgerton was preparing to call elections and convene the new territorial government, and seems not to have responded at all to the renewed activity of the vigilantes.[31]

In early October 1864, the first of the federal territorial justices appointed by President Lincoln arrived in Montana. Hezekiah Hosmer was a lawyer with a literary bent who had written a novel, *Adela, the Octoroon,* that proved popular in antislavery circles. A native of New York, Hosmer settled as a young man in Toledo, Ohio, and served as editor of the *Toledo Blade* before traveling to Washington in 1861 to seek the post of librarian of Congress. Instead, he became secretary to the House committee on territories chaired by James Ashley and took an active hand in the political wrangling that led to the creation of Montana Territory. He then agreed to serve as its first chief justice.[32]

Hosmer was not a handsome man. He had a protruding lower lip that one observer thought made him look like a member of the Hapsburg dynasty. At age forty-nine, he was gray and balding and appeared a decade older. Nonetheless, he arrived with a young second wife and two children from his first marriage and moved into cramped quarters as a guest in the Edgertons' home. The youngsters got along well together and soon put on a community theater production of both parts of Shakespeare's *King Henry IV,* complete with playbill. Though their political ambitions would eventually lead to friction, the governor and chief justice found common ground as radical Republicans and fellow Knights of Malta, and they joined forces to campaign for the election of a Union ticket to the Council and House—the upper and lower chambers—of the new territorial legislature. They also supported the candidacy of Edgerton's nephew, Wilbur Sanders, for the post of delegate to Congress.[33]

On October 17, 1864, a week before Election Day, the Republicans held a mass rally at Virginia City and launched several hours of invective at the "secesh" faction of the Democratic Party. Dimsdale, who acted as master of ceremonies, added his voice to the criticism of "that arch traitor, Jeff Davis." By lumping together all Democrats, even those who supported the war effort, the Republicans apparently overplayed their hand and created a backlash. Wilbur Sanders went down to stinging defeat at the hands of Samuel McLean, the portly Democratic lawyer who had brokered a peaceful outcome during the gold rush at Alder Gulch the year before. Even though the results for the legislature were a dead heat—a one-vote majority for the GOP in the Council and a one-vote majority for the

Democrats in the House—Sanders lost by the lopsided margin of 3,898 to 2,666.[34]

The Edgerton clan did not respond very graciously to the defeat. The governor's niece, Lucia Darling, wrote friends describing the three-hundred-pound McLean as "a man of small intellect but great bodily size [who] can swear and drink with the best (and worst) of them." Sanders warned his former commanding officer, James A. Garfield, then an Ohio congressman, "Do not regard him I beseech you as an intellectual specimen of our opposition. They have many better men but he is a very clever old fellow." Governor Edgerton groused to his wife that the secessionists had hijacked the election, and he decided to make Bannack the territorial capital rather than any of the larger towns in Alder Gulch. He issued a call for the new legislature to convene near his home in late December. The residents of Virginia City "do not like it very well," Mary Edgerton wrote her family. "They think it ought to be called there and it would have been if there had not been so many 'Copperheads' there. I am very glad it is to meet here because Mr. Edgerton can be at home all the time."[35]

In a subtle but important way, Edgerton's agitation of the war issue undermined the goal of reining in the vigilantes. Instead of governing from the population centers at Virginia City or Nevada City, where the Vigilance Committee was headquartered, Edgerton would remain seventy miles away, his influence diminished by distance. His rigid partisanship would make it virtually impossible for him to deal on a constructive basis with antiwar Democrats, whose ranks included the president of the Vigilance Committee. And his harsh rhetoric would alienate even pro-Union Democrats and damage his ability to play conciliator. As if to punctuate the fresh difficulties Edgerton had unleashed, the vigilantes struck next in Bannack, right under his nose.

On the morning of Monday, October 31, 1864, early risers in Bannack were greeted by the sight of "a man for breakfast"—a spectral figure dangling from the gallows just off Main Street. Unlike the executions conducted by the Vigilance Committee in Alder Gulch, this one had occurred with no pretense of a trial or hearing. The victim, a man named R. C. Rawley, apparently was hanged for the "crime" of having criticized the vigilantes. According to a scathing account written by Amede "Mitty" Bessette, a French Canadian saloonkeeper who knew him well and often served him whiskey, Rawley was a harmless drunk who had been banished the previous winter during the early days of vigilante activity. After losing

Amede "Mitty" Bessette, who criticized the vigilantes for hanging R. C. Rawley. Courtesy of the Montana Historical Society.

both feet to frostbite out in the countryside, Rawley had returned to Bannack and apparently wrote a letter or some other broadside complaining about his fate. According to Bessette, four unnamed vigilantes entered his saloon one afternoon and demanded a handwriting sample from Rawley. "They all looked at it carefully," Bessette recounted, "passing it to each other with the murmur, 'the same, the same, the same.'" The next morning Rawley was dead.[36]

Describing the scene with disgust, Bessette wrote that the body was clad in tattered clothes, and "two bones in place of human feet projected from the legs of the pants. His tongue hung about an inch out of his mouth." Dimsdale dismissed the incident with a brief item in the *Montana Post*, calling the execution "commendable" and explaining that Rawley had vanished the previous winter when "the citizens took unto themselves the right to exterminate a class of men who were a scourge and a curse upon us . . . " His return had marked him for death, making him the twenty-seventh victim of the vigilantes in the year 1864.[37]

Dimsdale's casual use of the word "exterminate" struck a chilling note. The vigilantes had graduated with far too much ease from their duty of conducting tribunals and meting out stern punishment to men who posed a genuine threat to the community, and now found themselves sliding without much of a toehold into the cold swamp of judgment by appearance, guilt by association, class hatred, and human eradication.

It seemed high time for someone in authority to take a stand.

CHAPTER EIGHTEEN

"No More Midnight Executions"

Setting up the first federal court in Montana Territory proved relatively easy. The chief justice, Hezekiah Hosmer, waited until the other guests had finished eating breakfast and then commandeered the dining room of the Planters House, the leading hotel in Virginia City, as a temporary court-room. According to his son, Hosmer ordered the dishes cleared, and "a bench was improvised by putting a number of tables close together and then placing another table on top of them, behind which the judge sat." Other tables were arrayed for the clerk of court and the two dozen lawyers who constituted the Alder Gulch bar association.[1]

The makeshift appearance of the scene belied the careful thought Hosmer had put into the task before him. Unlike Governor Sidney Edgerton, who remained behind in Bannack, Hosmer recognized the need to do business in the main population center of the territory. Leaving Edgerton's cramped household, Hosmer moved his family into new quarters in Virginia City and joined in a partnership with two leading merchants, Nathaniel Langford and Samuel D. Hauser, in opening a bank—evidence that the judge planned to rely on the profits of commerce to supplement his modest federal salary of $2,500 a year. Most of all, Justice Hosmer struggled with the challenge of dealing with the vigilantes. They had ignored the governor's tepid call for the rule of law, and Hosmer concluded that he must confront them directly if he hoped to establish the authority of the territorial courts.[2]

Hosmer picked December 5, 1864, the first Monday of the month, to convene a grand jury and charge its members with their duties. He began discreetly, by praising the early work of the Vigilance Committee. "It is no part of the business of this court to find fault with what has been done," Hosmer said, reading from a carefully prepared text, "but rather, in common with all good citizens, to laud the transactions of an organization, which in the absence of law assumed the delicate and responsible office of purging society of all offenders against its peace, happiness, and safety." He singled out Henry Plummer, the late sheriff, as the "greatest villain of them all—with hands reeking with the blood of numerous victims."

Hosmer's exoneration of the vigilantes for their acts to date might be dismissed as a matter of expediency and simple prudence, since two of their leaders—Thomas Baume and James Williams, the executive officer—were sitting directly in front of him as members of the grand jury. But the judge went on to take the bolder step of telling them they must stop. Summary executions, he said, "are no longer necessary. No law abiding citizen wishes their continuance. They should at once and forever be abandoned." Emphasizing his point with blunt language, he added, "Let us erect no more impromptu scaffolds. Let us inflict no more midnight executions." If anyone missed the point, he concluded by telling the grand jurors he would call on them to indict the vigilantes on charges of murder if they acted again.[3]

Hosmer's son believed that his father angered the vigilantes with his broadside. In a biographical sketch written many years later, the younger Hosmer recalled that an unnamed citizen approached his father at the end of the session of court and warned him, "We are glad the government has sent you here. We have some civil matters to attend to, but you had better let us take charge of the criminal affairs." Other sources, however, portray the vigilantes as far more guarded in their response. The son of Wilbur Sanders, prosecutor in the people's trial of George Ives, insisted that the vigilante leadership approached Hosmer privately in the days after his charge and vowed to support his court and give him a chance to demonstrate its effectiveness. Publicly, at least, the vigilantes had little choice but to pledge obedience. Their chief spokesman, Thomas Dimsdale, praised Hosmer in the pages of the *Montana Post* for his "masterly manner" and added, "We think that none of the Vigilantes can feel hurt, or even otherwise than gratified by the excellent remarks of the Chief Justice."[4]

Chief Justice Hezekiah Hosmer. Courtesy of the Montana Historical Society.

Whatever their true feelings, the vigilantes were now on formal notice that they must cease their activities or face the consequences. Most of their early executions had been carried out in full public view by leading men who did not feel it necessary to conceal their identities. More recently, the vigilantes had begun acting furtively, like nightriders, carrying out "private" hangings under the cover of darkness, with a resultant erosion of their moral authority. From now on, if they chose to continue, they might very well suffer criminal sanctions. And so, for a time, they stopped.

♦ ◇ ♦

As an example of political naivety, it is difficult to top Mary Edgerton's breathless joy at the profusion of gifts that began flooding her household in the late autumn of 1864. "Last week," she wrote her sister in late November, "we had given us some moose meat and a quarter of mountain sheep weighing over thirty pounds, and about six pounds of fresh pork." This largesse was not exactly a coincidence, since her husband, the governor, had called the newly elected legislature to convene in Bannack on Monday, December 12, and the lubricant of goodwill gestures followed accordingly. One admirer presented Mrs. Edgerton with a gold pin worth $25, while her sons, Wright and Sidney, were hired to serve as legislative pages at a rate of $5 a day. "The people here are very kind to us," she observed without irony.[5]

Francis Thompson, the banker turned merchant and erstwhile friend of Sheriff Plummer's, had returned to Bannack with his sawmill and was prospering selling lumber at $150 per thousand feet. His political ambitions had been churned during the period he spent in Washington lobbying for the creation of Montana Territory, and he stood successfully as a Republican candidate for election to the seven-member Council, the upper body of the legislature. His affection for the Edgertons, rooted in genuine feeling, deepened with the prospect of gaining even higher office. He made a cradle for their baby girl, Idaho, from a shoebox, and converted a ten-pound molasses keg into a chair for their five-year-old daughter, Pauline, who liked Thompson so much she began calling herself his "little wife" and insisted on being addressed as Mrs. Thompson. On behalf of the governor, Thompson ventured to Virginia City and bought an unfinished, two-story hotel building, which he had dismantled, shipped to Bannack, and refashioned into a meeting hall for the legislators.[6]

In turn, Edgerton forwarded Thompson's name to the White House and asked that he be named territorial secretary, a post left vacant when President Lincoln's first choice declined the appointment because of poor health. For some reason, quite possibly his preoccupation with General Sherman's decisive march through Georgia, which was then unfolding, Lincoln failed to respond. "If this petition ever reached the president," Thompson wrote later, "no notice was ever taken of it," and the post remained vacant—an oversight that would bear serious consequences in the months to come, beyond merely frustrating Thompson's ambitions. By law, the secretary was second-in-command in the territorial government and had exclusive control over the disbursement of federal funds.

Without a secretary, Montana would have no budget and no means of paying its officials their salaries.[7]

With no money, no secretary, and a judiciary that consisted of a lone, doughty justice single-handedly holding the Vigilance Committee at bay, Edgerton might have been well advised to greet the members of the new legislature with a message of conciliation and cooperation. And up to a point he did so, welcoming them to Bannack and pledging to work with them toward the goal of exploiting the "untold wealth" that lay about them. He spoke of the need for good roads, fair mining laws, a means of raising taxes, of building schools, mail facilities, and a penitentiary—and then, because he simply could not help it, he turned to the subject of the Confederacy and the Civil War. "This unhallowed rebellion," he intoned,

> had its origins in the lust for power and the insane desire to extend and perpetuate human bondage. For years this conspiracy had been plotting, till at length, under the imbecile administration of James Buchanan it threw off all disguise and assumed the defiant attitude of treason. Beginning in crime and perfidy, it has sought to establish its power by atrocities the most inhuman and appalling. Ignoring the long established rules of civilized warfare, it has prosecuted the war with a fiendish ferocity that would put to blush the most uncultivated savages. . . .

Edgerton's words, a sincere and even eloquent expression of his beliefs as an abolitionist and radical Republican, did not serve him well in a place where so many Southerners had settled, especially at a time when most of them were beginning to accept the likelihood of impending defeat, and while gentler voices, the president's among them ("with malice toward none"), were preaching a sermon of reconciliation and forgiveness. As Edgerton expressed it, the conflict between North and South was a simple case of "loyalty versus treason . . . and between them there is no middle ground."[8]

Even after delivering this harsh jeremiad, Edgerton might have emerged from his inaugural address with little damage other than chafing the tempers of his Southern listeners. But he also insisted on administering the so-called Iron Clad Oath to the incoming legislators, requiring them to swear loyalty to the Union and also to say that they had never borne arms against the United States. One of the new members of the House, John H. Rogers, had served briefly in the Missouri militia in the early days of the war, under the command of General Sterling Price, who had tried in vain to prevent Union troops from entering the state. Rather than join the Confederacy, Rogers had fled to the gold fields of the Rockies. He had not been a Rebel. He considered himself a patriot and volunteered to swear an oath to "support, protect, and defend" both the Union and the territory of Montana. But he could not honestly recite the part of the vow about bearing arms, and Edgerton stubbornly refused to admit him to the legislature.[9]

According to Thompson, who witnessed the scene, "the excitement was intense" as Edgerton demanded that Rogers, a very well-respected man, exit the building before the other members of the legislature could take office. Charles Bagg, the lawyer who had prosecuted George Ives alongside Wilbur Sanders, and who later defended the work of the vigilantes, was elected to the Council as an ardent antiwar Democrat and made plain his distaste for the oath by uttering a stream of loud asides in the Council chambers. "That means obey Abe Lincoln," he hissed at one point. "I guess not!" Thompson said he and Bagg nearly came to blows before the formalities ended. Edgerton's niece, Lucia Darling, wrote friends that the political venom and cursing directed at her uncle by Southern sympathizers before the incident "was faint in comparison to what they did now."[10]

It is entirely possible, of course, that the bitter residue of the war's passions would have afflicted the territory no matter how much healing balm flowed from its governor, but with his partisan ferocity Edgerton guaranteed a long-lasting rift that hindered the functioning of the government in Montana for years to come. John Lott, the secretary of the Vigilance Committee, said later he believed the antagonisms of the period engendered a sense of enduring hostility toward government itself. The legislature toiled at various duties during the coming six weeks, but eventually its members adjourned in complete defiance of the governor without adopting the necessary ground rules that would allow them to meet again legally. Thus the apparatus of territorial government was thrown further into stalemate.[11]

On January 14, 1865, Thomas Dimsdale marked the anniversary of the public hanging of five men in Virginia City with an editorial in the *Montana Post* recalling the work of the vigilantes. "There are but few of our present inhabitants who knew the desperate character of the ruling spirits here then," Dimsdale wrote. "Money was demanded of our merchants as a loan, when they knew they could not hope for a return, and if refused was met with threats—sometimes with personal violence." Dimsdale's account was noteworthy in several respects. He seemed to be saying that the executions were ancient history and that the population of Alder Gulch had turned over so thoroughly that few remaining residents were even aware of the problem that had existed at the time. And the problem, as he described it, was not highway robbery or the existence of a band of outlaws led by the late sheriff or the commission of more than a hundred homicides, but rather the occasional act of intimidation directed at merchants who might be asked to give unsecured credit to men who frightened them. In sum, the article was incriminating and defensive in tone, and could as easily have been written in modern times by a revisionist historian arguing that the vigilantes were out to protect their own property rights at the expense of due process.[12]

Dimsdale apparently recognized the damning nature of his article because he followed up two weeks later with another editorial in the *Post* stressing how times had changed. He cited Virginia City's two churches, theater, and lyceum, its lectures and social clubs, the wide availability of books and newspapers, and concluded with emphasis, "Law now reigns supreme."[13]

In truth, law reigned only marginally. The Vigilance Committee remained fully intact and operational, serving as a self-appointed shadow government that kept a very skeptical watch on the doings of the territory's courts. Some modern critics have argued that the vigilantes were unpopular and acted through intimidation, much as they accused their targets of doing. A more accurate analysis would be to say that the vigilantes were *popular* and acted through intimidation, much as they accused their targets of doing. As we have seen, very few settlers criticized the vigilantes, even in the privacy of their diaries or letters home. This interpretation is reinforced by the results of the municipal election held in Virginia City in early February 1865: Paris Pfouts, the president of the Vigilance Committee, was elected mayor, enjoying a strong vote of confidence by secret ballot.[14]

It would be a mistake to ignore the continuing, highly coercive power of the vigilantes. After his banishment from Alder Gulch, James Thurmond, the lawyer who had helped defend George Ives, moved to Salt Lake City and tried to resume his practice. He found that his reputation had suffered as a result of his clash with the vigilantes, and he began filing lawsuits against members of the committee if they happened to pass through town. While traveling in Salt Lake City in January 1865, Jeremiah M. Fox, the ex-sheriff and vigilante organizer from Alder Gulch, was served with notice of a defamation suit seeking $10,000 in damages. According to a newspaper account, Thurmond's suit alleged "that Fox was one of the leaders in hunting him from Virginia City," causing him loss of property, physical suffering, and a "stigma upon his name and reputation."[15]

Fox contested the suit. A jury trial ensued in Probate Court and lasted fully two weeks. "The witnesses were almost innumerable," according to the *Union Vedette,* a newspaper published by federal troops in Salt Lake City, "and the testimony took the widest possible range. The case was contested at every point by the respective attorneys, who were not only numerous but 'talky.'" The jury deliberated at length before returning a divided, eleven-to-one verdict in favor of Thurmond, awarding him slightly more than $3,000 in damages. Because the verdict was split, the judge ordered a new trial, and after another marathon session Thurmond won again, this time unanimously and in the amount of $8,000. The judge upheld the result.[16]

Word of Thurmond's victory triggered great consternation back in Virginia City. In conducting research for this book, the author was struck by the discovery of a letter written by Nathaniel Langford, one of the prominent chroniclers of the vigilante period, to his partner, Samuel T. Hauser, the merchant who was then traveling east on his way to raise capital for their bank and other ventures. In his influential book, *Vigilante Days and Ways,* Langford conceded that vigilante activity had continued after the organization of the territorial court system, but he insisted that the committee's leaders took swift and decisive steps to disband, "and the men who had misused its powers were given to understand that any further employment of them would probably cause it to react on themselves." Or so Langford said for publication in 1890, a quarter-century after the fact. On May 8, 1865, in the privacy of a missive to his partner and confidant, Langford wrote, "The Vigilantes had a meeting last week and sent Sanders to Salt Lake to see Thurmond. . . . Sanders has two indictments and two requisitions from Edgerton upon the Gov. of Utah, and unless Thurmond 'dries up' completely he will bring him back, and then of course the Vigilantes will hang him."[17]

And then of course the Vigilantes will hang him! It is simply not possible to maintain that the vigilantes avoided succumbing to the corruption of power when they used the threat of hanging to silence critics and undo the verdict of a duly constituted court of law. The record does not specify exactly what instruments of persuasion Wilbur Sanders carried to Utah to apply to Thurmond, but according to the *Montana Post* the "blockade" at Salt Lake City was soon lifted and Thurmond settled his case out of court "on terms assuredly discouraging to those who desire further litigation with the Vigilance Committee or any of its members." As smoking guns go, Langford's letter seems decisive enough: a champion of the vigilante cause caught in an unguarded moment, with his hypocrisy freshly fired.[18]

In the early months of 1865, as the vigilantes continued their fragile armistice with Judge Hosmer, they turned their energies to protecting their reputations and defending what they had done, engaging in what would be known in modern times as public relations, or "spin."

One of the acts adopted by the territorial legislature before its abrupt adjournment was the chartering of the Montana Historical Society, an institution of admirable scholarly independence in our own day and time, but one whose birth can only be interpreted as an attempt to ensure that the authorized version of the territory's early history would be written by the victors. Among the founding members were Wilbur Sanders, Francis Thompson, James and Granville Stuart, and Charles Bagg. Justice Hosmer also was chosen, which suggests that he agreed not to use his position to embarrass the original vigilantes. (Walter B. Dance, the merchant who had served as mining district president in Bannack in the early days, wrote a friend that he had been offered an "onorary" membership, presumably in spite of his shortcomings as a speller.)[19]

While the actions of the vigilantes were supported, for the most part, in Montana, the same cannot be said of neighboring territories. At the same time a jury in Salt Lake City was taking Thurmond's side against the vigilantes, a judge in Boise refused to honor a writ signed by Governor Edgerton seeking extradition of a man named Buckner back to Alder Gulch on a murder charge. Neil Howie, the sheriff of Madison County, traveled to Boise to take custody of the prisoner, only to face a near riot at the hands of Buckner's supporters. "It is the popular delusion over there," Dimsdale complained in the *Montana Post*, "that this place was ruled by an excited mob whose vengeance was more summary than discriminating. Many believe that Plummer, Ives, Carter, and the leaders of the cut-throats—executed for murder and highway robbery committed again and again—*were perfect gentlemen.*" (Italics in original.) Actually, the district attorney in Boise argued in favor of sending the defendant back to Montana and wrote Edgerton in praise of Sheriff Howie and his conduct, saying the judge's refusal had been a matter of local politics rather than a condemnation of the vigilantes. Nonetheless, the prosecutor added, the judge in effect had spent an entire week "trying the Vigilance Committee of Montana."[20]

The problem was not just that the vigilantes had critics looking over their shoulders. Their friends could be troublesome as well. In the summer of 1865, a book appeared called *The Banditti of the Rocky Mountains and the Vigilance Committee of Idaho,* purporting to be a first-hand account of the recent events by an unnamed eyewitness. Speculation has settled on an itinerant Chicago newspaperman named John Lyle Campbell, who passed through the area during the period, but whoever the author was, he mangled facts, manufactured dialogue, and endorsed the vigilantes so one-sidedly and in such purple prose as to lose all credibility. Dimsdale, who had begun work on his own version of affairs, labeled the competing volume "vulgar and disgusting" and full of falsehoods—an accurate assessment, even if prompted by jealousy at being scooped. Weeks later, Dimsdale began the serialization of his own account in the *Montana Post,* and the articles were collected and published the following year, 1866, as the territory's first book.[21]

Dimsdale's bias in favor of the vigilantes is a matter of record, and while his motive in large part was to exonerate his friends and colleagues from charges of criminal excess, he seems to have had another purpose as well: to articulate and publicize a justification for them to continue. Had the vigilantes truly agreed to retire from the field after Justice Hosmer's warning to them, much of what Dimsdale wrote in the *Post* would have been unnecessary. Historians at the time seemed inclined to treat the vigilantes kindly, and their detractors in neighboring communities would have had nothing further to criticize if they disbanded. There was no realistic likelihood of any of the vigilantes being charged, tried, or punished for their actions, in the territorial courts or elsewhere.

But the vigilantes did not see their work as complete. The inability of the infant territorial government to get a grip on the challenges facing the community—not just in controlling crime, but in enforcing a wide blueprint of social conduct—left the Vigilance Committee frustrated, with many of its members eager to resume taking a hand in local affairs. Frequent editorials in the *Post* implored the legislature to enact gun control measures, including a ban on carrying weapons within the city limits, to prevent the shootings that erupted in saloons on many a weekend evening. But the gunplay continued. No apparatus for charity existed. (A poignant item in the paper chastised a local gambler for abandoning his three daughters and urged a relief effort on their behalf; the eldest, Martha Jane Canary, age twelve, would survive and go on to fame as Calamity Jane.) In private, leading men began discussing their disappointment in Governor Edgerton and his leaden political touch. Borrowing an especially biting metaphor from gold mining terminology, the federal attorney for the territory, Edward Neally, a fellow Republican, wrote of Edgerton, "It is . . . possible that when they come to pan him out it will be difficult to find color." His government seemed inept, especially in dealing with the arrival of a fresh crisis, a food shortage.[22]

The winter of 1865 was not as frigid as the year before, but a great deal more snow fell, clogging the mountain passes that led from Salt Lake City north into the Montana gold camps. Freighters could not reach the settlements with perishable goods, and the price of various foodstuffs began rising to alarming levels. "The snow is so deep between here and Salt Lake," Mary Edgerton wrote her family in March 1865, "that our mail is much behind the time. I do hope that we shall have warmer weather before long. We have had such a long, long, cold winter. I am tired of it." But the weather did not break. As the cold lingered into early spring, the passes remained closed, and supplies of rice, bacon, beans, and other staples began to run out. The price of a hundredweight of flour, about $1.50 in "the States" and ordinarily less than $10 in the camps, reached $28 in late March, then $38 in early April, and finally shot up to $100.[23]

As the flour crisis worsened, Governor Edgerton declined to intervene. Merchants and settlers began hoarding their dwindling supplies, selling at inflated prices or refusing to sell at all. On April 2, 1865, a group of hungry miners gathered in the streets of Nevada City, organized themselves as "Regulators," and went about town confiscating and redistributing all of the flour they could find. Continuing two miles up the road to Virginia City, they were met by Sheriff Howie and an armed guard of twenty-three deputies who ordered them to halt and go home. They did so. The resultant standoff lasted for two weeks, until April 18, when the regulators—led by James Williams and Charles Bagg—gathered again, forced their way into stores and private homes up and down Alder Gulch, and seized the flour supplies. Molly Sheehan, the reliable observer of so many episodes in the gold camps, recalled her stepmother hiding their modest supply of flour under beans in a barrel. Conrad Kohrs, the merchant and future cattle king, was less fortunate. He had four hundred pounds of flour stashed at his partner's general store, and the regulators took all of it.[24]

The flour riots, as they came to be called, were not really riots at all. "The search was orderly," according to Granville Stuart, "but very thorough and disclosed sundry lots of flour concealed under coats, in boxes and barrels, and under haystacks." The regulators established what they considered a fair price for the flour, paid for the supplies they seized, and resold the flour at the same price to the needy. In his memoirs, miner George Bruffey recalled seeing Charles Bagg stopping a group of the vigilantes in the street and warning them sternly, "Go on, take all of the flour, rice, and beans that you can find, but be men, not fiends. Don't burn the town." No acts of violence or looting occurred.[25]

The flour seizures could be seen as fair or not, depending on one's economic philosophy, but the important point was that the vigilantes had decided to take matters into their own hands again, asserting a renewed role in deciding public policy and maintaining public order. One of the great ironies of the flour episode was the response of Paris Pfouts, who issued a public notice warning against future extralegal activities and promising the rule of law. His duties as mayor of Virginia City had trumped his leadership position in the Vigilance Committee, and he sided with Sheriff Howie and other officers of the legitimate government against the regulators.[26]

As with all other things in the nation, affairs in Montana were interrupted and changed in fundamental ways with the assassination of President Lincoln, who was shot on the night of April 14, 1865, and died the next morning. Word arrived in the gold camps, which were still beyond the reach of telegraph lines, about a week later, reducing even the most ardent of the president's enemies to numbness. The Southern men, James Fergus's daughter wrote, "were very quiet." The Edgerton household went into bitter mourning. "It is *terrible* to think of it!" Mary Edgerton wrote her mother. "*What do these traitors expect to gain by such deeds?*" (Emphasis in original.) She added, "I never saw Mr. Edgerton as excited about anything as he is about this. I do not wonder at it because it is enough [to] excite anyone."[27]

The governor could not know it at the time, but his uncertain grip on territorial governance would be loosened and ultimately broken in the aftermath of Lincoln's death. Before adjourning, the legislature had voted to move the territorial capital from Bannack to Virginia City, a decision that reflected the realities of population and left Edgerton in virtual political exile. He thought about moving to one of the nearby valleys where the winters were milder and later about buying a house in Virginia City, only to abandon both plans and stay put in Bannack. Because the territory remained without a secretary, Edgerton's salary went unpaid, and he apparently contemplated running for the post of delegate to Congress so he could pursue his interests in Washington. But he concluded that the Democratic majority would make it impossible for him to win office, and he began to accept the reality that he and his wife might do best by returning home to Ohio. Mary Edgerton was reluctant to let their daughter, Mattie, attend any of the parties in town, for fear that the fourteen-year-old girl, who looked mature for her age, would "associate with the 'set' that generally attend them." A woman of extraordinary warmth and kindness within the confines of her own family, Mrs. Edgerton made plain her dislike of the "drinking, loafing set" in Bannack, even though she realized that the townspeople—her husband's constituents—resented her attitude.[28]

In May 1865, restive Blackfeet Indians killed ten white travelers near Fort Benton, and the governor responded by announcing that he would raise a militia of five hundred men. He also asked the War Department to send troops and supplies. Edgerton's alienation from the vast majority of his fellow settlers had become a serious problem by now, and his abject failure to recruit a fighting force left him a laughingstock. He and Hosmer had drifted apart, and the chief justice observed with contempt, "The result was, after a fortnight [of] recruiting, boys and all, the company numbered about 30, and broke up in disgust." The federal government failed to respond. All in all, Hosmer said, the affair was a "great fizzle" that reflected very poorly on the governor: "It was a tremendous exhibition of windy patriotism, out of which no Buncombe could be made for any body."[29]

Hosmer had shortcomings of his own to answer for, notably an inability to preside over convictions in his courtroom. The first four capital cases tried before him ended in acquittal, souring the vigilantes on his abilities. One critic described him scornfully as "vacillating in opinion and wavering in decision." In June 1865, a store clerk named A. J. McCausland was found not guilty of murdering his partner, even though dozens of people had witnessed the shooting, which took place in a dry goods store in downtown Virginia City on the previous Christmas Day. The delay in conducting the trial and the refusal of the jury to convict left Hosmer wondering only half in jest if the grand jury might indict the prosecutors and other court officials "for swindling the county." He might more pertinently have asked how long the vigilantes intended to indulge his authority and refrain from resuming executions on their own.[30]

In a remarkable irony, the acquitted killer, McCausland, was himself slain just a month later, on July 13, 1865, when robbers again ambushed the stagecoach from Alder Gulch to Salt Lake City at Portneuf Canyon. In the deadliest holdup since the Magruder affair, four of the passengers were shot and killed and two others seriously wounded, underlining the point that the vigilantes had failed to create the climate of stability and order they liked to imagine. Confronted with this latest outrage, they organized another posse bent on tracking down the robbers, but failed to capture anyone. An account of the incident in the Montana Post added insult to injury by quoting one of the robbers as bragging that they "were even with those damned vigilanter s——s of b——s, now, for hanging and robbing their friends."[31]

In Helena, meanwhile, the courts had yet to be organized, even though thousands of settlers had swarmed there to make claims on the fertile gold discoveries in Last Chance Gulch. On June 7, 1865, a miner named John Keene was walking past a saloon on Bridge Street when he recognized an enemy—a man named Harry Slater, with whom he had feuded in Salt Lake City—and responded by pulling a pistol and shooting him several times at point-blank range, killing him instantly. Keene was arrested, turned over to the sheriff, and then seized by a group led by "X" Beidler, the diminutive lawman who had ridden with James Williams and the Vigilance Committee in Bannack and Alder Gulch.

After a two-day trial by a people's court, Keene was convicted and sentenced to death. On June 9, Beidler presided over the inaugural use of Helena's famous "Hanging Tree," a tall pine where Keene's body was left swaying in the midday breeze. According to Dimsdale, the scene closely resembled earlier executions in Alder Gulch. "Many familiar faces, known to Virginia [City] men in the trying times of the winter of '64, were visible," he wrote. In the aftermath of the execution, the leading men in

Helena formed a vigilance organization called the Committee of Safety, and the question arose whether its members would agree to suspend their activities once the territorial courts began operating there.[32]

Indeed, the territory as a whole faced a vital question in the summer of 1865. Would vigilante justice become a thing of the past? Or did the leaders of the vigilance movement believe they had a continuing right— even an obligation—to fill in the gaps of governance left by Edgerton and the territorial justices? The moratorium on extra-legal executions in Bannack and Alder Gulch had lasted more than six months, but as the hanging of John Keene in Helena demonstrated, there was a limit to the vigilantes' patience. At some point, they would have to decide whether to retire or reassert their dominance.

Appropriately, perhaps, an influential audience of one was headed to Montana to witness the answer. James Ashley, the Ohio congressman who as chairman of the House committee on territories had given Montana its name and labored over establishing its boundaries, took a cross-country trip in the summer of 1865 to look at the lands he had helped organize during the Civil War. As he approached the Rocky Mountain foothills of southwest Montana in the third week of July 1865, the town fathers of Alder Gulch organized a colorful welcoming ceremony: They arranged an "ambush" of the congressman's stagecoach at Laurin's ranch on the Stinking Water River, as if he were being attacked by Sioux Indians. Ashley was then accompanied to Virginia City amid great pomp and greeted by a large crowd of townspeople. On the evening of Saturday, July 22, he gave a lengthy, formal address to the settlers in Virginia City, praising their progress and advocating the forcible submission of Indians in the region.[33]

Symbolically, at least, Ashley's visit provoked no hint of squeamishness about the vigilante executions that had taken place during the previous year and a half. The ambush at Laurin's was staged at the exact site where Erastus "Red" Yeager and George Brown were hanged at the outset of the movement, and Ashley gave his speech at the corner of Wallace and Van Buren streets, where the five men had been hanged side by side on the vigilantes' deadliest day. Plainly no one thought it indiscreet to associate Ashley's visit with reminders of the vigilantes' work.

But one did not have to interpret signs or engage in other subtleties to discern the thinking of the Vigilance Committee. During the week of Ashley's visit, James Williams saddled his horse and rode to Diamond City, a mining settlement about forty miles east of Helena, to carry out a piece of business in his capacity as the committee's executive officer. A man called Jack Silvie had been seized there and accused, in Dimsdale's words, of "robbery, obtaining goods under false pretenses, and various other crimes of a kindred sort." Williams and Beidler rode at the head of a party of five who fetched Silvie from Diamond City to Helena to answer the charges. According to Dimsdale, Silvie broke under close questioning, confessed to having murdered a man on the Snake River, and was sentenced to death. The Vigilance Committee, Dimsdale said, "thought that it was high time that the world should be rid of such a monster." Its members joined hands on the end of a rope thrown over a branch of the "Hanging Tree" and hoisted Silvie into the air, killing him by strangulation.[34]

In his book, Dimsdale fudged the timing of Silvie's execution, so that a careless reader might think it was carried out before the arrival of the territorial justices and their establishment of legitimate courts. But in fact Silvie's death occurred nearly nine months after Justice Hosmer's charge to the grand jury insisting that the vigilantes cease their activities. It happened three weeks after Lyman Munson, the last of the territorial justices to arrive in Montana, reached Helena after difficult travels and set up his courtroom. And it took place right in the very midst of Ashley's visit to the gold camps, on the evening of Saturday, July 29, 1865.[35]

If the congressman objected in any way to the display of summary justice, he left no record of it.

CHAPTER NINETEEN

Thomas Francis Meagher

After presiding over the hanging of Jake Silvie, James Williams resigned as executive officer of the Vigilance Committee and went back to running his stable and corral in Nevada City. A neighbor's son who got to know him in later years claimed that he "quit his gruesome work with a sigh of great relief and retired as quietly as he could." Perhaps so. Silvie's death coincided with a sense of change in Montana, for individuals and families as well as the territory itself.[1]

In ways large and small, Montana was maturing. In the spring of 1865, Nathaniel Langford took up his duties as federal tax collector and began imposing levies, including a $10 license fee on miners. Maria Slade remarried, choosing a respectable merchant named James Kiskadden to take the place of the legendary Slade of the Overland. Alexander Davis, the erstwhile judge of the people's court, borrowed a book from James Fergus, the county commissioner, and later left him a note saying he had passed it along in turn to lawyer William Pemberton and pioneer settler Granville Stuart, as if four of the scrappiest men in the land had decided, in effect, to form a book club.[2]

Montana's mining industry stood second only to California's in the production of gold. The territory's cities were increasingly cosmopolitan, their early tents and log cabins gone in favor of frame houses, their main streets lined with two-story shops and hotels. Visiting singers, actors, and lecturers competed for audiences. Boxing matches, bull fights, and horse and human races drew crowds in the hundreds. A resident of Helena recalled listening to the din one Sunday morning as a preacher and a horse auctioneer tried to outshout each other. "What shall a man give in exchange for his soul?" cried the preacher to his congregation, while on the street, the auctioneer answered, "I am only offered forty-five dollars! Do I hear any more?"[3]

For some, it was a time of leave-taking. Francis Thompson, the banker turned lumberman and politician, made his way out of Fort Benton on a steamer bound for St. Louis and the East. As always, he marveled at his encounters with Indians along the way. A shower of arrows and bullets pelted the boat on a bend in the Missouri River without doing serious damage, and later Thompson witnessed a Sun Dance ceremony near Fort Union, in which young braves of the Gros Ventre tribe, in order to demonstrate physical courage, were hoisted and held aloft by means of pegs inserted into cuts in their breasts. It was a scene, he wrote in his memoirs, "worthy [of] the pencil of Frederic Remington."[4]

Thompson carried with him more than a ton of gold-enriched ore, sewn inside packets sealed with rawhide, each tagged with a sworn affidavit identifying the mining claim that yielded it. His first destination was his native Massachusetts, where he married his longtime sweetheart. Then he opened an office on Broadway, in New York City, and began selling shares in the discoveries he owned in Montana in partnership with Governor Sidney Edgerton and two other men.

From his office window, Thompson wrote, he could see regiment after regiment of returning Union soldiers marching up Courtland Street, "ragged and dirty heroes, keeping step to patriotic music, and as they turned the corner into Broadway, they were greeted by thousands of cheers and the shouts of an enthusiastic populace." When he was not watching parades, Thompson arranged to have his ore samples assayed by the superintendent of the School of Mines at Columbia College, who vouched for their quality. The extra care paid off. While other western prospectors had trouble convincing investors of the value of their claims, Thompson said, "I think I was the only one who met with much success." In all, he sold claims for "upwards of one hundred thousand dollars," making a remarkable profit for his time in Montana.[5]

Governor Edgerton had no way of knowing that his claims would fetch so much money, but he had decided to leave Montana anyway, frustrated by his growing political insularity and worried about raising his children—

fourteen-year-old Mattie in particular—in a rough-and-tumble environment far from the cultured precincts of Tallmadge, Ohio. Before he could pack for home, though, Edgerton awaited the appointment and arrival of a territorial secretary, the long-overdue second-in-command who could act as governor in his absence. Edgerton had not distinguished himself in office, but at least he accepted his obligation to remain until a substitute was in place.[6]

On August 4, 1865, President Andrew Johnson finally filled the position of territorial secretary, and his choice added quite a pungent flavor to the spicy soup of Montana politics. Thomas Francis Meagher, a thirty-five-year-old Irishman, had been banished from the land of his birth for agitation against the English. He escaped exile in Tasmania in the early 1850s and fled to the United States, where he led an Irish brigade in the Union army during the Civil War and rose to the rank of general. President Johnson, at odds with the radical Republicans in Congress, decided to give Meagher, a pro-Union Democrat, the job in Montana. Meagher accepted enthusiastically, responding that he was ready to provide the settlers there with "a strong infusion of . . . Celtic blood."[7]

While Meagher was still on his journey west, vigilantes in several Montana towns chose to answer the unresolved question of whether they intended to continue the use of extralegal justice. Despite fresh signs of settlement and civility around them, they decided to carry on as before. In September 1865, a suspected horse thief named Jack Howard was hanged in Diamond City with a piece of paper reading "Robber" pinned to his leg. In Helena, on the morning of Monday, September 18, 1865, the body of a man named Tommy Cooke was found dangling from the "Hanging Tree" with another handwritten note attached, saying "Pickpocket." And nine days later near Virginia City, according to an account in the *Montana Post,* suspected horse thieves John Morgan and John Jackson "were found hanging from a hay frame leaning [on] the corral of the slaughter house, up the gulch." A note on the bodies said, "Road Agents Beware."[8]

Making explicit what their actions advertised, the leaders of the Vigilance Committee posted a public notice in Virginia City on September 19, 1865, announcing that they had determined "to inflict summary punishment upon any and all malefactors in any case where the civil authorities are unable to enforce the proper penalty of the law." As a token gesture of respect for the legitimate courts, the notice added, "In all cases the Committee will respect and sustain the action of the civil authorities." But no one was fooled. Lyman Munson, who had recently taken up his duties as a territorial justice, claimed in his memoirs that he urged his fellow judges, Hezekiah Hosmer and Lorenzo Williston, to stand up to the vigilantes and renounce their notice, yet there is no evidence that any of the justices paid more than lip service to the matter. Hosmer's brave charge to the grand jury in Virginia City nine months earlier, demanding an end to "impromptu scaffolds," was a dead letter.[9]

All four of the latest executions were reported in matter-of-fact detail in the *Montana Post,* the weekly four-page broadsheet whose editor, Thomas Dimsdale, was concurrently running his serialized, highly lauda-tory account of the initial vigilante actions against Sheriff Henry Plum-mer and his gang in the winter of 1864. Dimsdale's view of the renewed reliance on summary judgment was mild, to say the least. He reported that Wilbur Sanders, the governor's nephew and the prosecutor in the people's trial of George Ives, had fended off an attacker while walking home one night recently, and added blithely that a "hempen solution" might be just the answer to such breaches of public safety. In early October, Dims-dale was the honoree at a ceremony called by the city fathers, who pre-sented him with a silver-plated revolver and leather belt in recognition of his defense of the vigilantes.[10]

The protests that greeted some of the executions late in 1864 were not repeated with the renewal of hangings in 1865. Partly, one supposes, this reflected the acts of intimidation the vigilantes had visited on critics, including James Thurmond, the banished lawyer. Yet various diarists and letter-writers also were mute on the subject in their private observations, hinting that the eradication of these particular chronic offenders did not greatly trouble them. To be executed as a pickpocket strikes a modern observer as the supreme penalty for a petty crime, but the target evidently was considered quite a nuisance. The inability of the territorial justices to operate their courts in an efficient manner, coupled with the inherent dif-ficulty of preventing crime before it occurred, apparently hardened many Montana settlers and numbed their respect for due process.

A fair question is why Montana entertained such a high level of vigi-lantism when other western states and territories did not. At the same time Montana's vigilantes were becoming active again in 1865, an incident occurred in Idaho City in which settlers surrounded the jail and prevented a group of vigilantes from hanging a man who had killed the ex-sheriff. In October 1865, meanwhile, the *Montana Post* reported four more hangings in various spots around the territory, prompting the editors of the *Carson Appeal,* in Carson City, Nevada, to admonish the Montana vigilantes for their casual and profligate approach to summary judgment. "Human depravity," they wrote, "is developed very often among men who take the law into their own hands."[11]

Responding angrily, Dimsdale answered in the *Post* that the peace-loving majority in Montana's towns had a right to preserve order "even if the sun of every morning should rise upon the morbid picture of a malefactor dangling in the air." Taken literally, Dimsdale seemed to be justifying an execution rate of 365 people a year in a place that had about 20,000 residents, an almost genocidal number. Perhaps a bit unnerved at his own expression of blood lust, Dimsdale went on to argue in his editorial that the vigilantes in Montana were acting solely to complement the work of the legitimate courts, not to co-opt them. He explained, "This 'Vigilance Committee'—the existence of which, we suppose, cannot be questioned—is not a mob. Society here is in a state of profound tranquility—the merchant, mechanic and laborer again begin to feel secure in their lives and the proceeds of their industry."[12]

And so the executions continued. On November 21, 1865, one George Sanders was found on Helena's "Hanging Tree" with a lengthy bill of particulars pinned to his back: "This man was hung for robbing A. Slane of $1,180, and for other small stealings." Another man, never identified, was hanged from the same tree in the same week. The level of killing was such that the *Post* carried a small item from Helena one week in early December 1865 remarking, "'Hangman's Tree,' in Dry Gulch, is barren this week—no crop, not a sign of one." That is, the fact that no one had been hanged was considered newsworthy.[13]

By the end of 1865, vigilantes in Montana Territory had executed thirty-seven men, making theirs the deadliest campaign of vigilante killing in American history. A word on the superlative is in order. The standard text on American vigilantism, Richard Maxwell Brown's thoroughly researched *Strain of Violence,* catalogues extralegal movements in North America from colonial days into the twentieth century and credits the vigilance committees of Bannack and Virginia City with a total of thirty killings from 1863 through 1865, calling it the largest number in American history. Adding the targets of the Committee of Safety in Helena to the total cements Montana's dubious record. Of course, vastly larger numbers of Americans were killed in the carnage of the Civil War, including

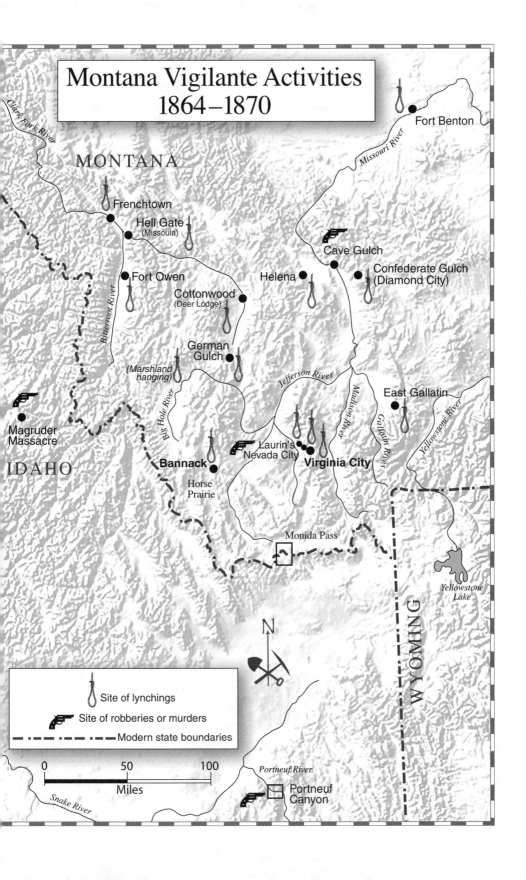

Montana Vigilante Activities
1864–1870

Clark Fork River

MONTANA

Fort Benton

Missouri River

Frenchtown

Hell Gate
(Missoula)

Cave Gulch

Helena

Confederate Gulch
(Diamond City)

Fort Owen

Bitterroot River

Cottonwood
(Deer Lodge)

German
Gulch

(Marshland
hanging)

Jefferson River

East Gallatin

Madison River

Gallatin River

Yellowstone River

Big Hole River

Magruder
Massacre

IDAHO

Laurin's
Nevada City

Virginia City

Bannack

Horse
Prairie

Monida Pass

Yellowstone
Lake

WYOMING

N

Site of lynchings

Site of robberies or murders

Modern state boundaries

0   50   100

Miles

Portneuf River

Snake River

Portneuf
Canyon

civilians caught in various riots and paramilitary operations, and the South's subsequent long use of lynching as a tool of intimidation toward blacks is a matter of wretched record. But Brown accords western vigilance committees the distinction of being "conservative mobs," whose members represented the forces in favor of order and the status quo. "Vigilantism," Brown writes, "was a violent sanctification of the deeply cherished values of life and property." By that measure, Montana stood alone.[14]

The author would add that Montana's relative isolation seems to have played a part in its continued reliance on lynching as a tool of social control. The telegraph would not arrive in the Montana gold camps until November 1866, when Virginia City finally hooked up with Salt Lake City. "Montana forms a part of the Civilized World!" crowed a celebratory headline in the *Montana Post*. "Citizens! Hang your Banners on the Outer Walls!" By implication, perhaps, Montanans had not felt themselves entirely a part of the civilized world and its constraints before then. The territory had no army forts or posts of consequence, and thus no federal soldiers whose uniformed presence might have discouraged the imposition of private justice. More than physical remoteness, however, the responsibility for the record-breaking level of vigilantism in Montana probably should be laid at the feet of the territory's political leaders, starting with Governor Edgerton. As we have seen, the earliest executions were justifiable. Afterward, when legitimate courts were in place, the few courageous voices lifted in opposition to summary judgment went unheeded by the men in charge of the territorial government, who refused to break their addiction to the easiest and cheapest means of maintaining order.[15]

With Sidney Edgerton's departure for home in September 1865, Thomas Francis Meagher became the acting governor of Montana Territory. To say the least, he brought a fresh perspective to the job. While Edgerton looked the part of a Biblical prophet and obeyed a rigid political code that alienated him from a majority of his constituents, Meagher enjoyed the sunny blarney of a born orator and the flexibility—some would say the laxity—of a man willing to change his mind.

On arriving in New York in 1852, Meagher married well and earned a public following with his speeches and articles in favor of Irish independence.

He soon learned, however, that making a living as a revolutionary parti-san was a difficult undertaking. He was residing in straitened circumstances under his father-in-law's roof when the Civil War broke out, and he seized the chance to fight for glory and fresh opportunity on the Union side. He helped recruit an Irish Brigade that fought with distinction in the first and second battles of Manassas, in the Seven Days' battles, and at Freder-icksburg and Chancellorsville, eventually suffering so many casualties that Meagher had to return to New York City to try to replenish its ranks. There he found growing opposition to the war among his Irish country-men and he openly criticized them for participating in the antidraft riots of the summer of 1863. Burning his bridges, he gave an ill-advised speech attacking the Irish for joining the Democratic Party and "following with gross stupidity and the stoniest blindness certain worn out old path-ways described for them by their drivers, but never doing anything worthy of the intellectual and chivalrous reputation of their race."[16]

Meagher's hopes of receiving another major command were frustrated by the staff of the regular army, who considered him a "political" general, and his military career ended in disgrace when he was accused of drunken incompetence moving a battalion of men from Tennessee to Maryland in the final days of the war. Having ruined his political future in New York, he lobbied President Andrew Johnson for a job in the territories. "Like many another gambler whose luck had played out," Meagher's biographer wrote, "he looked to the West." When Johnson offered him the position of secretary of Montana Territory, Meagher quickly accepted. Enduring three weeks of stagecoach rides, he arrived in Bannack around the end of September 1865 and relieved Edgerton of his duties as governor. Dubbed "the Acting One" by the newspapers, Meagher immediately began agi-tating for the establishment of forts and the placement of federal troops in Montana to protect against Indian attacks and to police the trails against the continued activity of highway robbers.[17]

Though nominally a Democrat, Meagher at first sided with the Repub-lican leadership in the territory, including the three federal justices. Echoing the party line handed him by Edgerton, Meagher dismissed the Democrats in Montana as "favourers and abettors of treason" who supported "slavery and Sectionalism." The pressing issue of the day was the matter of calling the territorial legislature back into session. Fearing that fresh elections would yield a Democratic majority, the Republicans argued that the first territorial assembly had adjourned improperly and could not meet again without the intervention and permission of Congress. Absent an elected body of legislators, Montana would be run by its chief executive and the judiciary, an idea that appealed to Meagher's vanity and appetite for power. When a group of leading citizens petitioned him to call an election and convene the legislature, he refused. Then, sensing that Edgerton had no intention of returning to the territory, Meagher had his wife, Elizabeth, send a telegram to President Johnson asking for his appointment as governor if and when Edgerton resigned.[18]

But Meagher soon saw another, brighter side to the coin. If by some chance Montana should become a state, its legislature would choose two United States senators, and Meagher decided he would very much like to be one of them. True, the territory was only a year and a half old and the idea of statehood entirely premature, but Meagher's ambition was a thing of grand scale and the potential for enrichment in Washington proved a strong lure. "I'm resolved," he wrote a friend, "not to turn my back on the Rocky Mountains until I have the means to whip my carriage and four through the New York Central Park, and sail my own yacht, with the Green Flag at the Mizen-peak, within three miles of the Irish coast." In a long letter to President Johnson dated January 20, 1866, Meagher urged support for Montana's admission to the Union as a state, arguing that otherwise the area and its people would remain "dumb and inactive." He pressed his case with Secretary of State William Seward as well, hoping their old friendship would gain him an ally.[19]

Anticipating the need to lobby support among the Democratic majority that could be expected to control the new state legislature, Meagher abruptly turned his back on the leaders of the Republican Party in Montana. "I have frankly to confess that I was greatly in error," he wrote Seward, adding that Edgerton and his crowd had been guilty of "unrelenting bitterness" toward the Democrats, most of whom actually were loyal to the Union. Meagher complained to President Johnson, who was having his own difficulties with the Republican leadership in Congress, that the GOP in Montana had been captured by "radicals and extremists." He aimed particular scorn at a man he now considered his chief rival for power, Wilbur Sanders, telling the president that Edgerton's nephew was "an unrelenting and unscrupulous extremist." (For his part, Sanders said of Meagher, "Among decent men of all parties, he is dead beyond hope of resurrection.")[20]

Meagher's about-face was triggered by more than simple opportunism. He feared that his personal conduct had become a target for criticism and

THOMAS FRANCIS MEAGHER.*

RIDES THROUGH MONTANA.

Acting Governor Thomas Francis Meagher, as depicted in *Harper's Monthly*, October 1867. Courtesy of the Montana Historical Society.

might give his enemies the ammunition to block his ascent to power. The unhappy truth was that Meager had a weakness for whiskey, and much of his time after arriving in Montana was spent in a drunken stupor. William Chumasero, a Republican lawyer, summed up the case against the "Acting One" in a withering letter to Lyman Trumbull, the influential U.S. senator from Illinois, saying Meagher's habits were "beastly and filthy in the extreme—on his first arrival in Virginia City he became intoxicated and remained so for a number of days in his room, polluting his bed and person in the most indecent and disgusting manner—and has in fact been drunk nearly every day since he has been in the Territory." Calling him a "drunken madman," Chumasero added that Meagher had brought "the vilest prostitutes" to his office and entertained them there. Fearing the accusations would take root, Meagher complained to the president that he was the target of a "cowardly conspiracy" and warned that the Republicans intended to "disable me by slander, or overthrow me in Washington by scandalous misrepresentations."[21]

When Meagher announced that he planned to call the Montana legislature back into session, the battle lines hardened. Hezekiah Hosmer and the other federal justices, his allies just two months earlier, now threatened to defy Meagher and declare any and all acts of the territorial assembly null and void. Meagher responded angrily in a speech in Virginia City that if necessary he would enforce the will of the legislature by calling out the militia.[22]

Montana's young government, fragile and flawed from its beginning, moved closer than ever to crisis. Not surprisingly, the issue of vigilantism seeped into the dispute between Meagher and the federal judges, with predictably damaging results. On the evening of Wednesday, November 29, 1865, a drifter named James B. Daniels stabbed and killed another man, Andrew Gartley, during a drunken brawl at a saloon in Helena. Daniels was arrested by Neil Howie, now serving as U.S. marshal, and the vigilantes stood back waiting to see how Lyman Munson, the territorial justice assigned to Helena, would handle the case. At trial a month later, after a change of venue to Virginia City, Daniels was convicted of manslaughter, sentenced to three months in jail, and fined one thousand dollars. Though fairly lenient, the punishment satisfied the leaders of Helena's Committee of Safety, who tended to care more about crimes against property than the inevitable fights of young men in bars. Some of Daniels's friends, however, thought he had acted in self-defense and petitioned Meagher for a pardon, setting the stage for a terrible fiasco.[23]

With little deliberation, Meagher signed a reprieve for Daniels and ordered him released immediately. As justification, the acting governor said he believed the victim had instigated the crime, but it seems more likely that Meagher was moved by empathy for a fellow Irishman, or for the thirty-two men, mostly Irish and Democrats, who signed the petition seeking his release. Writing in the *Montana Post,* editor Dimsdale suggested that Meagher must have been "misled by evil counselors." Justice

Justice Lyman Munson, who presided at the trial of James Daniels. Courtesy of the Montana Historical Society.

Munson insisted that Meagher had acted on drunken impulse, or as he put it in his memoirs, "while under the influence of an unfortunate habit." Whatever the motive, the fact was Meagher grossly exceeded his authority. Under territorial law, he had the right to suspend the death penalty in capital cases and refer appeals to the president of the United States. But he had no power to lift a sentence or free a prisoner.[24]

Hastening to the territorial capital at Virginia City, Justice Munson confronted Meagher and found him "still in his debauch," as he put it, refusing to rescind his decision. Munson ordered the prisoner re-arrested. But by then Daniels was headed back to Helena, where he made the mistake of threatening the lives of some of the witnesses who had testified against him. Sensing that his life might be in danger, Daniels asked to be taken back into custody. Instead, on the night of March 2, 1866, he was seized by the vigilantes and lynched on the "Hanging Tree," with his reprieve still tucked in his pocket.[25]

If this affront to his authority sobered Meagher, either literally or figuratively, he gave no sign of it. When the territorial assembly convened three days later in Virginia City, on March 5, 1866, the acting governor was "very drunk," according to an entry in Neil Howie's diary. On the same day the legislature gathered, lawyers involved in the Daniels case held an "indignation meeting" in Helena's Central Hall to vent their anger at the outcome, with a large audience in attendance. Branding the death a political murder, prosecutors and defense lawyers alike blamed the hanging on the feud between the governor and the judiciary.

The vigilantes, meanwhile, held themselves above politics. A correspondent calling himself "Index" explained in the *Montana Post* that the Committee of Safety had reacted predictably to the sight of Daniels back in Helena "as if returning to triumph over those whose feelings he had outraged, and whose lives he had threatened." Sounding like a proctor lecturing misbehaving schoolboys, Index added, "This attempt to make a political thing out of it, and to create jealousies between Republicans and Democrats, between east-side and west-side men, may create confusion for a time, but in the final result will not overthrow the power of the people." Let the politicians bicker, he seemed to be saying—the vigilantes would rule.[26]

Who were these vigilantes, who meant to govern when the government itself could or would not? In terms of general membership, the answer is just about everybody. By 1865, all able-bodied men who arrived in the territory were expected to join, and occasional public dances were held with the proceeds earmarked to benefit the organization. The leadership

James Daniels, lynched with his pardon in his pocket. Courtesy of the Montana Historical Society.

was meant to remain secret, of course, but the names of several top officers became a matter of record. In Helena, Charles J. D. Curtis, a merchant
who served as city clerk and helped organize the town's first fire department, also bore the private title of "chief" of the Committee of Safety. A
hint of the authority he assumed may be gleaned from a strange account
in the *Montana Post*. After he single-handedly broke up a raucous bridal
party, the newspaper reported, Curtis was challenged by a deputy federal
marshal and responded by firing his pistol in the air and claiming that he
was "higher than any civil officer." Though Curtis denied the story and
managed to secure a retraction, it had the ring of accuracy.[27]

Nathaniel Langford, who insisted in his memoirs that the vigilantes disbanded for good shortly after imposing order in the mining camps, was far
more candid in letters he wrote to his business partner, Samuel T. Hauser.
Referring to the robbery of the Pontneuf Canyon stagecoach, in which
four men were killed, Langford reported that the driver had come under
suspicion of involvement in the ambush and was captured and hanged by
vigilantes in January 1866 near Denver. "I was collecting money to ferret
out the matter," Langford reminded Hauser, "when you were here." As a
federal officer, Langford was sworn to uphold the Constitution, yet he collected funds for the vigilantes at the very same time he collected revenue
for the government. He was partner in a banking venture with Chief
Justice Hosmer, yet he made only a pretense of supporting the authority
of the territorial courts.[28]

The brazenness of the vigilantes could be remarkable. As the killing
outside Denver attested, they were willing to export their brand of justice
beyond the boundaries of Montana Territory. In the same month, January
1866, the Vigilance Committee in Virginia City hired an officer named
George Hurst to track down and arrest one Michael Duffy for unspecified
crimes. According to the *Salt Lake Telegraph*, Hurst found Duffy in Utah,
fought with him, took him into custody, and hauled him into court. A
judge ruled that Hurst had no jurisdiction and ordered him held instead
of Duffy. Hurst then escaped, resumed his search for Duffy—and killed him.
Thus it appears an agent for the Montana vigilantes committed homicide
on the sovereign soil of another territory.[29]

Within the confines of Montana Territory, meanwhile, the list of targets
of the vigilance committees continued to grow. In February 1866, in Gallatin City, a man named Jewett was hanged along with an accomplice after
wounding another man in a bar shooting. In Deer Lodge a month later,

the *Montana Post* reported, "The morning's bright sun shone down full upon the ghastly and disfigured countenance of Leander W. Johnson, who had been, a short time before, convicted of cattle stealing . . ." Johnson was seized from a sheriff's guard and hanged by a group of vigilantes whose ranks apparently included an assistant federal assessor, another official who seemed untroubled by his oath of office. In May 1866, a people's court in German Gulch carried out the execution of J. L. Goones after he stabbed his mining partner during a drunken dispute.[30]

This last action provoked a critical editorial in the *Idaho World* and fueled another fierce defense of the vigilantes from the pen of Thomas Dimsdale. Dimsdale's tenure as editor of the *Montana Post* was nearing an end. His tuberculosis had returned, choking his scarred lungs, and he would soon have to give up his duties to try recuperating in the countryside. As if to prove that illness could not bank his fires, though, Dimsdale unleashed a passionate attack on Idaho Territory, arguing that by its failure to embrace extralegal justice, Montana's neighbor was responsible for encouraging an exodus of rowdies east over the Bitterroots. In what would prove to be his valedictory on the subject, Dimsdale wrote, "There is no jury as immovably fair, impartial and unassailable, as the cold, stern, lynx-eyed, iron-willed and even-handed Executive Committee." He added, "In Montana there is peace, order and security. In Idaho there is insecurity, bloodshed and rampant lawlessness. We have made our choice."[31]

That Dimsdale firmly believed in his cause seems self-evident. His defensive tone might have given evidence of a twinge or two of dormant conscience, but he would not likely have written as he did, in a newspaper with his name on the masthead, if he thought the vigilantes were on the wrong side of a moral divide. Indeed, the policy of extending near universal membership in the vigilance committees in Montana appears to have resulted in widespread acquiescence in their activities. Dimsdale's successor as editor of the *Post,* a Boston lawyer named Henry Nichols Blake, arrived in Virginia City in the spring of 1866 and "was notified after a residence of two weeks . . . that I had been elected a member of the Vigilantes, which was virtually a certificate of an investigation and finding [that] I was of good moral character." Far from being disturbed at the anonymous invasion of privacy, Blake expressed approval of the vigilantes' mission. "This organization," he wrote in his memoirs, "rendered splendid work in upholding good order and punishing evildoers in Montana."[32]

While occasional cries of protest against the Montana vigilantes were raised in Utah, Idaho, and other western territories and states, one searches in vain for parallel criticism in the eastern press or in the halls of the nation's capital. Most itinerant journalists—among them A. K. McClure, who wrote favorable articles on the vigilantes for several New York newspapers and praised their actions in his book, *Three Thousand Miles through the Rocky Mountains,* published in 1869—took their cue from the leading citizens they interviewed, who were themselves vigilantes. Most members of "the establishment" in the Montana mining settlements belonged to vigilance committees and championed their deeds accordingly.

Reinforcing the reach and power of the vigilantes, Montana's territorial government continued to suffer from paralysis brought on by the political feud between acting Governor Meagher and his antagonists on the federal bench. The territorial legislature, controlled by Democrats, responded to Meagher's entreaties in March 1866 by cutting off the justices' salary supplements, leaving them to survive on their modest federal pay of $2,500 a year. In response, the judges turned to their Republican allies in Congress for relief, and a bill was circulated raising their salaries. For good measure, James Ashley, the Republican chairman of the House committee on territories, proposed an amendment declaring all acts of the territorial legislature to be "null and void," a harsh remedy that passed the House on May 3, 1866. The next day, Montana's congressional delegate, Democrat Samuel McLean, the three-hundred-pound lawyer, arose in the House and objected vehemently to what he considered an attack on Montana's territorial integrity. For obvious reasons, his speech is best remembered because he concluded it with a vivid threat that Montana might secede from the Union and join the Canadian province of British Columbia, a notion freighted with melodrama in the aftermath of the Civil War. Less noted at the time, but of greater significance, McLean disparaged the ability of the territorial courts to adjudicate criminal cases.[33]

From the beginning, McLean argued, Montana's laws "were not of sufficient force or sufficiently carried out to be of any positive benefit in dealing with crime in the Territory. The consequence of this condition of affairs is that justice, instead of being administered through the ordinary channels, has been compelled to give way to the vigilante system of condemnation and execution." While motivated by partisan politics, McLean's assertion entered the congressional record as nothing less than a blanket justification for a campaign of extralegal executions that by now had claimed more than forty lives. As a nonvoting delegate to Congress, McLean's authority was more symbolic than tangible, yet it is important to note that the duly elected representative of the people of Montana Territory, speaking in his official capacity on the floor of the U.S. House of Representatives, articulated a rationale for vigilante justice that did not provoke a single peep of disagreement and was left to stand, in effect, as the last word on the subject.

The U.S. Senate, hesitant to interfere in an intramural spat, rejected Ashley's amendment without debate and declined, for the moment at least, to pass any legislation affecting Montana. Given what amounted to a reprieve, the leaders of the territory's three branches of government might have chosen to work out their differences in a spirit of chastened cooperation, but they did not. In June 1866, after receiving word that Congress had passed on the matter, Justice Munson issued an order declaring all acts of the territorial legislature null and void, assuring that the dispute would continue for the foreseeable future. Days later, as if to punctuate the point, one John "Frenchy" Crouchet was lynched on Helena's "Hanging Tree" with a notice on his back saying, "A robber and perjurer, and one who has tried to swear away the lives of innocent men. An old offender, caught at last."[34]

It was Montana's lawyers who sensed the peril in the impasse afflicting the territorial government. Putting aside their partisan differences, a dozen members of the bar approached Chief Justice Hosmer in the summer of 1866 and urged him to repeat his charge to the grand jury insisting on the primacy of the courts and the rule of law. The roster of petitioners included Alexander Davis, the courageous anti-vigilante who had served briefly as judge of a people's court in Virginia City, and John D. Ritchie, who had acted as defense counsel in the trial of George Ives, the first man executed by the vigilantes. Most telling, the signatories also included Ritchie's adversary in that contest, Wilbur Sanders, the prosecutor whose fierce advocacy had placed Ives on the gallows. Sanders gave no explanation of his epiphany on the issue of summary justice at the time, but in later years he made plain his belief that while he and the original vigilantes had confronted a genuine menace, their successors were using their methods on mere riffraff and public nuisances.[35]

Hosmer's response to the petition, given in the form of a renewed charge to the grand jury, on August 7, 1866, was a model of discretion and might as easily have been written by Dimsdale in an editorial in the

Post. "Justice demands that I should accord the Vigilantes of Montana a thorough devotion to principle in all their operations," Hosmer said. "They have not taken life wantonly, or for the mere purpose of killing. Their desire has been—still is—for a condition of society exempt from crime . . ." Echoing Dimsdale, Hosmer criticized neighboring territories for laxity in law enforcement, adding that "ours is as nearly exempted [from crime] as any society similarly exposed could expect to be."[36]

Raising his point almost apologetically, Hosmer went on to note that some of the targets of the vigilantes within the past six months could have been handed over to the legitimate courts for trial. Then, in language remarkable for its trepidation coming from a federal judge, Hosmer added, "From frequent conversations with influential members of the Vigilantes, who understand the unfavorable tendencies of their society, I learn that as soon as they can feel assured that the Courts and the Juries will meet the demands of society, they will freely disband." The vigilantes would disband on their own terms, that is, and not Hosmer's. As if to acknowledge the realities of the balance of power, Hosmer concluded with a plea to the grand jury to pursue its duties diligently, in order to satisfy the criteria of the vigilantes and convince them to come to bay.

How did the vigilantes respond to this appeal to their softer side? As before, they promised Hosmer privately that they would give the courts a chance. And for the balance of the autumn of 1866, following the chief justice's admonition, they remained inactive. But they most emphatically did not disband. They came to see themselves as a necessary and permanent auxiliary to the legitimate authorities, performing such duties as making arrests, investigating crimes, and putting the fear of Jesus into various deadbeats, wife beaters, vagrants, and ne'er-do-wells.

On December 14, 1866, a claim-jumping incident led to a savage shootout among prospectors in Cave Gulch, a mining settlement about thirty miles northeast of Helena, leaving five men dead. A posse was dispatched by Helena's Committee of Safety to make arrests. Acting in place of the sheriff and federal marshal, its members rounded up nine suspects and returned them to Helena, where they were turned over to law enforcement officials to face arraignment and trial in the territorial courts. The vigilantes then decided to announce their intentions publicly. On December 27, 1866, leaders of the committee visited the newly opened offices of the *Helena Weekly Herald* and ordered a stack of posters. A. J. Fisk, the younger brother of editor Robert Fisk, recorded in his diary that the printing business had been given a boost, as the committee "had a lot of bills struck off . . . warning evil doers that it will commence operations again soon if they dont [*sic*] keep quiet."[37]

"Read and Reflect," the notice warned:

> In view of the fact that crime has run riot to such an alarming extent in the Territory of Montana (particularly east of the Missouri River) during the past six months, and that murders and high handed outrages have been of such frequent occurrence as to excite the just indignation of all good citizens, it is believed that it is now time that the good work should be re-commenced. Therefore, this is to notify all whom it may concern, that crime must and will be suppressed; and, to that end, all offenders will be summarily dealt with, and punished as of old. By order of the Vigilance Committee.[38]

Perhaps a final word on the subject should go to Nathaniel Langford, the territorial tax collector whose personal correspondence contained so many candid revelations that his later memoirs did not. "The Vigilantes have just been reorganized," he wrote his grandfather on January 16, 1867, adding:

> I have been solicited to take the position of "Chief," but have not the time, for the responsibility of the "Chief" is very great; at his call, 5,000 of our best citizens stand ready for any service. The civil authorities could not arrest the murderers in Cave Gulch. A hundred Vigilantes went over, made the arrests, and delivered the prisoners to the civil authorities. An executive committee of 10 try all offenders. I am one of that committee. The only crimes we punish are horse stealing, highway robbery and murder. We have nothing to do with *petty* crimes. [Emphasis in original.]
>
> The committee inflict but one punishment: Death. Of the other nine of the executive committee, I can only say that I never saw 9 more conscientious and thoroughly good, and *fearless* men than they. [Emphasis in original.] It's not every man that is willing to have 3 or 4 desperadoes brought before him for trial, and be discharged for want of evidence to convict, and go forth vowing vengeance against him, as a Vigilante.

Members of the Ex Committee would be regarded as very careless, if they ever, even now, should make known the fact that they [unreadable] journeying here or there, for our country is still full of bad men, who would kill a Vigilante if they could do it without detection, as soon as they would a hostile Indian.[39]

And so the vigilantes continued on their mission of imposing justice without law—three years after the hanging of Henry Plummer, two years after the establishment of territorial courts, and one year after the "indignation" meeting over James Daniels, with the very finest of Montana's citizens leading the way.

CHAPTER TWENTY

Pax Vigilanticus

On February 25, 1867, Benjamin Wade of Ohio rose in the U.S. Senate to urge passage of a bill meant to bring an end to the political feuding in Montana. "That territory," he intoned ominously, "is in a state of anarchy."[1]

Those listening from a modern perch might be forgiven for thinking that Senator Wade spoke of the continued activities of the vigilance committees in Montana's cities and mining settlements. Instead, he was referring to the unresolved spat between acting Governor Thomas Francis Meagher and the justices of the territorial Supreme Court. Demonstrating that no gesture of defiance was too petty to pursue, Meagher had convinced his fellow Democrats in the territorial legislature to banish two of the Republican judges to circuits in the remote, uninhabited reaches of Montana. Then he talked the county commissioners into withholding all supplies—including pens and paper—from the judges' courtrooms. Angry that its reprieve of the year before had been ignored, the Republican majority in Congress responded by raising the justices' salaries from $2,500 to $4,000 and then, for good measure, by nullifying the acts of the territorial legislature. "I am afraid," pioneer settler Walter Dance wrote a friend, "[that] this will make a good deal of confusion and lawsuits."[2]

Montana in 1867 was a contentious place, where political enemies continued to rake each other in the harsh language of the Civil War. The Democrats who controlled the territorial legislature, in the words of one Republican critic, were "men reeking with treason and boasting their copper head proclivities still." No one could tell exactly who was in charge. President Andrew Johnson had forced the resignation of Governor Sidney Edgerton upon his departure from the territory and replaced him with a moderate Democrat from Kentucky, Green Clay Smith, who tried to calm the partisan rancor. But like many territorial officials before him, Smith believed he could do the most for Montana's interests by going to Washington to lobby for them in person, and his journey there after two short months in office elevated Meagher once again to the position of "Acting One," where he continued to do as he pleased.[3]

The vigilantes, for their part, suffered a crisis of leadership that mirrored the political chaos going on around them. In mid-February 1867, an unusual notice was posted in Highland City, a mining district near Butte, apparently spurred by the lynching of a man named Rosenbaum. According to the *Montana Post,* which offered few other details, Rosenbaum had been whipped and banished by the vigilantes the previous autumn. He had returned to Nevada City and was hanged, the newspaper reported, adding ungenerously, "and the world is well rid of him." In his memoirs, Henry Nichols Blake, the editor of the *Post,* recalled Rosenbaum as a butcher who initially got into trouble for stealing a calf.[4]

Whatever the merits of the case, Rosenbaum's death evidently offended some of the original vigilantes. Under the headline "Notice!" they issued a warning: "We, now, as a sworn band of law-abiding citizens, do solemnly swear that the first man that is hung by the Vigilantes of this place, we will retaliate five for one, unless it be done in broad daylight, so that all may know what it is for." They continued:

> We are all well satisfied that, in times past, you did do some glorious work, but the time has come when law should be enforced. Old fellow-members, the time is not like it was. We had good men with us; but, now, there is a great change. There is not a thief comes to this country but what "rings" himself into the present committee. We know you all. You must not think you can do as you please. We are American citizens, and you shall not drive, and hang, whom you please.
>
> [Signed] Five for One[5]

Not surprisingly, most historians have interpreted the notice as a statement of anti-vigilante sentiment and some have claimed that it marked the end of the vigilance movement in Montana. Closer consideration, however, suggests a different conclusion. The original vigilantes had indeed gone their separate ways. Some, like James Williams, had retired. Others, Wilbur Sanders among them, had come to believe that vigilante methods were too harsh a remedy for a later generation of petty criminals. Many favored giving the courts a chance to operate. Paris Pfouts, the chief of the vigilantes, who moved with his family back east to St. Louis in 1867, wrote in his memoirs a year later, "The Committee still maintains its organization, but it has fallen into different hands and other men control its actions, and the people have ceased to repose that confidence in it which they did when every good man in the territory was an active member of it."[6]

In sum, the vigilantes of Montana were evolving in ways that some of their original leaders disliked. As in any thriving organization, the passage of time and the changing of the guard allowed various jealousies and disagreements to emerge and put a crack in a once-solid façade. But the vigilantes were not by any means disbanding or becoming extinct. The key phrase in the notice posted in Highland City was the demand that *future* vigilante activities be carried out in "broad daylight," a plain recognition that their work would go on. Blake, the editor of the *Montana Post,* interpreted the notice correctly as a call for reform in the vigilance committees, so that their mission could be continued.[7]

In coming weeks, the vigilantes remained active. They made several arrests, banished a handful of undesirables, and carried out at least one flogging. They did not conduct any executions, indicating that they took the public warning to heart. But their activities, like all other enterprises in Montana, were overshadowed by the sharp drama of a rise in reports of hostile encounters with Indian tribes in the region. John Bozeman, whose trail through the Big Horn Mountains had begun funneling hundreds of new settlers into Montana, wrote Meagher asking for protection, warning that Chief Red Cloud and his Sioux warriors were menacing white travelers in the Gallatin Valley. Meagher, who longed to ride again in command of men in uniform, responded by pestering the army for troops, munitions, and funds. At first, leery of Meagher's reputation and doubting the seriousness of the threat, the War Department declined to act. Then, in April 1867, Bozeman was ambushed and killed by a small party of Blackfeet on the Yellowstone River, and General William T. Sherman reluctantly sent 2,500 surplus muskets to Montana and agreed to guarantee federal reimbursement for the expenses of a militia.[8]

Seizing his opportunity, Meagher issued vouchers on the federal government and quickly raised a ragtag army of about two hundred men. "It was a marvelous opportunity to raid the treasury," Meagher's biographer observed, and the acting governor took full advantage. His requisitions would eventually cost the taxpayers more than $500,000, even though his troops never encountered any Indians in actual combat. When the muskets arrived by steamboat at Fort Benton, Meagher traveled from Virginia City with an entourage of fellow officers to claim them. Arriving hot and tired on the night of July 1, 1867, Meagher famously gulped down several doses of blackberry wine to quench his thirst and restore himself. Later that night, unsteady afoot, he berthed down on the *G. A. Thompson* as the guest of the ship's pilot. A sentry heard a loud splash over the deck rail in the wee hours, and Meagher was never seen again.[9]

Meagher's accidental death—"Another victim of Whiskey," in the assessment of one diarist—restored a measure of peace to territorial politics.[10] Governor Smith returned from Washington and helped oversee the legislature's chore of reenacting the many legitimate laws that had been sacrificed in the fight that led to nullification. The federal courts resumed operations and adjudicated several criminal cases. The government at last seemed to be functioning. The threat posed by Indians proved evanescent. But the summer of 1867 turned out to be unusually violent among the white men in Montana's cities and settlements. The *Montana Post* reported no fewer than seven homicides in the territory in the weeks after Meagher's death, and the discovery of an eighth victim, a farmer robbed and murdered in the Gallatin Valley on September 13, 1867, triggered a revival of lynching.[11]

On September 25, 1867, at a quarry just outside Virginia City, the vigilantes hanged an old associate of J. A. Slade's named Charles Wilson, an out-of-work stagecoach driver who had been behaving badly in recent days. In a pattern that was familiar by now, someone from the Vigilance Committee went to the *Montana Post*'s offices on Wallace Street and explained—off the record—the rationale for Wilson's execution. "Since mustered out of the volunteer service [militia]," the newspaper duly recounted, "he has been drinking hard; importuned the stage company for employment, and, on being refused, has made terrible threats of vengeance." Furthermore, the *Post* said, Wilson had been in league with a secret band of highway robbers, whose ranks included thirty-five active agents and one hundred accomplices, and whose plans called for setting fires, carrying out robberies, and targeting various individuals in and around Virginia City for death. Hard evidence to prove these dramatic accusations was not to be found, of course. But the newspaper insisted that Wilson had confessed before dying, and that was that. Wilson was hoisted up on a tripod, his feet nearly scraping the ground, with a piece of paper bearing the word "Vigilantes" pinned to his back, and then buried on the hill above town near the graves of the five men who were hanged side by side in 1864.[12]

In Helena, the editors of the Democratic *Rocky Mountain Gazette* lent a bipartisan flavor to the incident by applauding Wilson's demise, saying that "we think that few beside his accomplices will regret the summary and informal hanging of this man." It seemed as if Thomas Dimsdale, who had succumbed to his chronic illness in September 1865, still spoke from beyond the grave as the editorial voice of the vigilantes. Fittingly, perhaps, the *Post* wrapped up its coverage of the lynching by advertising his book, *The Vigilantes of Montana,* and offering a free copy as a bonus with every one-year, $10 subscription.[13]

Montana's reliance on extralegal justice, accompanied by cheerleading in the territorial press, continued until 1870. In that year, the lynching of a Chinese man, Ah Chow, in a domestic dispute in Helena, finally provoked the sort of heated public debate one might have expected much earlier. The facts of the case were dismally muddled. A miner named John R. Bitzer was walking home one Saturday night when he passed Ah Chow's cabin and heard the sounds of a struggle. Rushing inside, he found Ah Chow beating a woman and tried to intervene. Ah Chow pulled a pistol and shot Bitzer in the groin, fatally wounding him. Or so Bitzer told witnesses before he died. A rival version suggested that Ah Chow had happened upon Bitzer already inside his cabin, dallying with his woman, perhaps forcibly, and reacted accordingly.[14]

Either way, Ah Chow disappeared and a reward was posted for his capture. After a weeklong search, the legendary lawman "X" Beidler found the fugitive and turned him over to the vigilantes, who promptly lynched him on the "Hanging Tree." A sign was fastened to his back warning, "Beware! The Vigilantes still live!" Beidler then claimed the $600 prize on Ah Chow's head. It was this mercenary postscript to the proceedings that seemed to tip the balance in the community's sense of fair play. After riding with the original vigilantes, Beidler had served as a deputy sheriff and, since 1865, as a deputy U.S. marshal. Now he appeared to be trading on his position to play bounty hunter, which offended the sensibilities of some of his neighbors and turned them against him. He was handed a note, signed "200 Anti-Vigilantes," that threatened his life and warned, "We shall live to see you buried beside the poor Chinaman you murdered."[15]

For the first time, the newspapers openly criticized vigilante justice. Given the prevailing attitude toward Chinese in the American West at the time, it may seem odd that Ah Chow would emerge as a martyr, but he was a familiar figure around town and had friends across racial and ethnic divides. A correspondent called "Citizen" wrote an "earnest protest," published on the front page of the *Helena Daily Herald,* claiming Ah Chow had been an innocent victim. Robert Fisk, the editor of the *Herald,* wrote a companion article that concluded, "We hold to the view, ourself, that Montana is now sufficiently advanced toward an enlightened civilization to have done with the court of Judge Lynch, and to maintain and execute the law through the legal tribunals of the land." In starker language, the editors of the *New North-West* in Deer Lodge labeled the hanging "a grave wrong" and "an advertisement of anarchy in Montana."[16]

The gathering sentiment against lynching reached critical mass three months later, in April 1870, when two common thieves who had rolled a drunk were seized from the sheriff in Helena, tried by an informal people's court, and hanged side by side on the "Hanging Tree" while a large crowd looked on. A photograph of the scene was circulated, and it seems finally to have embarrassed the remaining vigilantes into suspending their activities. While it lacked the racial component that gave a specter of evil madness to the carnival photographs of lynching scenes in the American South—some of them crafted, literally, into postcards—the picture of Joseph Wilson and Arthur Compton dangling side by side with scores of adults and children gathered below their feet was more than adequate to disturb a viewer's sense of decorum, propriety, and justice. No formal announcement was made, but these would prove to be the final targets of the Committee of Safety. They were the forty-ninth and fiftieth victims of Montana's experiment with vigilante justice—a big, round number that seemed to mark a good stopping place.[17]

The lynching of Joseph Wilson and Arthur Compton. Courtesy of the Montana Historical Society.

The last use of Helena's "Hanging Tree." Courtesy of the Montana Historical Society.

The 1870s brought a sort of *pax vigilanticus* to Montana. Political stability arrived at last in the person of Governor Benjamin F. Potts, a three-hundred-pound Ohio Republican appointed by President Ulysses S. Grant. Potts, who served twelve years in the post, avoided the partisan extremism of his predecessors and made peace with the territory's Democratic leaders, including the congressional delegate, Martin Maginnis, another moderate. A territorial penitentiary was built in Deer Lodge in 1871, the courts gradually gained legitimacy, and Montana's first legal execution finally took place in 1875, more than a decade after the initial rush of settlement. Later that year, a Methodist minister bought the lot where the "Hanging Tree" stood and chopped it down, claiming it was dead and in danger of collapse. A few of his neighbors grumbled, but the *Herald* expressed a sense of nostalgia and also confidence that its day had been outlived.[18]

By the time of the national centennial, in 1876, the leading citizens of Montana faced a sharp irony. Their cities and settlements were now largely free of crime, as they had long wished, but the reason was an exodus to the Black Hills of Dakota Territory, where the latest gold rush was underway. Montana's surface mining was nearly played out, and as many as ten thousand settlers, a third of the population, had packed up and moved away. Alder Gulch was emptying out, and Helena became the territorial capital. Returning from a four-month visit east, Robert Fisk of the *Herald* wrote a lengthy article assessing Montana's prospects, which he admitted seemed "disheartening" in light of the loss of "our footloose citizens." Prosperity, according to Fisk and every other booster in the territory, depended on the arrival of the railroads, whose advance had been stalled by the Panic of 1873. Without railroads, one businessman warned, "in a few years there will not be enough of us left to make a corporal's guard."[19]

Regaining population became an urgent priority for Montana's political and business leaders, because it was the key to attaining the holy grail of statehood. As Fisk, a progressive Republican, preached in an editorial in the *Herald,* fresh settlement was essential, "for we want company, we want our resources developed, we want new kinds of business opened and all kinds of business extended; we want population to build up towns, open farms, multiply our herds, and help us the sooner to secure self-government and become a State." Governor Potts hounded his old commanding officer, General of the Army William T. Sherman, for military reinforcements to suppress Indian activity and encourage the resumption of railroad construction. Following the pyrrhic victory of the Sioux over Custer at the battle of Little Bighorn in 1876, Potts got what he wanted and the Indians were removed from the Yellowstone River corridor as an impediment to white settlement.[20]

The problem with inviting newcomers, of course, was that Montana's leaders had no control over the guest list and no easy way of keeping out undesirables. Eleven days after writing his editorial urging fresh settlement, in May 1878, Fisk rode to Fort Benton to greet the passengers arriving on the first steamer of the season. Appalled at their scruffy appearance, he laid out a rude headline proclaiming, "We Don't Want Them." With the easing of economic conditions in the late 1870s, crews began laying railroad track again, and the trickle of new settlers became a flood. The Northern Pacific approached Montana from the east and west and the Utah and Northern from the south, bringing a vanguard of young, single, rootless men who fit almost exactly the same demographic profile as the gold rush settlers who arrived in 1862 and 1863. The price for repopulating, it seemed, would be the return of vagrancy, disorder, and crime. And so, just a few short years after they retired, the vigilantes became the focus of a tremendous wave of nostalgia.[21]

Despite the praise lavished on them by Dimsdale and other chroniclers, the vigilantes had never enjoyed much success preventing trailside holdups, nor had they kept young men from getting drunk in bars and shooting at each other. But they had done a good job of terrorizing the bullies in the territory during their six-year reign, driving large numbers of them into exile. Confronted with newcomers who could not easily be intimidated, Fisk and some of his counterparts in the territorial press took it on themselves to trumpet the legacy of the vigilance committees, hoping to exploit the reputation of the vigilantes without inviting them to resume their actual practices. In the early part of 1879, Fisk wrote worriedly in the *Herald* about the "horde on our borders" and added that he hoped they might be held back "by public notice to the world that Montana is an unhealthy place for beggars."[22]

With the deck of history stacked in their favor, the vigilantes of Montana were bound for heroic stature in any case, but the wistful memories summoned by Montana's newspaper editors in 1879 cinched the deal. In Helena, which had been ravaged four times by catastrophic fires, people were especially fearful of vagrants, who often built bonfires to warm themselves and occasionally engaged in acts of arson to divert attention and create a cover for burglary. Fisk complained of a "coterie of petty offenders" who were loitering around Helena and warned, "The day approaches when an hour's notice will send them tramping from town. . . . It's the sovereign remedy and should be applied. Public opinion will uphold it." He turned out to be right about public sentiment.[23]

The brutal murder of a liquor store proprietor named John Denn in Helena on the evening of Monday, October 27, 1879, provoked widespread outrage in the community and led to a remarkable campaign aimed at forcing the vagrants out of the city. Writing in the *Herald,* a combative Fisk called for the organization of a new vigilance committee. "There is no disguising the fact," he wrote,

> that Helena at this time is the rendezvous of a score or more of very hard characters—men that have no visible means of a livelihood and that are watching for opportunities to rob and even murder, if necessary, to carry out their infamous purposes. Would it not be a wise precautionary step to invite some of these desperate characters to "take a walk," or shall we wait for other murders and robberies, or perhaps until they burn the town again?[24]

On the following Saturday night, the numbers 3-7-77 were posted on fences and walls in several locations around Helena, signaling a revival of the Committee of Safety. The men responsible for posting the numbers did not see fit to give a public explanation of their meaning, but the message appears to have been an ultimatum directed at some two dozen roughnecks to get out of town, using a $3 ticket on the 7 A.M. stagecoach to Butte, by order of a secret committee of seventy-seven—or so the author believes, based on extensive research undertaken for this book. Other plausible answers to the riddle have been a staple of Montana folklore for years. The important point is that the vigilantes were back in business. The targets of the warning did, in fact, leave Helena en masse, and the city fathers of Butte, sixty miles away, complained that their streets were suddenly "getting filled with tough characters" as a result of the purge.[25]

The prospect of a return to vigilante justice struck some in Montana as a dangerous idea, and several newspaper editors published calls for the rule of law. "It is well to look before we leap," the *Missoulian* argued, "to see where we will land if we allow law and order to be replaced by mobs and anarchy." But the new vigilantes quickly sent assurances that they did not intend to carry out summary executions. They would honor the primacy of the courts, they said, and meant only to advertise the fearful memory of their predecessors to scare vagrants and other undesirables out of town. They made a persuasive case. W. A. Woolfolk, editor of the *Independent,* Helena's Democratic weekly, wrote that the new Vigilance Committee was "composed of many of our best citizens," and he said they had given him their word in private that they did not intend to resort to violence. Thus placated, the editorial voices quieted down.[26]

The work of the 1864 vigilantes, meanwhile, was remembered in the warmest of terms. "Montana, for years succeeding the reign of the vigilantes, contained probably the most law abiding people of their number to be found anywhere," according to the *New North-West* of Deer Lodge. "Crime of every character and degree was almost unknown . . . " Newspapers outside the territory, once skeptical, now embraced legend as fact. According to the *San Francisco Chronicle,* the Vigilance Committee of 1864 "was not a mere local mob, the creature of an impulse of passion, but an organized body of stern, determined men, with branches in every camp." It had been formed, the newspaper said, in response to "an absolute reign of terror" fomented by an "organized band of robbers and murderers" whose ranks included officers of the law.[27]

Over the next few years, as the railroad tracks reached Butte and Billings and approached other cities and settlements in Montana, vigilance committees sprang up throughout the territory. The "mystic numbers," as they were called, appeared on tent flaps, sidewalks, thresholds, and in the newspapers, and scores of vagrants were driven from their flophouses, typically to the next stop on the railroad line. In Fort Benton, a "billiardist" named Blackburn was hounded onto a steamship headed back east. Simple intimidation worked for a time, but eventually the vigilantes' bluff was called, putting their vow of respect for the law to a crucial test.[28]

In 1883, a mob in Dillon seized an accused killer named John A. Jessrang and attempted to wring a confession from him by putting a noose around his neck and repeatedly hauling him off the ground to the point of near-strangulation. When Jessrang refused to admit the crime, his chastened tormentors concluded he might be innocent and returned him to jail. Fisk, writing in the *Herald,* responded angrily that Jessrang was guilty "beyond all doubt" and deserved to be lynched. With this open call for a return to summary judgment, the most influential newspaperman in Montana crossed an important line. Three weeks afterward, another mob broke into the jail at Dillon and hanged Jessrang in his cell. Other executions followed.[29]

Soon afterward, reflecting on the summary execution of a man in Salt
Lake City, Fisk's thinking crystallized, and he wrote his editorial advocating "decent, orderly lynching"—giving this book its title and suggesting
the remarkable extent to which the good folk of Montana had allowed
themselves to rationalize a practice that offends our modern sensibilities
as primitive and barbaric.[30]

In 1884, the shadow of lynching passed from Montana's cities to its
vast, unsettled central plain, where Granville Stuart, one of the territory's
earliest pioneers, led some of his fellow cattlemen in a famous raid along
the Musselshell River and shot or hanged some thirteen suspected horse
rustlers. Stuart's partner, James Fergus, the Scot who once had stood
courageously against vigilante justice, applauded the campaign, in which
his son was a participant. "The vigilantes in all their time never did a
braver, nobler, or more necessary act or one that paid better in its results,"
he insisted in a letter to a friend. Stuart's Stranglers, as they were nicknamed, became the stuff of legend, not least because a gentleman cattle
rancher from nearby Dakota Territory, Theodore Roosevelt, admired them
and tried to join their ranks. Roosevelt's enthusiasm for vigilante justice,
forged in Montana, continued into his presidency and helped shape his
belief in the need for American imperialism.[31]

(Applauding the U.S. conquest of the Philippines in 1899, Roosevelt
called Americans a "fighting race" and dismissed the islanders as "Apaches."
Later, in 1915, as World War I unfolded, Roosevelt used the analogy of
western vigilantism to explain his belief that "Superior" nations had a
duty to conquer and civilize lesser peoples. "Before there was law in California and Montana," he wrote, "and indeed as a requisite of bringing
peace there, Vigilantes had to be organized and had to hang people. Tech-
nically, this was murder; practically, it was the removal of murderers." The
same circimstances, he continued, justified British colonial rule in Egypt
and the Sudan, French rule in Algeria, German rule in East Africa, and
Russian rule in Turkistan.)[32]

The work of the urban vigilance committees in Montana, meanwhile,
continued unabated. In 1885, a prisoner named Con Murphy sawed his
way out of the Helena jail—his second escape—and was captured after a
shoot-out in which he wounded a policeman. A mob seized him, hanged
him, and pinned a card with the numbers 3-7-77 on his back. A young
man who witnessed the event took the card from Murphy's back and presented it as a gift to Fisk's thirteen-year-old daughter, Grace. Afterward,

Fisk's wife, Lizzie, wrote her mother in Connecticut, asking, "What did you think of the hanging? I have wondered how it would impress eastern people."[33]

Eastern people, for the most part, were not impressed one way or the other. Montana's resumption of summary justice caused little stir in the national press, and lynching continued right on through the achievement of statehood in 1889 and into the twentieth century. The "mystic figures" continued to appear and took on a sort of split personality. They were used with obvious, malicious intent by anonymous agents from time to time to terrorize various groups and individuals, but they also were bandied about lightly as a token of frontier nostalgia. As early as 1882, the members of a men's glee club in Helena styled themselves the "3-7-77 Boys." Because of the confusion about their meaning, an erroneous idea took hold from the outset that the numbers had been used by the earliest vigilantes. And the gallant reputation of those first vigilantes was reinforced at almost every turn by historians and journalists.[34]

In 1917, radical labor leader Frank Little, a member of the far-left Industrial Workers of the World, or Wobblies, arrived in Butte and began attacking America's recent entry into World War I. Speaking before large crowds of copper miners, Little called President Woodrow Wilson a "lying tyrant" and denounced United States soldiers as "scabs in uniform." This proved to be free speech at its most dangerous. In the early morning hours of August 1, 1917, six masked men seized Little in his boarding house, dragged him through the streets, and hanged him from a bridge. A sign was placed on his back with the numbers 3-7-77 and the initials of six other men threatened with the same fate.[35]

Far from tarnishing the memory of the first vigilantes, the lynching of Frank Little heralded the beginning of a period when their reign would be elevated to mythical heights. In 1920, hoping to profit from the advent of family vacations by automobile, state officials renamed the routes in southwest Montana from Yellowstone National Park to Butte and Helena the Vigilante Trail and designed distinctive red, white, and blue disks with the numbers 3-7-77 in the middle to mark the way. Two years later, in 1922, the numbers appeared in Missoula, not to frighten anyone, but in recognition of a meeting of the Montana Society of Pioneers.[36]

For the most part, these celebrations of vigilante history were undertaken innocently, free of any intent to promote or even contemplate extralegal justice. The thought that the vigilantes had overstepped the bounds of propriety and abused power simply did not occur to anyone who was writing, teaching, or shaping history at the time. In the 1920s, the principal of Helena High School, hoping to invent a fresh tradition to replace the staging of an annual fistfight between junior and senior boys, inaugurated a Vigilante Day Parade through downtown Helena with students competing peacefully to build prizewinning floats. It took hold, and in 1931 Twentieth-Century Fox and Paramount both filmed the parade for newsreel features, giving it a national audience. The *Saturday Evening Post* ran a series of articles on the original vigilantes in 1929 that echoed Dimsdale's version of events and cemented the popular view of Sheriff Henry Plummer as a villain and his executioners as brave and just.[37]

Putting a final gloss of respectability on the legend of the vigilantes, the numbers 3-7-77 were added to the shoulder patch and car door shield of the Montana Highway Patrol in 1956. Promoted to superintendent that year, Alex Stephenson personally designed the new insignia as a tribute to law and order. A rock-jawed, old-school lawman, Stephenson was entirely ignorant of the numbers' convoluted history and believed they simply honored the vigilantes of 1864. "We chose the symbol," he explained later, "to keep alive the memory of this first people's police force."[38]

To this day, the vigilantes are honored in Montana as heroes. Despite the determined efforts of a small school of revisionists, no lasting damage has been done to the reputations of the men who brought order to the gold camps in the winter of 1864. Those who extended the reign of extralegal justice for years afterward have been conveniently and almost totally ignored. Lynching in Montana finally faded from acceptance in the first half of the twentieth century, and today no one fears the midnight tramp of boots outside a cabin or the sight of a scaffold on a barren hillside lit by torch and moonlight.

It is hard, though, to imagine any Montanan not feeling a shiver of apprehension if he found 3-7-77 chalked on the front door one morning. Given Montana's continued, fretful association with various scofflaw organizations and its unwanted reputation as a place without speed limits or other boundaries on personal behavior, we might do well to acknowledge the excesses and inherent abuse of power carried out by men who for too many years refused to bow to the police and courts and rule of law.[39]

Epilogue

What became of our cast of characters? Did their later lives shed any further light on the activities of the vigilantes?

Not long after her husband, the sheriff, was hanged, Electa Bryan Plummer joined her sister and brother-in-law, Martha Jane and James Vail, on a farm outside Vermillion, Dakota Territory. On January 19, 1874, she was remarried to a widowed rancher named James Maxwell and later bore him two sons. "She had no children by Henry Plummer," her stepdaughter, Mrs. Ida Stafford, wrote in 1930. "She never spoke of her life in Montana and I knew little of it. She never returned to Montana after leaving there." Had she considered Henry Plummer an innocent victim, Electa might have spoken out against the men who executed him. She did not. She died in 1912 and was buried in Wakonda, South Dakota.[1]

James Williams, the executive officer of the vigilantes, was married in Virginia City in 1866 to Elizabeth Ledford, with Chief Justice Hezekiah Hosmer presiding. He fathered seven children and ran a cattle ranch that did not prosper. According to a neighbor, Mrs. Williams developed a "shrewish turn of mind" and often nagged her husband about his shortcomings. At one point he cosigned a bank note with Don Byam, the man who served as judge in the people's trial of George Ives, and when Byam failed to make good the creditors liquidated Williams's ranch and sold off his herd. He regrouped, only to face fresh disaster as the deadly winter of 1887 killed off thousands of head of cattle across Montana. With his herd

about to die, Williams wandered into his pasture on a bitterly cold night—
a night that might have reminded him of some of the vigilantes' rides—
and committed suicide by drinking laudanum. Those who considered his
actions as a vigilante improper, or worse, could contemplate his fate as a
form of rough justice.[2]

Francis Thompson, the banker turned lumberman who befriended and
ultimately betrayed Henry Plummer, returned to his hometown of Greenfield, Massachusetts, and entered upon a life of public service. He was
elected register of the Probate Court in 1870 and held that post for nearly
thirty years. In 1899, having studied law, he was appointed judge of the
court. He wrote a two-volume history of Greenfield that was well
received and completed his memoirs of life in Montana shortly before he
died on New Year's Day, 1916. "He was helpful, generous, and forward-
looking," according to his obituary.[3]

Wilbur Sanders, the prosecutor in the people's trial of George Ives, ran
four times without success for the post of territorial delegate to Congress.
He nonetheless earned the nickname "Mr. Republican" for his efforts on
behalf of the party, and was rewarded with election to the U.S. Senate
when Montana became a state in 1889. He wrote his friend Thompson
in 1904 to say that death was near and that he did not fear it, only the end
of his long fight to make Montana a better place. "[T]his poor debouched
state," he wrote, "it needs me, being woefully lacking in men of sensitive
natures who resent civic treachery as a crime. . . . I have fought bribery
and every form of civic corruption for forty years and now that it has
become triumphant, I fight it still." He died the next year in Helena.[4]

Mary and Sidney Edgerton returned to Tallmadge, Ohio, with enough
money from their mining claims to set up a comfortable household. He
resumed the practice of law and eventually softened in his political lean-
ings. During his only return visit to Montana, in 1882, he admitted in an
interview with the *Helena Daily Herald* that he had been too tough on
the Democrats. His daughter, Mattie, married, moved back to Montana,
and wrote extensively about the pioneer years.[5]

Nathaniel Langford, another prominent chronicler of the vigilantes,
came very close to realizing his dream of high office in Montana. In
December 1868, lame-duck President Andrew Johnson nominated him
for the post of territorial governor, to succeed Green Clay Smith. But with
incoming President Ulysses S. Grant awaiting inauguration, the Senate
declined to act. In Langford's place, Grant nominated James Ashley, the

congressman who played a vital role in creating Montana Territory and who lost his seat after taking the lead in impeaching Johnson. Ashley's brief service as governor was marred by a return to partisan bickering. Grant removed him in favor of Benjamin F. Potts.[6]

James Fergus, Granville Stuart, and Samuel Hauser went into the cattle business together and led the vigilante movement of 1884 known as "Stuart's Stranglers" aimed at curtailing cattle rustling in central Montana. They suffered dramatic losses in the deadly winter of 1887. Fergus and his beloved wife, Pamelia, enjoyed a long and fruitful union. Hauser was appointed territorial governor in 1885 by President Grover Cleveland, a fellow Democrat. Stuart was named a special envoy to Uruguay and Paraguay by Cleveland in 1894.[7]

Paris Pfouts returned to St. Louis in 1867 and became a partner in a wholesale grocery business. He continued his Masonic activities. He died at the home of a son in Dallas, Texas, in 1910 at age eighty-one.[8]

"X" Beidler served as a lawman in various capacities for years. He was regarded lightly as a "picturesque character" by some, but when he died in Helena in 1890 he was buried beneath a gravestone that proclaimed, "Public Benefactor, Brave Pioneer, To True Occasion True."[9]

Appendix

Targets of the Montana Vigilantes

1.	"Red" Yeager	Jan. 4, 1864	Laurin's ranch, Alder Gulch
2.	George Brown	Jan. 4, 1864	Laurin's ranch, Alder Gulch
3.	Henry Plummer	Jan. 10, 1864	Bannack
4.	Ned Ray	Jan. 10, 1864	Bannack
5.	Buck Stinson	Jan. 10, 1864	Bannack
6.	"Dutch John" Wagner	Jan. 11, 1864	Bannack
7.	José Pizanthia	Jan. 11, 1864	Bannack
8.	George Lane	Jan. 14, 1864	Virginia City
9.	Frank Parish	Jan. 14, 1864	Virginia City
10.	Hayes Lyons	Jan. 14, 1864	Virginia City
11.	Jack Gallagher	Jan. 14, 1864	Virginia City
12.	Boone Helm	Jan. 14, 1864	Virginia City
13.	Steve Marshland	Jan. 16, 1864	Big Hole Valley
14.	Bill Bunton	Jan. 19, 1864	Cottonwood (Deer Lodge)
15.	George Shears	Jan. 24, 1864	Frenchtown or Bitterroot Valley
16.	Cyrus Skinner	Jan. 25, 1864	Hell Gate (Missoula)
17.	Alex Carter	Jan. 25, 1864	Hell Gate
18.	John Cooper	Jan. 25, 1864	Hell Gate
19.	Robert Zachary	Jan. 25, 1864	Hell Gate
20.	Bill Graves	Jan. 26, 1864	Fort Owen (Bitterroot Valley)
21.	William Hunter	Feb. 3, 1864	Gallatin Valley (Emery's cabin)
22.	Unknown	Feb. 17, 1864	Virginia City
23.	J. A. Slade	Mar. 10, 1864	Virginia City
24.	James Brady	June 15, 1864	Nevada City
25.	Jem Kelly	Sept. 5, 1864	Snake River Ferry

26. John Dolan	Sept. 17, 1864	Nevada City
27. R. C. Rawley	Oct. 31, 1864	Bannack
28. John Keene	June 9, 1865	Helena
29. Jack Silvie	July 29, 1865	Helena
30. Jack Howard	Sept. 15, 1865	Diamond City
31. Tommy Cooke	Sept. 18, 1865	Helena
32. John Morgan	Sept. 27, 1865	Virginia City
33. John Jackson	Sept. 27, 1865	Virginia City
34. Con Kirby	Oct. 3, 1865	Helena
35. Unknown	Oct. 1865	Prickly Pear Tollgate
36. Unknown	Oct. 1865	Prickly Pear Tollgate
37. Unknown	Oct. 1865	Confederate Gulch
38. George Sanders	Nov. 21, 1865	Helena
39. Unknown	Nov. 23, 1865	Helena
40. Unknown	Nov. 23, 1865	Helena
41. Frank Williams	Jan. 1866	Denver
42. Michael Duffy	Jan. 1866	Salt Lake City
43. Charles Jewett	Feb. 5, 1866	East Gallatin
44. Unknown	Feb. 5, 1866	East Gallatin
45. James Daniels	Mar. 2, 1866	Helena
46. Leander Johnson	Mar. 12, 1866	Deer Lodge
47. J. L. Goones	Apr. 20, 1866	German Gulch
48. "Frenchy" Crouchet	June 5, 1866	Helena
49. Rosenbaum	Feb. 1867	Nevada City
50. Charles Wilson	Sept. 25, 1867	Virginia City
51. J. M. Douglas	Nov. 13, 1867	Red Mountain City
52. George Ballou	May 18, 1868	Reynolds City
53. Jack Varley	Aug. 13, 1868	Beartown
54. William Hinson	Aug. 18, 1868	Fort Benton
55. Ah Chow	Jan. 24, 1870	Helena
56. Arthur Compton	Apr. 30, 1870	Helena
57. Joseph Wilson	Apr. 30, 1870	Helena

Sources for the first twenty-one victims are Thomas J. Dimsdale's *The Vigilantes of Montana* and the Merrill Burlingame Papers at the Montana Historical Society; sources for all other victims are the *Montana Post* and the Burlingame Papers.

Note on Sources

Every historian who tackles the subject of the Montana vigilantes confronts the same dilemma—the need to challenge the one-sided version written by Thomas Dimsdale while also relying on it as a primary resource. The series of articles Dimsdale wrote in 1865 for his weekly newspaper, the *Montana Post*, gives us a highly detailed, nearly contemporaneous account of the vigilantes' activities. But it also presents the vigilantes as unblemished heroes who did nothing wrong and their targets as evildoers requiring immediate execution. How much credibility should we grant Dimsdale?

In my view, there is no reason to ignore Dimsdale just because he is opinionated and partisan. I have elected to treat him, in effect, as a hostile witness: I have examined his story closely and carefully, and I have struck his testimony whenever he strayed from fact to feeling. Fortunately, Dimsdale was not writing in a vacuum. His account can be checked against various diary entries, letters, miners' claims, contracts, memoirs, oral histories, and other primary source materials. I have relied on more than forty eyewitness descriptions of events in this book to balance what Dimsdale has to say, and I am more than satisfied that, while some errors may remain, the basic story of the vigilantes can be told accurately, impartially, and without exaggeration.

In general, I have given the greatest weight to diary entries and letters, on the theory that they are contemporaneous and, as private observations, likely to be candid. Similarly, miners' claims and contracts have the advantage of being legal documents executed within the time frame of the events in the book. Oral histories and memoirs have their inherent weaknesses, and I have tried to weigh and assess them on a case-by-case basis. Nathaniel Langford, for instance, is given to obvious flights of melodrama and occasionally to outright fiction. I have relied on him very judiciously and only when he is writing about events he experienced first-hand. In the case of Francis Thompson, who became a well-respected amateur historian in his later years, I felt comfortable assigning a higher level of trust.

Just as Dimsdale dominates the early histories of the vigilantes, Ruth Mather has staked a claim on Henry Plummer with a highly revisionist view of the vigilantes of Montana in three books of modern vintage: *Hanging the Sheriff*, *Vigilante Victims*, and *Gold Camp Desperadoes*. Along with her co-author, F. E. Boswell, Mather paints a picture as one-sided as Dimsdale's, but with Plummer as the white hat and his prosecutors as venal bullies. Mather and Boswell have done a prodigious amount of research for which they deserve credit, and I have made grateful use of their trail markers in tracking fresh primary sources. But I am unable to embrace their conclusions.

Many other historians have contributed to the vigilante canon over the years, in both research and interpretation, and I appreciate the opportunity to build on their work. A special word of thanks is due Art Pauley, the author of *Henry Plummer, Lawman and Outlaw*, published in 1980 by the Meagher County News, White Sulphur Springs, Montana. An amateur historian, Pauley combed the newspaper archives of northern California and pieced together a detailed, even-handed look at Plummer's life there in the 1850s and early 1860s. Regrettably, Pauley failed to annotate his text, so his sources occasionally are a matter of guesswork. According to his editor, Verle L. Rademacher of the *Meagher County News*, Pauley drove around with great reams of paper files stacked in heaps in the back seat of his car, an old-fashioned method of scholarship one can respect if not endorse.

My purpose in writing this book is to bring the Montana vigilantes into a wider context and to a wider audience than previous treatments. Therefore, I have chosen not to interrupt the narrative by debating and rebutting every disputed point in the main text. But where there are material disagreements among historians on key matters, I have addressed those issues in the endnotes. For example, in their account of Plummer's murder trial in *Hanging the Sheriff*, p. 154, Mather and Boswell state unequivocally, "Vedder's shot passed through the kitchen and out the front door, lodging in the gate." Actually, while one witness testified that a bullet was lodged in the gate, several other witnesses said the hole in the gate was old and painted over, and other persuasive testimony and physical evidence strongly suggested that Vedder did not fire his gun at all—an important reason, in my view, that two juries found Plummer guilty of second-degree murder. I hope readers will agree that I have struck the right balance between storytelling and scholarship.

On another ticklish point, I have adopted a policy of using direct quotes if they are sourced to my satisfaction. This is a subjective standard, obviously. Where one party to a conversation has provided a plausible exchange whose basic content is supported by secondary accounts, I have elected to include it for the simple reason that the people in this book did in fact speak, and I think readers will appreciate the chance to hear their words. I have not invented dialogue. Some legendary utterances—"Men, do your duty," and "Ask him how long he gave the Dutchman!"—were heard by hundreds of men and seem genuine beyond dispute.

Finally, as a glance at the bibliography will show, I believe I have tracked down and studied every significant history of the Montana vigilantes. All have contributed to my interpretation of what happened in the Rocky Mountains in the 1860s and afterward. But the judgments in this book, right or wrong, are mine alone.

Notes

AUTHOR'S NOTE

1. For a discussion of the superlative "deadliest," please see text and endnotes for Chapter 19.

2. Regarding the numbers 3-7-77, see Frederick Allen, "Montana Vigilantes and the Origins of 3-7-77," *Montana: The Magazine of Western History*, 51 (Spring 2001): 2–19.

3. Charles Bagg, Francis Thompson, William Rheem, George Bruffey, Walter Dance, James Fergus, Anton Holter, Conrad Kohrs, Perry McAdow, William Steele, and Granville Stuart all served as territorial legislators; John X. Beidler was a deputy sheriff and Neil Howie a federal marshal; Samuel Hauser was a territorial governor (Nathaniel Langford was appointed governor but not confirmed); Henry Nichols Blake and William Pemberton were territorial Supreme Court justices. John Creighton was a founder of Creighton University. See Ellis Waldson, *Montana Legislators*; Owings, *Montana Directory*; Bob Reilly, "World of the Creightons," *Window*, Creighton University (Winter 1996-97): 4–11.

4. *Helena Daily Herald*, August 27, 1883.

5. Phinney, *Jirah Isham Allen*, pp. 18–27. Ike Allen was the son of my great-grandfather's brother, thus my first cousin twice removed.

6. Memo to file, Allis Stuart, September 15, 1942, Worthen-Fergus papers, MSU.

INTRODUCTION

1. Palmer's discovery: Dimsdale, *Vigilantes of Montana*, p. 82; Sanders, "*The Story of George Ives*" (published in Sanders and Bertsche, *Beidler*, pp. 40–79.) The dead boy's last name is variously rendered as Tbalt, Tbolt, and Tiebolt.

2. High-pitched, shrieking sound: Lovell, oral history, pt. 2, MHS.

3. "The ground . . . turned inside out": W. Hillhouse Raymond, WPA Oral Histories, MSU. Palmer description: Sanders, *Beidler*, p. 51.

4. Clark had been riding: William Herron in Sanders, *Beidler*, p. 34.

5. San Francisco as hamlet of eight hundred: Greever, *Bonanza West*, p. 7. 175,000 pounds of gold: Manning, *One Round River*, p. 131. There are other estimates of the yield from California. Malcolm J. Rohrbaugh, in *Days of Gold: The California Gold Rush and the American Nation* (Berkeley, University of California Press, 1997) states on p. 3: "In the six years from 1849 to 1855, the Argonauts harvested some three hundred million dollars in gold from California." Miners did not steal: Boorstin, Americans, p. 82.

6. Gold discovered in Nevada, Colorado, Idaho, Montana: Greever, *Bonanza West*.

7. Strike at Grasshopper Creek: Toole, *Montana*, p. 78.

8. "Three oxen, some beans": Fergus to wife, November 2, 1862, cited by Horn, "James Fergus," p. 73.

9. "Twenty to thirty families here": Ibid., December 13, 1862, Worthen-Fergus Papers, MSU. (Fergus's letters come from three main sources: Many of his letters were transcribed by Clifton B. Worthen, a Montana history teacher, and copied in Collection 913, the Worthen-Fergus Papers, in the archives of the Montana State University Special Collections department. Other letters are cited verbatim in *The Gold Rush Widows* by Peavy and Smith, and in a doctoral thesis, "James Fergus" by Horn.)

10. "Forty-rod" whiskey: West, *Saloon*, p. 13.

11. Robbers active in autumn: Langford, *Vigilante Days*, p. 141.

12. Alder Gulch discovery: Hughes interview, *Virginia City Times*, November 5, 1909; Sweeney, Reminiscences, MHS; Edgar journal.

13. Dimsdale claimed 102 murders on p. 22. The figure is repeated by such respected Montana historians as Merrill Burlingame, Ross Toole, and Michael Malone. My figure of eight homicides represents only white victims, as Indian deaths did not contribute to the rise of vigilantism.

14. Palmer quick to relate: Dimsdale, pp. 82–83.

15. Coffin cobbled: Ibid.

16. Clark a man of "iron resolution": Barbour, "Two Vigilance Committees": 287. Clark active in San Francisco, drew up document: Lott bio, Wheeler Papers, MHS.

17. "Avenger of God": Lovell, oral history, pt. 1, MHS.

18. "Come on, Cap": Callaway, *Montana's Righteous Hangmen*, p. 25.

19. "Great American pie-eater": Langford, p. 191; Purple, *Perilous Passage*, p. 133.

20. Ives's background: Mather and Boswell, *Gold Camp Desperadoes*, pp. 125–31. "like a swan": Sanders, *Beidler*, p. 44. Back horse into saloons: Dimsdale, p. 79. Shot by Carrhart: Purple, p. 131. Ives in Yellowstone: Thrapp, *Vengeance!*, p. 89.

21. "Old Man" Clark encountered Ives: Herron in Sanders, *Beidler*, p. 35.

22. Posse's ride: Dimsdale, p. 83; Callaway, pp. 25–6. The narrative of the capture of Ives comes mainly from Dimsdale. However, Callaway and others make a strong case that Dimsdale was mistaken in saying Franck was found by the posse near the spot where Palmer discovered Tiebolt's body. My conclusion is that Tiebolt was killed on land that Franck and Hilderman leased from Robert Dempsey. After Palmer's discovery, Franck fled to a campsite some six or seven miles distant, on or near Ives's ranch on Wisconsin Creek, in company with Ives, while Hilderman returned to Dempsey's ranch.

23. "Long John . . . prepare for another world": Dimsdale, p. 84.

24. Williams's background: Callaway, p. 6. "Did you hear what I said?": Ibid., pp. 7–10. "I had some leather": Williams, Reminiscence, SC 975, MHS. (Williams denied joining the posse in this account, but Callaway insists that Williams acknowledged participating: Callaway speech text, June 8, 1938, SC 213, MHS.)

25. Franck identified Ives: Dimsdale, p. 85.

26. "I guess I'll have to go": Callaway, p. 27.

27. Ives's escape: Ibid.

28. Debate about Ives at Nevada City: Dimsdale, p. 89.

CHAPTER 1: MAINE TO CALIFORNIA

1. "No place for sissies": Rich, *Coast of Maine*, pp. 266–68.

2. Plummer's ancestry: *Early Pleasant River Families of Washington County, Maine* (Camden: Picton Press, 1997), pp. 462–74. Mather and Boswell, in *Hanging the Sheriff*, pp. 193–99, discuss Plummer's lineage and conclude that he was one William Henry Handy Plumer, son of Jeremiah and Elizabeth Handy Plumer, born in 1832 in Addison, Maine. They give their source as "Maine, Machias Vital Records, Hannah Weston Chapter of the DAR." In *Vigilante Victims*, pp. 176–77, they give the names of Plumer's brother and sister as Wilmot and Rebecca. However, records in *Early Pleasant River Families* suggest that the authors are mistaken. Jeremiah Plumer was married to Elizabeth "Bestey" Wass, not Elizabeth Handy, and while the couple had children named Wilmot and Rebecca, they did not have a son named Henry. They had a son named Marion Handy Plumer, who died in 1853. It appears far more likely that Henry Plummer was the son of Jeremiah Plumer's brother, Moses Plumer IV, as the records show an unnamed son born to Moses Plumer IV and his wife, Abigail "Nabby" Wass, in the years 1830–35. Lending further credence to this theory is the fact that "Nabby" Wass had an older brother named Henry, for whom she might well have named a son.

3. *Addison, Maine: A Bicentennial History*, 1997. Black bear: p. 11.

4. See *Early Pleasant River Families*. Great Wass Island: *New York Times*, Travel Section, July 13, 1997.

5. Maine after 1820, "thrifty" farms: Judd, *Maine*, p. 250. *Sarah Ann*, "hauling bee": Ibid., p. 232.

6. Joshua Chamberlain: Roberts, *Trending into Maine*, p. 43.

7. Moses Plummer III household: Federal Census, 1840.

8. Polk: message to Congress, December 5, 1848, cited by Holliday, *Rush for Riches*, p. 87. Voyage of *Belgrade*, Jared Nash diary: *Addison Bicentennial*, pp. 22–23.

9. Plummer booked passage on *Golden Gate*: Louis J. Rasmussen, *San Francisco Passenger Lists* (Baltimore, Dedford, 1965), cited by Mather, *Hanging the Sheriff*, p. 121.

10. California, "hog-hole" hotels: Holliday, p. 101. Voyage of *Golden Gate*, "pandemonium": Mather, *Hanging the Sheriff*, pp. 120–21.

11. Description of San Francisco in 1852, rudiments of zoning: Lotchin, *San Francisco*, p. 12. Vigilance Committee of 1851: Quinn, *Rivals*, p. 109–25. Plummer on Bush, Montgomery Streets, *Directory of San Francisco for 1853*, cited by Mather, *Hanging the Sheriff*, p. 121. "From treasure hunt to an industry": Holliday, p. 151. $5 per day: Holliday, p. 160fn. Plummer's skill at cards: no primary source states that Plummer was a gambler, but the *Nevada Journal* of Nevada City, California, seemed to include him in a blanket condemnation of local gamblers (issue of December 2, 1859).

12. Letter to Plummer, July 3, 1853: *Nevada Journal*, cited by Mather, *Hanging the Sheriff*, p. 122. "Triangular figure": *Nevada Journal*, October 14, 1853, cited by Mather, *Hanging the Sheriff*, p. 122.

13. Salesman for a bakery: Pauley, *Henry Plummer*, p. 24. Plummer vital statistics, *Register and Descriptive List of Convicts*, cited by Mather, *Hanging the Sheriff*, p. 162–63.

14. Nevada City by 1854: State of California Census, 1853, cited by Mather, *Hanging the Sheriff*, p. 123; Pauley, p. 23. National Hotel, Lola Montez: Kelly, *Falcon Guide*, p. 144.

15. "Fresh peaches": *Nevada Journal*, April 28, 1854, cited by Pauley, p. 25.

16. Courting daughter of merchant: Mather, *Hanging the Sheriff*, p. 126. *Banditti*, p. 43, has Plummer engaged to a "Miss B." "Merchants, ministers": Mann, *After the Gold Rush*, p. 197. "Live and Let Live": *Nevada Journal* ads, April 1854.

17. Fire of 1855: Mather, *Hanging the Sheriff*, p. 124. Lippart, Polka: Pauley, p. 26. Plummer sold house to Heyer: Mather, *Hanging*, p. 125.

18. Evans resigned, Plummer hired: Pauley, p. 29.

19. Know-Nothing background: Quinn, p. 163. J. Neely Johnson elected governor: Johnson, *Founding the Far West*, p. 200.

20. Plummer joined Democrats: Pauley, p. 30. Profile of Democrats: Johnson, pp. 244–45; Starr and Orsi, *Rooted in Barbarous Soil*, p. 264.

21. Johnson, Wright in American Party: Pauley, pp. 30, 32. Rolph praised, "arrested too many": *Nevada Journal*, May 2, 1856, cited by Pauley, pp. 30–31. Plummer won, "cursing, hiccupping": Ibid.

22. Plummer expected "to possess": Mann, p. 76. Duties: Mather, *Hanging the Sheriff*, p. 127–28.

23. Incident of June 6, 1856, in saloon: Pauley, p. 32–33, from *Nevada Journal*, undated.

24. San Francisco Vigilance Committee of 1856: Lotchin, pp. 194-201; Quinn, pp. 186-99; Holliday, pp. 180–81; Gould, *Cast of Hawks*, pp. 35–55; Senkewicz, *Vigilantes*, pp. 105–70; Ethington, *Public City*, pp. 89–126. Ethington makes a persuasive case, on p. 89, that the vigilance movement of 1856 was a political "rebellion" by the business community against City Hall. "Proof against this country": Quinn, p. 175.

25. "Irresponsible organization": Gould, p. 52. "bevy of . . . bullies": Lotchin, p. 195.

26. Plummer and fire of July 19, 1856: Pauley, p. 34.

27. Jail escape of October 1856: *Nevada Journal*, October 10, 1856, cited by Pauley, p. 35.

28. Incident with Sheriff Wright: *Nevada Journal*, November 7 and 14, 1864, cited by Pauley, pp. 36–46.

29. Plummer's letter, *Nevada Democrat*, November 19, 1856. Williams answers: *Nevada Journal*, November 25, 1856.

30. "Considerable ingenuity": *Nevada Journal*, April 15, 1857, cited by Mather, *Hanging the Sheriff*, p. 139. Plummer had fined Waite: *Nevada Journal*, March 25, 1857, cited by Mather, *Hanging*, p. 140. Plummer won reelection: Pauley, p. 50.

31. Nominated for assembly: Pauley, p. 51. Plummer accused of taking money from proprietor of brothel: Ibid., p. 50. Plummer "leader of reckless, rowdy": *Sacramento Union*, August 19, 1857.

32. Rolph, "not been in the last dog fight": *Nevada Democrat*, August 26, 1857, cited by Pauley, p. 50.

33. Plummer defeated by Know-Nothing: Pauley, p. 54.

CHAPTER 2: "A SEDUCER" ON TRIAL

1. Unless otherwise noted, my account of the Vedder homicide and trial comes from the trial transcript, *People v. Plumer*, Nevada County, California State Archives, Sacramento. The transcript, written in longhand, gives verbatim phrases from witnesses' responses but does not include counsel's questions. Also, accounts of the shooting were carried in the *Nevada Journal*, October 2, 9, and 16, 1857, the *Nevada Democrat*, September 29, 1857, and the *Sacramento Union*, September 28, 1857—cited in Mather, *Hanging the Sheriff*, and Pauley. Vedder cursed Lucy, pinched her nose: H. W. Rice testimony, *People v. Plumer*.

2. Vedder injured by rocket, *Nevada Democrat,* July 8, 1857, cited by Mather, *Hanging the Sheriff*, p. 144. Vedder called on Belden: Belden testimony.

3. Vedder pulled Bowie knife: William Draper testimony.

4. Lucy went to Hotel de Paris, Plummer stayed there: O. Cheaval testimony.

5. Plummer knew Vedder suffered "hard lot": B. H. Barker testimony. Plummer had "no intention of letting Vedder shoot him down": Ibid.

6. Stop milk deliveries: H. C. Mills testimony. Offered chair for sale: Draper testimony. Asked Van Young to guard daughter. Ibid.

7. Divorce papers, "think I'm a damn fool?": Belden testimony.

8. Asked Vedder if he was sick: Draper testimony. Borrowed a gun: George McFadden testimony.

9. Description of house on Spring Street: Mather, *Hanging the Sheriff*, p. 151. Lucy had dinner with Corbett: Lucy Vedder testimony.

10. Four shots, "I'll take that pistol": Couts testimony.

11. Vedder was dead: Mallory testimony.

12. Plummer "in a fuss": Van Hagan testimony. The most important dispute among historians is whether Vedder fired a gun at Plummer. Mather, *Hanging the Sheriff*, p. 154, states, "Vedder's shot passed through the kitchen and out the front door, lodging in the gate." A close reading of the transcript indicates that defense counsel Belden *argued* that a shot flew from the kitchen, through the sitting room, out the front door and into the gatepost. But William C. Asher testified that the hole in the gate was old and painted over, and four other witnesses testified that after making a thorough search of the premises, they could find no evidence that Vedder had fired his gun.

13. Judge bound Plummer over, set bond: Mather, *Hanging the Sheriff*, p. 150. "Plummer's conduct . . . condemned": *Nevada Journal,* October 2, 1857. "An intimacy" existed: *Sacramento Union*, September 28, 1857. "Seducer": Mather, *Hanging the Sheriff*, p. 160. "A man who would take": Stephen E. Southwick affidavit, January 2, 1858, appeal record, *People v. Plumer.*

14. Lucy gave up custody . . . ordered to return child: *Nevada Journal*, October 16, 1857.

15. Grand jury indicted Plummer: Mather, *Hanging the Sheriff*, p. 150.

16. Seven qualified jurors: appeal brief, Belden testimony. Getchell: affidavits filed by Belden, January 2, 1858, appeal record.

17. Lucy Vedder's testimony is from the trial transcript.

18. Exhibit A: trial record.

19. Jury pronounced Plummer guilty: *Nevada Journal*, January 1, 1858.

20. Three jurors prejudiced: Belden brief, appeal record. "The people ought to . . . hang him": W. F. Pulse affidavit, appeal record. Judge sentenced Plummer: *Nevada Journal*, January 22, 1858.

21. California Supreme Court reversed: Supreme Court April Term 1858, *California Reports*, IX, pp. 298-313, cited by Mather, *Hanging the Sheriff*, pp. 156–57. Description of Terry: Gould, *Cast of Hawks*, p. 15; Quinn, *Rivals*, p. 192.

22. Retrial in Marysville: transcript of second trial; *Nevada Journal* and *Nevada Democrat*, September 15, 22, and 29, cited by Pauley, *Henry Plummer*, p. 68. New witness: Mrs. St. John testimony.

23. Plummer reported to San Quentin: Mather, *Hanging the Sheriff*, p. 161.

24. Description of San Quentin: Pauley, p. 69. (Pauley cites a series, "The Ten Years of San Quentin, 1851–1861," in the *San Francisco Bulletin,* June 13–July 16, 1918.) Also, Mather and Boswell, *Gold Camp Desperadoes*, p. 25. "Make the heart sick": Pauley, p. 75.

25. Convict Number 1573: Mather, *Hanging the Sheriff*, pp. 162–63, Pauley, p. 69.

26. Status of trusty: Plummer to San Rafael: Ibid., pp. 70–71.

27. Taliaferro and Heiry sent petition: Governor's File on Henry Plummer, California State Archives, Sacramento, cited by Mather, *Hanging the Sheriff*, p. 164. Corbett petition re "entraps": Ibid.

28. Weller issued pardon: Pauley, p. 87. Plummer hired by Tompkins: Pauley, p. 91. Capture of "Ten Year" Smith: *Nevada Journal*, September 26, 1859, cited by Pauley, p. 92.

29. Tompkins defeated: Ibid. "A gentleman worthy of sympathy": Thomas B. Lewis letter, August 9, 1859, reprinted in Pauley, p. 84.

30. Plummer to Comstock: Mather, *Hanging the Sheriff*, p. 167. Showed off cache: *Nevada Democrat*, October 9, 1860, cited by Mather, p. 168.

31. "Increasing immorality": *Nevada Journal*, December 2, 1859, cited by Mather, *Hanging the Sheriff*, p. 169. Incident at Irish Maggie's: *Nevada Journal*, February 14, 1861, cited by Pauley, p. 93. Muldoon died, Plummer not charged: Pauley, pp. 93–95.

32. Plummer killed Riley: *Nevada Journal,* October 29, 1861, cited by Pauley, p. 95. Plummer escaped jail: Ibid, p. 96. "If Plummer shows": *Nevada Democrat*, October 31, 1861, cited by Mather, *Hanging the Sheriff*, pp. 170–71.

33. Plummer to Carson City: Pauley, p. 97. Mayfield 'hid Plummer: both Pauley and Mather cite Sam P. Davis, ed., *The History of Nevada* (Reno, Elms Publishing, 1913).

34. Mayfield killed Blackburn: Pauley, p. 98.

35. Plummer rumored in Walla Walla: Mather, *Hanging the Sheriff*, p. 174; Pauley, p. 100. Plummer signed guest book: Luna House Register, Luna House Museum, Nez Perce County Historical Society, Lewiston, Idaho, cited by Mather, p. 175. Pauley mistakenly has Plummer arriving in Lewiston in January 1861.

36. Plummer's stand against lynching: Byron Defenbach, *Idaho: The Place and Its People* (Chicago: American Historical Society, 1933), vol. I, p. 324, cited by Mather, *Hanging the Sheriff*, p. 177; Pauley pp. 105–6.

37. Checked back into Luna House: Register. Pat Ford incident: Pauley, pp. 106–7.

38. Mayfield raid: *Sacramento Daily Union*, November 1, 1862, cited by Mather, *Hanging the Sheriff*, p. 178. Rumors about Plummer: *Sacramento Daily Union*, June 17, 1863.

CHAPTER 3: WOOING ELECTA BRYAN

1. Fewer than one hundred white men: This is my estimate, supported by the number of voters—thirty—who participated in the election of July 14, 1862, in Missoula County, as reported in Stuart, *Montana Frontier*, p. 214ff.

2. "As soon as we had crossed the divide": Ibid., p. 124.

3. Legislature in Olympia created Missoula County: Spence, *Territorial Politics*, p. 6.

4. "Met two fine-looking young men": Stuart, *Montana Frontier*, p. 223ff.

5. Stuart could recognize "bad man": Ibid., p. 218. Woody noted Plummer liked whiskey: *Madisonian*, January 1, 1915, cited by Mather and Boswell, *Vigilante Victims*, p. 50.

6. Plummer and Reeves departed for Bannack: Stuart, *Montana Frontier*, p. 223.

7. Plummer arrived in Fort Benton with Jack Cleveland: Thompson, "Reminiscences" (January 1913): 36. (Happily, Thompson's memoirs are to be reprinted in book form. They were originally published as an eight-part serial in *The Massachusetts Magazine,* beginning with supplement to Vol. V, 1912, including the four issues of 1913 [January, April, July, and October], three issues of 1914 [January, April, and July], and concluding in January 1915.) Cleveland was John Farnsworth: Francis S. Goss recollection, ca. 1915, SC 762, MHS; Mather

and Boswell, *Gold Camp Desperadoes*, pp. 109–10, 113. The authors assert that Cleveland was stalking Plummer, a plausible theory but not established fact.

8. Fort Benton occupied by "Indians, half breeds": Chancellor Hoyt, undated letter to the *St. Louis Democrat*, cited by Thompson (Supplement to Vol. V, 1912, hereafter Supp.): 165.

9. Vail at Fort Benton looking for help: Thompson (July 1913): 124, and (October 1913): 159.

10. My description of the voyage of the *Emilie* is based on the diaries of Samuel T. Hauser and James Harkness and the memoirs of Francis Thompson. "Balance are Gentlemen": Hauser Papers, May 20, 1862.

11. "As fine a set of men": Thompson, Supp.: 161. Hoyt on "little faith" in enterprise: Ibid.: 162.

12. Electa Bryan's background: Mather and Boswell, *Hanging the Sheriff*, p. 19. Electa as "pure" and "pretty": Thompson (July 1913): 118, 124.

13. "Burned and ruined buildings": Thompson (Supp.): 151. Description of Sioux at Fort Randall, Ibid.: 153. "Swindle the Indians": Hauser Papers, undated. "Gross in all their appetites": Thompson, Supp.: 167. Indians ate elk: Ibid.: 156. Water "seemed alive" with buffalo, fusillade: Ibid.: 155.

14. Incident with *Spread Eagle*: Ibid.: 156–57; Hauser diary, undated entry, Hauser Papers; Harkness, *Contributions*, II, p. 347; Phinney, *Jirah Isham Allen*, p. 20.

15. Vails and Thompson at Sun River, "no Indians were taking lessons": Thompson (January 1913): 36; Morley, Diary, June 29, 1862, MHS.

16. Vail residence "not fit . . . no crop of consequence": Harkness diary entry, June 27, 1862, in *Contributions*, II, p. 350. Mosquitoes, rattlesnakes, flooding: Ibid., pp. 351, 356.

17. Plummer and Cleveland put to work: Thompson (July 1913): 124.

18. Electa "isolated in a palisaded log house": Ibid. The recollections of Francis S. Goss, ca. 1915, SC 762, MHS, give a plausible account of his recognition of Cleveland as Farnsworth, but in other respects are plainly inaccurate.

19. Plummer and Cleveland left for Bannack: Thompson (October 1913): 159.

20. Arrived in Bannack: Dimsdale, *Vigilantes of Montana*, p. 24; Stuart, *Montana Frontier*, p. 231. "Secesh whiskey rowdies": Fergus to wife, November 2, 1862, Worthen-Fergus papers, MSU. "Infidel and 'secesh'": Emily Meredith to father, April 30, 1863, cited in Spence, *Territorial Politics*, p. 21.

21. Cabin as "quite cozy": Stuart, *Montana Frontier*, p. 231. Fiddlers, "became the custom to go armed": Ibid., p. 232.

22. Plummer "is my meat": Dimsdale, p. 24.

23. Plummer "a general favorite": Langford, *Vigilante Days*, p. 80. "Men might be seen running": Purple, *Perilous Passage*, p. 130. "Could pan gold out of the sagebrush," Stuart, *Montana Frontier*, p. 232.

24. Both Mather and Pauley insist that Plummer was an accomplished gambler; I can find no primary source establishing this as fact, but it certainly seems plausible, given his background. "An inoffensive, gentlemanly man": Undated Fergus MS, Coll. 913, box 1, folder 17, Worthen-Fergus Papers, MSU.

25. Cyrus Skinner at San Quentin: Mather, *Gold Camp Desperadoes*, p. 168.

26. "It is charitable to believe": Langford, p. 80. Cleveland the "vilest character": Ibid. "Perhaps the worst": Purple, p. 140. Purple misnames Cleveland as Cunningham. Cleveland threatened man who recognized him: Goss, Recollection, MHS.

27. Edwards's death: Dimsdale, p. 24; Purple, p. 134; Stuart, *Montana Frontier*, p. 234n. Crawford "caroused a good deal": Kohrs, *Conrad Kohrs*, p. 23.

28. Plummer at Goodrich, shooting of Cleveland: Dimsdale, pp. 25–26; Purple, p. 137–38; Morley, Diary, January 14, 1863, MHS.

29. Plummer "still at large, unmolested": Fergus journal entry, January 21, 1863, Worthen-Fergus Papers, MSU. "It was thought by many": Langford, p. 82.

CHAPTER 4: THE NEW SHERIFF

1. Bannock Indians: Malone, Roeder, and Lang, *Montana*, p. 19.

2. Aubony, "a fairly good cook": Stuart, *Montana Frontier*, p. 206. "Squaw men" lost prestige: West, *Contested Plains*, p. 187. In "'Mr. Montana' Revised: Another Look at Granville Stuart," *Montana* 36 (Autumn 1986): 14–23, William Kittredge and Steven M. Krauser describe Stuart's regrets at marrying Awbonnie (as they spell her name), his stubborn decision to remain with with her until her death in 1888, and his subsequent abandonment of their children after his remarriage in 1890.

3. Reeves's background: *Helena Herald*, January 3, 1882, cited by Mather and Boswell, *Gold Camp Desperadoes*, pp. 175–79.

4. Reeves and Indian woman, shooting incident: Dimsdale, *Vigilantes of Montana*, pp. 30–31; Langford diary, January 24, 1863, Langford Papers; Morley, Diary, January 22, 1863; Fergus to wife, January 27, 1863, MSU. "The squaws . . . howling": Fergus, letter to wife, January 27, 1863, Worthen-Fergus Papers, MSU. Fergus condemned "drunken rowdies": Ibid.

5. Bear Creek massacre: Madsen, *Shoshoni Frontier*, p. 192.

6. Reeves and Plummer fled, Rockwell pursued: Fergus, to wife, January 27, 1863, MSU. Plummer as negotiator: Langford, *Vigilante Days*, p. 84.

7. Plummer exonerated: Ibid.; Morley, Diary, January 22, 1863, MHS.

8. On "current of popular opinion": Langford, p. 85. Mass jury: Ibid., pp. 85–86. "Riotous gatherings in Paris": Ibid., p. 87. Hoyt elected judge: Ibid.

9. Mitchell acquitted: Langford diary entry of January 23, 1863, SC 215, Langford Papers, MHS.

10. "Meager" excuse for Reeves and Moore: Purple, *Perilous Passage*, p. 148.

11. Mitchell returned to town: Ibid., p. 149. Reeves and Moore in crude hut, subsisting on coffee and dried meat: Montana Newspaper Association "News Inserts" (afterward MNA), November 29, 1936.

12. Crawford gathered up guns: Dimsdale, p. 33. Crawford returned guns: Ibid., p. 34.

13. Crawford feared Plummer: Ibid., pp. 35–36.

14. Dance, "get the advantage": Langford, p. 107. "Little . . . bragadocio": Purple, p. 139. Eyes "like a rattlesnake's": Ibid.

15. Plummer complained of gossip: Purple, p. 154.

16. Plummer shot: Langford, p. 96; Dimsdale, p. 39; Langford diary entry, March 15, 1863, SC 215, Langford Papers, MHS. Crawford visibly shaking: Purple, p. 156.

17. Plummer's arm swelled, treatment by Dr. Glick: Langford, p. 97.

18. Creation of Idaho Territory: Schwantes, *In Mountain Shadows*, pp. 61–69. The failure of Congress to provide even a basic framework for civil and criminal laws in Idaho eventually led the territorial Supreme Court to declare that no criminal laws had been in effect during the first nine months of the territory's existence. See Limbaugh, *Rocky Mountain Carpetbaggers*, pp. 31–32. Limbaugh argues that the Supreme Court's decision was highly political and struck many observers as absurd.

19. Established cities wanted to rid: Arrington, *History of Idaho*, p. 213.

20. Ashley wanted to suit Mullan: *Idaho Yesterdays*, (Spring 1963): 43–58. Lincoln appointed Wallace: Arrington, p. 222.

21. Wallace got to Lewiston: McConnell, p. 112. In "Idaho's First Territorial Governor," *Idaho Yesterdays*, Annie Laurie Bird defends Wallace against criticism that he was slow getting to Lewiston.

22. James Stuart led prospecting party: Stuart, p. 234. Granville Stuart went to Gold Creek: Ibid. Fergus wrote wife: letters of May 10 and 17, 1863, Worthen-Fergus Papers, MSU.

23. Fergus called himself "Americanized": Fergus to family, March 16, 1863, MSU. "I like the prairies": Fergus to Dr. E. A. Wood, November 6, 1841, MSU.

24. Bannack gained hundreds: Fergus to wife, May 17, 1863, MSU. Surviving contracts: material supplied author by Bill Neal; Purple, p. 161. Black preacher: Wolle, *Montana Pay Dirt*, p. 52. Rumor that Lincoln captured: Wilbur Sanders MS, "Sketches of Early Settlers in Montana," MHS, cited by Thane, p. 38n. Masons applied for charter: Wolle, p. 52.

25. Davenports robbed: Langford, p. 108. "Infested by robbers": Fergus to wife, May 17, 1863, Worthen-Fergus Papers, MSU. "Wholesale plunder": Langford, p. 108.

26. On trip with Purple: Stuart, *Montana Frontier*, p. 234. On trip with Stuart: Purple, p. 164.

27. Elkhorn shooting, death of Carrhart: Dimsdale, pp. 42–43. Indian killed: Ibid., p. 44. "Dangerous to pass along the streets": Langford, p. 109.

28. Dance called election: Purple, p. 186n. Plummer won: Ibid. "I can be a good man": Langford, pp. 114–15.

CHAPTER 5: THE DILLINGHAM KILLING

1. Plummer left for Sun River: Purple, *Perilous Passage*, p. 186.

2. Plummer appointed deputies: Dimsdale, *Vigilantes of Montana*, p. 64.

3. Plummer formed partnership with Skinner and Ridgley: *Sacramento Union*, June 17, 1863. In *Vigilante Days*, Langford states (p. 106) that after being shot in the right arm, Plummer practiced until he gained dexterity drawing and shooting with his left. The description of his crippled left hand in records from San Quentin indicates otherwise. Dimsdale, on p. 25 of his book, asserts: "Plummer was the quickest hand with his revolver of any man in the mountains. He could draw the pistol and discharge the five loads in three seconds."

4. Richardson was wanted: Mather and Boswell, *Gold Camp Desperadoes*, pp. 22–35.

5. Stuart found Crow Indians: Malone et al., *Montana*, p. 65. Discovery of gold at Alder Gulch: Hughes interview, *Virginia City Times*, November 5, 1909; Sweeney Reminiscences, MHS; Edgar, Journal. "God is good": Thrapp, *Vengeance*, p. 111. Fairweather and rattlesnake: Pace, *Golden Gulch*, p. 9; Thrapp, p. 105.

6. Six miners in vanguard, "strung out for a quarter of a mile": Stuart, *Montana Frontier*, pp. 246–47.

7. "Our horses will die": Thrapp, p. 118.

8. Varina City, "no such blot": Pace, p. 6.

9. Molly Sheehan on "creaking in the warm sunshine": Ronan, *Frontier Woman*, p. 15. Fire swept gulch: Ibid.

10. Gold at $18.50 per ounce: Toponce, *Reminiscences*, p. 42. Bannack "quiet as a grave-yard": Purple, p. 194.

11. Thompson returned to Sun River: Thompson, "Reminiscences" (October 1913): 160.

12. Thompson's background: Thompson (Supp. 1912): 123.

13. "To her unsophisticated soul": Thompson (October 1913): 160.

14. Swift admired Plummer, Ibid.: 161.

15. On Iron, "best Indian I ever knew": Thompson (July 1913): 116. Thompson and Mrs. Vail confronted by Blackfeet: Ibid.

16. Description of Plummer: Thompson (October/1913): 161.

17. Trip to Great Falls: Thompson (July 1913): 117.

18. Steamships stuck at Milk River: Ibid.: 118.

19. Wedding of Plummer and Electa Bryan: Ibid.: 118–19.

20. Alder Gulch filled: Fergus to wife, June 15, 1863, cited in Peavy and Smith, *Gold Rush Windows*, p. 149.

21. "Gold dust . . . medium of exchange": Stuart, *Montana Frontier*, p. 266. Grocery prices: Ibid., p. 262. Boots escalated by an ounce per size: Sanders and Bertsche, *Beidler*, p. 32. Stove went for $250: *Newark Sunday Call*, November 26, 1893 (afterward Steele interview). Wagons in bottleneck: Jackson, "Fisk Expeditions to the Montana Gold Fields."

22. Todd a "stupid, ignorant fellow": Steele interview.

23. Dillingham on "a lot of robbers": Purple, p. 188.

24. Stapleton warned companions, encountered Lyons: Dimsdale, p. 64.

25. Courtroom: Steele interview. "Nonsuit": Langford, p. 129. Steele's hat: *Helena Daily Herald*, July 12, 1939.

26. Dillingham fell "like an empty sack": Dimsdale, p. 65.

27. Trial organized: Ibid., pp. 65–66. "Don't shoot!": Langford, p. 130.

28. Forbes's appearance: Dimsdale, p. 68. Cry of "Hang 'em!": Langford, p. 131.

29. Forbes's testimony: Dimsdale, p. 68.

30. H. P. A. Smith's background: Thrapp, p. 49. "My boy!" Dimsdale, p. 68.

31. Women cried: Dimsdale, p. 69; Fergus to wife, July 5, 1863, in Peavy and Smith, p. 153.

32. Crowd voted on verdicts: Langford, pp. 133–34. "Let them go!": Ibid., p. 134.

33. Steele in a "melancholy reverie": Ibid. Believed Forbes fired fatal shot: Steele interview.

34. Defendants "belonged to a group of highwaymen": Ferus to wife, July 5, 1863, in Peavy and Smith, p. 153. "Graves to Let": Sanders, *Beidler*, p. 29.

35. Fourth was somber: Fergus to wife, July 12, 1863, Worthen-Fergus Papers, MSU.

CHAPTER 6: "CUT-THROATS AND ROBBERS"

1. Plummer returned to Bannack: Mather and Boswell, *Hanging the Sheriff*, p. 47. (A surviving contract shows Plummer bought a cabin on Second Cross Street on May 23, 1863, three days before he was elected sheriff, apparently in anticipation of his marriage: Noyes, *Dimsdale's Vigilantes*, p. 204.) Plummer given a corner: Ibid., p. 51. Store was "news bureau": Thane, *Governor's Wife*, p. 40n. "Marked change": Langford, *Vigilante Days*, p. 114. Plummer "forsook the saloons": Ibid. Plummer "a very nice man": Journal of N. H. Webster, *Contributions*, III, p. 300.

2. Wore hat to hide scar: Pauley, *Henry Plummer*, p. 169.

3. Plummer's trip home with Electa, "gorgeous sunsets": Ronan, *Frontier Woman*, p. 14. It is possible that they rushed home fearing Indian attacks, but I prefer to imagine a happy honeymoon.

4. Electa not at dances: Mather, *Hanging the Sheriff*, p. 51. Caven played fiddle: Stuart, *Montana Frontier*, p. 215.

5. Plummer started subscription for jail: Mather, *Hanging the Sheriff*, p. 54. Document with Plummer's signature: MNA, January 24, 1930. Settled estate of Carrhart: Ibid.

6. Plummer and Pemberton: Typed memoir, undated, Pemberton Papers, MHS.

7. "Fancy ladies": Ronan, p. 18. Dance for a dollar: West, *Saloon*, p. 48.

8. Father lodged "discovery men": Ronan, p. 19. Fergus reminded wife: Fergus to family, July 12, 1863, Worthen-Fergus Papers, MSU.

9. Stagecoach lines: Pace, *Golden Gulch*, p. 31.

10. Father Giorda: Ronan, p. 21.

11. "Napoleon . . . an exile": Langford, p. 115. Stuart learned of Vicksburg: Stuart, *Montana Frontier*, p. 256.

12. Wallace proclaimed Lewiston capital: Arrington, *History of Idaho*, p. 215. Wallace made plans to run for delegate: Bird, "Idaho's First Territorial Governor."

13. Payne at Gold Creek "to estimate population": Stuart, *Montana Frontier*, p. 256

14. Payne at Bannnack: Langford, p. 138. Langford urged to run: Ibid.

15. Langford's suspicions of Plummer, "weatherbeaten appearance": Ibid., p. 115.

16. Plummer's name suggested to Union League: Ibid., p. 139.

17. Hauser warned against Plummer, Ibid. Hauser's background: Spence, *Territorial Politics*, p. 159. Historians have assumed: Mather, in *Vigilante Victims*, p. 50, suggests that Plummer was a political ally of fellow Democrat Samuel McLean and that Edgerton, a Republican, meant to remove him from the office of sheriff for partisan reasons. She makes the same case in *Hanging the Sheriff*, p. 74.

18. "Talked over the whole matter": Langford, p. 139.

19. Plummer hanged Horen: Pauley, pp. 170–71.

20. Plummer formed mining partnership: contractin Noyes, *Dimsdale's Vigilantes*, p. 207, cited by Mather and Boswell, *Vigilante Victims*, p. 51.

21. Fergus sent wife $1,000: letter to wife, September 27, 1863, Worthen-Fergus Papers, MSU.

22. Trying to track down supplies: Thompson, "Reminiscences" (July 1913): 119.

23. Vail gave Swift livestock: Ibid.: 120.

24. Thompson and Swift travel, see "not a spear of grass": Ibid.: 120–22.

25. Thompson went to Fort Benton: Ibid.

26. Thompson's trip with "Doc" Howard, conversation with Plummer, Electa's departure: Ibid., p. 122–23.

CHAPTER 7: THE RELUCTANT CHIEF JUSTICE

1. Mather and Boswell, *Hanging the Sheriff*, p. 60, speculate on a more benign reason Electa might have left: her husband's frequent absences from home. But Mather also reports rumors, on p. 56, that Plummer and his wife quarreled.

2. Plummer rode along stage on horseback: Martha Plassmann, *Rocky Mountain Husbandman*, November 13, 1930. (Martha Plassmann's last name is spelled variously with one or two *n*'s; according to the Helena city directory and the U.S. census, she was married to Theodore Plassmann for less than a year in 1895–96; sources conflict on the spelling of his family name.)

3. Edgerton journey west: Thane, *Governor's Wife*, p. 1. Mary Edgerton's "wishes were always subordinate": Plassmann, "Daughter," p. 63, cited by Thane, p. 7.

4. Edgerton background, political career: Plassmann, *Contributions,* III, p. 331.

5. Edgerton's group to Cleveland: Thane, pp. 11–12. Pleasant trip: Mary Edgerton to sister, June 10, 1863, in Thane, p. 15.

6. Edgerton shaved eyebrows: Mary Edgerton to family, August 6, 1863, in Thane, p. 29.

7. Animals moaning from thirst: Plassmann, "Daughter," p. 105. Party reached South Pass: Thane, p. 29.

8. Telegraph man rode up: Thane, p. 30. Lewiston "far pleasanter" than Bannack: Sanders diary, August 15, 1863, cited by Thane, p. 30.

9. Party reached Blackfoot Creek: Thane, p. 31n.

10. Martha Edgerton thrilled at encounter with "bad man": Plassmann, "Daughter," p. 118.

11. Ives encounter: Sanders and Bertsche, *Beidler*, p. 44.

12. "'Bangup' is a humbug": Sanders diary, September 18, 1863, cited by Thane, p. 31. "Keen sense of disappointment": Plassmann, "Daughter," p. 113.

13. Decided to stay in Bannack: Some historians have mistakenly asserted that William Wallace, the governor of Idaho Territory, assigned Edgerton a remote judicial district east of the Bitterroot Mountains because of political jealousy. But Merle W. Wells, in "The Idaho-Montana Border," *Idaho Yesterdays,* argues persuasively that Wallace was on friendly terms with Edgerton and would have welcomed him in Lewiston. Edgerton bought cabin: Deed, Leggatt Papers, MSU.

14. No one to administer oath: Plassmann, "Daughter," p. 117.

15. Got gold fever, "shake a pan": Mary Edgerton to mother, October 4, 1863, cited by Thane, p. 64. "Don't think I am finding fault": Ibid. Slept by whooshing sound: Plassmann, "Daughter," p. 113.

16. Fisk left howitzer: Plassmann, *Rocky Mountain Husbandman*, November 13, 1930.

17. Electa moved near Cedar Rapids: Birney, *Vigilantes*, p. 100. Plummer sold part interest in claim, sold cabin to Vail: MNA, January 24, 1930. Kept misgivings to himself: Thompson, "Reminiscences" (October 1913): 167.

18. Bannack "very quiet": Mary Edgerton to sister, October 18, 1863, cited by Thane, p. 65. Settler complained of "hard looking set" near Dempsey's: entry of November 5, 1863, Journal of N. H. Webster, *Contributions,* III, p. 300.

19. "A loveable man": Thompson (October 1913): 167. "I became certain": Ibid.

20. Howard signed on with Magruder: Ladd Hamilton's footnoted historical novel, *This Bloody Deed*, and Julia Conway Welch's *Magruder Murders* are both good accounts of the crime. (Hamilton imagines that Plummer was involved in the massacre, while Welch concludes persuasively that he was not.) Magruder sold inventory: trial testimony, cited by Welch, p. 43. Dimsdale, p. 105, makes the amount of the proceeds $14,000. Magruder left Oct. 5: Welch, p. 66.

21. Plummer and Magruder in California: Welch, pp. 19, 25.

22. Magruder a Copperhead candidate for delegate: *Lewiston Golden Age,* September 5, 1863, cited by Welch, pp. 41–42.

CHAPTER 8: A *RASHOMON* NIGHT

1. Payne reported to Wallace: Bird, "Idaho's First Territorial Governor": 8–15.

2. Payne padded the vote totals: Ibid.

3. Magruder disappeared, wife's fears: Welch, *Magruder Murders*, p. 129. Travelers who had left Bannack after Magruder did arrived in Lewiston on October 23, 1863.

4. My account of the night of October 18, 1863, and the subsequent actions of Hill Beachy comes from Welch, pp. 54–55. Ladd Hamilton's novel, *This Bloody Deed*, recreates the

scene using Page's testimony from the later trial transcript, as well as an interview with Chester Coburn, cited in *An Illustrated History of North Idaho*, 1903, p. 35.

5. Complaint signed by acting governor: Welch, p. 55.

6. "Bummer" Dan McFadden holdup: Dimsdale, *Vigilantes of Montana*, pp. 55–61. Bill Neal has found a sale of a claim on Chapman Bar in Alder Gulch dated October 3, 1863 by McFadden and a partner for $2,000, which probably accounts for the money he was carrying. McFadden filed a claim dated January 15, 1863 on 9W on the Dakota Lode, which gave him his first valuable strike.

7. Bill Bunton's background: Mather and Boswell, *Vigilante Victims*, pp. 108–21.

8. "I've got a big thing": Toponce, "Reminiscences," p. 73.

9. Bunton as "soul of hospitality": Mather, *Vigilante Victims*, p. 121.

10. "Unusual excitement": Stuart, *Montana Frontier*, p. 258.

11. "No steps . . . to discover" robbers: Ibid., p. 161.

12. "Can tell you an easier way": Langford, *Vigilante Days*, p. 141.

13. Hauser on stagecoach with Plummer: November 13, 1863: Ibid., pp. 157–58.

14. Hauser and Langford's trip: Ibid., pp. 158–61. Thompson, "Reminiscences" (October 1913): 169, gives an eyewitness account of the scene in the hotel.

15. Competing tale: Langford, p. 164.

16. "Most conspicuous citizen of eastern Idaho": Sanders, *History of Montana*, I, p. 188.

17. "Open secret" about silver: Ibid., 188.

18. Sanders' version of trip to Rattlesnake: Ibid., p. 188. Any notion that Edgerton and Sanders were hostile to Democrats, and thus political enemies of Plummer, seems to be refuted by Sanders' association with McLean at this time. Thompson opened shop, shipping cost $4,762: Thompson (July 1913): 123. "Likely to be rough times": Ibid., (October 1913): 162.

19. Governor and nephew "intimate friends": Thompson (July 1913): 168.

20. Henry Tilden's ride: Dimsdale, p. 47; Plassmann, "Daughter," p. 123.

21. Sanders and Gallagher: Sanders, *History*, I, p. 188. Gallagher "tall and striking looking": Ronan, *Frontier Woman*, p. 13.

22. Bunton suggested horse trade: Sanders, *History*, I, p. 188. Langford "afterwards ascertained": Langford, p. 160.

23. Plummer returned to Bannack, spoke to Tilden: Plassmann, *The Meagher Republican*, MNA insert undated but ca. 1925, Sidney Edgerton vertical file, MHS.

24. "*Henry Plummer!*": Thompson (October 1913): 168. The timing of Thompson's exclamation is unclear, but the context indicates it was shortly after the Tilden incident.

CHAPTER 9: THE SOUTHMAYD ROBBERY

1. Plummer and Mrs. Vail called on Edgertons: Plassmann, *Rocky Mountain Husbandman*, MNA insert, November 13, 1930. "Unusual . . . to take off hat": Plassmann, "Daughter," p. 118.

2. "An excellent meal": Mary Edgerton to sister, November 29, 1863, cited by Thane, *Governor's Wife*, p. 67. "Delicately cooked," excerpt, Harriett Sanders diary, Merrill Burlingame Papers, MSU.

3. Mather and Boswell, *Hanging the Sheriff*, p. 72. Plummer "soul of hospitality": Sanders, *History*, I, p. 219.

4. Budding romance: Burlingame speculates on this possibility in notes he took while evaluating Mather's manuscript of *Hanging the Sheriff*, Merrill Burlingame Papers, MSU.

5. Chrisman chosen in election: Leeson, *History of Montana*, p. 470. "Acquiesced in rather than approved": Thompson, "Reminiscences, (October 1913): 167.

6. Southmayd incident: Dimsdale, *Vigilantes of Montana*, p. 71. Dimsdale misspells Southmayd's name with an *e* at the end.

7. Broadwater and Ives: MNA, August 17, 1936. Sweeney and Ives: Sweeney Reminiscences, SC 823, MHS. Other accounts of violent exchanges with Ives: Anton Holter (in Cushman, *Montana*, p. 109); Lovell memoir, Wheeler Papers, MHS; Tom Baker, in MNA, August 17, 1936; Jim Sheehan in Ronan, *Frontier Woman*, p. 26; Kohrs, *Conrad Kohrs*, pp. 28, 30–31; Johnny Grant in Meikle, *Very Close to Trouble*, p. 100. Bruffey, *Eighty-One Years*, p. 34, has Ives being rude to Pete Daly's wife.

8. Langford, *Vigilante Days*, p. 150 has a detailed account of the Southmayd incident that closely tracks Dimsdale's. Dimsdale appears to have interviewed Southmayd and Caldwell after the robbery, and perhaps other participants, including "Tex" Crowell, as well. Southmayd was a prominent miner in Alder Gulch until his death in 1883: Obituary, *Helena Daily Herald*, May 30, 1883. Mather and Boswell dismiss the robbery in a single paragraph on p. 76 of *Hanging the Sheriff* and do not mention Southmayd by name. I consider the robbery significant because Southmayd reported it publicly to Plummer immediately after it happened and because Southmayd's pistol was recovered later in the possession of George Ives. Incidentally, George McMillan's *Making of an Assassin* (Boston: Little, Brown, 1976), p. 12, contains family speculation that James Earl Ray, the killer of Dr. Martin Luther King, Jr., was the great-grandson of Ned Ray, but I can find no evidence to support the notion.

9. Moody robbery: Dimsdale, pp. 50–54.

10. Holter a bank director: *Helena Daily Herald*, January 2, 1877. Would "yump" on it: Ibid., May 5, 1882, story told by Samuel T. Hauser. Holter shot at by Ives: Dimsdale, pp. 79–80; also, Cushman, p. 109; Bruffey, p. 37.

11. "Certainly an organized band": Stuart, *Montana Frontier*, p. 262. "Ferret out the mail robbers": Fergus to Ignatius Donnelly, December 10, 1863, cited in Horn, "James Fergus," p. 70.

12. "Spit in my face": Kohrs, p. 25.

13. "I'm a coward": Dimsdale, p. 36.

14. "With increasing certainty": Sanders and Bertsche, *Beidler*, pp. 46–47.

15. "Clubfoot George" Lane rode to Bannack: Dimsdale, p. 90.

CHAPTER 10: THE IVES TRIAL

1. Pale sun, thaw: Dimsdale, *Vigilantes of Montana*, p. 90. Paul Adams in *When Wagon Trails Were Dim* (Montana Conference Board of Education of the Methodist Church, 1957) has a poetic description of "gumbo," p. 39.

2. Posse brought in Ives: Sanders and Bertsche, *Beidler*, pp. 51–52.

3. Sanders encountered lawyers: Ibid., p. 52.

4. Lott brothers ask to see Sanders: Ibid., p. 53.

5. Sanders' background: profile, A. C. McClure, *Contributions*, VIII, p. 25–35. Sanders withdrew from military to protest Fugitive Slave Act: *Bozeman Avant Courier*, October 28, 1886 and November 11, 1886, in Burlingame Papers, MSU.

6. Recalled songs, "There's a Light": Sanders to Plassmann, n.d., Plassman Papers, MHS. Booming voice: Plassmann, "Daughter," p. 145. Tried to ford river: Ibid., p. 109.

7. Hattie cut up Belgian rug: Ronan, *Frontier Woman*, p. 29. "I had made up my mind": Sanders, *Beidler*, p. 54.

8. Debates and crowd votes: Ibid., pp. 54–56; Dimsdale, p. 91. "The crowd looked at me curiously": Sanders, *Beidler*, p. 56.

9. Confrontation with Caven, "whole tumult": Sanders, *Beidler*, pp. 57–59.

10. Outdoor courtroom: Dimsdale, pp. 92–93; Sanders, *Beidler*, p. 59–60.

11. Bagg as "short, stubby, hairy": Sanders, *Beidler*, p. 59.

12. Pemberton on Ives: Notes, speech at Unity Club, May 12, 1908, Pemberton Papers, MHS. Ives "stood head and shoulders above": Ronan, p. 20.

13. Hereford and Davis backed by Williams: Callaway, *Montana's Righteous Hangmen*, p. 31.

14. Bagg's opening argument: Lovell memoir, Wheeler Papers, MHS.

15. Palmer spoke: Sanders, *Beidler*, p. 61. Ives gunned down suspected informant: Dimsdale, p. 80; Meikle, *Very Close to Trouble*, p. 100.

16. "One of the worst-looking men": Bruffey, *Eighty-one Years*, p. 37.

17. Franck "came in for the seven vials": Sanders, *Beidler*, p. 65.

18. Amos Hall's ledger: Leeson, *History of Montana*, p. 1269 (cited by Bill Neal, draft monograph on Southmayd).

19. "Prudent to excuse them": Sanders, *Beidler*, p. 65.

20. Overheard conversation "that left no doubt": Lovell memoir, Wheeler Papers, MHS.

21. "Worst man in community on trial": Dimsdale, p. 92.

22. "Order without law": Sanders, *Beidler*, p. 70.

23. Sanders interrupted by Wall, taken to Nye & Kenna's: Pfouts, Four Firsts, p. 98. I am indebted to Lew Callaway for an intelligent discussion of the origins of the Vigilance Committee, beginning on page 37 of his book, *Montana's Righteous Hangmen*. He is mistaken about Pfouts having been in San Francisco, but otherwise his facts and reasoning seem sound. The notion that the vigilantes were united by membership in the Masons is thoroughly debunked by Merrill Burlingame in "Montana's Righteous Hangmen: A Reconsideration," *Montana* 28 (Autumn 1978): 36–49. Nor were they all Republicans, as assumed by James Kirkpatrick in Noyes, *Dimsdale's Vigilantes*, p. 235. Speculation continues to this day that Union sympathizers targeted Plummer in hopes of obtaining his supposed cache of gold for the Confederacy. I can find nothing to support such a notion. Mather and Boswell (*Hanging the Sheriff*, p. 115; *Vigilante Victims*, p. 169) embrace the idea that the vigilantes were mostly merchants while their targets were mostly miners, making a distinction by occupation and class that was not, in my view, nearly so clear-cut in practice.

24. Plummer would not leave Bannack: Dimsdale, p. 96.

CHAPTER 11: "MEN, DO YOUR DUTY"

1. Sanders nervous, Ives calm: Sanders and Bertsche, *Beidler*, pp. 65–67.

2. Three o'clock deadline: Grannis, Diary, entry of December 21, 1863, SC 301, MHS. Lovell claims he was the miner who insisted on a 3 p.m. deadline: Lovell, Oral History, MHS.

3. Sanders' closing argument, Ives "belonged to the criminal classes": Sanders, *Beidler*, pp. 66–67.

4. Ives "a little wild": Ibid., p. 68.

5. "Gentleman from Oberlin": Ibid., p. 69.

6. Spivey declined to vote for conviction: Langford, *Vigilante Days*, p. 187.

7. Sanders moved for verdict, sentence: Sanders, *Beidler*, p. 71.

8. Ives's speech, "I am a gentleman": Ibid., p. 72.

9. "Ask him how long he gave the Dutchman!": Sanders, *Beidler*, pp. 72–73.

10. Ives "imperturbable": Dimsdale, *Vigilantes of Montana*, p. 95. Reply to Ritchie: Sanders, *Beidler*, pp. 73–74; MNA, September 11, 1922.

11. Hereford and Davis unable to find suitable gallows: Sanders, *Beidler*, p. 75. Pemberton and Ives spoke: Pemberton memoir, undated, Pemberton Papers, MHS.

12. "Aleck Carter killed the Dutchman": Dimsdale, p. 98.

13. "Men, do your duty": Lovell, Oral history, MHS. Granville Stuart wrote in ink in the margin of Lovell's manuscript that it was Williams who gave the order. According to family members, Nelson Story, the cattle baron, claimed he kicked the box.

14. Hanging Ives a miscarriage: Mather and Boswell, *Gold Camp Desperadoes*, pp. 147–52.

15. Meade's abuse: Sanders, *Beidler*, p. 77. Letter from George Wing to editor, *Helena Daily Herald*, February 18, 1879, saying of Sanders, "His prosecution of Geo. Ives, on Alder Gulch, still lingers in my memory as the grandest picture of the heroic."

16. Two committees: Callaway, *Montana's Righteous Hangman*, p. 37; Pfouts, *Four Firsts*, p. 98. Lott formed second committee: Upon providing the signed charter of the second vigilance committee to the Montana Historical Society in 1900, Lott said it "was signed in the back room of our store in Nevada City[;] as host I passed it to my guests . . . [I] didn't need to sign it": MS, history of Madison County, article by Frances G. Albright, Melvina Lott Papers, all in Madison County Federated Women's Club Writings, SC 1382, MHS. Callaway further notes that the handwriting in the document is similar to that in correspondence he had from Lott.

17. Ives on the noose: Dimsdale, p. 100. "A weak, foolish man": Sanders, *Beidler*, p. 78. Smith called Dr. Glick: Dimsdale, p. 101.

18. Banish, shoot on sight: Sanders, *Beidler*, p. 78.

19. "If every Road Agent cost as much": Dimsdale, p. 102.

20. "We the undersigned" document presented to the Montana Historical Society by John Lott, 1900; *Madison County Monitor*, March 2, 1900.

21. Franck with posse: Dimsdale, p. 108. Posse to Camp Creek, Big Hole River: Beehrer memoir in Noyes, *Dimsdale's Vigilantes*, pp. 265–67. Carter "lying drunk" at Cottonwood: Dimsdale, p. 109.

22. Organization of formal vigilance committee, text of by-laws, "DEATH": Birney, Vigilantes, pp. 218–21. Complementing the research and reasoning of Callaway, Birney makes the most plausible case for the creation of the two committees.

CHAPTER 12: THE VIGILANTES

1. Pfouts's background: Unless otherwise noted, all material on Pfouts's family and early life is from Pfouts's autobiography, *Four Firsts for a Modest Hero*. Elected because absent: p. 99.

2. Ancestry, grandfather, p. 10.

3. Father and mother, "belle": p. 15. Father's career: pp. 15–24.

4. Pfouts sent to Ohio: pp. 39–42.

5. Pfouts's politics, pp. 43, 86–87.

6. Pfouts in Pittsburgh: pp. 44–46. "The more I heard the subject of the mines discussed": p. 51.

7. "Hundreds of idle men:" p. 54.

8. Pfouts on drinking, "Hardly a day went by": p. 74.

9. Pfouts returned to St. Joseph, married: pp. 78–82.

10. As Freemason, card player, pp. 83–85.

11. Pfouts in Denver: p. 85.

12. Pfouts on Civil War sympathies: pp. 86–87. Trip from Denver to Bannack, Pfouts forced to swear oath: p. 94.

13. Pfouts attended miners' court, Judge Bissell: pp. 95–96.

14. Bought cabin on Wallace Street: pp. 96–97. "Adopting some measures of redress": p. 98.

15. Pfouts and Sanders urged "immediate and decisive action": p. 98. Committee formed "three or four days" later: Ibid. Meeting at Fox's "blue house": Adriel Davis memoir, cited by Callaway, *Montana's Righteous Hangmen*, p. 41.

16. A thousand joined: Pfouts, p. 99.

17. Plummer in Bannack warned: Dimsdale, *Vigilantes of Montana*, p. 96. Plummer signed power of attorney: Contract, December 27, 1863, Noyes, *Dimsdale's Vigilantes*, p. 207.

18. Mary Edgerton wrote family: letter, December 27, 1863, cited by Thane, *Governor's Wife*, pp. 68–69.

19. Williams led men into Cottonwood: Dimsdale, p. 109. Paid for meat: Beehrer memoir in Noyes, p. 265–67. Working from Dimsdale, Beehrer, Beidler, and other sources, I have pieced together the itinerary and timetable of the posse's journey.

20. Severe weather on trip: Dimsdale, p. 110; Sanders and Bertsche, *Beidler*, p. 80. "I never saw such weather": Williams quoted by Callaway, p. 54.

21. Weather turned worse at Beaverhead: Ibid.

22. New Year's Eve, Williams to Rattlesnake, meets Beidler: Sanders, *Beidler*, p. 84; Dimsdale, pp. 110–11. "As cold a night": Sanders, *Beidler*, p. 80.

23. Beidler encounters Wagner: Sanders, *Beidler*, pp. 82–83.

24. Beidler in Durant's: Ibid., pp. 83–84.

25. Williams to Rattlesnake Ranch, arrests Yeager, "It's mighty cold": Dimsdale, pp. 110–11.

26. Williams's horse stumbled: Ibid.

27. Brown, Yeager's confession: Ibid., pp. 112–13.

28. Men "to vote": Dimsdale, p. 113.

29. Vigilante dissents, others level guns: Ibid., pp. 113–14.

30. Hanging of Yeager and Brown: Ibid.

31. "I merit this": Dimsdale. Yeager's background in Iowa: Mather and Boswell, *Vigilante Victims*, pp. 22–25.

32. Yeager's full confession: Dimsdale, pp. 114–15. Cushman, *Montana*, p. 105, is among those expressing doubt about the supposed secret signals and rituals of the road agents.

33. Execution of Yeager and Brown: Dimsdale, pp. 115–17.

34. Yeager's venom toward Bunton: Ibid., p. 115. The usually reasonable Art Pauley speculates without foundation that Yeager and Brown were hanged on the orders of J. A. Slade. See, *Henry Plummer*, pp. 207–8.

CHAPTER 13: "RED" YEAGER'S LIST

1. Williams reported to Lott: Callaway, *Montana's Righteous Hangmen*, p. 61.

2. By-laws called for committee of seventeen: Pfouts, *Four Firsts*, p. 99; photocopy of by-laws, Coll. 953, MHS.

3. "Pleasant and agreeable": Thompson, "Reminiscences" (October 1913): 183. New Year's Day confrontation involving Plummer, Ibid.: 184.

4. Committee extended jurisdiction, targeted Plummer: Pfouts, *Four Firsts*, p. 99. Believed Plummer part-owner of Rattlesnake Ranch: Thompson, "Reminiscences" (October

1913): 167. Lott and three others left: Callaway, p. 61. Mather and Boswell, (*Vigilante Victims*, p. 29, and *Hanging the Sheriff*, p. 83) have Beidler as one of the four, but no other source names him. Pauley, *Henry Plummer*, pp. 206, 208, has the slaying of T. M. Kinna by A. J. McCausland taking place at this time, but the incident occurred a year later, on Christmas Day, 1864.

5. "Dutch John" Wagner captured, examined: Dimsdale, *Montana's Vigilantes*, pp. 118–22.

6. Howie encountered Plummer: Ibid., p. 123. "This new way": Langford, *Vigilante Days*, p. 222.

7. Lott meeting in cabin with Chrisman, others: Dimsdale, pp. 125–26. Plassmann, *Rocky Mountain Husbandman*, November 13, 1930, confirms that Sanders attended the meeting.

8. Fetherstun and Wagner at Durant's: Dimsdale, pp. 123–25.

9. Wagner's refusal to implicate Plummer: Ibid., p. 125; Plassmann, *Husbandman*, November 13, 1930.

10. Sanders suggested "someone warn Plummer": Plassmann, *Husbandman*, November 13, 1930.

11. Tilden gave account: Ibid.

12. Daylight broke, Vails' breakfast table: Thompson (October 1913): 180–81. "Terrible secret": Ibid. Thompson strikes me as making an honest admission of his ambivalence and human weakness at this moment.

13. Meeting with Edgerton, "men were very nervous": Ibid., p. 181.

14. Small parties removed horses: Dimsdale, pp. 126–27.

15. Thompson at Edgerton house, choir practice cancelled, "You will not go": Thompson (October 1913): 181.

16. The account of the arrests is from Thompson. "Company! Forward march!" and other quotes: Dimsdale, p. 127.

17. Young man embraced Plummer: Most historians have assumed this was Joseph Swift. But Plassmann, *Husbandman*, November 13, 1930, says it was a different young man.

18. Ray and Madam Hall: Dimsdale, pp. 128–29.

19. Porter's recollection, "No, Henry": E. J. Porter, *Helena Independent*, March 24, 1886, cited in Sanders and Bertsche, *Beidler*, p. 90.

20. Informed Martha Jane Vail: Thompson (October 1913): 182.

21. Plummer "confessed his numerous crimes": Dimsdale, p. 128.

22. Plummer an "oily and snake-like demon": Dimsdale, p. 130. Plummer "open-minded . . . civilizing the mining frontier": Mather, *Hanging the Sheriff*, p. 191.

23. Pizanthia episode: Dimsdale, pp. 130–32. Pizanthia smashed window: McLatchy, "From Wisconsin to Montana," pp. 91–92.

24. "I'm shot!": Dimsdale, p. 130. Howitzer: Plassmann to R. S. Ellison, October 14, 1934, Plassman Papers, MHS.

25. "Every time a bullet struck": McLatchy, p. 92.

26. "Wild and ungovernable passion": Dimsdale, p. 132. "Cowardly mutilation": Lovell, Oral history, pt. 2, MHS.

27. "When the order came ": Plassmann to Ellison, see note 24 above.

CHAPTER 14: FIVE HANGED SIDE BY SIDE

1. Beachy likened to Huck Finn: Welch, *Magruder Murders*, p. 47. Beachy's background is taken from Welch, pp. 47–50.

2. Beachy's dream: Welch, pp. 104–5, discusses the origins of the dream story (recounted with fictional flourishes by Langford, *Vigilante Days*, p. 197).

3. Beachy journeys to San Francisco, confronts four fugitives in jail: Welch, p. 55, citing Joe Bailey, "The Magruder Murder," *The Pacific Northwesterner* (Spring 1962).

4. Renton background: Governor's file on David Renton, California State Archives, Sacramento, cited by Mather and Boswell, *Vigilante Victims*, pp. 49–53. Welch, on pp. 88–96, quotes from several contemporary but undated issues of the *Lewiston Golden Age* on Renton, Lower, and Romaine.

5. Lower's background: Mather, *Vigilante Victims*, pp. 48–49. Also, article from *San Francisco Journal*, reprinted in [Salem] *Oregon Statesman*, November 23, 1863, cited by Hamilton, p. 235.

6. Page's background: Mather, *Vigilante Victims*, p. 47.

7. Romaine's background: Ibid., pp. 47–48. Both Welch and Hamilton also cite Joe Bailey, "The Magruder Murder," Spokane *Spokesman-Review*, March 17, 1963.

8. Four men hired lawyer, appealed: Hamilton, pp. 104–5, citing the *San Francisco Bulletin*, reprinted in (Salem) *Oregon Statesman*, November 16, 1863. Merits of appeal, Hamilton, pp. 128–29. *Oregonian* warned of "necktie party": undated issue, cited by Hamilton, p. 130. Stanford signed extradition: order signed by Gov. Stanford, November 2, 1863, cited by Hamilton, p. 236n.

9. Renton tried bribe, tried escape: Welch, p. 56. "We have not heard a single expression": *Golden Age*, n.d. but December 1863, cited by Hamilton, p. 247n.

10. Page confessed, gave account of crime: Trial records, Idaho State Historical Society, Boise, cited by Welch and Hamilton.

11. "Dirty work": Page's testimony, ibid.

12. Prosecutor Grey's strong case: Hamilton, pp. 183–85.

13. Idaho adopted common law: Arrington, *History of Idaho*, p. 153.

14. Parks on Edgerton's "high moral and official character": *Boise News*, February 27, 1864, cited by McConnell, *Early History*, p. 128. Frush penmanship "defies deciphering": Welch, p. 61. Renton glared with savage anger: *Portland Oregonian*, n.d., cited by Welch, p. 69n.

15. Guilty verdict: Welch, p. 81.

16. Parks on "degraded and abandoned outcasts": *Golden Age*, n.d., reprinted by *Oregon Statesman*, February 8, 1864, cited by Hamilton, p. 238n.

17. Wagner showed dignity: Plassmann, *Rocky Mountain Husbandman*, November 13, 1930. Wagner "begged hard for his life": Dimsdale, *Vigilantes of Montana*, p. 134.

18. Wagner's letter: Ibid. "Quite a little sum": Thompson, "Reminiscenes" (October 1913): 186. $42.50 for coffin: Pauley, *Henry Plummer*, p. 222, citing a receipt signed by G. D. French dated January 12, 1864, MHS records.

19. "Not long": Dimsdale, p. 135.

20. "Marked for slaughter": Ibid., p. 136. Pfouts and committee met January 13, 1864, made list of six: Ibid.

21. Background of Boone Helm: Langford pp. 45–52; Mather, *Vigilante Victims*, pp. 76–92. "Helm was the most hardened": Dimsdale, p. 139. "One of those hideous monsters": Langford, p. 45. Harrison "fired off his pistol": Pfouts, *Four Firsts*, p. 100.

22. Grannis "obeying a notice": Diary entry, January 14, 1964, SC 301, MHS. "I saw them march": Barbour, *"Two Vigilance Committees"*: 288. Dismissed as cowards: Ibid.: 289. Details of arrests: Dimsdale, pp. 137–38.

23. Helm "innocent as the babe": Dimsdale, p. 138. "Ask Jack Gallagher": Ibid., p. 139.

24. Parish admitted "Bummer Dan" robbery: Ibid., p. 137. Released "because no positive proof": Pfouts, p. 100.

25. Hanging of the five: Dimsdale, pp. 141–45. Clayton & Hall's drug store: Pauley, p. 227. "Your dealings with me": Langford, p. 239, identifies the speaker as Dance. Lyon asks Beidler: Dimsdale, 165.

26. Helm's quotes: Dimsdale, p. 143.

27. "All of them said they were innocent": Stuart diary entry, January 14, 1864. Morley, "Such wholesale hanging": Diary entry, January 14, 1864, MHS. John Jones: letter to wife, January 12, 1864, addendum, in the possession of Jones's great-granddaughter, Mitzi Grover. "I don't think they made a mistake": Toponce, *Reminiscences*, p. 143.

An alphabetical list of first-hand accounts: David J. Bailey, Chauncey Barbour, Charles Beehrer, J. X. Beidler, Amede Bessette, C. A. Broadwater, George Bruffey, Lucia Darling, Henry Edgar, Mary Edgerton, James Fergus, John W. Grannis, Johnny Grant, Samuel T. Hauser, Sara Waddams Howard, Barney Hughes, John Jones, Robert Kirkpatrick, Conrad Kohrs, Nathaniel Langford, Mortimer Lott, George Lovell, James Knox Polk Miller, James H. Morley, Charles Ohle, William Y. Pemberton, Joseph Pennington, Paris Pfouts, Martha Edgerton Plassmann, Horace Pope, Edwin Ruthven Purple, Mary Ronan, Harriett Sanders, Wilbur Sanders, Charles Schafft, William L. Steele, Granville Stuart, James Stuart, James "Bill" Sweeney, Francis Thompson, Alexander Toponce, Carolyn Tyler. Please see Bibliography for details.

28. "Far from the control": Thompson (October 1913): 188. "Broken-down gamblers": Barbour: 285.

29. "Written notices were handed" to Smith and Thurmond: Stuart, diary, entry of January 14, 1864.

30. Alexander Davis: Walter N. Davis, "Hung for Contempt of Court," unpub. MS, MHS.

31. Davis held court: Langford, p. 286. "After the execution of the five men": Dimsdale, p. 167.

32. Committee organized twenty-one riders: Dimsdale, p. 147.

33. "Looked almost like highway robbery": Kohrs, *Conrad Kohrs*, p. 35.

34. Grant "told them they were as bad": Meikle, *Very Close to Trouble*, p. 108. Grannis's pony commandeered by "the vigilance": Diary entry of January 23, 1864. "Ferreting fund": Lott brothers' ledger, copy, vertical file, "Vigilantes," MHS.

CHAPTER 15: ONE HUNDRED AND TWO!

1. Mary Edgerton's letter of January 17, 1864: cited by Thane, *Governor's Wife*, pp. 73–75.

2. "By discoveries of the bodies . . . one hundred and two": Dimsdale, *Vigilantes of Montana*, p. 22.

3. "Known" dead: Burlingame, *Montana Frontier*, p. 100.

4. Dimsdale "marred by propaganda": Mather and Boswell, *Vigilante Victims*, p. 171.

5. "I never knew such cold weather": Mary Edgerton letter, January 17, 1864. "In sending dry goods": Mary Edgerton to sister, November 29, 1863, cited by Thane, *Governor's Wife*, p. 67. "Now this next that I write": Mary to sister, February 21, 1864, cited by Thane, p. 78.

6. "They were very anxious to know": Mary Edgerton's letter of January 17, 1864. "No danger . . . now": Ibid. Sewed ingots in lining of coat, "to dazzle the eyes": Plassmann, *Contributions*, III, p. 331.

7. Edgerton carried $2,000: Thompson, "Reminiscences" (January 1914): 15. Edgerton wore fisher fur cap: Plassmann, "Daughter," p. 128.

8. Detail led by Thomas Pitt: Birney, *Vigilantes*, p. 299. Marshland in poor health: Dimsdale, p. 147.

9. Body had to be buried that night: Dimsdale, p. 148.

10. "No. 84" was Pitt:Thompson (January 1913): 25.

11. Posse rode to Cottonwood, captured Bunton: Dimsdale, pp. 148–49; Kohrs, *Conrad Kohrs*, p. 35.

12. Bunton executed: Dimsdale, p. 150. Meiklejohn: *Fallon County Times*, December 21, 1936, cited by Mather, *Vigilante Victims*, p. 108, 126.

13. Crowell "a highwayman and a common thief": Dimsdale, p. 150. Tribunals conducted "in absentia": I can find no specific accounts of such tribunals, but it is clear that the posse led by Williams started out with a specific list of targeted men provided by the Executive Committee.

14. Ride toward Hell Gate, capture of Skinner: Dimsdale, pp. 152–53. Idaho legislature created ten counties: Madison County Records, Coll. 295, MSU.

15. Skinner and Carter questioned: Dimsdale, p. 153; Kohrs, p. 36. Description of Cooper: Meikle, *Very Close to Trouble*, p. 107.

16. Pitt rode to O'Keefe's, arrested Zachary: Dimsdale, pp. 154–55.

17. Shears, "Taking a walk with [Pitt]": Ibid., p. 155. "Shall I jump off or slide off?": Ibid.

18. Higgins and Worden suspected Carter and Skinner: Kohrs, p. 36. Cooper accused by girl's father: Dimsdale, p. 157.

19. Hanging of Graves: Dimsdale, p. 156.

20. "Tired and worn": Ibid., p. 159.

21. Magruder robbery planned by Plummer in "council" with Skinner: Dimsdale, p. 105. Skinner "ingratiated himself into the favor of Page": Ibid., p. 154. Skinner served killers a drink: Page testimony, Magruder trial record, cited by Welch, *Magruder Murders*, p. 63. Skinner borrowed from Chrisman: promissory note, reprinted in Noyes, *Dimsdale's Vigilantes*, p. 239.

22. Skeptics argued Dimsdale made up list ex post facto: Mather, *Vigilante Victims*, p. 167.

23. Smith joined Thurmond in Salt Lake City: obit of Thurmond, *Helena Daily Herald*, March 22, 1882. *Sacramento Union* re "greatest astonishment": issue of February 15, 1864, cited by Mather and Boswell, *Hanging the Sheriff*, p. 182. *Sacramento Union* questioned case against Lane, wondered "whether organization . . . as great as reported": Ibid. Mather also cites articles on the vigilante executions in the *Rocky Mountain News*, February 14, 1864, February 18, 1864, and February 19, 1864; (Salt Lake City) *Union Vedette*, February 5, 1864; *Portland Oregonian*, March 30, 1864, April 13, 1864; *Oregon Statesman*, May 23, 1864; *Boise News*, March 19, 1864; (Idaho City) *Idaho World*, June 3, 1865. *Portland Oregonian* suggested posse was bullies: issue of April 13, 1864, cited by Mather, *Vigilante Victims*, p. 144.

24. Account of meeting Plummer's brother and sister: Langford, *Vigilante Victims*, p. 227.

25. Charles Ohle letter: Mendenhall Papers, MHS.

26. Miners joined "grand stampedes": Stuart diary, entry of January 21, 1864. "Horses are selling very high": Ibid., entry of January 24, 1864.

27. Capture and hanging of Bill Hunter: Callaway, p. 70; Dimsdale, pp. 159–66.

28. "Dreadful and disgusting duty": Ibid., p. 166.

29. Miners' meeting of February 7, 1864, "very foolish": Stuart diary entry, February 8, 1864.

CHAPTER 16: SLADE OF THE OVERLAND

1. On Slade: Dimsdale, *Vigilantes of Montana*, p. 166. Twain on Slade: *Roughing It*, chapters X and XI. Dickens on Dimsdale: William McDevitt, *The Collector's Journal* (April–June, 1933); article, n.d. but ca. 1889, *St. Louis Globe-Democrat*.

2. Sheehan, "I was alarmed": Ronan, *Frontier Woman,* p. 24.

3. Incident with Slade over lumber: Langford, *Vigilante Days,* pp. 283–84.

4. Posse lost to Slade's wife at poker: Callaway, *Montana's Righteous Hangmen,* p. 70, quoting Adriel Davis.

5. Slade fined twice for mischief: Bruffey, *Eighty-one Years,* p. 44. Unnamed man hanged February 17, 1864: Grannis, Morley diary entries, MHS.

6. Slade and Moll Featherlegs: Birney, *Vigilantes,* pp. 329–31, citing an undated letter from John Lott to Lew Callaway. Bancroft, *Popular Tribunals,* I, p. 689, says Featherlegs brought suit against Slade and won damages.

7. Slade arrested, taken before Judge Davis: Dimsdale, pp. 169–73. Davis gave a detailed account of the incident to the *St. Louis Globe-Democrat,* reprinted in the *Helena Daily Herald,* July 20, 1878.

8. Mrs. Slade "possessed of . . . personal attractions": Dimsdale, p. 172.

9. Slade hanged: Dimsdale, pp. 172–73. "I found her sobbing": Ronan, p. 25.

10. Sheehan's family disapproved: Ibid. Case exemplified need for jail: Lovell, Oral history, pt. 2, Wheeler Papers, MHS. "Stern necessity": Dimsdale, p. 173.

11. Idaho legislature created counties, appointed officials: Commission, Fergus as county commissioner, February 6, 1864, Worthen-Fergus Papers, MSU. Edgerton reached Tallmadge: *Summit County Beacon,* February 25, 1864, cited by Thane, *Governor's Wife,* p. 81n. Hauser, Langford, others in Washington: Letter from Hauser, Langford et al. to President Lincoln, March 17, 1864, asking him to appoint Edgerton governor, cited by Jackson, "The Appointment and Removal of Sidney Edgerton": 293.

12. Thompson carried ingot, "gold ran down into the cinders": "Reminiscences" (January 1914): 16. Thompson's trip east: Ibid.: 16–17.

13. Ashley's plan for interior mining territory: Wells, "The Idaho-Montana Boundary." Wells argues persuasively that Edgerton was not banished to a judicial district east of the Bitterroots by Governor Wallace, a mistaken idea propounded by W. Turrentine Jackson (see note above) and repeated by James H. Hamilton, *From Wilderness to Statehood: A History of Montana* (Portland, 1957).

14. Wallace supported the "panhandle" boundary of Idaho, which ruined him politically: Edgerton interview, *Helena Daily Herald,* August 22, 1882. Spence, *Territorial Politics,* p. 11, correctly notes that Wallace was an ally of Edgerton's. Bill reached House, "Let a man . . . go westward": *Congressional Globe,* 38th Cong., 1st sess., (March 17, 1864), p. 1169.

15. Letter to Lincoln: see note above.

16. Spaulding's objection, Beaman response, "I am informed": *Globe,* p. 1168.

17. House votes down amendment: Ibid. "Gem of the Mountains": Schwantes, *In Mountain Shadows,* p. 59. Samuel Cox, debate on name of Montana: *Congressional Globe,* 38th Cong., 1st sess., pp. 1168–9.

18. Civil War politics: McPherson, *Battle Cry,* pp. 698–713.

19. Wilkinson amendment re "male citizen": *Congressional Globe,* 38th Cong., 1st sess., pp. 1346, 1362.

20. Reverdy Johnson, "They may go": Ibid., p. 1345.

21. Amendment approved: Ibid., p. 1361. Name strikes Sumner as "peculiar": Ibid. Sumner and Johnson argue, Senate votes 29–8: Ibid.

22. Senate debate April 19, 1864, Sherman, Doolittle, Hale: *Congressional Globe,* 38th Cong., 1st sess., p. 1704.

23. Wilkinson Speech, April 20, 1864: Ibid., p. 1744.

24. Langford asks meeting with Doolittle, Doolittle speech of April 25, 1864: Ibid., p. 1842.

25. General Burnside marching: Ibid.

26. Senate voted, Hale grumbled: Ibid., p. 2349.

27. Lincoln signed: Spence, *Territorial Politics*, p. 15.

CHAPTER 17: "THE WOUNDED MAN RECOVERED"

1. Edgerton meeting with Lincoln, "Dosheimer" story: Plassmann, *Contributions*, III, p. 331. Wilkinson letter to Lincoln: dated may 20, 1864, cited by Spence, *Territorial Politics*, p. 17n.

2. Mary Edgerton gave birth: Thane, *Governor's Wife*, p. 56, 86n. Edgerton reached Tallmadge, found stack of letters: Thane, p. 86n. Mary Edgerton letter to sister, April 27, 1864: Thane, pp. 84–86.

3. Thompson proposed, invested in sawmill: Thompson, "Reminiscences" (January 1914): 19.

4. Fergus sent wife $750: letter, March 7, 1864, cited in Peavy and Smith, *Gold Rush Widows*, p. 183. Fergus and wife quarreled: Ibid., pp. 193–97.

5. "'Biz' begins to look up a little": Stuart diary entry, February 9, 1864. Mary Edgerton notes arrival of thirty settlers: letter to sister, March 19, 1864, in Thane, p. 82. Magruder killers executed: Welch, *Magruder Murders*, pp. 85–87. Page led group to crime scene: *Golden Age*, June 11, 1864, cited by Welch, pp. 117–18.

6. Shooting on night of June 14, 1864: Dimsdale, *Vigilantes of Montana*, p. 178.

7. Brady caught, taken to Nevada City: Ibid., p. 179.

8. Brady's affairs put in order, Brady executed: Ibid., pp. 180–81.

9. Murphy survived; "Now, we have always held": Ibid., p. 177.

10. "The most cynical passage": Smurr, "Afterthoughts on the Vigilantes": 8–20, referring to Birney, *Vigilantes*, p. 340.

11. Edgerton received telegram, had to buy horse, saddle: letter from Mary Edgerton to sister, July 13, 1864, in Thane, pp. 89–90. "A wonderful child": Ibid.

12. Edgerton, Sanders fired howitzer on July 4, 1864: Ibid. Lovell saw armed men: Lovell, oral history, pt. 2, MHS. Mattie saw "drunken horsemen": *Contributions*, III, p. 331.

13. Torsey declined position: Spence, pp. 18, 235. Hauser petitioned for secretary, Langford for surveyor: Ibid., p. 17

14. Gold discovered at Last Chance: Malone et al., *Montana*, p. 67; Toole, *Montana*, p. 71. Two prospectors killed at Highland: Morley diary, April 11, 1864, cited by Pace, *Golden Gulch*, pp. 64–65.

15. Edgerton's commission arrived July 30, 1864: letter from Mary Edgerton to sister, July 31, 1864, in Thane, p. 91. "It is so much work to move": letter from Mary Edgerton to mother, September 18, 1864, in Thane, p. 95.

16. Edgerton treated to "serenade": *Montana Post*, August 27, 1864.

17. Poster on "summary punishment," editors of *Post* on "not a 'myth'": Ibid.

18. Ambush at Portneuf Canyon: Ibid. Williams and posse chased suspects: Dimsdale, p. 182. "Ferreting fund," $5 "for rope": copy of Lott's account book, vertical file 2, "Vigilantes," MHS.

19. Williams departed, found and executed Kelly: Dimsdale, pp. 182–87. "A trial was called": Ibid., p. 186.

20. Indians retched: Callaway, *Montana's Righteous Hangmen*, pp. 115–16.

21. Edgerton commissioned census, appointed Howie, Bissell, Fergus: *Montana Post*, September 17, 1864.

22. Fergus's open letter: September 10, 1864, cited by Horn, "James Fergus," p. 92.

23. Edgerton appointed Lott auditor: *Montana Post*, October 1, 1864. Howie appointed Beidler: *Billings Gazette*, March 8, 1964.

24. *Montana Post* bought by Tilton: issue of September 10, 1864. Dimsdale "small, delicate-looking": Ronan, *Frontier Woman*, p. 23. Virginia City boasted bookstore, stationer's: *Montana Post*, September 10, 1864, September 17, 1864.

25. Dolan tracked, arrested: *Montana Post*, September 24, 1864; Dimsdale, pp. 187–91.

26. "Little knot of men": L. A. Fenner to Mrs. Laura E. Howey, March 4, 1902, Fenner Letters, MHS. Williams, "Don't try it": Dimsdale, p. 189.

27. "The dull sound of the drop" Dimsdale, p. 190.

28. "Gentleman of Nevada" spoke: Ibid.

29. "Solemnity and decorum": Ibid., p. 191.

30. Prize fight: *Montana Post*, September 24, 1864. Bull fight: Morley diary, cited by Pace, p. 25.

31. "Dirtiest kind of work": Letter from Mary Edgerton to mother, September 18, 1864, in Thane, p. 95.

32. Hosmer arrived: *Montana Post*, October 22, 1864. Description of Hosmer: Plassmann, MNA, April 13, 1925. Wanted to be librarian of Congress: J. H. Hosmer, "Biographical Sketch of Hezekiah L. Hosmer," *Contributions*, III, p. 288.

33. Youngsters stage *Henry IV*: Playbill, cited by Thane, p. 51n.

34. Republican meeting: *Montana Post*, October 22, 1864. Dimsdale on "that arch traitor, Jeff Davis": Spence, *Territorial Politics*, p. 23. Sanders defeated by McLean: Spence, p. 24.

35. Lucia Darling on McLean as "small intellect": letter from Darling to "Friends," January 7, 1865, Plassmann Papers, MHS. "Do not regard him": letter from Sanders to Garfield, November 24, 1864, cited by Spence, p. 23. Capital at Bannack, Virginia Citians "do not like it": letter from Mary Edgerton to sister, November 6, 1864, in Thane, pp. 98–99.

36. "A man for breakfast": Bessette MS, "The Last Bandit Hanged in Bannack," SC 420, MHS.

37. Dimsdale dismissed hanging as "commendable": *Montana Post*, November 6, 1864.

CHAPTER 18: "NO MORE MIDNIGHT EXECUTIONS"

1. Hosmer's court, "a bench was improvised": J. H. Hosmer, *Contributions*, III, p. 291.

2. Hosmer joined Langford and Hauser in bank: biographical sketch of Samuel T. Hauser, Hauser Papers, MHS.

3. Hosmer's charge to the grand jury, December 5, 1864: text, reprinted in *Montana Post*, December 10, 1864. Baume and Williams were members of grand jury: *Montana Post*, December 10, 1864.

4. Hosmer's son quoted citizen, "let us take charge": Hosmer, *Contributions*, III, pp. 288–99. Sanders' son said vigilantes supported courts: James U. Sanders, paper dated August 5, 1917, Sanders Papers, MHS. Dimsdale praised "masterly manner": *Montana Post*, December 10, 1864.

5. Mary Edgerton's description of gifts, "some moose meat": Letter to sister, November 27, 1864, in Thane, *Governor's Wife*, p. 103. Sons worked as pages for $5 a day: letter to mother, January 15, 1865, in Thane, p. 108. "The people here are very kind to us": Ibid.

6. Ran for council: Thompson, "Reminiscences" (January 1914): 22. Thompson made cradle and chair for Edgerton's daughters: Ibid., p. 27.

7. Edgerton forwarded Thompson's name, "no notice was taken": Ibid., p. 23.

8. Edgerton welcomed legislature, spoke of "untold wealth": text, reprinted in *Montana Post*, December 24, 1864.

9. Edgerton administered Iron Clad Oath, refused to admit Rogers: Plassmann, *Contributions*, III, p. 331; Thane, p. 58.

10. Bagg, "That means obey Abe Lincoln": Thompson (January 1914): 23–24. Lucia Darling said venom "was faint in comparison": letter to "Friends," January 7, 1865, Plassmann Papers, MHS.

11. Lott on enduring hostility to government: *Montana Post*, April 1, 1865, cited by Athearn, "The Civil War and Montana Gold." Legislature adjourned without rules: Spence, *Territorial Politics*, p. 31.

12. Anniversary of vigilante hanging of five men: *Montana Post*, January 14, 1865.

13. "Law now reigns supreme": Ibid., January 28, 1865.

14. Pfouts elected mayor: Ibid., February 11, 1865.

15. Thurmond's suit against Fox for "stigma upon his name": *Union Vedette*, January 18, 1865.

16. "Witnesses were almost innumerable": Ibid., February 6, 1865. Jury awarded $3,000: *Deseret News*, February 8, 1865. Second trial, damages of $8,000: *Union Vedette*, February 27, 1865.

17. On disbanding of vigilantes: Langford, *Vigilante Days*, p. 297. "Vigilantes will hang him": Langford to Hauser, May 8, 1865, Hauser Papers, MHS.

18. "Blockade" lifted at Salt Lake City: *Montana Post*, June 3, 1865.

19. Chartering of Montana Historical Society: text of Act, February 2, 1865, *Contributions*, II, p. 19. Dance as "onorary" member: Dance to Hauser, March 27, 1865, Hauser Papers, MHS.

20. Judge refused to extradite Buckner, "popular delusion": *Montana Post*, April 8, 1865.

21. Speculation on Campbell as author: Peltier in *Banditti*, p. 17. Dimsdale called book "vulgar and disgusting": *Montana Post*, July 1, 1865. Dimsdale's series on the vigilantes began in the *Montana Post* on August 26, 1865.

22. Editorial calling for gun control: *Montana Post*, December 24, 1864. Item on Martha Jane Canary: Ibid., December 31, 1864. "Difficult to find color": Letter from Neally to Hosmer, May 7, 1865, cited by Spence, p. 30.

23. "The snow is so deep" letter from Mary Edgerton to sister, March 6, 1865, in Thane, p. 112. Price of flour: Fergus to family, May 17, 1863, Worthen-Fergus Papers, MSU, sets price of a hundredweight at $8; price rose to $38, Mary Edgerton to mother, April 2, 1865, in Thane, p. 117; price rose above $100, Jean Baptiste Laurin, WPA Oral Histories, MSU.

24. "Regulators" gathered: Pace, *Golden Gulch*, p. 51. Flour seized: Athearn, "The Civil War and Montana Gold." Molly Sheehan on stepmother hiding flour: Ronan, *Frontier Woman*, p. 28. Confiscated flour: Kohrs, *Conrad Kohrs*, p. 39.

25. "Go on, take all of the flour": Bruffey, *Eighty-one Years*, p. 53.

26. Pfouts issued notice: *Montana Post*, April 22, 1865.

27. Re Lincoln, Southern men "very quiet": letter from Luella Fergus to father, April 1865, cited in Peavy and Smith, *Gold Rush Windows*, p. 199. "It is *terrible*": letter from Mary Edgerton to mother, April 23, 1865, in Thane, p. 121.

28. Capital moved to Virginia City: Spence, p. 27. Edgerton thought about moving: letter from Mary Edgerton to mother, May 7, 1865, in Thane, pp. 122–23. Mary Edgerton reluctant to let Mattie attend parties: Ibid.

29. Blackfeet killed ten: Spence, p. 33. Hosmer on "great fizzle": Ibid., citing letter to Hauser, June 24, 1865.

30. First four capital cases ended in acquittal: Spence, p. 219. Hosmer described as "vacillating in opinion": Bailey, "Reminiscences," MHS. McCausland not guilty: *Montana Post*, June 24, 1865. Hosmer on "swindling the county": letter to Hauser, June 24, 1865, Hauser Papers, MHS.

31. McCausland slain at Portneuf Canyon: *Montana Post*, July 22, 1865. *Post* reports, "those damned vigilanters": Ibid.

32. Keene shot Slater: *Montana Post*, June 17, 1865. Keene seized, hanged: Ibid.; Dimsdale, pp. 194–207. "Many familiar faces": Dimsdale, p. 203. Committee of Safety organized in Helena: Leeson, *History of Montana*, p. 730.

33. Ashley's visit, "ambush" at Laurin's: *Montana Post*, July 29, 1865. Ashley's speech, text, Ibid.

34. Execution of Jake Silvie: Dimsdale, pp. 207–16. "Rid of such a monster": Ibid., p. 213.

35. Execution of Silvie: *Montana Post*, August 5, 1865.

CHAPTER 19: THOMAS FRANCIS MEAGHER

1. Williams "quit his gruesome work": Callaway, *Montana's Righteous Hangmen*, p. 119.

2. Langford collected taxes: Michael Kennedy, "'Infernal' Collector," *Montana* (Spring 1954). Maria Slade remarried: *Montana Post*, March 25, 1865. Davis borrowed book, left note: Davis to Fergus, May 25, 1865, Worthen-Fergus Papers, MSU.

3. Montana second to California in production of gold: Malone, *Battle for Butte*, p. 6. "What shall a man give": Thomas J. Farrell testimony, WPA Oral Histories, box 50, Coll. 2336, MSU.

4. Left for St. Louis: Thompson, "Reminiscences" (January 1914): 30–31; (April 1914): 85–87. "Worthy [of] . . . Remington: Ibid., p. 87.

5. Thompson in New York: Ibid.

6. Edgerton left for Ohio: Thane, *Governor's Wife*, p. 60.

7. President Johnson appointed Meagher: Spence, *Territorial Politics*, p. 18. Background of Meagher: Athearn, *Thomas Francis Meagher*, p. 13. Meagher to provide "strong infusion of . . . Celtic blood": Spence, p. 36n.

8. Jack Howard hanged: *Montana Post*, September 30, 1865. Cooke hanged: Ibid., September 23, 1865. Morgan and Jackson "found hanging": Ibid., September 30, 1865.

9. Vigilantes, "to inflict summary punishment": notice reprinted in Sanders and Bertsche, *Beidler*, pp. 107–8. Munson against vigilantes: Greever, *Bonanza West*, p. 229; "Personal Recollection," Munson Papers, MHS.

10. Dimsdale on "hempen solution": *Montana Post*, September 9, 1865. Dimsdale presented revolver: Ibid., October 7, 1865.

11. Idaho City settlers prevented lynching: *Montana Post*, September 30, 1865. Four more hangings: Ibid., October 7, 1865. *Carson Appeal* on "Human depravity": reprinted in *Montana Post*, November 4, 1865.

12. Dimsdale answered, " sun of every morning ": *Montana Post*, November 1865, cited by Gard, *Frontier Justice*, p. 185n.

13. Sanders hanged: Ibid., December 2, 1865. Second man hanged: Ibid., November 25, 1865. Tree "is barren this week": Ibid., December 2, 1865.

14. Thirty-seven men executed: My count of targets is taken from Dimsdale and from the *Montana Post*. It is the same as a list compiled by Merrill Burlingame, Burlingame Papers,

folder 21, box 26, MSU. For a discussion of Brown's count of victims in Montana, see Frederick Allen, "Montana Vigilantes and the Origins of 3-7-77," *Montana* (Spring 2001): n. 58, p. 16. Re "conservative mobs": Brown, *Strain of Violence*, p. 94. On "violent sanctification": Ibid., p. 97.

(Brown appears to have overestimated the number of horse and cattle thieves hanged by "Stuart's Stranglers" in central Montana in 1884. In *Strain of Violence*, p. 101, he calls the 1884 episode "the deadliest of all American vigilante movements," a superlative supported by his book's Appendix III, which cites thirty-five victims, p. 313. The actual number, however, appears to be considerably smaller. In "The Central Montana Vigilante Raids in 1884," which appeared in the premier issue of *Montana: The Magazine of Western History* (January 1951), Oscar O. Mueller argues that fifteen to eighteen men died at the hands of Stuart's posse. In a 1980 University of Oregon master's thesis, "Granville Stuart and the Montana Vigilantes of 1884," Richard K. Mueller, no relation to Oscar Mueller, puts the figure at nineteen to twenty-two. My own count shows a maximum of seventeen, while Malone, Roeder, and Lang's reasonable and reliable *Montana: A History of Two Centuries,* p. 163, estimates "at least fifteen" victims. Meanwhile, Brown's appendix cites thirty victims of vigilantism in Montana from 1863 to 1865, while my examination of the *Montana Post* and other sources raises that number to at least thirty-five. In either case, the distinction of being "deadliest of all American vigilante movements" properly belongs to Montana's earliest vigilantes.)

15. Telegraph arrived November 1866, "Citizens!": *Montana Post*, November 3, 1866.

16. Meagher's career is taken from Athearn, p. 88. Attacked Irish for "following with gross stupidity": Ibid., p. 134.

17. Accused of drunken incompetence: Ibid., p. 137. "Like many another gambler": Ibid., p. 139. Dubbed "the Acting One": *Montana Radiator*, February 28, 1866.

18. Democrats dismissed as "favourers and abettors of treason": Spence, p. 36. Refused to convene legislature: Ibid., pp. 36–37. Had wife send telegram to President Johnson: Athearn, p. 147.

19. "I'm resolved ": John Francis Maguire, *The Irish in America* (Chicago, Ayer, 1969), p. 549n, cited by Athearn, p. 154. Meagher letter to President Johnson, January 20, 1866, cited by Spence, p. 37. Meagher wrote Seward: Ibid.

20. "I was greatly in error": letter from Meagher to Seward, February 20, 1866, cited by Spence, p. 37. Montana Republicans "radicals and extremists": letter to Johnson, January 20, 1866, cited by Athearn, p. 150. Sanders as "unrelenting . . . extremist": letter to Johnson, January 29, 1866, cited by Spence, p. 38. "Among decent men ": letter from Sanders to Fergus, February 14, 1866, Worthen-Fergus Papers, MSU.

21. Chumasero to Trumbull: letter dated March 12, 1866, cited by Athearn, p. 153. Meagher complained to president of "cowardly conspiracy": letter dated January 29, 1866, cited by Athearn, p. 154.

22. Justices threatened to declare, Meagher threatened to call out: Langford to Hauser, February 27, 1866, Hauser Papers, MHS.

23. Daniels stabbed Gartley: *Montana Post*, December 9, 1865. Daniels convicted: Ibid., December 30, 1865.

24. Meagher signed reprieve: Text, February 22, 1866, reprinted in *Montana Post*, February 24, 1866. "Misled by evil counselors": Ibid., March 10, 1866. Meagher "under the influence": Lyman Ezra Munson, "Hon. Lyman E. Munson, U.S. Judge, Third Judicial District Montana," Munson Papers, MHS. Governor had no power to lift sentence or release prisoner: MNA, May 15, 1939.

25. Meagher "still in his debauch": Munson, Munson Papers, MHS. Daniels hanged: *Montana Post*, March 10, 1866.

26. Meagher "very drunk": Howie diary, March 5, 1866, cited by Spence, p. 38. "Indignation meeting": *Montana Post*, March 10, 1866. "Index" article: Ibid., March 17, 1866.

27. All able-bodied men join vigilantes: Blake, "Proper Bostonian," 39. Dance proceeds earmarked for vigilantes: *Montana Post*, January 20, 1866. Curtis incident: Ibid., December 29, 1866. Retraction: Ibid., January 12, 1867.

28. Langford on hanging near Denver, "I was collecting money": letter to Hauser, January 14, 1866, Hauser Papers, MHS.

29. Hurst tracked down Duffy, killed him: *Salt Lake Telegraph*, January 16, 1866, reprinted in *Montana Post*, January 27, 1866.

30. Jewett hanged: *Montana Post*, February 14, 1866. Leander Johnson "ghastly and disfigured": Ibid., March 24, 1866. Goones executed: Ibid., May 12, 1866.

31. Critical editorial in *Idaho World*, fierce defense by Dimsdale: Ibid.

32. "Notified . . . that I had been elected": Blake, p. 39.

33. Legislature cut justices' salary supplements: Spence, p. 41. Ashley proposed amendment: *Congressional Globe*, 39th Cong., 1st sess., p. 2368. McLean's speech: Ibid., Appendix, p. 202.

34. Senate rejected amendment: Spence, p. 42. Munson declared acts of legislature null and void: *Montana Post*, June 9, 1866. Crouchet lynched: Ibid.

35. Lawyers petitioned Hosmer: *Montana Post*, August 11, 1866.

36. Hosmer's charge: text, reprinted in Ibid.

37. Cave Gulch incident: *Montana Post*, December 22, 1866. Vigilantes visited offices of *Helena Weekly Herald*: A J. Fisk, diary entry, December 27, 1866, Fisk Family Papers, MHS.

38. "Read and Reflect": text reprinted in *Montana Post*, January 5, 1867.

39. "The Vigilantes have just been reorganized": Langford to Will Doolittle, January 16, 1867, Langford Papers, MHS.

CHAPTER 20: *PAX VIGILANTICUS*

1. Wade, "anarchy": *Congressional Globe*, 39th Cong., 1st sess., pp. 1816–17.

2. Meagher, legislature banished judges, withheld supplies: Spence, *Territorial Politics*, p. 44. Congress raised justices' salaries, declared acts null and void: Ibid., p. 45. "I am afraid": Dance to Hauser, March 23, 1867, Hauser Papers, MHS.

3. "Men reeking with treason": Spence, p. 45. President Johnson forced resignation of Edgerton: Jackson, "Appointment and Removal of Sidney Edgerton." Jackson cites a letter, Edgerton to President Johnson, March 27, 1866, asking for a leave of absence, which Johnson denied. Edgerton then resigned. Johnson appointed Green Clay Smith, Smith went to Washington: Spence, p. 43.

4. Rosenbaum lynching: *Montana Post*, February 2, 1867; Blake, p. 39.

5. "Notice!" posted in Highland City: Text, reprinted in *Montana Post*, March 2, 1867. I assumed, as have most historians, that the notice was posted in the Highland District of Alder Gulch, but it appears to have been in Highland City instead.

6. "The Committee . . . has fallen into different hands": Pfouts, *Four Firsts*, p. 101.

7. Blake interpreted notice correctly: *Montana Post*, March 2, 1867.

8. Vigilantes made arrests, banished men, carried out a flogging: *Montana Post*, March 16, April 13, May 5, 1867. Bozeman wrote Meagher, asking protection: letter dated March 25, 1867, cited by Athearn, *Thomas Francis Meagher*, p. 157. Meagher telegraphed Grant, April 9, 1867, cited by Athearn, p. 157. Army declined to respond: Athearn, pp. 159-60. Bozeman killed, Ibid.

9. Meagher issued vouchers, "marvelous opportunity to raid": Athearn, p. 162. Meagher's death: Ibid., p. 165.

10. "Another victim of Whiskey": A. J. Fisk diary, July 3, 1867, cited by Athearn, p. 166. Some of Meagher's supporters believed he was assassinated, possibly by vigilantes, but I can find no evidence whatsoever to support such a conclusion.

11. *Montana Post* reported seven homicides: Issues of July 7, July 14, July 27, August 3, 1867. Farmer robbed, killed in Gallatin Valley: Ibid., September 21, 1867.

12. Vigilantes hanged Charles Wilson, gave rationale: *Montana Post*, September 28, 1867.

13. "Few beside his accomplices": *Rocky Mountain Gazette*, reprinted in *Montana Post*, October 5, 1867.

14. Ah Chow: *Helena Daily Herald*, January 16, 1870; *Rocky Mountain Daily Gazette* (Helena), January 18, 1870. Bitzer dallying with woman: letter signed "Citizen," *Helena Daily Herald*, January 25, 1870.

15. Fugitive found, lynched: Ibid. Beidler claimed reward: *Helena Daily Herald*, January 27, 1870. Note signed "200 Anti-Vigilantes": Sanders, *History*, I, p. 193n.

16. "Citizen": *Helena Daily Herald*, January 25, 1870. Fisk article: Ibid. "A grave wrong": (Deer Lodge) *New North-West*, January 28, 1870.

17. Photograph of dual hanging: Photo in MHS Archives. (The targets were Arthur Compton and Joseph Wilson: *Helena Daily Herald*, April 30, 1870.) Forty-ninth and fiftieth victims: My earlier count has been augmented by lynching incidents reported in the *Helena Daily Herald*.

18. The remainder of this chapter appeared in slightly different form in the author's "Montana Vigilantes and the Origins of 3-7-77," *Montana* (Spring 2001): 2–19. Notes on sources are repeated. Penitentiary: Spence, p. 220. First legal execution: Cornelius Hedges, "Historical Sketch of Lewis and Clark County, Montana," July 4, 1876, *Contributions*, II, p. 107. "Hanging Tree" chopped down, day outlived: *Helena Daily Herald*, September 7, 1875.

19. Fisk on "disheartening" prospects: *Helena Daily Herald*, July 24, 1876. "Enough of us left to make a corporal's guard": P. W. "Bud" McAdow to Margin Maginnis, Maginnis Papers, MHS.

20. Fisk, "we want company": *Helena Daily Herald*, April 29, 1878. Potts hounded Sherman: letter to Sherman, March 7, 1873, Potts Papers, MHS.

21. "We Don't Want Them": *Helena Daily Herald*, May 10, 1878.

22. Fisk on "horde on our borders": *Helena Daily Herald*, January 16, 1879.

23. Fisk on "coterie of petty offenders": Ibid., August 1, 1879.

24. Murder of Denn: Allen, *Montana*: 2–19. "There is no disguising the fact": *Helena Daily Herald*, October 29, 1879.

25. Numbers posted: *Helena Herald*, November 3, 1879. Butte leaders complained of "tough characters": *Butte Miner*, November 12, 1879.

26. *Missoulian* on "anarchy": issue of November 21, 1879. Woolfolk said committee "composed of many of our best citizens": *Helena Independent*, November 16, 1879.

27. "The most law-abiding people": (Deer Lodge) *New North-West*, November 7, 1879. San Francisco *Chronicle*: December 4, 1881, reprinted in *Helena Daily Herald*, December 20, 1881.

28. "Billiardist" left Fort Benton: *Helena Daily Herald*, June 19, 1882.

29. Jessrang incident: Ibid. February 10 and 12, March 10, 1883.

30. Fisk on "decent, orderly lynching": Ibid., August 27, 1883.

31. Stuart raid on Musselshell: Allen, "Montana Vigilantes": 16, n. 58. "The vigilantes in all their time": letter from Fergus to Conrad Kohrs, May 5, 1887, cited by David Remley,

"Granville Stuart, Cowman." On Roosevelt and the vigilantes, see Allen, "Montana Vigilantes": 16, n. 59.

32. "Fighting race": Slotkin, p. 106, citing Stuart Creighton Miller, *"Benevolent Assimilation": The American Conquest of the Philippines, 1899–1903* (New Haven: Yale University Press, 1982), pp. 22–23. "Before there was law": Letter to William Roscoe Thayer, July 10, 1915, cited in Elting E. Morison, ed., *The Letters of Theodore Roosevelt* (Cambridge: Harvard University Press, 1951–54), vol. 8, p. 945. Slotkin is Richard Slotkin, *Gunfighter Nation: The Myth of the Frontier in Twentieth-Century America* (New York: Antheneum, 1992). Paperback, University of Oklahoma Press, 1998.

33. Con Murphy: Jacob Mathews Powers, "Tracking Con Murphy," *Montana* (Autumn 1980): 52–56; grand jury charge, Decius Wade Papers, January 1885, Coll. 54, MHS. "What did you think?": Letter from Lizzie Fisk to mother, February 15, 1885, Fisk Family Papers, MHS.

34. Lynching continued into twentieth century: folder 30, box 40, Roeder Papers, MSU. Roeder kept handwritten notes on lynching from 1865 into the early 1900s. Glee club called "3-7-77 Boys": *Helena Daily Herald*, July 17, 1882.

35. Frank Little: MNA, August 6, 1917; (Butte) *Montana Standard*, June 5, 1992; Gutfeld, *Montana's Agony*, pp. 23–36.

36. Vigilante Trail: State Department of Agriculture, Labor, and Industry, *Montana: Resources and Opportunities Edition* (Helena, 1920), p. 60; MNA, March 15, 1920. Society of Pioneers: (Missoula) *Missoulian*, August 25, 1922.

37. Vigilante Day Parade: *Helena Independent Record*, May 28, 1939, May 13, 1999. *Saturday Evening Post*: published in book form as Birney's *Vigilantes*.

38. 3-7-77 added to shoulder patch: *Spokane Spokesman-Review*, February 11, 1968.

39. Montana's brief experiment with a "reasonable and prudent" daytime speed limit ended with a ruling by the state Supreme Court in 1998 that the language was unconstitutionally vague and the legislature's adoption of numerical speed limits the following year. See *Bozeman Daily Chronicle*, June 30, 2000.

EPILOGUE

1. Electa Bryan Plummer: letter from Ida Stafford and Mrs. John Slattery to David Hilger, Montana Historical Society, 1930, copy in Burlingame Papers, folder 6, box 5, MSU.

2. James Williams: Callaway, *Montana's Righteous Hangmen*, pp 137–39, 175–82.

3. Francis Thompson: obit, *Greenfield Recorder*, January 5, 1916. "helpful, generous" *History of Greenfield*, III, p. 1547.

4. Wilbur Sanders: Thompson, "Reminiscences" (January 1915): 15, has the text of a letter Sanders wrote him, dated January 20, 1904, saying the prospect of impending death "holds no terror." But Sanders complained bitterly about corruption in Montana: "What with the R. Roads and copper companies, and the millionaires, everything is pecuniarily appraised, except the scars on a soldier. I have fought bribery and every form of civic corruption for forty years and now that it has become triumphant, I fight it still."

5. Edgertons: Thane, *Governor's Wife*, pp. 60–61. Interview with *Helena Daily Herald*: issue of September 9, 1882.

6. Langford, Ashley: Spence, pp. 57–69.

7. Fergus, Stuart, Hauser in cattle business: Remley, "Granville Stuart, Cowman." And see Stuart, *Pioneering in Montana*, p. 234 on the severe winter of 1887.

8. Reid Gardiner, grand secretary, Grand Lodge A.F. & A.M., Helena, Montana.

9. "X" Beidler: tombstone in Helena.

Bibliography

MANUSCRIPT COLLECTIONS

Merrill Burlingame Papers, Collection 2245, Montana State University Special Collections Department (MSU).

Fisk Family Papers, Collection 31, Montana Historical Society Archives (MHS).

Samuel T. Hauser Papers, Collection 37, MHS.

Nathaniel Langford Papers, Collection 215, MHS.

Leggatt Papers, Collection 781, MSU.

Madison County Federated Women's Club Writings, Collection 1382, MHS.

Madison County Records, Collection 295, MSU.

Martin Maginnis Papers, Collection 50, MHS.

John S. Mendenhall Papers, Collection 925, MSU.

Lyman Ezra Munson Papers, Collection 553, MHS.

William Y. Pemberton Papers, Collection 629, MHS.

Pioneer Reminiscences, Collection 64, MSU.

Martha Edgerton Plassmann Papers, Collection 78, MHS. Includes "Judge Edgerton's Daughter," unpub. MS.

Richard B. Roeder Papers, Collection 2346, MSU.

James Upson Sanders Papers, Collection 66, MHS.

Virginia City Vigilantes, Collection 953, MHS.

William F. Wheeler Papers, Collection 65, MHS.

Clifton B. Worthen–James Fergus Papers, Collection 913, MSU.

DIARIES, MEMOIRS, REMINISCENCES, AND ORAL HISTORIES

Bailey, David J. Reminiscences, Collection 1471, MHS, 1905.

Barrett, Martin. Reminiscences, Collection 64, MSU, undated.

Bessette, Amede. Manuscript, "The Last Bandit Hanged in Bannack by the Vigilantes," Collection 420, MHS, undated.

Edgar, Henry. Journal, *Contributions to the Historical Society of Montana, Helena*, III, p. 124.

Fenner, L. A. Letters, Collection 64, MHS, 1902.

Goss, Francis S. Recollection, Collection 762, MHS, ca. 1915.

Grannis, John. Diary, Collection 301, MHS.

Hughes, Barney. Interview in *Dillon Tribune*, reprinted in *Virginia City Times*, November 5, 1909.

Kinerk, Tim. Memoir, Collection 175, MHS, 1921.

Lott, Mortimer. Oral history, Collection 65, MHS, Octiber 1, 1885.

Lovell, George. Oral history, Collection 65, MHS, November 1, 1886.

Mills, James H. Reminiscence, Collection 70, MHS.

Morley, James. Diary, Collection 533, MHS.

Munson, Lyman Ezra, Reminiscence, Collection 553, MHS, 1899.

Steele, William L. Interview in *The Sunday Call*, Newark, N.J., November 26, 1893.

Sweeney, James "Bill." Reminscences, Collection 823, MHS, 1921.

Williams, James. Reminiscence, Collection 975, MHS, n.d.

WPA Oral Histories, Collection 2336, MSU.

BOOKS

Anonymous. *Banditti of the Rocky Mountains and Vigilance Committee in Idaho*. Minneapolis: Ross & Haines, Inc., 1964.

Arrington, Leonard J. *History of Idaho*. 2 vols. Moscow: University of Idaho Press, and Boise: Idaho Historical Society, 1994.

Athearn, Robert G. *Thomas Francis Meagher: An Irish Revolutionary In America*. Boulder: University of Colorado Press, 1949.

Bancroft, Hubert Howe. *Popular Tribunals, Vols. I and II*. San Francisco: The History Company, Publishers, 1887.

Birney, Hoffman. *Vigilantes*. Philadelphia: Penn Publishing Company, 1929.

Boorstin, Daniel. *The Americans: The National Experience*. New York: Random House, 1965.

Brown, Richard Maxwell. *Strain of Violence: Historical Studies of American Violence and Vigilantism*. New York: Oxford University Press, 1975.

Bruffey, George A. *Eighty-One Years in the West*. Butte: The Butte Miner Company, 1925.

Burlingame, Merrill G. *"The Montana Frontier*. Helena: State Publishing Company, 1942. Paperback reprint, Bozeman: Big Sky Books, Montana State University, 1980.

Callaway, Lew. L. *Montana's Righteous Hangmen: The Vigilantes in Action*. Norman: University of Oklahoma Press, 1982.

Connolly, Christopher P. *The Devil Learns to Vote: The Story of Montana*. New York: Covici, Friede, Inc., 1938.

Contributions to the Historical Society of Montana, Helena. 10 vols. Helena: State Publishing, 1917.

Cushman, Dan. *Montana: The Gold Frontier*. Great Falls: Stay Away, Joe Publishers, 1973.

Dimsdale, Thomas J. *The Vigilantes of Montana*. Virginia City: Montana Post Press, 1866. Reprinted by Time-Life Books, Inc., 1981.

Ethington, Philip J. *The Public City: The Political Construction of Urban Life in San Francisco, 1850–1900*. Cambridge: Cambridge University Press, 1994.

Gard, Wayne. *Frontier Justice*. Norman: University of Oklahoma Press, 1949.

Gould, Milton S. *A Cast of Hawks: A Rowdy Tale of Scandal and Power Politics in Early San Francisco.* La Jolla: Copley Books, 1985.

Greever, William S. *The Bonanza West: The Story of Western Mining Rushes, 1848–1900.* Norman: University of Oklahoma Press, 1963.

Guice, John D. W. *The Rocky Mountain Bench: The Territorial Supreme Courts of Colorado, Montana, and Wyoming, 1861–1890.* New Haven: Yale University Press, 1972.

Gutfeld, Aaron. *Montana's Agony: Years of War and Hysteria, 1917–1921.* Gainesville: University Presses of Florida, 1979.

Hall, Frank. *History of the State of Colorado.* 4 vols., Chicago: Blakely Printing Co., 1891.

Hamilton, Ladd. *This Bloody Deed: The Magruder Incident.* Pullman: Washington State University Press, 1994.

Holliday, J. S. *Rush for Riches: Gold Fever and the Making of California.* Berkeley: Oakland Museum of California and University of California Press, 1999.

Hollon, W. Eugene. *Frontier Violence: Another Look.* New York: Oxford University Press, 1974.

Judd, Richard W. et al. *Maine: The Pine Tree State from Prehistory to the Present.* Orono: University of Maine Press, 1995.

Johnson, David Alan. *Founding the Far West: California, Oregon, and Nevada, 1840–1890.* Berkeley: University of California Press, 1992.

Kelly, Leslie A. *Traveling California's Gold Rush Country: A Falcon Guide.* Helena: Falcon Publishing Inc., 1997.

Kohrs, Conrad. *Conrad Kohrs: An Autobiography.* Deer Lodge: Platen Press, 1977.

Langford, Nathaniel P. *Vigilante Days and Ways.* Boston: J. G. Cupples, 1890. Citations are from 1996 edition published by American & World Geographic Publishing, Helena.

Leeson, Michael A. *The History of Montana, 1739–1885.* Chicago: Warner, Beers & Co., 1885.

Limbaugh, Ronald H. *Rocky Mountain Carpetbaggers: Idaho's Territorial Governors, 1863–1890.* Moscow: University Press of Idaho, 1982.

Lotchin, Roger W. *San Francisco, 1846–1856: From Hamlet to City.* New York: Oxford University Press, 1974. Reprint, University of Illinois Press, Illini Books edition, 1997.

Madsen, Brigham D. *The Shoshoni Frontier and the Bear River Massacre.* Salt Lake City: University of Utah Press, 1985.

Malone, Michael P. *The Battle for Butte: Mining and Politics on the Northern Frontier, 1864–1906.* Seattle: University of Washington Press, 1981. Reprinted 1995 by the Montana Historical Society, Helena.

Malone, Michael P., Richard B. Roeder, William L. Lang. *Montana: A History of Two Centuries.* Seattle: University of Washington Press, 1976, revised 1991.

Mann, Ralph. *After the Gold Rush: Society in Grass Valley and Nevada City, California.* Stanford: Stanford University Press, 1982.

Manning, Richard. *One Round River: The Curse of Gold and the Fight for the Big Blackfoot.* New York: Henry Holt, 1998. .

Marx, Jennifer. *The Magic of Gold.* New York: Doubleday, 1978.

Mather, R. E., and F. E. Boswell. *Hanging the Sheriff: A Biography of Henry Plummer.* Salt Lake City: University of Utah Press, 1987.

———. *Gold Camp Desperadoes: Violence, Crime, and Punishment on the Mining Frontier.* San Jose: History West Publishing, 1990.

———. *Vigilante Victims: Montana's 1864 Hanging Spree.* San Jose: History West Publishing, 1991.

McConnell, W. J. *Early History of Idaho.* Glendale, Calif.: Arthur H. Clark Co., 1913.

McPherson, James M. *Battle Cry of Freedom: The Civil War Era*, New York, Oxford University Press, 1988.

Meikle, Lyndel, ed. *Very Close to Trouble: The Johnny Grant Memoir*. Pullman: Washington State University Press, 1996.

Miller, Joaquin. *An Illustrated History of the State of Montana*. Chicago: The Lewis Publishing Company, 1894.

Mommer, Hope. *Look Out West! Here Comes Robert Dempsey, 1848–1908*. Chicago: Adams Press, 1994.

Myers, Rex C. *Lizzie: The Letters of Elizabeth Chester Fisk, 1864–1893*. Missoula: Mountain Press Publishing Company, 1989.

Noyes, A. L. *Dimsdale's The Vigilantes of Montana*. 4tth ed. Helena: State Publishing Company, 1915.

Pace, Dick. *Golden Gulch: The Story of Montana's Famous Alder Gulch*. Virginia City: Bovey Restorations, 1962.

Pauley, Art. *Henry Plummer: Lawman and Outlaw*. White Sulphur Springs: The Meagher County News, 1980.

Peavy, Linda, and Ursula Smith. *The Gold Rush Widows of Little Falls*. St. Paul: Minnesota Historical Society Press, 1990.

Pfouts, Paris Swazy. *Four Firsts for a Modest Hero*. Helena: Grand Lodge, Ancient Free and Accepted Masons of Montana, 1968.

Phinney, Mary Allen. *Jirah Isham Allen: Montana Pioneer*. Rutland, VT: Tuttle Publishing Co., n.d.

Purple, Edwin Ruthven. *Perilous Passage: A Narrative of the Montana Gold Rush, 1862–1863*. Helena: Montana Historical Society Press, 1995.

Quinn, Arthur. *The Rivals: William Gwin, David Broderick, and the Birth of California*. Lincoln: University of Nebraska Press, 1994. Originally published by Crown, New York, 1994.

Rich, Louise Dickinson. *The Coast of Maine: An Informal History*. New York: Thomas Y. Crowell Co., 1956.

Roberts, Kenneth. *Trending into Maine*. New York: Doubleday, Doran & Company, 1945.

Rohrbaugh, Malcolm J. *Days of Gold: The California Gold Rush and the American Nation*. Berkeley: University of California Press, 1997.

Rolle, Andrew, ed. *The Road to Virginia City: The Diary of James Knox Polk Miller*. Norman: University of Oklahoma Press, 1960.

Ronan, Margaret. *Frontier Woman: The Story of Mary Ronan*. Edited by H. G. Merriam. Missoula: University of Montana, 1973.

Sanders, Helen Fitzgerald, and William H. Bertsche, Jr., eds. *X. Beidler: Vigilante*. Norman: University of Oklahoma Press, 1957.

Sanders, Helen Fitzgerald. *A History of Montana*. 3 vols. Chicago: Lewis Publishing Company, 1913.

Schwantes, Carlos A. *In Mountain Shadows: A History of Idaho*. Lincoln: University of Nebraska Press, 1991.

Senkewicz, Robert M., S.J. *Vigilantes in Gold Rush San Francisco*. Stanford: Stanford University Press, 1985.

Spence, Clark C. *Territorial Politics and Government in Montana, 1864–1889*. Urbana: University of Illinois Press, 1975.

Starr, Kevin, and Richard J. Orsi, eds. *Rooted in Barbarous Soil: People, Culture, and Community in Gold Rush California*. Berkeley ; University of California Press, 2000.

Stiles, T. J. *Jesse James: Last Rebel of the Civil War*. New York: Alfred A. Knopf, 2002.

Stout, Tom. *Montana: Its Story and Biography*. Chicago: The American Historical Society, 1921.

Stuart, Granville. *The Montana Frontier, 1852–1864*. Lincoln: University of Nebraska Press, 1977. Originally published as Vol. 1 of *Forty Years on the Frontier* by Arthur H. Clark Company, 1925.

———. *Pioneering in Montana: The Making of a State, 1864–1887*. Lincoln, University of Nebraska Press, 1977. Originally published as Vol. 2 of *Forty Years on the Frontier* by Arthur H. Clark Company, 1925.

Thane, James L., Jr., ed. *A Governor's Wife on the Mining Frontier: The Letters of Mary Edgerton from Montana, 1863–1865*. Salt Lake City: University of Utah Tanner Trust Fund, 1976.

Thrapp, Dan L. *Vengeance! The Sage of Poor Tom Cover*. El Segundo: Upton & Sons, Publishers, 1989.

Tibbetts, Leonard F., and Darryl B. Lamson. *Early Pleasant River Families of Washington County, Maine*. Camden: Picton Press, 1997.

Toole, Ross K. *Montana: An Uncommon Land*. Norman: University of Oklahoma Press, 1959.

Toponce, Alexander. *Reminiscences of Alexander Toponce*. Norman: University of Oklahoma Press, 1971.

Twain, Mark. *Roughing It*. New York: Harper & Brothers, 1871.

Welch, Julia Conway. *The Magruder Murders: Coping with Violence on the Idaho Frontier*. Helena: Falcon Press Publishing Co., 1991.

West, Elliott. *The Saloon on the Rocky Mountain Mining Frontier*. Lincoln: University of Nebraska Press, 1979.

———. *The Contested Plains: Indians, Goldseekers, and the Rush to Colorado*. Lawrence: University Press of Kansas, 1998.

Wolle, Muriel Sibell. *Montana Pay Dirt: A Guide to the Mining Camps of the Treasure State*. Athens: Ohio University Press, 1963.

ARTICLES

Athearn, Robert G. "West of Appomattox." *Montana: the Magazine of Western History* (Spring 1962): 2.

———. "The Civil War and Montana Gold." *Montana: the Magazine of Western History* (Spring 1962). Reprinted from *Pacific Historical Review* (February 1960).

Barbour, Chauncey. "Two Vigilance Committees." *Overland Monthly*, 2d ser., 10, no. 57 (September 1887): 285–91.

Bird, Annie Laurie. "Idaho's First Territorial Governor." *Idaho Yesterdays* (Summer 1966).

Blake, Henry Nichols. "Proper Bostonian, Purposeful Pioneer." Edited by Vivian Paladin. *Montana: The Magazine of Western History* (Autumn 1964).

Burlingame, Merrill. "Montana's Righteous Hangman: A Reconsideration." *Montana: The Magazine of Western History* (Autumn 1978).

Fergus, James. "Early Mining Life at Bannack and Alder Gulch." *Rocky Mountain Magazine* 1, no. 4, 265–69.

Jackson, W. Turrentine. "The Appointment and Removal of Sidney Edgerton, First Governor of Montana Territory." *Pacific Northwest Quarterly* (July 1943).

———. "The Fisk Expeditions to the Montana Gold Fields." *Pacific Northwest Quarterly* (July 1942).

Kittredge, William, and Steven M. Krauzer. "'Mr. Montana' Revised: Another Look at Granville Stuart." *Montana: the Magazine of Western History* 36 (Autumn 1986): 14–23.

Malone, Michael P. and Richard B. Roeder. "1876 in Montana: Anxiety and Anticipation." *Montana: The Magazine of Western History* (January 1975).

———. "The Centennial Year in Montana: In the Gulches—Mining in Field and Pasture—Agriculture." *Montana: The Magazine of Western History* (Spring 1975).

Mueller, Oscar O. "The Central Montana Vigilante Raids of 1884." *Montana: The Magazine of Western History* (January 1951).

Myers, Rex C. "Vigilante Numbers: A Re-examination." *Montana: The Magazine of Western History* (Autumn 1974).

Remley, David. "Granville Stuart, Cowman." *Montana: The Magazine of Western History* (Summer 1981).

Schafft, Charles. "Memoirs" *Montana: The Magazine of Western History* (Winter 1960).

Smurr, J. W. "Afterthoughts on the Vigilantes." *Montana: The Magazine of Western History* (Spring 1958).

Spence, Clark C. "The Territorial Bench in Montana, 1864–1889." *Montana: The Magazine of Western History* (Winter 1963).

Thompson, Francis M. "Reminiscences of Four-Score Years." *The Massachusetts Magazine*: Supplement to Vol. V, (1912): 123–67; Vol. VI, no. 1 (January 1913): 28–45; Vol. VI, no. 2 (April 1913): 63–81; Vol. VI, no. 3 (July 1913): 99–124; Vol. VI, no. 4 (October 1913): 159–90; Vol. VII, no. 1 (January 1914): 11–31; Vol. VII, no. 2 (April 1914): 85–94; Vol. VII, no. 3 (July 1914): 129–36; Vol. VIII, no. 1 (January 1915): 15–22.

Wells, Merle W. "The Idaho-Montana Boundary." *Idaho Yesterdays* (Winter 1968–69).

———. "A Year without A Code." *Idaho Yesterdays* (Spring 1981): 13.

THESES AND DISSERTATIONS

Horn, Robert M. "James Fergus: Frontier Businessman, Miner, Rancher, Free Thinker." Master's thesis, University of Montana, 1971, published in Bozeman, Fergus Family Associates, 1982.

McKanna, Clare V., Jr. "Nineteenth Century Vigilantism in Montana: Changing Historical Interpretations." Master's thesis, University of Nebraska–Lincoln, 1990.

McLatchy, Michael Gene, ed. "From Wisconsin to Montana and Life in the West, 1863–1889, The Reminiscences of Robert Kirkpatrick." Master's thesis, Montana State University, 1961.

Mueller, Richard K. "Granville Stuart and the Montana Vigilantes of 1884." Master's thesis, University of Oregon, 1980.

Raffety, Robert O. "The History and Theory of Capital Punishment in Montana." Masters thesis, University of Montana, 1968.

Thane, James L., Jr. "Montana Territory: The Formative Years, 1862–1870. Master's thesis, University of Iowa, 1972.

Acknowledgments

An author in need of help seems to bring out the generous side of just about everybody. As I have learned before and confirmed anew on this project, the most rewarding aspect of researching and writing a book is the arrival of cavalry in times of need. I have in my office a remarkable document—a copy of the *Sacramento Daily Union* from a crucial date in 1863, fashioned out of small strips of photocopied microfilm laboriously Scotch-taped together to form a full-size, precise replica of that day's edition, the work of a public librarian in Sacramento, Jill Stockinger, who answered my request for assistance with thoroughness and dedication above and beyond the call of duty.

As I write my thank-you notes, I begin with the late Michael P. Malone, an extraordinary man who somehow found time to write first-rate histories while also serving as president of Montana State University. I barged into Mike's life in the middle of a street festival in downtown Bozeman one evening in the summer of 1997. He became a good friend and mentor and went out of his way to vouch for me with other Western scholars who might not otherwise have rushed to embrace an ex-journalist from Atlanta venturing into a new field. Mike encouraged my interest in the Montana vigilantes as a serious subject in need of serious treatment.

In the course of my research, I became fascinated with the mystery behind the meaning of the vigilantes' warning sign, "3-7-77." Mike supported my investigation into the "mystic numbers" in part, I suspect, because he enjoyed conspiracy theories. He died, too young, before I could share all of my findings with him. I think he would have liked the article I wrote about the numbers for *Montana: The Magazine of Western History*, and I am sure he would have been pleased that the Western History Association saw fit to grace the piece with its inaugural Michael P. Malone Award. It is an honor I treasure.

Among my guides in the early going were Dave Walter, the historian at the Montana Historical Society in Helena, and Kim Allen Scott, the head of the special collections department at Montana State. Dave volunteered what was, in effect, a syllabus for vigilante studies, while Kim directed me to several sources of fresh information. Other scholars who tutored and advised me include Greg Nobles, Jim Hendrix, Elliott West, Tom Wessel, Tom Chaffin, Clyde Milner, Clark Spence, Carlos Schwantes, Richard Maxwell Brown, and Ken Owens.

At the Montana Historical Society, I benefited from the assistance and good company of Brian Shovers, Angela Murray, Ellie Arguimbau, Ellen Baumler, Bob Clark, Tom Cook, Lory Morrow, Patricia Spencer, and Tammy Ryan. In the same building, I thank the staff of *Montana: The Magazine of Western History*—Clark Whitehorn, Martha Kohl, Molly Holz, and Glenda Bradshaw—for polishing, publishing, and promoting my article on the numbers "3-7-77." In Bozeman, Marilyn Wessel, dean and director emerita of the Museum of the Rockies, arranged several speaking engagements for me.

Among the many librarians and archivists who dropped what they were doing and aided me: Lisa Prolman of the Greenfield Public Library, Greenfield, Massachusetts; Ellen Cordes at Yale University; Brian Kenney of the Denver (Colorado) Public Library, Larry Jones at the Historical Society of Idaho; Jon Axline, historian of the Montana Department of Transportation; Valerie Komor of the New-York Historical Society; Edwin L. Tyson of the Searls Historical Library, Nevada City, California, and Jeff Brown, archivist at the Maine State Archives. At Emory University, Linda Matthews helped pilot me through the Interlibrary Loan program.

Chad Jones of Logan, Utah, mined microfilm for me in Salt Lake City. Mitzi Grover of Helena, Montana, gave me a copy of a previously unpublished letter her great-grandfather, John Jones, wrote about the vigilantes. Mick Seeberg of Bozeman shared his knowledge of nineteenth century guns and ammunition (and late twentieth century Scotch). Merilee Lovit of Addison, Maine, sent me valuable material on that town's history. Valdine Atwood of Machias, Maine, provided me with thorough, up-to-date genealogical material on the Plummer family. Henry Nichols Blake Clark, known as "Nick," my friend from the High Museum of Art in Atlanta, directed me to biographical material on his great-grandfather and namesake, Henry Nichols Blake.

At the Grand Lodge of the Ancient Free & Accepted Masons in Helena, Dean Lindahl, the grand secretary, gave me the run of the library and also counseled me on matters Masonic to the limit the proprieties of his organization would allow. Verle Rademacher, editor of the *Meagher County News* in White Sulphur Springs, Montana, helped me get a copy of Art Pauley's book on Henry Plummer and described Pauley's old-fashioned research habits.

The determined revisionists who are laboring to restore Henry Plummer's reputation will not agree with my conclusions in this book. Nonetheless, they have extended me every courtesy in our various encounters, and I especially appreciate Ruth Mather's willingness to engage in a long discussion about the sheriff over the course of an afternoon in Virginia City, Montana. Louis Schmittroth's web site on the Vigilantes of Montana is a valuable source of information and worth a cyber-visit.

As always, I was encouraged by my board of editorial advisers—friends who read the manuscript in various incarnations and offered good advice and gently applied the blue pencil: Peggy Galis, Pam Meredith, Doug Mullins, George Watkins, Jerry Dobson, Mary Chapman Webster, and Eric Redman.

My greatest debt is to a man who volunteered to perch on my shoulder and accompany me through every twist and turn of the vigilantes' story. Bill Neal of Helena is a geologist and gold miner by profession, and a first-rate historian, researcher, and map maker by avocation. A keen, impartial student of the Montana vigilantes, Bill was generous with his time and insights, devoting countless hours to helping me referee the many disputed points of what actually happened in the gold camps east of the Bitterroots during the winter of 1864. He shared his research on contracts and mining claims that are published in this book for the first time. One memorable day in the summer of 2001, Bill drove me up into the hills above Virginia City and showed me how to go panning for gold—"mucking and moiling," in his words—and in a matter of minutes I understood, through excruciating, first-hand experience, what a hard job it is and why men banded together so quickly to gain the economies of scale. His collaboration with Kathy Fehlig on the maps in this book will help readers figure out where they are (just as they helped the author).

My friendship with my publisher, Charles E. Rankin, dates back to his days as editor of *Montana: The Magazine of Western History*, when he shepherded me through the rigorous and valuable process of review and revision of my article on the vigilantes' numbers, "3-7-77." Chuck's relocation to Norman, Oklahoma, to become Editor-in-Chief of the University of Oklahoma Press, left a big void in Helena, Montana, but I am delighted that my book traveled with him and that I enjoyed the thoughtful, hands-on editing that so many authors miss these days. Our collaboration has improved this work in countless ways, and we've had many a laugh, too, along the way. Chuck's colleagues at the Press as well as copyeditor Jay Fultz and indexer Galen Schroeder have been a pleasure to work with, and have made this a book we're proud to put on the new release table (or better yet, right up there on the counter next to the cash register).

My agent, Kris Dahl of International Creative Management, has given me her typical wise counsel and this book her strong advocacy.

Finally, a word of gratitude to my wife and best friend, Linda. She has endured my moodiness through three books now, and I appreciate her unstinting efforts to keep my chin up. There is a reason I have nicknamed her Sisyphus. Even though this book has a colorful cast of characters and a strong narrative tug, the plain truth is that lynching is a disturbing subject, one that's tough to have loitering around the house like a brooding boarder. I know Linda shares my relief that the project is completed, and she should know that I love her all the more for sharing its burdens with me. We both believe it was worthwhile.

Index

Abolition. *See* Slavery

Acculturation and assimilation, 64–68. *See also* American Indians

Adobetown mining district, 101. *See also* Alder Gulch

African-Americans, 87, 283–89, 330

Alcohol, frontier crime and role of, 8

Alder Gulch: crime at, 107–108, 163–67; discovery and naming, 8–9, 92–95; growth and settlement of, 100–101; law enforcement, 154–55; Plummer as sheriff, 109–10; Vigilance Committee, 183–84. *See also* Nevada City, Mont.; Virginia City, Mont.

Allen, Charley, 238

Allen, Jirah Isham ("Ike"), 67, 371n5

American Fur Company, 62, 65

American Indians: Bear Creek massacre, 79; hostile encounters with, 12, 91–92, 320, 347–48, 354–55; relationship with whites, 6, 77–78, 299; status of women, 68, 98; unrest and western migration, 64; vigilantism and, 372n13; white attitudes toward, 66, 78–79, 325. *See also* Acculturation and assimilation

American Party, 26–27, 31–32, 202–203

American Revolution, 17–18

Anti-vigilante reactions: Ah Chow lynching, 349–50; beginning evidence of, 249–53, 268–69; Brady lynching, 294–95; Committee of Safety, Helena, 350–52; organized resistance as, 302–303; resurgence of vigilantism and, 346–47

Ashley, James: Idaho Territory and, 84–85; Montana Territory creation, 280–82, 304; as territorial governor, 362–63; territorial politics and, 340; vigilante justice and, 322–23

Bagg, Charles S., 177–79, 186–87, 314–19

Ball, Smith, 230–31

Banishment: George Hilderman, 194; J. A. Slade, 275–77; Meagher and territorial, 345; people's court punishment, 81–82; Reeves and Moore, 163–64; Rosenbaum, 346; as vigilante action, 250–51, 253, 300, 305–306

Bannack mining camp: area map of, 156; creation of, 6–8; crime at, 107–108, 163–67; description of, 70–71; George Edwards murder, 73–74; governing the,